The

Clean Water Act

Handbook SECOND EDITION

Mark A. Ryan
editor

Defending Liberty
Pursuing Justice

The publications of the Section of Environment, Energy, and Resources have a commitment to quality. Our authors and editors are outstanding professionals and active practitioners in their fields. In addition, prior to publication, the contents of all of our books are rigorously reviewed by the Section's Book Publications Committee and outside experts to ensure the highest quality product and presentation.

The materials contained herein represent the opinions of the authors and editors and should not be construed to be the action of either the American Bar Association or the Section of Environment, Energy, and Resources unless adopted pursuant to the bylaws of the Association.

Nothing contained in this book is to be considered as the rendering of legal advice for specific cases, and readers are responsible for obtaining such advice from their own legal counsel. This book and any forms and agreements herein are intended for educational and informational purposes only.

Library of Congress Cataloging-in-Publication Data

Clean Water Act / by Mark Ryan, editor.— 2nd ed.
        p. cm.
Rev. ed. of: The Clean Water Act handbook / Parthenia B. Evans, editor.
Includes index.
    ISBN 1-59031-217-1
    1. Water—Pollution—Law and legislation—United States. 2. United
States. Federal Water Pollution Control Act. I. Ryan, Mark, 1957– II.
American Bar Association. Section of Environment, Energy, and Resources.
III. Clean Water Act handbook.

    KF3790.C545 2003
    344.73'046343—dc21

                        2003010677

CONTENTS

About the Editor   xiii

About the Contributors   xv

Preface to the Second Edition   xxi

Preface to the First Edition   xxv

Chapter 1
Overview of the Clean Water Act   1
Theodore L. Garrett
   I. The Permit Program and Enforcement   1
   II. Water Quality– and Technology-Based Controls   2
   III. Spills of Hazardous or Toxic Substances   4
      A. Enforcement and Judicial Review   4
      B. Historical Background   5

Chapter 2
Water Pollution Control Under the National Pollutant Discharge Elimination System   9
Karen M. McGaffey
   I. Applicability and Scope   9
      A. Definitions   9
      B. Exclusions from the NPDES Program   14
      C. Discharges to Groundwater and Wells   15
   II. Conditions Applicable to All NPDES Permits   16
      A. Technology-Based Limitations   16
      B. Water Quality–Based Limitations   16
      C. Monitoring   16
      D. Standard Conditions   17
      E. Special Conditions   18

III. *Technology-Based Limitations*   18
  A. Levels of Control   19
  B. Developing Technology-Based Limits   23
  C. Variances   24
IV. *Water Quality–Based Effluent Limitations*   26
  A. Elements of a Water Quality Standard   26
  B. Standards Review and Approval Process   32
  C. Supplemental Water Quality–Based Effluent Limitations: Section 302   33
  D. Total Maximum Daily Loads: Section 303(d)   34
  E. Individual Control Strategies: Section 304(1)   35
  F. Implementation   38

Chapter 3
NPDES Permit Application and Issuance Procedures   41
Randy Hill

  I. *Applicability and Scope*   41
 II. *Types of NPDES Permits*   41
  A. Individual Permits   42
  B. General Permits   42
III. *Application Requirements*   43
  A. Who Must Apply?   43
  B. Timing of Application   44
  C. Content of Application   44
  D. Signature Requirements   45
IV. *Permit Issuance Process*   45
  A. Review for Completeness   45
  B. Effective Date of Application   46
  C. Tentative Permit Decision, Issuance of a Draft Permit, and Public Notice   46
  D. Public Comment/Hearing   47
  E. Final Permit Decision   47
  V. *State Certification of EPA-Issued Permits and EPA Review of State-Issued Permits*   48
  A. State Certification   48
  B. EPA Review   49
 VI. *Effect of Permit Issuance—Permit Shield*   53
VII. *Permit Term, Expiration, and APA Extension*   53
VIII. *Special NPDES Program Requirements for New Sources*   54
 IX. *Permit Appeals*   56
  A. EAB Hearing Process   57

B. Judicial Review of Final Agency Permit Action   58

C. Effect of Appeal on the Issued Permit   59

D. Appeal of General Permits   59

X. *Permit Modification, Revocation, Termination, and Transfer*   60

A. Permit Modification or Revocation and Reissuance   60

B. Permit Termination   63

C. Permit Transfers   64

D. Procedures for Modification, Revocation and Reissuance, or Termination of Permits   64

E. Antibacksliding Prohibitions   66

Chapter 4

Publicly Owned Treatment Works (POTWs)   69

Alexandra Dapolito Dunn

I. *Applicability and Scope*   69

II. *Effluent Limitations Applicable to POTWs*   70

A. Technology-Based Limitations   70

B. Water Quality–Based Limitations   71

III. *POTW NPDES Permit Requirements*   71

IV. *POTW Pretreatment Programs*   72

A. Applicability   73

B. Pretreatment Standards   73

C. Substantive POTW Pretreatment Program Requirements   74

D. Pretreatment Program Submission and Approval Procedures   75

E. POTW Pretreatment Program Modifications   75

V. *Sewage Sludge Use and Disposal*   76

A. Round One Sludge Regulations   76

B. Round Two Regulations   78

VI. *Sewer Overflows*   78

A. Combined Sewer Overflows   79

B. Sanitary Sewer Overflows   80

Chapter 5

Pretreatment and Indirect Dischargers   83

Corinne A. Goldstein

I. *Overview*   83

A. Objectives   83

B. Definitions   84

C. Applicability   84

II. *The General Pretreatment Requirements*   85

III. Categorical Pretreatment Standards 87
    A. Applicability of and Basis for the Standards 87
    B. The Combined Wastestream Formula 90
    C. Deadlines 90
    D. Innovative Technology Deadline Extensions 90
IV. Modifications of and Variances from Categorical
    Pretreatment Standards 91
    A. Removal Credits 91
    B. Fundamentally Different Factors Variances 92
V. Reporting, Monitoring, and Record Maintenance Obligations 93
    A. Industrial Users Subject to Categorical Standards 93
    B. Industrial Users Not Subject to Categorical Standards 94
    C. Reporting Obligations Applicable to All Industrial Users 95
    D. Records Maintenance 96
VI. Enforcement of Pretreatment Standards 96

Chapter 6
Wetlands: Section 404   **97**
Sylvia Quast
Steven T. Miano
I. Introduction and Scope 97
II. The Scope of Jurisdiction under Section 404 98
    A. The Definition of Wetlands 98
    B. Adjacent Wetlands 100
    C. Isolated Wetlands and the Migratory Bird Rule 101
    D. Wetlands Delineation Manuals 104
    E. Longevity of Wetlands Delineations 105
III. State Authority in Light of SWANCC 106
IV. The Section 404 Permit Program 107
    A. Activities Covered 107
    B. Types of Permits 109
    C. The Individual Permit Process 112
    D. Mitigation Policy and Banking 118
V. Enforcement: Potential Liabilities for Violating Section 404 119
    A. Agency Roles and Administrative Enforcement 119
    B. Civil Enforcement 120
VI. The Takings Issue 123
VII. State Authority to Implement a Section 404 Permit Program 130
VIII. "No Net Loss" Policy 130
IX. Practical Suggestions for Addressing Section 404 131

Chapter 7
Oil and Hazardous Substances Spills: Section 311   133
David G. Dickman
  I. Introduction and Scope   133
     A. The Comprehensive Environmental Response, Compensation, and
        Liability Act (CERCLA)   134
     B. The Oil Pollution Act (OPA)   135
     C. Definitions   135
     D. The General Discharge Prohibition in CWA Section 311   135
     E. Exemptions From the General Discharge Prohibition
        of Section 311   136
     F. Spill Notification Requirement   138
 II. Spill Prevention   138
     A. SPCC Plans: Nontransportation-Related Facilities   139
     B. Marine Facilities and Vessels   143
III. Removal and Response Authority   144
     A. Authority to Act   145
     B. Substantial Threats to Public Health or Welfare   145
     C. Federal Response Units   146
     D. Responder Immunity   146
 IV. Response Planning   147
     A. Federal Response Contingency Plans   147
     B. Facility and Vessel Response Plans   148
  V. Liability for Response Costs and Damages   154
     A. Liability for Oil Discharges Under the OPA   155
     B. OPA Limits of Liability for Response Costs and Damages   156
     C. Defenses and Exclusions to Liability Under the OPA   157
     D. Financial Responsibility Requirements Under the OPA   158
     E. Oil Spill Liability Trust Fund (OSLTF)   159
 VI. Enforcement of Penalties   160
     A. Enforcement Provisions   160
     B. Civil Penalties   161
     C. Criminal Sanctions   162

Chapter 8
"Wet Weather" Regulations   163
Randy Hill
David Allnutt
  I. Stormwater   163
     A. Phase I Stormwater Discharges   165

B. Phase II Stormwater Discharges   175
II. *Concentrated Animal Feeding Operations*   178
    A. Definition of CAFO   179
    B. CWA Requirements Applicable to CAFOs   183
    C. Proposed Revisions to the CAFO Regulations   186
III. *Other "Wet Weather" Discharges*   186
    A. Silviculture   186
    B. Aquatic Animal Production or Aquaculture   188
    C. Combined Sewer Overflows and Sanitary Sewer Overflows   190

Chapter 9
Nonpoint Source Pollution Control   191
Edward B. Witte
David P. Ross

I. *Introduction*   191
II. *The Definition of Nonpoint Source Pollution*   192
III. *Original Control Provisions in the Clean Water Act of 1972*   193
    A. Clean Water Act Section 208   194
    B. Clean Water Act Section 303(e)   194
    C. Development of Water Quality Management Plans
       Under Sections 208 and 303(e)   194
IV. *Enactment of Section 319 in the Water Quality Act of 1987*   195
    A. State Assessment Reports Under Clean Water Act
       Section 319(a)   195
    B. State Management Programs Under Clean Water Act
       Section 319(b)   195
    C. Federal Grants for State Management Program Implementation
       Under Section 319(h) of the Clean Water Act   196
V. *Selected Milestones in the Section 319 Program21*   196
    A. 1987: EPA Issues Nonpoint Source Guidance   196
    B. 1991: Creation of Section 319 National Monitoring Program   197
    C. 1992: EPA Issues Final Report to Congress
       on Section 319 Activities   197
    D. 1996: New Focus for Section 319 Program Guidance   198
    E. 1998: Clean Water Action Plan   199
    F. 2002 and Beyond: Supplement Guidelines
       for the Award of Section 319 Grants Issued   199
VI. *Related Programs for the Control of Nonpoint Source Pollution*   200
    A. Coastal Zone Act Reauthorization Amendments of 1990   200
    B. Unified Federal Policy for Watershed Management
       on Federal Lands   201

C. Enforceable State Mechanisms   202

D. Effluent Trading Programs   203

VI. *Looking Towards the Future of Nonpoint Source Pollution Control*   204

Chapter 10
TMDLs: Section 303(d)   205
Laurie K. Beale
Karin Sheldon

I. *Introduction*   205

II. *TMDL Basics*   206

   A. Components of a TMDL   206

   B. The TMDL Process   207

   C. Trading   208

   D. Multistate Issues   209

III. *TMDL Litigation*   210

   A. Judicial Review   210

   B. The Constructive Submission Theory   210

   C. Challenges to the Substance of TMDLs   212

   D. EPA's Expanded Authority   213

IV. *Sources Subject to TMDL Limitations*   213

   A. Sources of Heat   213

   B. Sources of Pollution   214

V. *Implementation of TMDLs*   215

   A. Point Sources   215

   B. Nonpoint Sources   216

   C. Sources Requiring Section 401 Certification   217

VI. *TMDLs and the Endangered Species Act*   217

VII. *The July 2000 TMDL Rule: Future Issues*   218

Chapter 11
Enforcement: Section 309   221

I. *Civil Judicial Enforcement*   221

Beth S. Ginsberg
Jennifer E. Merrick

   A. Statutory Authority   221

   B. Enforcement Trends   222

   C. EPA's Enforcement Jurisdiction   223

   D. Venue and Statutes of Limitations   224

   E. Standards of Liability   225

   F. Elements of Proof   225

   G. Trial Considerations   228

1. The Right to a Jury   228
H. Defenses   228
I. Remedies   232
II. *Civil Administrative Enforcement*   235
Mark A. Ryan
A. Administrative Compliance Orders   236
B. Information Requests   236
C. Administrative Penalties   237
D. Effect of Administrative Proceedings on Other Enforcement Actions
242
III. *Criminal Enforcement*   243
James Oesterle
A. Introduction and Overview   243
B. The Mental State Requirement   244
C. Common Criminal Offenses   248
D. Related Water Pollution Statutes   256
IV. *Citizen Suits*   257
Laird Lucas
A. Statutory Authority   258
B. Legislative Intent and Authority   258
C. Types of CWA Citizen Suits   259
D. Statutory Requirements for Citizen Suits   262
E. Standing   265
F. Defenses   267
G. Intervention   269
H. Remedies   269

Chapter 12
Judicial Review: Section 509   273
Karen M. McGaffey
I. *Jurisdiction*   273
A. Federal Court of Appeals   273
B. District Court Jurisdiction   276
II. *Justiciability: Ripeness and Exhaustion of Administrative Remedies*   277
A. Ripeness   277
B. Exhaustion of Remedies   278

Table of Cases   279

Index   295

ABOUT THE EDITOR

Mark A. Ryan is with the EPA Region X Office of Regional Counsel. Mark has been with the EPA since 1990, and he currently works in the Region X Idaho Office in Boise, Idaho. Mark's work focuses primarily on Clean Water Act litigation and counseling. Mark has tried numerous administrative enforcement cases for EPA and he is an adjunct faculty member with the EPA National Trial Advocacy Institute in Boulder, Colorado. He received his B.S. in Natural Resources in 1981 from the University of Michigan, and studied environmental policy at Albert-Ludwigs-Universität, Tübingen, Germany as a University of Michigan Tübingen Fellow. Mark received his law degree in 1988 from Indiana University School of Law.

ABOUT THE CONTRIBUTORS

David Allnutt is with the Office of Regional Counsel for Region X of the U.S. Environmental Protection Agency, located in Seattle, Washington. In this capacity, he represents the agency in enforcement cases, advises on permitting matters, and coordinates with the Department of Justice and EPA Headquarters on a variety of issues arising under the Clean Water Act, the Safe Drinking Water Act, CERCLA, and other environmental statutes. He has also served on details with EPA's Offices of Enforcement and Compliance Assurance and General Counsel. He has earned degrees from Colgate University (B.A., 1988) and the University of Washington (J.D., 1994). As a westerner, he pronounces "CAFO" with a soft "A."

Laurie K. Beale practices with the law firm Stoel Rives LLP in Seattle, Washington. She specializes in environmental litigation and appellate law, with a focus on matters relating to the Clean Water Act, the Endangered Species Act, NEPA, the Magnuson-Stevens Fishery Conservation and Management Act, and state environmental laws. Ms. Beale received a B.A. from the University of Notre Dame and a J.D. from the University of Washington School of Law.

David G. Dickman is with the firm of Venable LLP (Venable, Baetjer, Howard & Civiletti, LLP) in Washington, D.C. He specializes in environmental criminal defense, maritime and environmental regulatory compliance, international marine safety and environmental law, and homeland security issues with an emphasis on the marine and transportation industries. Mr. Dickman received his B.S. from the United States Coast Guard Academy and his J.D. from St. Louis University School of Law.

Alexandra Dapolito Dunn is General Counsel of the Association of Metropolitan Sewerage Agencies (AMSA). Ms. Dunn provides legal and strategic counsel to AMSA on association matters and on environmental regulatory development and implementation, permitting, and legislation, with a particular focus on the Clean Water Act. Ms. Dunn represents AMSA in litigations and *amicus* activities across the nation. Ms. Dunn is the author of several articles and speaks regularly at conferences on a variety of environmental and administrative law topics. She is the 2002-2003 Chair of the American Bar Association's (ABA) Section of Environment, Energy and Resources' In-House Counsel Committee. She also is a Vice Chair of the ABA's *32nd Annual Conference on Environmental Law,* and will Chair the Conference in 2005. Ms. Dunn received her J.D., *magna cum laude,* in 1994 from the Columbus School of Law, Catholic University of America in Washington, D.C., where she was Editor-in-Chief of the *Catholic University Law Review.* She received her B.A., *cum laude,* in 1989 from James Madison University.

Theodore L. Garrett is a senior partner in the law firm Covington & Burling in Washington, D.C., and is Co-Chair of the firm's environment practice. He has been extensively involved in litigation and administrative proceedings throughout the country involving federal and state environment and natural resource matters. Mr. Garrett recently served as Chair of the ABA Section of Environment, Energy and Resources, and served for several years as a member of the Section's Executive Committee. Mr. Garrett is a member of the editorial board of the *Environmental Law Reporter* and a member of the Advisory Committee on Hazardous Waste of the Center for Public Resources. He is listed in Who's Who in America. He earned his B.A. from Yale College and his J.D. from Columbia Law School. He served as U.S. Supreme Court law clerk to Chief Justice Warren Burger.

Beth S. Ginsberg is a partner in the environmental and natural resource practice group at Stoel Rives LLP. Her practice focuses on environmental, wildlife and natural resource litigation, and counseling for both public and private interests, including port authorities, counties, private landowners, mining, oil and gas, timber, pulp and paper, sport and commercial fishing entities. She has been litigating environmental and natural resource cases for seventeen years. She previously worked for the U.S. Department of Justice and the U.S. Environmental Protection Agency, where she served as a Senior Advisor to the Assistant Administrator of the Office of Solid Waste and Emergency Response. She graduated from Northwestern University, Phi Beta Kappa, in 1982, and obtained her J.D. in 1985 from the State University of New York at Buffalo, where she was the recipient of Fellowships from the Baldy Center for Law and Public Policy and the New York State Sea Grant Association. She currently is the Co-Chair of the ABA's Water Quality and Wetlands Committee.

Corinne A. Goldstein is with the firm of Covington & Burling in Washington, D.C., where she concentrates in environmental law, including counseling and litigation related to the Clean Water Act, Superfund, and RCRA. She also counsels clients in the environmental aspects of corporate transactions and toxic tort litigation. Ms. Goldstein is a graduate of Wellesley College and the University of Michigan Law School.

Randolph L. Hill is Assistant General Counsel in the Water Law of the Office of General Counsel at the U.S. Environmental Protection Agency. Since 1997, he has led a team of attorneys responsible for counseling and litigation arising under the Clean Water Act and Safe Drinking Water Act. Prior to that, he spent nearly ten years as a staff attorney in the same office, and was recognized as the Agency's national legal expert in a number of areas related to the Clean Water Act, including the regulation of point and nonpoint sources of so-called "wet weather" pollution and the implementation of the Act on Indian lands. He received a prestigious EPA award for Leadership Excellence in 2001. Mr. Hill is an Adjunct Associate Professor at the University of Maryland, University College, where he has taught for 14 years, teaching courses in public sector management business-government relations, problem-solving, and small business planning. Mr. Hill obtained his J.D. and a Master of Public Policy degree from the University of California, Berkeley and was elected to the Order of the Coif; he obtained his B.A. from UC San Diego.

Laird J. Lucas is Executive Director of Advocates for the West, a public interest environmental law nonprofit based in Boise, Idaho. Laird is a 1986 graduate of Yale Law School. He clerked for a federal district judge in Texas, and worked in private practice for several years in San Francisco before moving to Boise in 1993 to focus on environmental law. Since then, he has won many precedent-setting citizen suits under the Clean Water Act and other federal environmental statutes.

Steven T. Miano is a Partner in and Co-Chair of the Environmental Practice Group at WolfBlock, LLP in Philadelphia, PA. He has been practicing environmental law for over seventeen years, concentrating in all areas of environmental law, including complex cases arising under the federal Clean Water Act, Resource Conservation and Recovery Act, Comprehensive Environmental Response Compensation and Liability Act, Toxic Substances Control Act, brownfields redevelopment laws, and comparable state laws. Before private practice, Mr. Miano was an Assistant Regional Counsel for the U.S. Environmental Protection Agency, Region III, Hazardous Waste Branch. Mr. Miano is currently an Adjunct Professor at Rutgers University Law School where he teaches environmental law. Mr. Miano received his B.S. in Environmental Studies from George Washington University in 1982 and his J.D. from Franklin Pierce Law

Center in 1985. He was a law clerk to the Honorable Martin F. Loughlin, U.S. District Court for the District of New Hampshire. He is the Co-chair of the ABA Section's Water Quality and Wetlands Committee.

Karen McGaffey is a partner with the Perkins Coie LLP in Seattle,Washington. Her practice emphasizes energy facility siting, water quality permitting and compliance, air permitting, endangered species issues, natural resources and environmental litigation. Ms. McGaffey earned an A.B.. degree from Dartmouth College, and a J.D. from Harvard Law School.

James D. Oesterle is the Regional Criminal Enforcement Counsel for Region X of the U.S. Environmental Protection Agency, located in Seattle, Washington. In addition, he is a Special Assistant United States Attorney in the Western District of Washington, and the Districts of Alaska and Idaho. He prosecutes environmental crimes under all of the environmental statutes, including the Clean Water Act. Mr. Oesterle received his B.S. degree from the University of Minnesota, M.S. degree from Michigan State University, and J.D. from the University of Washington.

Sylvia Quast is an Attorney-Advisor with the U.S. Department of Justice in the Law and Policy Section of the Environment and Natural Resources Division in Washington, D.C. Her litigation practice currently focuses on the Clean Water Act, NEPA, and the ESA, and she deals with a broad spectrum of environmental and natural resource issues as a speechwriter and policy advisor. Ms. Quast received a B.A. from the University of Minnesota and a J.D. from Harvard Law School.

Mark A. Ryan is with the EPA Region X Office of Regional Counsel. Mark has been with the EPA since 1990, and he currently works in the Region X Idaho Office in Boise, Idaho. Mark's work focuses primarily on Clean Water Act litigation and counseling. Mark has tried numerous administrative enforcement cases for EPA and he is an adjunct faculty member with the EPA National Trial Advocacy Institute in Boulder, Colorado. He received his B.S. in Natural Resources in 1981 from the University of Michigan, and studied environmental policy at Albert-Ludwigs-Universität, Tübingen, Germany as a University of Michigan Tübingen Fellow. Mark received his law degree in 1988 from Indiana University School of Law.

Karin P. Sheldon is Professor of Law, Dean of the Environmental Law Program, and Director of the Environmental Law Center at Vermont Law School. Professor Sheldon teaches and writes in the areas of federal natural resources law and policy, watershed management and protection, and environmental policy. She received her A.B. from Vassar College and her J.D. from the University of Washington.

Edward B. Witte (Ned) is a partner with Foley & Lardner and works out of its Milwaukee, Wisconsin office. Ned is a member of Foley's Environmental Law Practice Group and focuses his practice on land use (including siting, zoning, water resources, riparian regulations, nonpoint pollution and wetlands), Brownfields redevelopment, environmental due diligence and liability allocation and enforcement in transactions. Ned is a 1989 graduate of Vermont Law School (JD, *cum laude,* and MSEL, *magna cum laude*). Ned has published numerous articles regarding environmental law related topics in national law journals and periodicals.

PREFACE TO THE
SECOND EDITION

I started working with the Clean Water Act not long before the time the first edition of this Handbook was written. Since that time, CWA litigation and counseling has accounted for the bulk of my practice. After years of concentrated practice in the area, I had naturally become familiar with the case law, rule makings, EPA guidance documents, etc. When I agreed to take on editing the new edition of this book, I naively thought that it was be an easy task because (1) Congress has not amended the CWA since 1987, and (2) I have closely followed developments under the CWA since the first edition was published. I took for granted how many developments there have been since that time. Only after beginning work on the second edition did I realize what I had gotten myself into. Publishers, I am sure, love such naivete. It makes it easier to recruit editors.

The many small and some large changes to the law have resulted in substantial changes in the Handbook. Every chapter was significantly rewritten to reflect the new judicial and regulatory interpretations given the Act. Also, we have added two new chapters to deal with areas of the law that have expanded dramatically since 1994. Up until the early 1990s, EPA and the states focused on the low-hanging fruit of the CWA, the traditional point sources such as factories and sewage treatment plants. Beginning in the early 1990's, but not taking hold until the late 1990's, did regulatory agencies begin to grapple with the far more difficult problems inherent in regulating nonpoint source and storm water runoff. The first new chapter deals with total maximum daily loads, or TMDLs. TMDLs are the CWA's main hook into nonpoint source control, and they have quickly becoming that tail that wags the dog. Today, TMDLs consume significant federal, state, and local resources in their design and implementation, and few areas of the country can escape their effects. Second, we've added a chapter on wet weather regulations, namely storm water and feed lot regulations. Like TMDLs, these areas have matured significantly since 1994. Anyone working with the CWA will encounter TMDL and storm water issues, and we hope these new chapters will assist in those efforts.

This Second Edition also reflects the growth and importance of the Internet in our everyday lives. When the first edition was published, the World Wide Web was in its infancy. This edition incorporates URLs extensively to give the reader quick access to government documents that formerly were difficult, if not impossible, to find. The reader will find web site addresses for government offices, such as the EPA's Office of Administrative Law Judges (*www.epa.gov/oalj*) and EPA's Environmental Appeals Board (*www.epa.gov/eab*), where the reader can quickly and at no cost access all of the agency's recent ALJ and appeals decisions on the CWA and other statutes. These and similar sites are invaluable resources that were unavailable ten years ago.

Finally, this Second Edition comes out at an important time in the evolution of the Act. Alhough Congress has not amended the Act since 1987, recent court rulings and a change in administration in Washington has resulted in a very significant shift in the Act. Cases such as the Supreme Court's decision in *SWANCC,* and the Courts of Appeals decisions in *American Mininig Assoc., Talent Irrigation,* and *Forsgren,* to name a few, have altered many time-honored tenets of the CWA. *SWANCC* and its progeny virtually guarantees that uncertainty will exist over basic questions of CWA jurisdiction for some time to come. I hope this Handbook will help guide you through these changes and others that are sure to occur.

Acknowledgments

Without a doubt, it is easier to build on the good work of others than it is to start from scratch. I and the contributing authors to this second edition had the good fortune of a solid and well-organized book on which to build and expand. We are indebted to Parthenia Evans and the first set of authors, some of whom miraculously agreed to assist with the second edition. Without their solid groundwork, this book would not be as useful as you will find it to be.

I would like to thank all of the authors of this book for there considerable contributions of time and expertise. They are: David Allnutt, Laurie Beale, Dave Dickman, Alex Dunn, Ted Garrett, Beth Ginsberg, Corinne Goldstein, Randy Hill, Laird Lucas, Karen McGaffey, Steve Miano, Jim Oesterle, Sylvia Quast, Professor Karen Sheldon, and Ned Witte. Without their assistance, this wonderful practice guide would not be as up-to-date or as useful as it is. I would like to extend special thanks to Beth Ginsberg and Kathleen Carr who helped me recruit the small army of writers who have contributed to this second edition. Finding experienced CWA attorneys who have the time and willingness to work on a book while attending to their busy practices is a challenge. Thanks go to Adrianne Allen of the EPA Region 10 Office of Regional Counsel for her bottomless knowledge of the TMDL program, water quality standards law and her deft review of the TMDL chapter. Thanks to Rick Paszkiet at the ABA for his support and understanding when my litigation practice sometimes took precedence over my editing of this book. I worked on this project mostly on evenings and weekends. Inevitably, however, I needed to do some of the work during the day in the office. And for that privilege, I thank EPA Region 10 Management, who graciously allowed me the time to parlay the knowledge I have gained working with the Clean Water Act at EPA into this book.

Mark Ryan
Boise, Idaho

PREFACE TO THE
FIRST EDITION

Pardoning the pun, this book is intended to clear muddy waters. Although water pollution control has a nearly one hundred-year history in the United States, before this book there has not been a single-volume, practically oriented, and definitive resource for the practitioner wading through the complex business of understanding the federal Clean Water Act (CWA).[1] In part, this may be attributable to the difficulty encountered in finding the experts and extracting the time and experience needed to put together such a work. The American Bar Association through its Section of Natural Resources, Energy, and Environmental Law has the unique ability to gather the experts when there is a need for service to the bar and to facilitate the creation of a book such as this.

The writers of this book are a group of fifteen of the most experienced and recognized Clean Water Act experts in this country. In some ways, this book is too good because it offers an understanding of the Clean Water Act that takes years to develop in an environmental law practice—a resource not commonly shared among members of the bar. The authors deserve special thanks for their willingness to share with the bar the cumulation of their years of experience. Their generosity is unparalleled and the value of their contribution cannot be overstated.

A lineage of eleven major federal enactments leading to the present-day CWA began with the Rivers and Harbors Appropriations Act of 1899, which aimed at preventing nineteenth- century folk from tossing into our nation's waterways large objects that would inhibit navigation. Over a period of nearly one hundred years, there has evolved a complex statute and even more complex set of implementing regulations and guidelines that continue to have as a focal point a variation of the blanket prohibition developed in 1899 against discharging pollutants to the nation's waters.

The sheer bulk of statutes, regulations, and agency guidance under the CWA presents challenge enough to the practitioner. Complicating that challenge is the uncertainty Congress and the U.S. Environmental Protection Agency (EPA) each has displayed over the preferred approach to water pollution control. For nearly fifty years, the dilemma has been whether water pollution control should be technology-based or water quality–based, or both.

The technology/water quality dichotomy was established with the first two of the eleven clean water enactments. The Rivers and Harbors Appropriations Act of 1899[2] used a water quality–based approach while the Federal Water Pollution Control Act of 1948[3] used an effluent limitations or technology-based approach. Since 1948, the CWA has been amended nine times and the technology/water quality issue has taken a turn in preference with nearly each enactment.

The schizophrenic approach[4] to water pollution control first noticeable in 1948 persists today. Technology-based controls and water quality–based controls have many mutually exclusive components and, when coupled, often do not serve to further the goals and objectives of the CWA. Even more frustrating is the effect that the dichotomous approach has for the CWA practitioner. The controlling element in disputes regarding permit conditions frequently hinges on whether the permit requirement is technology driven or water quality driven. Unfortunately, Congress has not given any more direction on the subject than a few overriding choice directives in CWA section 301(b).[5] Moreover, there is no indication on the horizon that Congress or EPA will unravel the problems created by the dichotomy or will make a clear choice.

This book squarely addresses issues such as the practical implications of the technology/water quality issue, as well as pieces together the CWA and EPA's implementing regulations in a fashion that permits confidence in CWA problem solving. The editor and the authors of this book are confident that the book will accomplish for users its intended purpose of providing a single-volume, definitive tool for use in addressing CWA issues.

The history of water pollution control will have a new chapter in the 1990s when Congress faces the long overdue CWA reauthorization. A new edition of this book will be written immediately following reauthorization, to address changes in the CWA and interpretation and implementation of those changes.

Parthenia B. Evans
Kansas City, Missouri

Notes

1. 33 U.S.C. §§ 1251 *et seq.* The CWA also is referred to as the Federal Water Pollution Control Act, which is the title used by Congress in its second water pollution control endeavor: the Federal Water Pollution Control Act of 1948, Pub. L. No. 80-845, ch. 750, 62 Stat. 1155.

2. 30 Stat. 1151.

3. Pub. L. No. 80-845, ch. 750, 62 Stat. 1155.

4. Appropriately labeled as such by William H. Rodgers, Jr., Environmental Law 356 (1977).

5. 33 U.S.C. § 1311(b).

CHAPTER 1

Overview of the Clean Water Act

THEODORE L. GARRETT

Virtually all manufacturing companies discharge process wastewater and/or stormwater. Those discharges are extensively regulated under the Clean Water Act (CWA or the Act)[1] through a collaborative federal and state program of permits and standards. This book describes the complex framework of federal and state controls and will be a valuable reference to the environmental lawyer. A brief overview of the law and a road map of the topics covered in this book follow.

I. The Permit Program and Enforcement

A person responsible for a "discharge of pollutants" into "waters of the United States" from a "point source " (a discrete conveyance)[2] is subject to various provisions of the CWA. The key requirement is to obtain and comply with a permit under the National Pollutant Discharge Elimination System (NPDES) program pursuant to section 402 of the CWA.[3] Permits must be obtained from EPA or from a state that has an EPA-approved permit program. NPDES permits apply the technology- and water quality–based requirements of the Act to a particular discharger. Permits also contain schedules of compliance and requirements for

---

1. 33 U.S.C. § 1251, *et seq.*
2. EPA also implements programs to control nonpoint source discharges. *See infra* chapter 9.
3. 33 U.S.C. § 1342.

monitoring and reporting. Permits may be issued for a term of up to five years and thus must periodically be reissued. See infra chapter 3.

Compliance with a permit constitutes compliance with most of the operative provisions of the CWA.[4] Discharges without a permit and violations of permit conditions are subject to federal and state civil and criminal penalties and citizen suits.[5] Violations of EPA regulations governing toxic pollutant standards and pre-treatment standards are also subject to enforcement.[6]

In deference to the established role of the Army Corps of Engineers, section 404 of the CWA gives the Corps the authority to issue permits for the discharge of dredged or fill material to waters of the United States.[7] See infra chapter 6. An environmental impact statement may be required if the Corps issues the permit. The Corps must choose a disposal site through application of EPA guidelines, but EPA has the final authority to prohibit a disposal site. The Corps may issue general permits for categories of activities. States with approved programs may also issue section 404 permits. The regulation of wetlands has evolved rapidly and remains controversial—in particular, concerning the scope of "waters of the United States" and what constitutes a "wetland" for purposes of the Section 404 Program.[8]

II. Water Quality– and Technology-Based Controls

As discussed above, a discharger of pollutants to waters of the United States must obtain an NPDES permit. The effluent limits set out in such permits are dictated largely by two basic kinds of regulatory controls under the CWA: water quality–based and technology-based requirements. Compliance with the more restrictive of applicable water quality– and technology-based requirements is required.

Technology-based requirements are designed to reflect the levels of effluent quality achievable through the use of pollution control technology. See infra chapter 2. Effluent limitations reflecting the application of the "best practicable control technology currently available" (BPT) were required to be achieved by July 1, 1977.[9] The Act requires the achievement of limits reflecting "best avail-

---

4. 33 U.S.C. § 402(k).

5. 33 U.S.C. §§ 1319, 1365.

6. 33 U.S.C. §§ 1317, 1319.

7. 33 U.S.C. § 1344.

8. *See* Solid Waste Agency of Northern Cook County v. U.S. Army Corps of Engineers, 531 U.S. 159 (2001), invalidating the Corps's "migratory bird" rule and curtailing the Corps's jurisdiction over wetlands. *See also Federal Wetlands Policy: Protecting the Environment or Breaching Constitutional Rights?* Hearing before the House Committee on Government Reform, 106th Cong. (October 6, 2000).

9. 33 U.S.C. § 1311(b)(1)(A).

able technology economically achievable" (BAT) by July 1, 1984, for "toxic pollutants" and by July 1, 1987, for "nonconventional" pollutants.[10] In addition, "new-source" direct dischargers are subject to standards of performance for new sources (NSPS).[11] These requirements are defined by the U.S. Environmental Protection Agency (EPA or the Agency) in "effluent guidelines" regulations under 33 U.S.C. Section 1314(b), which sets forth the various factors EPA must take into account in establishing these limits.

"Indirect dischargers" to publicly owned treatment works (POTWs) must comply with pretreatment standards for pollutants that would interfere with or pass through the POTWs.[12] The new source and pretreatment standards are generally identical to BAT limits for existing direct dischargers. See infra chapters 4 and 5.

EPA's effluent limitations guidelines and standards are published at 40 C.F.R. part 400. The Agency has largely completed its initial round of regulations for 21 major industries. New and revised regulations are contemplated. In the absence of applicable BPT, "best conventional pollutant control technology" (BCT), or BAT guideline regulations, EPA exercises "best professional judgment" (BPJ) to establish effluent limitations for a particular plant in issuing a discharge permit.[13]

The initial focus of the Act was on these technology-based controls. In recent years, however, the emphasis has shifted back to water quality–based controls. Water quality requirements consist of a set of rules designed to achieve a given level of quality for a natural body of water. See infra chapter 2, section IV. They are based on scientific information about pollutant levels consistent with various uses of water, such as public water supply, recreation, industrial uses, and protection of fish and wildlife. Water quality standards are adopted by the states and submitted to EPA for approval.[14] These standards must take into account the uses of a body of water, such as public water supply; propagation of fish and wildlife; recreation; and agricultural, industrial, and other purposes.[15] EPA's criteria for

---

10. *Id.* at §§ 311(b)(2)(C) and (F). The list of toxic pollutants designated by EPA is contained in 40 C.F.R. § 401.15. Nonconventional pollutants cover every pollutant not identified as toxic or conventional. The Act also requires the achievement by July 1, 1984, for "conventional pollutants" of effluent limits reflecting the "best conventional pollutant control technology" (BCT). 33 U.S.C. § 1311(b)(2)(E). A list of conventional pollutants is set forth in 40 C.F.R. § 401.16. They include biological oxygen demand (BOD), total suspended solids (TSS), pH, and oil and grease.

11. 33 U.S.C. § 1316.

12. 33 U.S.C. § 1317(b). In addition, the Act imposes certain requirements on POTWs. *See* chapter 4.

13. 33 U.S.C. § 1342(a)(1).

14. 33 U.S.C. § 1313(c)(2).

15. *Id.*

reviewing state standards are set forth in 40 C.F.R. sections 131.5 to 131.6.[16] EPA also has developed certain toxic pollutant effluent limitations and has implemented a program to develop limits based on effluent toxicity.

In the last decade, there has been increasing emphasis on Total Daily Maximum Loads (TMDLs) (see infra chapter 10) and the control of nonpoint sources and stormwater. See infra chapters 8 and 9. Section 303(d) of the Act provides that the states shall (1) identify waters that failed to achieve water quality standards after application of technology-based controls; (2) determine the TMDLs that would be needed to comply; and (3) allocate these loads among dischargers in permits and water quality plans.[17] EPA issued guidance documents to the states in August 1997, clarifying the scope of listed waters and setting schedules for action. In February 1998, the president announced a Clean Water Action Plan, which emphasized that runoff is the most important source of water pollution, and that agriculture affects 70 percent of impaired rivers. Prompted by the 1987 amendments to the Act, EPA has been developing and implementing standards for various diffuse sources, such as animal feeding operations, municipal storm sewers, and stormwater.

III. Spills of Hazardous or Toxic Substances

Section 311 of the CWA authorizes EPA to determine by regulation "those quantities of oil and any hazardous substances the discharge of which may be harmful to the public health or welfare," known as "reportable quantities."[18] See infra chapter 7. The responsible person is required to notify the appropriate federal agency as soon as he or she has knowledge of any discharge of oil or a hazardous substance in a reportable quantity into or upon the navigable waters of the United States.[19] In addition, the federal government is authorized to arrange for the removal of oil or a hazardous substance, and to assess the costs of removal to the responsible party.

A. ENFORCEMENT AND JUDICIAL REVIEW

Several enforcement options and procedures are available to federal and state governments. See infra chapter 11. They include administrative orders, blacklisting, and civil and criminal suits. Section 309(a)(3) of the Act authorizes EPA to issue an administrative order whenever it finds that a person is in violation of enumerated provisions of the Act or an NPDES permit implementing these pro-

---

16. If EPA disapproves a state standard and the state does not adopt required changes, EPA may adopt a standard. 33 U.S.C. § 1313(c)(3).

17. 33 U.S.C. § 1313(d).

18. 33 U.S.C. § 1321(b)(4).

19. 33 U.S.C. § 1321(b)(5).

visions.[20] EPA may "blacklist"—or suspend from government contracting—any company convicted of an offense under section 309 of the CWA.[21] EPA's general regulations governing debarment are set forth in 40 C.F.R. part 32.

Sections 309(d) and 309(g) of the Act authorize EPA to sue for civil penalties for any violation of an NPDES permit, an EPA order, or the Act.[22] Section 309(c) of the CWA authorizes EPA to seek criminal penalties against responsible persons for willful or negligent violations and for knowingly making any false statement or report.[23] See infra chapter 11, section III. The term "person" for these purposes means a corporation or any responsible corporate officer.[24]

Section 505 of the CWA authorizes citizen enforcement and has been used since 1982 as the basis for hundreds of suits against discharges.[25] See infra chapter 11, section IV. Under this provision, any citizen may bring a civil action against any person who is alleged to be in violation of an effluent limitation or standard under the Act or an administrative order issued by EPA or a state. However, the courts have imposed limitations on the extent to which such citizen suits may be brought when the defendant has come into compliance.[26] The courts in such suits may award civil penalties under section 309(d) of the CWA and enforce appropriate limitations or orders. Citizen groups may be awarded their costs of litigation including attorneys' and expert witness fees.[27]

Section 509(b)(1) of the CWA provides that specified EPA actions are subject to exclusive jurisdiction in the U.S. Courts of Appeals.[28] See infra chapter 12. The enumerated actions are subject to appellate review if suit is commenced within 90 days from the date of EPA's action, unless new grounds subsequently arise. Suits may be commenced in the circuit court within which the petitioner resides or transacts business affected by EPA's action.[29] Other EPA actions not enumerated in section 509(b) are subject to judicial review in federal district court.

B. HISTORICAL BACKGROUND

The first federal statute governing water pollution control was the Rivers and Harbors Appropriations Act of 1899.[30] This statute prohibits the construction of

---

20. 33 U.S.C. § 1319(a)(3).
21. 33 U.S.C. § 1368.
22. 33 U.S.C. § 1319(d).
23. 33 U.S.C. § 1319(c).
24. 33 U.S.C. § 1319(c)(3).
25. 33 U.S.C. § 1365.
26. *See* Gwaltney of Smithfield v. Chesapeake Bay Found., 484 U.S. 49 (1987).
27. 33 U.S.C. § 1365(d).
28. 33 U.S.C. § 1369(b)(1).
29. *Id.*
30. 33 U.S.C. §§ 401–466n.

bridges and other structures (section 10) and the deposit of refuse matter (section 13) without approval or a permit from the Army Corps of Engineers. For decades these provisions, as administered by the Corps, were not thought to require permits for discharges that did not interfere with navigation.[31]

The Federal Water Pollution Control Act (FWPCA) was first enacted in 1948.[32] The 1948 act allowed a court to grant relief from pollution after considering the practicability and economic feasibility of abatement. The Water Quality Act of 1965[33] provided for the adoption of water quality standards for interstate waters. However, the approach in the 1965 act was later regarded as ineffective due to its limited scope, the difficulty in determining when a discharge violated the standards, and its cumbersome enforcement mechanism.

In late 1972, Congress passed a comprehensive revision and recodification of the FWPCA.[34] The 1972 act established a program for continuing existing water quality standards, while providing for their modification from time to time.[35] The act established a July 1, 1977, deadline for technology-based limits on discharges of pollutants to be achieved by direct industrial dischargers and POTWs or more-stringent water quality–based standards imposed by states. The act also called for the creation of pretreatment standards for indirect dischargers.[36] Finally, the Act established the NPDES permit program as a federal-state system to supplement and replace the Rivers and Harbors Act permit program.[37]

Based on experience with the 1972 amendments, Congress enacted mid-course corrections to the Act in 1977.[38] The highlights of the 1977 amendments were the provisions dealing with 65 so-called priority or toxic pollutants.[39] Rather than relying solely on water quality standards, Congress required "best-available

---

31. In 1968, the Corps of Engineers announced that it would consider factors other than protection of navigation in issuing permits under the Rivers and Harbors Act, and in 1970 the Corps announced that industrial dischargers would be subject to new permit procedures. *See* Zabel v. Tabb, 430 F.2d 199 (5th Cir. 1970), *cert. denied*, 401 U.S. 910 (1972); 35 Fed. Reg. 20,005 (1970). Hundreds of suits were commenced under the Rivers and Harbors Act against dischargers without a permit.

32. Pub. L. No. 80-845, 62 Stat. 1155 (1948).

33. Pub. L. No. 89-234, 79 Stat. 903 (1965).

34. Pub. L. No. 92-500, 86 Stat. 816 (1972).

35. 33 U.S.C. § 1313.

36. 33 U.S.C. § 1307, 1311, 1314.

37. 33 U.S.C. § 1342. *See infra* chapter 2. Permits issued under the 1899 act were deemed permits under the 1972 Act and vice versa. 33 U.S.C. § 1342(a)(4). Pending applications under the 1899 Act were deemed to be applications under the 1972 FWPCA, and no further permits were to be issued under the 1899 Act. *Id.* at § 1342(a)(5).

38. Pub. L. No. 95-217, 91 Stat. 1567 (1977).

39. The list of 65 toxic pollutants (or groups of pollutants) is set forth in H. Comm. Pub. Works and Transp., Comm. print 95-30, 95th Cong., 1st Sess. (1977).

technology" limitations for toxic pollutants to be achieved by July 1, 1984. Congress established a new requirement of "best conventional pollutant control technology" limitations to be achieved by July 1, 1984, for conventional pollutants such as suspended solids, biological oxygen demanding (BOD), fecal coliform, and pH.[40] The 1977 amendments also added provisions (discussed below) for best management practices, removal credits for pretreatment standards, and modifications of BAT requirements for nontoxic pollutants.[41]

In 1987, Congress adopted amendments to the CWA that established post–BAT water quality requirements, provided for administrative civil penalties, and codified the requirements for stormwater discharges and other features of the program that had been the subject of debate.[42] Section 319 of the Act was added to address the creation of nonpoint source management programs. New section 402(p) of the Act established a comprehensive new program for stormwater regulation. In 1995, EPA issued the "multisection general permit" for stormwater, which was reissued in 2000. In 1998 the Clinton administration published the *Clean Water Action Plan,* which would provide resources to targeted areas, focus on watershed-based planning, and implement a national strategy for control of contaminated runoff.

The provisions of the Act dealing with water quality and nonpoint sources have proven the most difficult to implement in practice. The Total Maximum Daily Load program under section 303(d) of the Act is another program—slow to be implemented—that will have a significant impact on both point and nonpoint sources. However, the mechanisms to control diffuse runoff remain limited, and imposing additional controls on point sources will not always address the root of the problem. An effluent trading program to address water quality compliance, similar perhaps to the trading program under the acid rain provisions of the Clean Air Act, has been suggested as a means to establish effective incentives.[43]

Additional amendments may be expected when the CWA is next reauthorized. Among the issues that have been discussed in hearings and bills are environmental taxes and fees, pollution prevention, nonpoint source control, regulation of wetlands, regional water quality issues, and enforcement.[44]

---

40. 33 U.S.C. § 1311(b).

41. 33 U.S.C. §§ 1314(e), 1317(b)(1), 1311(g).

42. Pub. L. No. 100-4, 101 Stat. 76 (1987).

43. *Water Quality Trading—An Innovative Approach to Achieving Water Quality Goals on a Watershed Basis,* Hearing before the House Committee on Transportation and Infrastructure, Subcommittee on Water Resources and Environment, 107th Cong. (June 13, 2002).

44. *See, e.g.,* S. 1114, 103d Cong., 1st Sess. (1993); *Improving Water Quality: States Perspectives on the Federal Pollution Water Control Act,* Hearing before the House Committee on Transportation and Infrastructure, Subcommittee on Water Resources and Environment, 107th Cong. (Feb. 28, 2001).

CHAPTER 2

Water Pollution Control Under the National Pollutant Discharge Elimination System

KAREN M. McGAFFEY*

I. Applicability and Scope

Section 301(a) of the Clean Water Act (CWA)[1] prohibits the "discharge of any pollutant" by any "person" into "navigable" waters, except as in compliance with sections 302, 306, 307, 318, 402, and 404 of the Act. In order to comply with section 301(a), dischargers typically obtain permits through either the section 402 National Pollutant Discharge Elimination System (NPDES) permit program or the section 404 dredge-and-fill permit program. This chapter addresses the primary substantive components of the NPDES program. Chapter 3 addresses procedural aspects of the NPDES program, such as applying for permits, the types of permits, and administrative procedures for permit issuance. The section 404 permit program is addressed in chapter 6.

A. DEFINITIONS

By prohibiting certain unpermitted activities, section 301(a) effectively prescribes the scope of the NPDES permit program. It is important to understand several key terms found in section 301(a)—"discharge," "pollutant," "point source," and "navigable waters"—in order to understand the scope of the NPDES program.

* The author acknowledges the contributions of Karen M. Wardzinski, David B. Sandalow, Sara M. Burgin, and Beth S. Ginsberg to the 1994 edition of this chapter.
    1. 33 U.S.C. § 1311(a).

1. Discharge

CWA section 501(12) defines the term "discharge of a pollutant" to mean "any addition of any pollutant to navigable waters from any point source."[2] This definition leads to questions about the meaning of the terms "addition," "pollutant," and "point source."

The statute does not define the term "addition," and its meaning is not always straightforward. For example, courts have come to different results in cases involving activities that affect the flow of water to the detriment of water quality. In *National Wildlife Federation v. Gorsuch*,[3] the U.S. Court of Appeals for the D.C. Circuit considered the flow of water over a dam that resulted in the supersaturation of entrained gases as adversely affecting water quality of water below the dam. The court concluded that the adverse effects on water quality were the result of in-stream water quality changes and, therefore, did not constitute the "addition" of pollutants to the water.[4] In *Rybacheck v. Environmental Protection Agency*,[5] however, the Ninth Circuit Court of Appeals considered placer mining activities that caused soil, rock, sand, and minerals from the streambed to be resuspended in the water column. In that case, the court concluded that pollutants were being added to the water, and that therefore a discharge had occurred.

Courts have also disagreed about whether the spraying of herbicides or insecticides may constitute the discharge of pollutants. In *No Spray Coalition, Inc. v. City of New York*,[6] the district court held that spraying insecticides into the atmosphere did not constitute a discharge into navigable waters, even though some de minimus amount of insecticide did drift into navigable waters. On the other hand, in *Headwaters, Inc. v. Talent Irrigation District*,[7] the Ninth Circuit held that spraying herbicides directly into surface waters to control vegetative growth in the waterway did constitute a discharge.

2. Pollutant

Section 502(6) of the CWA defines "pollutant" to mean "dredged spoil, solid waste, incinerator residue, sewage, garbage, sewage sludge, munitions, chemical

---

2. 33 U.S.C. § 1362(12). The definition also includes "any addition of any pollutant to the waters of the contiguous zone or the ocean from any point source other than a vessel or other floating craft."

3. 693 F.2d 156 (D.C. Cir. 1982).

4. *Id.; see also* National Wildlife Fed'n v. Consumers Power Co., 862 F.2d 580,585 (6th Cir. 1988) (pumped storage plant's release of generating water containing dead fish is not the "addition" of pollutants).

5. 904 F.2d 1276 (9th Cir. 1990).

6. 200 U.S. Dist. LEXIS 13919 (S.D. N.Y. Sept. 25, 2000).

7. 243 F.3d 526 (9th Cir. 2001).

wastes, biological materials, radioactive materials,[8] heat,[9] wrecked or discarded equipment, rock, sand, cellar dirt, and industrial, municipal, and agricultural waste discharged into water."[10]

Excluded from the definition of "pollutant" is sewage from vessels within the meaning of section 312 of the CWA, and water, gas, or other material injected into a well to facilitate oil or gas production, if the well is approved by the state.[11]

Courts have interpreted the definition of "pollutant" broadly. They have found the following to be pollutants: entrained gases naturally occurring in water that become supersaturated after the water is released from a dam,[12] chlorine and alum added to water by a water treatment plant for beneficial purposes,[13] bombs dropped during military target practice,[14] and dead fish and fish parts.[15]

3. Point Source

CWA section 501(14) defines the term "point source" to mean "any discernible, confined and discrete conveyance, including but not limited to any pipe, ditch, channel, conduit, well, discrete fissure, container, rolling stock, concentrated animal feeding operation, landfill leachate collection system,[16] or vessel or other floating craft, from which pollutants are or may be discharged."[17]

EPA's regulations specify that this definition includes surface runoff collected and channeled by human effort, and discharges through pipes, sewers, or other conveyances leading to privately owned treatment works.[18] However, the Act expressly excludes agricultural stormwater discharges and return flows from irrigated agriculture.[19]

---

8. Radioactive materials that are regulated under the Atomic Energy Act of 1954, 42 U.S.C. § 2011, are excluded from the CWA's definition of pollutant. Train v. Colorado Public Interest Research Group, 426 U.S. 1 (1976); Waste Action Project v. Dawn Mining Co., 137 F.3d 1426 (9th Cir. 1998). This exemption includes source, byproduct, or special nuclear materials.

9. *See, e.g.*, Piney Run Preservation Ass'n v. County Commissioners of Carroll County, 50 F. Supp. 2d 443 (D. Md. 1999).

10. CWA § 502(6), 33 U.S.C. § 1362(6); 40 C.F.R. § 122.2.

11. CWA § 502(6), 33 U.S.C. § 1362(6).

12. National Wildlife Fed'n v. Gorsuch, 693 F.2d 156 (D.C. Cir. 1982) (holding that these were pollutants even though they were not *added* to waters of the United States and, thus, were not subject to NPDES permit requirements).

13. Hudson River Fishermen's Ass'n v. City of New York, 751 F. Supp. 1088 (S.D.N.Y. 1990).

14. Weinberger v. Romero-Barcelo, 456 U.S. 305 (1982).

15. National Wildlife Fed'n v. Consumers Power Co., 657 F. Supp. 989 (W.D. Mich. 1987), *rev'd on other grounds,* 862 F.2d 580 (6th Cir. 1988).

16. CWA § 507, 33 U.S.C. § 1367.

17. CWA § 502(14), 33 U.S.C. § 1362(14); 40 C.F.R. § 122.2.

18. 40 C.F.R. § 122.2.

19. CWA § 502(14); 33 U.S.C. § 1362(14).

Courts have interpreted the term "point source" very broadly, expanding the term far beyond the traditional industrial or municipal outfall pipe. The following are examples of point sources: a gold leachate system capable of overflowing its series of sumps, ditches, and pumps;[20] overflows from mining spoil piles;[21] mushroom farming operations;[22] Navy planes;[23] a trap shooting range;[24] bulldozers and backhoes dumping fill materials into wetlands;[25] a cattle feedlot capable of discharging pollutants during an extreme storm event;[26] unintentional overflow from a lagoon at a hazardous waste facility;[27] leachate from a landfill that flowed into a pond and through a culvert to a marsh;[28] log transfer facilities;[29] and stormwater collected and channeled by pipes and culverts.[30]

4. Navigable Waters

CWA section 501(7) defines "navigable waters" to mean waters of the United States, including the territorial seas.[31] Thus, waters need not be capable of being navigated in order to fall within the scope of the NPDES program. Under EPA's regulations, navigable waters include:

1. All waters that are currently used, were used in the past, or may be susceptible to use in the future in interstate or foreign commerce, including all waters that are subject to the ebb and flow of the tide;
2. All interstate waters, including interstate "wetlands";
3. All other waters such as intrastate lakes, rivers, streams (including intermittent streams), mudflats, sandflats, wetlands, sloughs, prairie potholes, wet meadows, playa lakes, or natural ponds of which the use,

---

20. United States v. Earth Sciences, Inc., 599 F.2d 368 (l0th Cir.1979).

21. Committee to Save Mokelumme River v. East Bay Util. Dist., 13 F.3d. 305 (9th Cir. 1993); Trustees for Alaska v. EPA, 749 F.2d 549 (9th Cir. 1984); Sierra Club v. Abston Constr. Co., 620 F.2d 41 (5th Cir. 1980); Washington Wilderness Coalition v. Hecla Mining Co., 870 F. Supp. 983 (E.D. Wash. 1994).

22. United States v. Frezzo Bros., 546 F. Supp. 713 (E.D. Pa. 1982), aff'd, 703 F.2d 62 (3d Cir.), cert. denied, 464 U.S. 829 (1983).

23. Weinberger v. Romero-Barcelo, supra.

24. Stone v. Naperville Park District, 38 F. Supp. 651 (N.D. Ill. 1999).

25. United States v. Weisman, 489 F. Supp. 1331 (M.D. Fla. 1980).

26. Carr v. Alta Verde Indus., Inc., 931 F.2d 1055 (5th Cir. 1991); Community Ass'n for Restoration of the Env't v. Henry Bosma Dairy, 65 F. Supp. 2d 1129 (E.D. Wash. 1999).

27. Fishel v. Westinghouse Elec. Corp., 640 F. Supp. 442 (M.D. Pa. 1986).

28. Dague v. City of Burlington, 935 F.2d 1343 (2d Cir. 1991).

29. However, CWA section 407 directs EPA and the Corps of Engineers to enter into an agreement coordinating permitting for log transfer facilities under sections 402 and 404. 33 U.S.C. § 1347.

30. Driscoll v. Adams, 181 F.3d 1285 (11th Cir. 1999); NRDC v. Train, 396 F. Supp. 1393 (D.D.C. 1975), aff'd sub nom. NRDC v. Costle, 568 F.2d 1369 (D.C. Cir. 1977).

31. CWA § 502(7), 33 U.S.C. § 1362(7).

degradation, or destruction would affect or could affect interstate or foreign commerce including any such waters:

    a.   that are or could be used by interstate or foreign travelers for recreational purposes;

    b.   from which fish or shellfish are or could be taken and sold in interstate or foreign commerce; or

    c.   that are used or could be used for industrial purposes by industries in interstate commerce;

4.   All impoundments of waters otherwise defined as waters of the United States under this definition;

5.   Tributaries of waters identified in paragraphs 1 through 4 of this definition;

6.   The territorial seas; and

7.   "Wetlands" adjacent to waters (other than waters that are themselves wetlands) identified in paragraphs 1 through 6 of this definition.[32]

Publicly owned treatment works (POTWs) and waste treatment systems, including treatment ponds or lagoons designed to meet the requirements of the CWA, generally are not considered waters of the United States.[33]

For many years, courts followed EPA's lead, defining navigable waters to include nearly every type and form of surface water body that could be envisioned under any scenario to involve interstate commerce.[34] Courts have held that intermittent streams[35] and irrigation ditches[36] are navigable waters.

---

32. 40 C.F.R. § 122.2. Many disputes concerning the reach of the term "waters of the U.S." have arisen in the context of the Corps of Engineers exercising its jurisdiction over wetland fill activities under section 404 of the CWA. 33 U.S.C. § 1344. Wetlands, which are included in the definition of waters of the United States, are themselves defined to mean areas that are inundated or saturated by surface or groundwater at a frequency and duration sufficient to support, and that under normal circumstances do support, a prevalence of vegetation typically adapted for life in saturated soil conditions. Wetlands typically include swamps, marshes, bogs, and similar areas. 40 C.F.R. § 122.2. Chapter 6 of this book addresses wetlands and the Corps of Engineers' jurisdiction.

33. 40 C.F.R. § 122.2.

34. *See, e.g.*, United States v. Oxford Royal Mushroom Prod., Inc., 487 F. Supp. 852 (E.D. Pa. 1980) (term "navigable waters" does not require navigability in fact); United States v. Phelps Dodge, 391 F. Supp. 1181 (D. Ariz. 1975) (definition of waters of the United States includes normally dry arroyo which, when wet, flows into public waters constituting waters of the United States); United States v. Holland, 373 F. Supp. 665 (M.D. Fla. 1974) (waters of non-navigable, manmade mosquito canals, which emptied into bayou of Tampa Bay, were "waters of the U.S."); Leslie Salt Co. v. United States, 896 F.2d 354, 369 (9th Cir. 1990), *cert. denied,* 498 U.S. 1126, 111 S. Ct. 1089 (1991) (seasonal ponding in former salt pits sufficient to constitute "water of the U.S.").

35. Driscoll v. Adams, 181 F.3d 1285 (11th Cir. 1999); United States v. Edison, 108 F.3d 1336 (11th Cir. 1997).

36. Community Ass'n for Restoration of the Env't v. Henry Bosma Dairy, 65 F. Supp. 2d 1129 (W.D. Wash. 1999).

In 2001, however, the U.S. Supreme Court drew the line on the CWA's jurisdiction in *Solid Waste Agency of Northern Cook County v. United States Army Corps of Engineers (SWANCC)*.[37] Although *SWANCC* involved the proposed filling of a wetland under the section 404 permit program, the Court's interpretation of the term "navigable waters" has bearing on the scope of the NPDES program as well. In *SWANCC*, the Corps had concluded that an isolated wetland was a navigable water because migratory birds, which are in interstate commerce, used the wetland for habitat. The Supreme Court disagreed, holding that the mere use of isolated wetland by migratory birds did not render it a "navigable water" within the meaning of the CWA.

B. EXCLUSIONS FROM THE NPDES PROGRAM

Although the scope of the NPDES program is broad, there are several statutory and regulatory exceptions to the program's coverage. The following discharges do not require an NPDES permit:

1. Any discharge of sewage from vessels; effluent from properly functioning marine engines; laundry, shower, and galley sink wastes; or any other discharge incidental to the normal operation of a vessel. This exclusion does not apply to trash, garbage, or other materials discharged overboard, or to discharges when the vessel is operating in a capacity other than as a means of transportation, such as a storage, seafood-processing, mining, or energy facility, or when secured to any of these facilities or to the ocean floor;[38]

2. The discharge of pollutants (including sewage and industrial wastes) to a POTW;[39]

3. Any discharge in compliance with the instructions of an on-scene coordinator under the Comprehensive Environmental Response, Compensation, and Liability Act (CERCLA)[40] or 33 C.F.R. section 153.10(e) (Oil and Hazardous Substances Pollution);[41]

4. Any introduction of pollutants from nonpoint source agricultural or silvicultural activities, including stormwater runoff from orchards, cultivated crops, pastures, rangelands, and forest lands, unless otherwise explicitly covered in the NPDES regulation at 40 C.F.R. part 122;[42]

---

37. 531 U.S. 159 (2001).

38. 40 C.F.R. § 122.3(a).

39. 40 C.F.R. § 122.3(c). Chapter 5 provides a complete discussion of § 307 pretreatment requirements.

40. 42 U.S.C. § 9601 *et seq.*

41. 40 C.F.R. § 122.3(d).

42. 40 C.F.R. § 122.3(e).

5. Return flows from irrigated agriculture;[43]
6. Discharges to privately owned treatment works unless otherwise required to be permitted pursuant to 40 C.F.R. section 122.44(m);[44] and
7. Discharges of dredged or fill material regulated under section 404 of the CWA.[45]

C. DISCHARGES TO GROUNDWATER AND WELLS

The CWA does not generally require NPDES permits for discharges to groundwater or wells.[46] Some courts have held that an NPDES permit is not required for discharges to groundwater even if those discharges eventually migrate to surface waters.[47] Other courts have found NPDES permits to be required when discharges to groundwater result in the migration of pollutants to hydrologically connected surface waters.[48]

In states with approved NPDES permitting programs, the states must themselves demonstrate the legal authority "to control the disposal of pollutants into wells."[49] EPA is far less demanding in its review of a state's program for well disposal than it is of a state's program for surface water discharges. EPA's regulations require only that the state's authority enable it to protect public health and welfare and to impose whatever permit terms and conditions

---

43. 40 C.F.R. § 122.3(f); CWA § 502(14); 33 U.S.C. § 1362(14).

44. 40 C.F.R. § 122.3(g). 40 C.F.R. § 122.44(m) authorizes the NPDES permit-issuing authority to address discharges into a privately owned treatment works in one of three ways, in order to ensure compliance with applicable requirements of the NPDES regulations. The authority may (1) issue a permit that includes conditions expressly applicable to one or more users, as limited co-permittees; (2) issue separate permits to the treatment works and its users; or (3) simply issue a permit to the treatment works with no specific conditions applicable to any users.

45. 33 U.S.C. § 1344; 40 C.F.R. § 122.3(b).

46. Exxon Corp. v. Train, 554 F.2d 1310,1329 (5th Cir. 1977); *see also* Idaho Rural Council v. Bosma, 143 F. Supp. 2d 1169, 1180 (D. Idaho 2001); Potter v. Asarco, 49 ENV'T REP. CAS. (BNA) 1082 (D. Nebr. 1999); Allegany Env. Action Coalition v. Westinghouse Corp., 46 ENV.'T REP. CAS. (BNA) 1126 (W.D. Pa. 1998); United States v. GAF Corp., 389 F. Supp. 1379 (S.D. Tex. 1975).

47. Village of Oconomowoc Lake v. Dayton Hudson Corp., 24 F.3d 962, 965 (7th Cir. 1994); Umatilla Water Quality Protection Assoc. v. Smith Frozen Foods, Inc., 962 F. Supp. 1312, 1318 (D. Or. 1997).

48. Idaho Rural Council v. Bosma, 143 F. Supp. 1169, 1180 (D. Idaho 2001); Friends of Santa Fe County v. LAC Minerals, 892 F. Supp. 1333, 1357 (D.N.M. 1995); Washington Wilderness Coalition v. Hecla Mining Co., 870 F. Supp. 983, 989 (E.D. Wash. 1994); Sierra Club v. Colorado Refining Co., 838 F. Supp. 1428, 1434 (D. Colo. 1993). Independent of the NPDES, state laws and regulations may require permits for discharges to groundwater. *See, e.g.*, Ala. Admin. Code § 335-6-6-.03; Colo. Admin. Code § 6.4.0; Ill. Admin. Code § 309.102; N.Y. Admin. Code § 751.1(a); Tex. Admin. Code § 305(b).

49. 33 U.S.C. § 1342(b)(1)(D).

may be appropriate.[50] Generally, EPA will defer to state programs under the Underground Injection Program of the Safe Drinking Water Act for satisfaction of this requirement.

II. Conditions Applicable to All NPDES Permits

CWA section 402 requires that a NPDES permit assure compliance with all CWA requirements applicable to the discharge being permitted.[51] Permits have five general types of provisions: technology-based limitations, water quality–based limitations, monitoring and reporting requirements, standard conditions, and special conditions. The following sections address each of these components briefly. Parts III through VIII of this chapter address them in greater detail.

A. TECHNOLOGY-BASED LIMITATIONS

Technology-based limitations are limitations on the discharge of pollutants developed based on the availability and cost of pollution control technology. EPA has promulgated technology-based effluent limitation for many industries. If EPA has promulgated a guideline applicable to the industry group to which a facility belongs, the effluent limitation must be incorporated into the facility's NPDES permit.[52] If EPA has not yet issued an applicable effluent limitation guideline, the permitting authority must develop technology-based limitations for the facility being permitted based on its best professional judgment (BPJ).[53]

B. WATER QUALITY–BASED LIMITATIONS

Water quality–based limitations are limitations developed in order to achieve compliance with established water quality standards. Technological feasibility and economic reasonableness are not factors considered in developing water quality–based effluent limitations. Water quality–based limitations are included in NPDES permits if technology-based limitations alone are not sufficient to ensure compliance with applicable water quality standards.[54]

C. MONITORING

Monitoring is the primary means of determining whether a permittee is complying with limitations included in an NPDES permit. Permittees are required to

---

50. 40 C.F.R. § 123.28.

51. 33 U.S.C. §§ 1342(a) & (b).

52. CWA § 301(b), 33 U.S.C. § 1311(b); 40 C.F.R. § 125(b).

53. CWA § 402(a)(1)(B), 33 U.S.C. § 1342(a)(1)(B); 40 C.F.R. §§ 125(3)(d).

54. CWA §§ 301(b)(1)(C), 303(e)(3)(A), 33 U.S.C. §§ 1311(b)(1)(C), 1313(e)(3)(A); 40 C.F.R. § 122.44(d).

monitor their own discharges and report the results of their monitoring in Discharge Monitoring Reports (DMRs) submitted to EPA or the state agency administering the NPDES permit program.[55]

An NPDES permit identifies the pollutant parameters that must be sampled, the place where sampling must be conducted,[56] the frequency of sampling, the type of samples that must be taken (grab or composite), the method to be used to analyze the samples, and the frequency of reporting.[57] In establishing permit conditions concerning each of these requirements, the permitting authority will consider the facility's design capacity, the treatment method to be used, the significance of the pollutants discharged, and the feasibility and cost of monitoring.

D. STANDARD CONDITIONS

EPA regulations found at 40 C.F.R. sections 122.41 and 122.42 set forth "boilerplate" conditions that must be included in all NPDES permits, either expressly or by incorporating these regulations by reference. The following are the most significant boilerplate conditions:

1. An express duty to minimize or prevent any permit violation that has a reasonable likelihood of adversely affecting human health or the environment;

2. A duty to properly operate and maintain the facility and its treatment equipment at all times;

3. A duty to allow the permitting authority to enter and inspect the premises, take samples, and have access to records;

4. A requirement to report planned changes to the facility, anticipated noncompliance, and transfers to new owners or operators;

5. A prohibition on bypassing any portion of the treatment facility unless the bypass is necessary for essential maintenance. This prohibition may

---

55. 40 C.F.R. § 122.41(1)(4). DMRs are one of the primary tools used to support enforcement actions against permittees who violate permit limits. However, permitting authorities also conduct periodic inspections of permitted facilities, and may base enforcement actions on observations made or samples taken during such inspections.

56. Samples are usually taken at the point of discharge. However, where imposing permit limitations at the point of discharge is impractical or infeasible, effluent limitations may be imposed on internal wastestreams before they are mixed with other wastestreams or discharged from the facility. 40 C.F.R. § 122.46(h). *See* Texas Mun. Power Agency v. EPA, 836 F.2d 1482, 1488 (5th Cir. 1988) (holding that EPA is authorized to regulate internal wastestreams because such controls are necessary to control adequately discharges into waters of the United States); *see also* Mobil Oil Corp. v. EPA, 716 F.2d 1187, 1190 (7th Cir. 1983), *cert. denied*, 466 U.S. 980 (1984) (upholding EPA authority to monitor internal wastestreams).

57. 40 C.F.R. §§ 122.44(i) & 122.48.

apply even if the permittee could bypass a part of the treatment system and still comply with its permit effluent limits;[58] and

6.   A provision authorizing a permittee to raise as an affirmative defense to a permit violation the occurrence of an upset, if the reporting conditions of 40 C.F.R. section 122.44(n) are met.[59]

E. SPECIAL CONDITIONS

In addition to "boilerplate" conditions required of all NPDES permits, permits may contain additional site-specific conditions appropriate to the particular facility being permitted. For example, permits include conditions specifying their duration,[60] and may include schedules of compliance for meeting applicable limitations.[61] Some permits also include conditions reflecting variances from otherwise applicable requirements.[62]

III. Technology-Based Limitations

The CWA requires all dischargers to comply with effluent limitations based on available pollution control technology.[63] These "technology-based limits" are established after consideration of technological feasibility and cost. EPA has established nationwide technology-based limitations for many industries.[64] All point sources have technology-based limits in their NPDES permits, whether they are based on EPA's nationwide guidelines or facility-specific BPJ.

Most of the Clean Water Act's success in reducing water pollution in the past 30 years has been the result of technology-based limitations on point sources. Technology-based limits could be developed and implemented relatively quickly, and they ensured that all dischargers implemented a certain level of pollution

---

58. 40 C.F.R. § 122.41(m); upheld in NRDC v. EPA, 822 F.2d 104 (D.C. Cir. 1987). *See* United States v. Weitzenhoff, 1 F.3d 1523 (9th Cir. 1993) for discussion of what constitutes "essential maintenance" for purposes of the bypass provision.

59. "Upset" is defined as an exceptional incident in which there is unintentional and temporary noncompliance with a technology-based permit effluent limitation due to factors beyond the control of the permittee. Operational error, design defects, or lack of preventative maintenance do not constitute an upset. Upsets are not recognized as defenses to water quality–based permit effluent limitations. 40 C.F.R. § 122.41(n)(1).

60. 40 C.F.R. § 122.46.

61. 40 C.F.R. § 122.47.

62. Available variances are discussed in more detail below and in 40 C.F.R. pt. 125, subpts. B–G.

63. 33 U.S.C. § 1311.

64. 40 C.F.R. pts. 425–71.

control. The use of technology-based limits also encouraged the development of new pollution control technology by essentially guaranteeing a market for technological improvements. At the same time, however, technology-based limits are not directly tied to the water quality goals underlying the CWA. In some instances, technology-based limits may be insufficient to achieve the desired levels of water quality, while in others they may require the installation of expensive control devices that are not needed to achieve the desired level of water quality. Most observers agree, however, that technology-based limits are a reasonable method, although not necessarily the only reasonable method, of limiting water pollution.

Although technology-based limits are set based upon an evaluation of available technology, permittees are generally not required to implement any specific pollution control technology to comply with the limits. With only limited exceptions,[65] a permittee may choose to use any pollution control technology as long as permit limits are met.

A. LEVELS OF CONTROL

The CWA creates an alphabet soup of technology-based standards. Effluent limitations based upon BPT and BCT (which stand for "best practicable control technology currently available" and "best conventional pollutant control technology," respectively) apply to discharges of conventional pollutants to surface water by existing sources. Effluent limitations based upon BAT (best available technology economically achievable) apply to discharges of toxic and nonconventional pollutants into surface waters by existing sources. NSPS, or "new source performance standards," apply to new sources discharging into surface waters. PSES (pretreatment standards for existing sources) and PSNS (pretreatment standards for new sources) apply to discharges to publicly owned treatment works. The following subsections discuss each of these in more detail.

1. Best Practicable Control Technology Currently Available (BPT)

All conventional pollutants[66] must be controlled through application of either the "best practicable control technology currently available" (BPT) or the "best conventional pollutant control technology" (BCT). BPT is the baseline level of control applicable in all circumstances.

---

65. *See* CWA § 304(e), 33 U.S.C. § 1314(e) (authorizing EPA to mandate "best management practices" in connection with the development of effluent guidelines).

66. The conventional pollutants are BOD (biological oxygen demand), TSS (total suspended solids), oil and grease, pH, and fecal coliform. *See* CWA § 304(a)(4); 40 C.F.R. § 401.16.

BPT limits are based on the "average of the best" performance in an industrial category or subcategory.[67] In setting BPT limits, EPA typically identifies a model technology used by a group of the best performers in an industry, and then sets limits based on the capabilities of that technology. However, if EPA determines that the technology used by an industry is uniformly inadequate, EPA may base BPT limits on technologies not currently used in the industry but transferable from elsewhere.[68]

CWA section 304(b)(1)(B) sets forth the following six factors to be considered in establishing BPT limits: (i) the age of the equipment and facilities involved, (ii) the process employed, (iii) the engineering aspects of the application of various types of control techniques, (iv) process changes, (v) non–water quality environmental impacts (including energy requirements), and (vi) such other factors as the administrator deems appropriate.[69] Each of these factors must also be considered when establishing BCT and BAT limits.[70]

In establishing BPT limits, however, EPA must also consider the "total cost of application of technology in relation to the effluent reduction benefits. . . ."[71] This amounts to a limited cost-benefit analysis in which EPA considers the benefits in terms of effluent reduction, but does not broadly compare the societal costs and benefits of the limitations.[72] The Act's legislative history states that the consideration of cost is intended "to limit the application of technology only where the additional degree of effluent reduction is *wholly out of proportion* to costs of achieving a marginal reduction of pollution. . . ."[73]

---

67. The "average of the best" formulation is found in the legislative history of the 1972 Federal Water Pollution Control Act (FWPCA). *See* Conf. Rep. on S. 2770 (October 4, 1972), Legislative History of the Federal Water Pollution Control Act of 1972 ("Legislative History") at 169–70 ("The Administrator should establish a range of 'best practicable' levels based upon the average of the best existing performance by plants of various sizes, ages, and unit processes within each industrial category."). No specific percentage of the industry must be included within the group of best performers. In the effluent guidelines for the organic chemicals, plastics, and synthetic fibers industrial category, for example, EPA set BPT limits based on the performance of a technology used by 72 percent of the industry; in the original effluent guidelines for the pulp and paper industry, EPA set BPT limits based on a technology used by approximately 30 percent of the industry. In contrast, the Clean Air Act requires EPA to set limits no less stringent than "the average emission limitation achieved by the best performing 12 percent of the existing sources." 42 U.S.C. § 7412(d)(3)(A).

68. *See, e.g.,* American Meat Inst. v. EPA, 526 F.2d 442, 453 (7th Cir. 1975); Tanners' Council of Am. v. Train, 540 F.2d 1188, 1192 (4th Cir. 1976).

69. CWA 304(b)(1)(B), 33 U.S.C. § 1314(b)(1)(B).

70. *Id.*

71. *Id.*

72. Legislative History, *supra,* note 58.

73. *Id.* at 170.

2. Best Conventional Pollutant-Control Technology (BCT)

In 1972, when Congress first enacted the CWA, it required NPDES to include effluent limits based on BPT by 1977, and effluent limits based on BAT by 1983.[74] In 1977, however, Congress amended this scheme because it felt that limits on conventional pollutants should be increased beyond BPT only if more-stringent limits were reasonable in light of their cost.[75] Congress established BCT as a new category of limitations, at least as stringent as BPT, but typically not as stringent as BAT.

Under the current statutory scheme, NPDES permits include BCT limits only if they are deemed to be cost-effective in light of two complex cost tests. The first such test is the "POTW cost-comparison test." In performing this test, EPA identifies a candidate BCT technology and looks at the cost of using that technology to remove additional conventional pollutants beyond those removed at the BPT level of control. If this cost is less than a benchmark of $0.46 per pound in 1986 dollars, then the candidate technology "passes" the POTW cost-comparison test. The $0.46-per-pound benchmark is based upon EPA's calculation of the cost of upgrading a POTW from secondary to advanced secondary treatment.[76]

The second BCT cost test is the "industry cost-effectiveness test." In performing this test, EPA identifies a candidate BCT technology and divides the cost per pound of the extra conventional pollutants removed using the candidate BCT technology instead of BPT, by the cost per pound of conventional pollutants removed using the BPT technology instead of no control. (For example, if the incremental conventional pollutant removals gained by using a candidate BCT technology cost $0.30 per pound, and the incremental conventional pollutant removals gained by using BPT technology cost $0.15 per pound, then the ratio would be 2.0.) If this ratio is less than a benchmark of 1.29, the candidate technology "passes" the industry cost-effectiveness test. The 1.29 benchmark is based upon EPA's calculation of the cost per pound to upgrade a POTW from secondary treatment to advanced secondary treatment, divided by the cost per pound to upgrade from no control to secondary treatment.[77]

Both of these cost tests are highly complex, and neither has any basis in the statutory language. Nothing in the statute requires EPA to establish specific benchmarks, much less to choose $0.46 per pound or a ratio of 1.29 as the benchmarks. Instead, EPA could have compared the cost of pollution-control technologies on an industry-by-industry or case-by-case basis.

---

74. *See* Public Law 92-500 (Oct. 18, 1972).

75. *See* 3 Legislative History of the Clean Water Act of 1977 at 266-69 (Oct. 1978).

76. *See* 51 Fed. Reg. 24,974,24,976 (July 9,1986) (setting forth EPA's "BCT methodology").

77. *Id.*

3. Best Available Technology Economically Achievable (BAT)

Under the CWA, all toxic and nonconventional pollutants[78] must be controlled through use of the BAT. BAT limits are based on the "best of the best" performance within an industrial category or subcategory.[79] In setting BAT limits, EPA looks to "the optimally operating plant, the pilot plant which acts as a beacon to show what is possible."[80] BAT limits may be based on actual plant operations, pilot plant studies, or bench scale studies.[81] In setting BAT limits, EPA is directed to consider the same section 304(b)(2)(B) core factors that must be considered in setting BPT and BCT—"the age of the equipment and facilities involved, the process employed, the engineering aspects of the application of various types of control techniques, process changes . . . non–water quality environmental impacts (including energy requirements), [and] such other factors as the Administrator deems appropriate."[82]

Congress intended cost to play a lesser role in setting BAT limits than in setting BCT or BPT.[83] The CWA does not require EPA to compare costs and effluent reduction benefits in establishing BAT, but instead requires only that EPA consider "cost" and whether such limits are "economically achievable."[84]

4. New Source Performance Standards (NSPS)

CWA section 306(b)(1)(B) requires all "new sources" to meet "new source performance standards" (NSPS).[85] EPA's CWA regulations define "new source," in almost all relevant circumstances, to mean a "building, structure, facility, or installation . . . the construction of which is commenced . . . [a]fter promulgation of standards of performance under section 306 of the CWA which are applicable

---

78. The toxic pollutants are those identified in CWA § 307(a)(1) and listed at 40 C.F.R. § 401.15. "Nonconventional" pollutants are those that are neither toxic nor conventional.

79. See Legislative History, supra note 58, at 170 ("the range should, at a minimum, be established with reference to the best performer in any industrial category.").

80. Kennecott v. EPA, 780 F.2d 445, 448 (4th Cir. 1985); see also National Ass'n of Metal Finishers v. EPA, 719 F.2d 624, 657 n. 51 (3d Cir. 1983); FMC Corp. v. Train, 539 F.2d 973, 983 (4th Cir. 1976); American Frozen Food Inst. v. Train, 539 F.2d 107, 117 (D.C. Cir.1976); American Iron & Steel Inst. v. EPA, 526 F.2d 1027,1061 (3d Cir. 1975).

81. See, e.g., American Paper Inst. v. Train, 543 F.2d 328, 353 (D.C. Cir. 1976); see also Conference Report at 170.

82. 33 U.S.C. § 1314(b)(2)(B).

83. Legislative History, supra note 58, at 170; see, e.g., American Petroleum Inst. v. EPA, 661 F.2d 340, 355 (5th Cir. 1981); Association of Pac. Fisheries v. EPA, 615 F.2d 794, 817 (9th Cir. 1980).

84. CWA §§ 301(b)(2)(A), 304(b)(2)(B).

85. 33 U.S.C. § 1316(b)(1)(B).

to such source. . . ."[86] That is, if EPA has not promulgated an NSPS applicable to a newly constructed facility, the facility is not considered to be a "new source." Such a facility is classified as a "new discharger," and BAT/BCT limits, instead of NSPS, apply.

NSPS limits are intended to reflect "the greatest degree of effluent reduction . . . achievable through application of the best available demonstrated control technologies, processes, operating methods or other alternatives. . . ."[87] NSPS may apply to any pollutant, whether conventional, nonconventional, or toxic. NSPS are at least as stringent as BAT and may be more stringent.[88] Costs often play even less of a role in establishing NSPS than they do in establishing BAT. In part, this is because whole categories of costs, such as the cost of retrofitting existing technologies or of purchasing additional land at current locations, are not relevant in determining NSPS. In requiring new sources to meet more-stringent limitations than existing sources, Congress expected that new sources could incorporate the newest and most efficient processes and treatment systems in plant design.[89]

5. Pretreatment Standards (PSES and PSNS)

PSES and PSNS stand for "pretreatment standards for existing sources" and "pretreatment standards for new sources," respectively. These standards may apply to the introduction of pollutants into publicly owned treatment works. Chapter 5 addresses pretreatment standards in detail.

B. DEVELOPING TECHNOLOGY-BASED LIMITS

Effluent guidelines are regulations establishing industrywide limitations on the discharge of pollutants. If EPA has established effluent guidelines applicable to a type of facility, then those guidelines serve as the basis for technology-based permit limits for each facility of that type. To date, EPA has promulgated more than 50 sets of effluent guidelines.[90] Any particular set of guidelines may include

---

86. 40 C.F.R. § 122.2; *see also* CWA § 306(a)(2), 33 U.S.C. § 1316(a)(2). If EPA were to promulgate an effluent guideline within 120 days of proposal (something the agency has never done), the new source performance standards within that effluent guideline could apply to any source the construction of which was commenced after *proposal* of the rule. *See* 40 C.F.R. § 122.2, NRDC v. EPA, 822 F.2d 104 (D.C. Cir. 1987) (upholding validity of "new source" definition in § 122.2). *But see* National Ass'n of Metal Finishers v. EPA, 719 F.2d 624 (3d Cir. 1983) (holding definition invalid), *rev'd on other grounds sub nom.* CMA v. NRDC, 470 U.S. 116 (1985).

87. 33 U.S.C. § 1316(b)(1)(A).

88. *See, e.g.,* American Iron & Steel Inst. v. EPA, 526 F.2d 1027, 1058 (3d Cir. 1975).

89. Legislative History, *supra* note 58, at 172, 797, 1476; *see, e.g.,* American Paper Inst. v. Train, 543 F.2d 328, 354 (D.C. Cir. 1976).

90. *See* 40 C.F.R. pts. 405–471.

some or all of the types of technology-based limitations discussed above as well as "best management practices" under CWA section 304(e).[91]

In order to develop an effluent guideline, EPA typically (i) gathers extensive information on the industry (through questionnaires, wastewater sampling, literature reviews, and other methods); (ii) performs detailed statistical analyses of this information; (iii) develops a set of proposed control options for the industry; (iv) estimates the effluent reductions, costs, economic impacts, and environmental effects of those options; (v) shapes the options into a proposed set of limits; (vi) explains the proposed limits in a *Federal Register* publication and additional supporting documents; (vii) reviews comments on the proposed limits; and (viii) incorporates those comments into a final regulation (again with considerable supporting documentation). From start to finish, this process often takes five years or more.

Every two years EPA publishes an *Effluent Guidelines Plan* that sets forth the agency's plan for developing new or revised effluent guidelines.[92] The plans are published pursuant to section 304(m) of the CWA and a consent decree in *NRDC v. Reilly*.[93] Pursuant to the consent decree, EPA will develop approximately 20 new or revised effluent guidelines, which began during the 1990s and continue into the early 2000s. Some of the industries that will be subject to these guidelines have been identified; others have not.

If EPA has not developed an effluent guideline applicable to a facility, the permit writer must develop technology-based limits based on "best professional judgment."[94] Even if EPA has developed guidelines, the permit writer may need to supplement the limits based upon EPA guidelines with additional BPJ limits for pollutants not addressed in the guideline.[95]

C. VARIANCES

The CWA authorizes a few limited opportunities for dischargers to receive variances from technology-based limits. EPA rarely grants such variances. The elements of these variances are summarized below.

1. Fundamentally Different Factors Variance

A facility that is "fundamentally different" from those upon which an effluent guideline is based may be eligible for a section 301(n) variance from the limits

---

91. 33 U.S.C. § 1314(e).

92. CWA § 304(m), 33 U.S.C. § 1314(m). The most recent *Effluent Guidelines Plan* was published at 65 Fed. Reg. 53,008 (Aug. 31, 2000).

93. Civ. No. 89-2980 (D.D.C. Jan. 30, 1992).

94. 33 U.S.C. § 1342(a)(1).

95. 40 C.F.R. § 122.44(e)(1).

set forth in that effluent guideline.[96] EPA rarely grants fundamentally different variances, and never with respect to New Source Performance Standards or Pretreatment Standards for New Sources. If a variance is granted, the permit writer uses BPJ to develop facility-specific technology-based limits.

Two requirements significantly limit the availability of the fundamentally different factors variance. First, applications for the variance must be submitted within 180 days of the date the effluent limitation guideline in question is established or revised.[97] Second, differences in the cost of controlling pollutants do not constitute a fundamental difference for purposes of this variance.[98] The only differences that may be considered are those with respect to (i) the age of the equipment and facilities involved, (ii) the process employed, (iii) the engineering aspects of the application of various types of control techniques, (iv) process changes, (v) non–water quality environmental impacts (including energy requirements), and (vi) other factors (excluding cost) that the EPA administrator considered in establishing the effluent guideline.

2. BAT Variances

The CWA authorizes EPA to grant two other types of variances from BAT limits. In practice, however, EPA almost never grants these variances.

The first such variance is for "economic incapability." CWA section 301(c) authorizes EPA to grant variances from BAT limits to dischargers that can demonstrate that proposed alternative limits "(1) will represent the maximum use of technology within the economic capability of the owner or operator; and (2) will result in reasonable further progress toward the elimination of the discharge of pollutants."[99] A discharger who receives such a variance is still required to comply with BPT limits for the pollutant at issue. The variance is not available for any toxic pollutant listed in CWA section 307(a)(1).[100]

The second type of variance from BAT limits set forth in an effluent guideline applies to only five specific nonconventional pollutants: ammonia, chlorine, color, iron, and phenols.[101] Dischargers must demonstrate that such a variance would not interfere with the attainment or maintenance of water quality, would not result in additional requirements on other point or nonpoint sources, and would not prevent

---

96. 33 U.S.C. § 1311(n); *see* 40 C.F.R. § 125.30–125.32.

97. CWA § 301(n)(2), 33 U.S.C. § 1311(n)(2). In addition, applications for this type of variance must be based solely on information submitted to the administrator during the development of the effluent guideline, unless the applicant did not have a reasonable opportunity to submit such information. CWA § 301(n)(1)(B), 33 U.S.C. § 1311(n)(1)(B).

98. CWA § 301(n)(1)(A), 33 U.S.C. § 1311(n)(1)(A).

99. 33 U.S.C. § 301(c).

100. CWA § 301(*l*), 33 U.S.C. § 1311(*l*).

101. CWA § 301(g), 33 U.S.C. § 1311(g).

the discharger from meeting BPT.[102] Procedures for covering additional pollutants under this variance (and for delisting pollutants) are set forth in the statute.[103]

IV. Water Quality–Based Effluent Limitations

Water quality–based effluent limitations are based upon the impact that a discharge makes on its receiving waters. The water quality standards established for a particular water body serve as the basis for imposing water quality–based treatment controls in NPDES permits beyond the technology-based levels of treatment required by CWA section 30l(b).[104]

The purpose of a water quality standard, as defined in CWA section l0l(a)(2), is to ensure that, wherever attainable, water quality provides for the protection and propagation of fish, shellfish, and wildlife, and provides for recreation in and on the water.[105] CWA section 303(c)(2)(A) further provides that water quality standards shall be established for waters taking into consideration their use and value for public water supplies; propagation of fish and shellfish; recreational purposes; and agricultural, industrial, navigation, and other purposes.[106]

Sections 301(b)(1)(C) and 303(e)(3)(A) of the CWA require that all NPDES permits include limitations as necessary to comply with water quality standards developed by the states pursuant to section 303.[107] NPDES regulations under 40 C.F.R. section 122.44(d)(1) specify the minimum requirements and general types of analyses necessary for establishing permit limits.[108]

A. ELEMENTS OF A WATER QUALITY STANDARD

"Water quality standards" are laws or regulations that consist of (i) the designated use or uses of a water body, (ii) the water quality criteria that are necessary to protect the use or uses, and (iii) an antidegradation statement.[109]

---

102. CWA § 301(g)(2), 33 U.S.C. § 1311(g)(2).

103. CWA §§ 301(g)(4), (5), 33 U.S.C. §§ 1311(g)(4), (5).

104. 40 C.F.R. § 131.2; *see also* 40 C.F.R. § 130.3.

105. 33 U.S.C. § 1251(a)(2).

106. 33 U.S.C. § 1313(c)(2)(A). Whereas section 101(a)(2) of the CWA establishes the *goal* of ensuring that the quality of all U.S. waters provides for protection and propagation of fish, shellfish, and wildlife, and for recreation in and on the water, section 303(c)(2) directs each state to consider all of the uses enumerated in section 303(c)(2) when establishing state water quality standards.

107. 33 U.S.C. §§ 1311(b)(1)(c), 1313(e)(3)(A). "States" include the fifty 50 states, the District of Columbia, Guam, the Commonwealth of Puerto Rico, Virgin Islands, American Samoa, the Trust Territory of the Pacific Islands, the Commonwealth of the Northern Mariana Islands, and Indian Tribes that EPA determines qualify for treatment as states for purposes of water quality standards. *See* 40 C.F.R. § 131.3(j), (k), & (l), and 40 C.F.R. § 131.8.

108. *See* U.S. EPA, Technical Support Document for Water Quality-Based Toxics Control ("Technical Support Document"), EPA 505/2-90-001, at 47 (Mar. 1991).

109. 40 C.F.R. § 131.6.

1. Designated Uses

Section 303(c) requires that each state designate uses for all water bodies within the state. A designated use can be either an existing use or a higher quality use even though that use is not currently an existing use.[110] Some uses to be protected under the CWA include protection and propagation of fish and shellfish, wildlife protection, recreation, public water supply, agriculture, navigation, and industry.[111] A state may designate several compatible uses for the same water body (for example, public water supply, contact recreation, high-quality aquatic habitat).[112]

The CWA makes distinction between "designated uses" and "existing uses" of a water body. Existing uses of a water body are those that were attained on or after the reference date of November 28, 1975.[113] Existing uses must be protected.[114] "Designated uses" are those specified in water quality standards whether or not the uses are being attained.[115] A state can remove a designated use—as long as it is higher than an existing use—if the state can demonstrate that attaining the designated use is not feasible.

Whenever a state attempts to demonstrate that attaining "fishable/swimmable" uses on a water body is not feasible, the state must prepare a scientific assessment called a use attainability analysis.[116] The use attainability analysis must be a comprehensive assessment of the physical, chemical, biological, and economic factors affecting achievement of a designated use. 40 C.F.R. section 131.10(g) lists only six conditions that may justify not attaining the designated use. The state's use attainability analysis must demonstrate to EPA that one or more of the 40 C.F.R. section 131.10(g) conditions exists. Use attainability analyses and the uses a state establishes based upon these analyses are subject to EPA's review and approval.

---

110. 40 C.F.R. § 131.3(f); 40 C.F.R. § 131.10. Subsection (d) of 40 C.F.R. § 131.10 states that, at a minimum, uses are deemed attainable if they can be achieved by the imposition of technology-based effluent limitations and cost-effective, reasonable best management practices for nonpoint source control.

111. 33 U.S.C. § 1313(c)(2)(A); 40 C.F.R. § 131.2.

112. 33 U.S.C. § 1370. One designated use that may be established for a water body is "outstanding national resource waters." This designation is intended for waters of the highest quality that have ecological uniqueness such as those within parks or refuges. *See* U.S. EPA, Introduction to Water Quality Standards ("EPA Introduction"), EPA-4401588-089 at 8–9 (Sept. 1988).

113. 40 C.F.R. § 131.3(e).

114. 40 C.F.R. § 131.12(a)(1).

115. 40 C.F.R. § 131.3(f).

116. 40 C.F.R. § 131.10(g) & (j); *see also* EPA Introduction at 16–17.

2. Water Quality Criteria

"Criteria" is used as a term in the CWA in two ways. The term is part of the definition of a state water quality standard—that is, a water quality standard is composed of designated uses and the water quality criteria necessary to protect those uses.[117] Upon adoption by a state, such "ambient criteria" become the applicable regulatory requirements for such waters. The other use of the term is in CWA section 304(a), which directs EPA to publish and periodically update water quality criteria reflecting the latest scientific knowledge on the effects on human health and welfare that may be expected from the presence of a certain pollutant in a body of water. Section 304(a) criteria are nonregulatory scientific assessments.[118] The following discussion focuses on ambient criteria.

Ambient criteria to protect uses of a water body designated by a state are expressed as (i) chemical-specific concentrations, (ii) toxicity levels, or (iii) narrative statements representing a quality of water that supports a particular use of a water body. Ambient criteria must contain sufficient parameters or constituents to protect the uses of a water body. When a water body has multiple use classifications, criteria must protect the most sensitive use.[119]

EPA regulations at 40 C.F.R. section 131.11(b) provide guidance to the states on the form of ambient criteria. Subparagraph (b)(l) indicates a preference for numerical criteria by directing states to establish criteria as numerical values based on section 304(a) guidance, section 304(a) guidance modified to reflect site-specific conditions, or other scientifically defensible methods. Two types of numerical criteria are discussed below. Numerical chemical-specific criteria focus on individual pollutants. Numeric whole-effluent toxicity criteria focus on combinations of pollutants.

Subparagraph (b)(2) requires that narrative criteria or criteria based upon biomonitoring methods be established where numerical criteria cannot be established, or when appropriate to supplement numerical criteria. When narrative criteria are adopted in lieu of numerical criteria to control toxic pollutants, the state must provide information identifying a methodology for how point sources will be regulated based upon the narrative criteria.[120]

a. Numeric Chemical-Specific Criteria. Numeric chemical-specific criteria are concentrations of individual pollutants that will be allowed in a water body based

---

117. 40 C.F.R. § 131.3(b).

118. 40 C.F.R. § 131.3(c); *see also* Preamble, Water Quality Standards: Establishment of Numeric Criteria for Priority Toxic Pollutants; States' Compliance ("National Toxics Rule"), 57 Fed. Reg. 60,848 & 60,850 (Dec. 22, 1992).

119. 40 C.F.R. § 131.11(a)(1).

120. 40 C.F.R. part 131; Technical Support Document, *supra,* at 1–42; *see also* U.S. EPA, WATER QUALITY STANDARDS HANDBOOK ("HANDBOOK"), at 3–24 (2d ed. Aug. 1994).

upon the uses of the water body. States traditionally have established numeric criteria for such parameters as dissolved oxygen, pH, and temperature. Prior to 1987, only some states have adopted numeric criteria for toxic pollutants.

In the Water Quality Act of 1987, Congress added section 303(c)(2)(B) to the CWA. Section 303(c)(2)(B) requires that each state, during its triennial water quality standards review, adopt criteria for all toxic pollutants listed pursuant to CWA section 307(a)(1) for which EPA has published criteria under section 304(a), and the discharge or presence of which in the affected waters could reasonably be expected to interfere with designated uses adopted by the state.[121] EPA has defined compliance with section 303(c)(2)(B) as state adoption and EPA approval of appropriate human health and aquatic life criteria for all priority pollutants that can reasonably be expected to interfere with designated uses in the state's waters.[122]

Under section 304(a)(1), EPA periodically publishes new and revised criteria documents or summaries of such documents.[123] EPA's criteria documents provide a toxicological evaluation of each chemical that is addressed. For toxic pollutants, the criteria documents tabulate available acute and chronic toxicity information for aquatic organisms and derive criteria maximum concentrations (acute criteria) and criteria continuous concentrations (chronic criteria). These are the criteria EPA recommends to protect aquatic life. For human health, the criteria document provides reference doses or carcinogenic slope factors for pollutants, and derives recommended criteria from available scientific information. EPA has published its methodologies for deriving aquatic life and human health criteria and has revised those methodologies over the years. EPA's methodologies for deriving these criteria and the factors and assumptions EPA uses in its calculations are a continuing source of controversy.[124]

Criteria documents are intended to serve as nonregulatory guidance and are not subject to the public notice and comment requirements of the federal Administrative Procedure Act.[125] Notification of a new or revised criteria document's availability is published in the *Federal Register.*

In establishing statewide numeric criteria for toxic pollutants, a state may adopt the same numeric limits as in the criteria EPA developed under section 304(a). States often adjust the national criteria to reflect local environmental conditions or

---

121. 33 U.S.C. § 1313(c)(2)(B). The 126 priority pollutants are listed at 40 C.F.R. § 423, Appendix A.

122. Notice, State Compliance with Clean Water Act Requirements for Adoption of Water Quality Criteria for Toxic Pollutants, 55 Fed. Reg. 14,350, 14,351 (Apr. 17, 1990).

123. *See* Preamble, National Toxics Rule, 57 Fed. Reg. at 60,850.

124. *See* Preamble, National Toxics Rule, 57 Fed. Reg. at 60,850 & 60,861.

125. U.S. EPA, Preamble, Quality Criteria for Water 1986, EPA 440/5-86-001 at 1 (May 1, 1986).

human exposure patterns. These state-specific criteria are then incorporated into statewide water quality standards as enforceable ambient water quality criteria.[126]

On December 22, 1992, EPA promulgated chemical-specific numeric criteria for priority toxic pollutants necessary to bring all states into compliance with the requirements of CWA section 303(c)(2)(B).[127] The rule establishes at least some criteria for fourteen jurisdictions.[128] States determined by EPA to comply fully with section 303(c)(2)(B) requirements are not affected by the rule.

Section 304(a) criteria documents formed this basis of EPA's federal numeric toxicity criteria.[129] Section 304(a) guidance for pollutants that are based on carcinogenicity presents concentrations for a range of risk levels from one excess cancer per 100,000 people (10^{-5}) to one excess cancer per 10 million people (10^{-7}). EPA's rule promulgates criteria according to the affected state's policy or practice with respect to acceptable risk level. EPA notes that there are waters where site-specific criteria could be developed, but it is up to the states to identify the waters and develop site-specific criteria.

b. Whole-Effluent Numeric Toxicity Criteria. CWA section 101(a)(3) provides that it is national policy that the discharge of toxics in toxic amounts should be prohibited. Whole-effluent toxicity (WET) criteria focus on the toxicological properties of combinations of pollutants in effluents or in mixtures of effluent and receiving waters. Where controls on individual pollutants through chemical-specific numeric criteria do not adequately protect uses of a water body, EPA has determined that assessing and controlling whole-effluent toxicity is necessary to reduce the toxic impact of the discharge. The CWA requires NPDES permits to include water quality–based effluent limitations, including whole-effluent toxicity limitations, when the permitting authority determines that a discharge causes, or has the reasonable potential to cause or contribute to, an excursion above any water quality standards.[130]

The whole-effluent approach to toxics control involves the use of acute and/or chronic toxicity tests to measure the toxicity of wastewaters. An acute test is defined as a test of 96 hours or less in which lethality or immobilization of

---

126. *See* 40 C.F.R. § 131.11 (b) for state authority in establishing criteria. *See* Preamble, National Toxics Rule, 57 Fed. Reg. at 60,862 for discussion of state adjustment authority regarding human health criteria.

127. Preamble, National Toxics Rule, 57 Fed. Reg. 60,848 *et seq.*

128. The fourteen jurisdictions are Alaska, Arkansas, California, the District of Columbia, Florida, Idaho, Kansas, Michigan, Nevada, New Jersey, Puerto Rico, Rhode Island, Vermont, and Washington. 40 C.F.R. § 131.36(d).

129. In some instances, human health recommendations are based upon the criteria in the 304(a) criteria document recalculated with latest information. *See* Preamble, National Toxics Rule, 57 Fed. Reg. at 60,863.

130. 33 U.S.C. § 1251(a)(3).

organisms is measured at the endpoint. A chronic test is a long-term test in which sublethal effects, such as impaired fertilization, growth, or reproduction, are measured in addition to lethality or immobilization.[131] The appropriateness of the acute or chronic toxicity test to a particular discharge is based upon the uses designated for the water body. Aquatic invertebrates, fish, and plants are used in both types of tests.

Terms commonly used to express the toxicity of effluent include the lethal concentration (LC) and the no-observed-effect concentration (NOEC). The LC is the concentration of an effluent at which a certain percentage of test organisms die (that is, the LC_{50} test measures the concentration of an effluent at which half of the test organisms die). The NOEC is the highest concentration of effluent that causes no observable adverse effects in test organisms.[132]

Because of concerns regarding possible toxicological properties of combinations of pollutants in effluents, state water quality standards may include both whole-effluent toxicity criteria and numerical water quality criteria for individual pollutants.[133]

c. Narrative Criteria. The most common narrative criteria are general statements designed to protect the aesthetics and health of a waterway. For example, narrative standards often preclude the formation of putrescent or otherwise objectionable bottom deposits, debris, oil, scum, objectionable color, odor, taste, or turbidity. Narrative standards may also prohibit discharges that injure or are toxic to humans, animals, or plants, or that produce undesirable or nuisance aquatic life.[134]

3. Antidegradation

As part of its water quality standards program, each state must establish an antidegradation policy consistent with 40 C.F.R. section 131.12. An antidegradation policy must, at a minimum, achieve the following:

1. maintain and protect existing instream water uses;
2. maintain and protect existing water quality where it exceeds levels necessary to support propagation of fish and recreation, unless the state finds, after full public participation, that allowing lower water quality is

---

131. Preamble, National Toxics Rule, 57 Fed. Reg. at 60,967.

132. *Id.*

133. *See* Technical Support Document at 33–41.

134. Office of Water Regulations & Standards, U.S. EPA, General Provisions/ Freedoms Water Quality Standards Criteria Summaries—A Compilation of State/Federal Criteria at i–ii (Sept. 1990).

necessary to accommodate important economic or social development in the area where the waters are located (existing uses still must be fully protected);

3.   maintain and protect high-quality waters that constitute an outstanding national resource, such as waters in national or state parks.

A state's implementation of its antidegradation policy must ensure that existing water quality is protected. Whenever an activity is proposed that may degrade existing high-quality water, EPA's *Water Quality Standards Handbook*[135] specifies that an opportunity must be provided for public and intergovernmental participation in the decision to allow the proposed degradation activity. Where the public response, taken as a whole, opposes the activity, the state may not allow the activity without a substantial and convincing justification.

B. STANDARDS REVIEW AND APPROVAL PROCESS

Section 303(c) establishes the structure for EPA review and approval of state water quality standards.[136] EPA's procedures and criteria for implementing section 303 are set out in regulations at 40 C.F.R. part 131.[137] Under section 303(c), states are primarily responsible for developing water quality standards applicable to state waters. Section 303(c)(1) requires that each state review and update its water quality standards every three years.[138] During the triennial review, each state is required to incorporate changes to its standards necessary to achieve compliance with any revisions to the CWA or EPA's implementing regulations.[139] Further, any water body segment that does not include the uses specified in section 101(a)(2) of the Act (that is, fishable/swimmable) must be examined every three years to determine if new information indicates that the section 101(a)(2) uses are attainable.[140] If so, standards must be revised accordingly. A state must provide notice to the public and hold a public hearing each time it revises its water quality standards.[141] New and revised standards are subject to EPA review and approval.[142]

---

135. HANDBOOK at 2-13 to 2-14. *See* Preamble, Proposed Water Quality Guidance for the Great Lakes System ("Proposed Great Lakes Rule"), 58 Fed. Reg. 20,820, 20,885 (Apr. 16, 1993).

136. 33 U.S.C. § 1313(c).

137. 40 C.F.R. § 131.1.

138. 33 U.S.C. § 1313(c)(1).

139. *See* HANDBOOK at 2-2 through 2-3.

140. 40 C.F.R. § 131.20(a).

141. 40 C.F.R. § 131.20(b).

142. 40 C.F.R. § 131.20(c). *See* HANDBOOK at 2-1 through 2-4.

EPA is required to review each state's new and revised standards to determine whether they meet CWA requirements. Specific elements of the review are set out at section 303(c)(2) and at 40 C.F.R. sections 131.5 and 131.6.[143] One aspect of the review is to determine whether the effluent limitations imposed by an upstream state would interfere with standards attainment in a downstream state.[144] If EPA determines that standards are not consistent with the CWA, EPA is to notify the state and specify revisions to be made.[145] If changes are not made by the state, EPA has a mandatory duty to promulgate for the state new or revised standards that comply with CWA requirements.[146]

Under section 303(c)(4)(B), EPA may also promulgate federal water quality standards, independent of this review process, whenever EPA determines that new or revised standards are necessary to meet CWA requirements.[147]

C. SUPPLEMENTAL WATER QUALITY–BASED EFFLUENT LIMITATIONS: SECTION 302

CWA section 302 authorizes EPA to promulgate water quality–based effluent limitations whenever discharges from a point source will interfere with the attainment of water quality standards even after the application of required technology-based effluent limitations.[148] Both the language of section 302 and the pertinent legislative history make clear that these limitations are supplemental in nature, to be established when the technology-based limitations required by section 301 are insufficient to produce the desired level of water quality.[149]

CWA section 301(b)(1)(C) requires EPA to implement any more-stringent limitations that are necessary to attain water quality standards by July 1, 1977.[150] The CWA does not, however, obligate EPA to establish section 302 limitations until (i) EPA has established the technology-based effluent limitations required by section 301 and (ii) those technology-based limitations have proven to be

---

143. EPA's decisions as to whether a state's standards satisfy the Act's requirements are deemed to be discretionary and not subject to section 505 citizen suit. Scott v. Hammond, 741 F.2d 992 (7th Cir. 1984).

144. 40 C.F.R. § 131.10(b).

145. 33 U.S.C. § 1313(c)(3); 40 C.F.R. § 131.21.

146. 33 U.S.C. § 1313(c)(3); 40 C.F.R. § 131.22(a); Scott v. Hammond, 741 F.2d 992 (7th Cir. 1984).

147. 33 U.S.C. § 1313(c)(4)(B); 40 C.F.R. § 131.22(b).

148. 33 U.S.C. § 1312(a); *see generally,* W. Rogers, 2 Environmental Law: Air & Water § 4.18(C)(2) (1986).

149. *See* 33 U.S.C. § 1312(a); *see also* S. Rep. No.92-414, 92d Cong., 1st Sess. 46–48 (1971) *reprinted in* 2 Legislative History at 1464–66.

150. 33 U.S.C. § 1311(b)(1)(C).

insufficient.[151] To date, EPA has established section 302 limitations only very rarely.

Before establishing a section 302 effluent limitation, EPA must determine that discharges from one or more point sources "would interfere with the attainment or maintenance" of basic water quality goals.[152] EPA must then establish effluent limitations that "can reasonably be expected to contribute to the attainment or maintenance of such water quality."[153]

Section 302 requires notice and a public hearing before a water quality–based effluent limitation becomes final.[154] The hearing process is designed to require EPA to consider "on a case by case basis . . . a balancing of the economic and social costs against the social and economic benefits sought to be obtained."[155] An effluent limitation established pursuant to section 302 for a non-toxic pollutant is subject to modification if the affected party is able to demonstrate that "there is no reasonable relationship between the economic and social costs and the benefits to be obtained."[156] In contrast, a section 302 effluent limitation for a toxic pollutant may be modified for a single period of no more than five years and only if the affected party demonstrates both that the proposed modification is the maximum control within the affected party's economic capability and that it will result in "reasonable further progress" toward the water quality goals.[157]

Section 302 does not authorize action by the states and, consequently, neither section 302's notice and hearing requirements nor its provisions for cost-beneficial modification apply to state-promulgated water quality–based effluent limitations.[158]

D. TOTAL MAXIMUM DAILY LOADS: SECTION 303(d)

CWA section 303(d) authorizes and in some cases requires the establishment of another kind of water quality–based effluent limitation called a "total maximum daily load" (TMDL).[159] A TMDL is a more stringent water quality–based efflu-

---

151. *See* Homestake Min. Co. v. EPA, 477 F. Supp. 1279, 1285 (D.S.D. 1979).

152. *See* 33 U.S.C. § 1312(a) (describing the water quality goals as assuring the "protection of public health, public water supplies, agricultural and industrial uses, and the protection and propagation of a balanced population of shell-fish, fish and wildlife, and allow recreational activities in and on water").

153. 33 U.S.C. § 1312(a).

154. 33 U.S.C. § 1312(b)(1); *see also* Homestake Min. Co., 477 F. Supp. at 1285 ("[s]ection 302 requires a cost-benefit hearing prior to the establishment of new effluent limitations").

155. S. Rep. No.92-414, 92d Cong., 1st Sess. 47 (1971) in 2 LEGISLATIVE HISTORY at 1467.

156. 33 U.S.C. § 1312(b)(2)(A).

157. 33 U.S.C. § 1312(b)(2)(B).

158. *See* Homestake Min. Co., 477 F. Supp. at 1286.

159. 33 U.S.C. § 1313(d); *see also* 40 C.F.R. § 130.7.

ent limitation established when the Act's technology-based limitations are not adequate to achieve existing water quality standards.[160] TMDLs and the process of developing TMDLs are addressed in greater detail in chapter 10.

E. INDIVIDUAL CONTROL STRATEGIES: SECTION 304(1)

In 1987, Congress amended the CWA, adding section 304(1).[161] At that time, Congress was particularly concerned with the problems posed by toxic pollutants[162] and felt that the CWA's requirements for use of best available technology would not always be sufficient to control toxic pollutants.[163] Section 304(1) creates a mechanism both for identifying waters in which technology-based effluent limitations have proven insufficient and for establishing supplemental water quality–based effluent limitations.[164]

1. State Responsibilities

States have primary responsibility for administering the 304(1) program.[165] Section 304(1) requires states to identify waters that are not attaining established water quality standards for toxic pollutants (the "A list" and "B list"), to identify the point sources contributing to the impaired water quality in those waters on the "C list," and to develop individual control strategies (ICSs) for those point sources.[166] Stressing an urgent need to control toxic pollution, Congress included strict deadlines in section 304(1).[167] Section 304(1)(1) required each state to submit its lists and ICSs by February 4, 1989.[168] Section 304(1)(1)(D) requires the ICSs to result in the attainment of water quality standards within three years of their establishment.[169]

a. The A List. Under section 304(1)(1)(A), each state is required to submit to EPA a list of all waters within the state that after application of effluent limitations

---

160. U.S. EPA, GUIDANCE FOR WATER QUALITY–BASED DECISIONS: THE TMDL PROCESS 1 (April 1991) (hereinafter "EPA TMDL GUIDANCE").

161. 33 U.S.C. § 1314(l).

162. *See* S. Rep. No.50, 99th Cong., 1st Sess. 3 (1985); *see also* Natural Resources Defense Council v. EPA, 915 F.2d 1314, 1318 (9th Cir. 1990).

163. S. Rep. No. 50, 99th Cong., 1st Sess. 22-23 (1985); H. Rep. No. 1004, 99th Cong., 2d Sess. 128–29 (1986).

164. Section 304(l) was designed to identify and control "toxic hot spots." 133 Cong. Rec. 1287 (1987) (statement of Sen. Moynihan).

165. U.S. EPA, FINAL GUIDANCE FOR IMPLEMENTATION OF REQUIREMENTS UNDER SECTION 304(l) iv (Mar. 1988) ("304(l) GUIDANCE").

166. 33 U.S.C. § 1314(l)(1).

167. *See* H. Rep. No.1004, 99th Cong., 2d Sess. 128–30 (1986).

168. 33 U.S.C. § 1314(l)(1); 40 C.F.R. § 123.46(a).

169. 33 U.S.C. § 1314(l)(1)(D).

required by CWA section 301(b)(2) "cannot reasonably be anticipated" to attain or maintain either water quality standards that have been established pursuant to CWA section 303(c)(2)(B) or the level of water quality necessary to assure protection of public health, various water uses, and fish and wildlife.[170] This is known as the "A list" or the "long list."

Under section 304(l)(1)(A), therefore, it appears that listing is not appropriate prior to establishment of best-available technology (BAT) effluent limitations pursuant to section 301(b)(2).[171] One could argue, however, that in some situations it may reasonably be possible to anticipate that the technology-based effluent limitations required by section 301(b)(2), but not yet established, will be insufficient to attain water quality standards and protect human health and wildlife. EPA has taken the position that if compliance with technology-based limits cannot be expected within three years, the water should be listed.[172]

b. The B List. Under section 304(l)(1)(B), each state must submit to EPA a list of all navigable waters in the state that, due entirely or substantially to discharges of toxic pollutants from point sources, are not expected to achieve the applicable standard under section 303 after the requirements of sections 301(b), 306, and 307(b) are met.[173] The B list is necessarily shorter than the A list because it includes only those impaired waters of which the impairment can be traced primarily to point source discharges.[174]

Listing under B, like listing under A, appears to require the prior implementation of the technology-based effluent limitations required under CWA sections 301(b), 306, and 307(b). Again, however, one could argue that in some instances it is possible to "expect" that the applicable water quality standard will not be met, even after technology-based limitations are developed and implemented.

Section 304(l)(1)(B) also presupposes the establishment of numeric water quality standards. Listing under B requires a determination as to whether the applicable standard under section 303 is being met. Section 303 specifically requires that numeric water quality standards be established for toxic pollutants.[175] At least one state administrative tribunal has ruled that 304(l) listings

---

170. 33 U.S.C. § 1314(l)(1)(A); 40 C.F.R. § 130.10(d)(1).

171. The legislative history of the 1987 CWA amendments makes clear that 304(l) was intended to establish a supplemental, post-BAT regulatory program. *See* S. Rep. No. 50, 99th Cong., 1st Sess. 22–23 (1985).

172. *See* 54 Fed. Reg. 23,868, 23,881 (Jun. 2, 1989).

173. 33 U.S.C. § 1314(l)(1)(B).

174. *Natural Resources Defense Council,* 915 F.2d at 1319.

175. 33 U.S.C. § 1313(c)(2)(B). *But see* 40 C.F.R. § 130.10(d)(4) (explaining the process of listing under B in the absence of a numeric water quality standard); 304(l) GUIDANCE at 20 (same).

are not valid in the absence of a properly established numeric water quality standard.[176]

c. The C List. Section 304(l)(1)(C) requires each state to submit to EPA a list of the point sources discharging into the waters included on either the A or B list.[177] The states must also identify the amount of toxic pollutants discharged from each point source listed.[178]

EPA initially promulgated regulations concerning section 304(l) that required states to identify point source dischargers only for those waters on a state's B list.[179] In *Natural Resources Defense Council v. EPA*,[180] however, the Ninth Circuit held that those regulations were invalid and that states must identify point source dischargers on waters included on either the A or the B list.[181]

d. Individual Control Strategies. For each discharger on the C list who discharges into waters on the B list, CWA section 304(l)(1)(D) and EPA regulations require the state to develop an ICS.[182] In *Natural Resources Defense Council v. EPA,* the Ninth Circuit did not reach the question of whether the statute also requires the states to develop ICSs for dischargers on the C list discharging into waters on the A list.[183]

The ICS must be sufficient, in combination with existing controls on other pollution sources, to achieve the applicable water quality standard within three years of its establishment.[184] The CWA does not specify the form that ICSs should take. EPA, however, has defined an ICS to be a draft or final NPDES permit accompanied by supporting documentation demonstrating that the effluent limits are sufficient to meet applicable water quality standards.[185]

2. EPA Responsibilities

EPA's role in the 304(l) process is intended to be primarily one of providing guidance and oversight.[186] States submit the A, B, and C lists to EPA for

---

176. See James River II, Inc. v. State of Washington, Nos. 91-140 *et al.* (Wash. Pollution Control Hrg. Bd. May 15,1992).

177. 33 U.S.C. § 1314(l)(1)(C).

178. *Id.*

179. *See Natural Resources Defense Council,* 915 F.2d at 1320.

180. 915 F.2d 1314 (9th Cir. 1990).

181. 915 F.2d at 1320.

182. 33 U.S.C. § 1314(l)(1)(D); *see* 304(l) GUIDANCE at iii.

183. 915 F.2d at 1323.

184. 33 U.S.C. § 1314(l)(1)(D).

185. *See* Municipal Auth. of St. Mary's v. EPA, 945 F.2d 67, 69 (3d Cir. 1991); *see also* 40 C.F.R. § 123.46(c).

186. 304(l) GUIDANCE at iv.

approval.[187] EPA may disapprove a part of a state's lists if it believes the state has failed to include certain water segments or dischargers.[188] If EPA disapproves a state's list, EPA must develop its own lists.[189]

The states also must submit their ICSs to the EPA for approval.[190] Within four months, EPA must either approve or disapprove these state submittals.[191] If the ICS is submitted in the form of a draft NPDES permit, EPA will either conditionally approve or disapprove the ICS.[192] Even after EPA conditionally approves an ICS, a state remains free to change the limitations established in the draft permit when it issues a final permit.[193] If the state submits a final NPDES permit as the ICS, EPA must either approve or disapprove it.[194]

If a state does not submit ICSs or if EPA does not approve those submitted, EPA must assume authority for issuing the ICSs in that state.[195] In such circumstances, the statutory deadline for promulgating ICSs was extended to June 4, 1990.[196]

F. IMPLEMENTATION

CWA section 303(e)(1) requires that each state establish and maintain a continuing planning process.[197] This planning process is subject to EPA approval. Minimum requirements of the document are set out at 40 C.F.R. section 130.5. One significant requirement is that the continuing planning process set out the state's plan for establishing and assuring adequate implementation of new or revised water quality standards, including schedules of compliance, under CWA section 303(c). Through the continuing planning process, states may, at their discretion, adopt procedures to effectuate their policies on issues such as site-specific criteria, variances, mixing zones, low flows, and compliance schedules.

1. Site-Specific Criteria and Variances

States may, at their discretion, in their water quality standards program provide for derivation of site-specific numeric criteria. Site-specific criteria may be

187. 33 U.S.C. § 1314(l)(1); 40 C.F.R. § 130.10(d).

188. 33 U.S.C. § 1314(l)(2); 40 C.F.R § 130.10(d)(8).

189. 33 U.S.C. § 1314(l)(2); 40 C.F.R. §§ 123.46(b), 130.10(d).

190. 33 U.S.C. § 1314(l)(1); 40 C.F.R. § 123.46(a).

191. 33 U.S.C. § 1314(l)(2); 40 C.F.R. § 123.46(b).

192. 40 C.F.R. § 123.46(c). States frequently submit ICSs in the form of draft NPDES permits. See Lake Cumberland Trust, Inc. v. EPA, 954 F.2d 1218, 1220 n.3 (6th Cir. 1992).

193. P.H. Glatfelter Co. v. EPA, 921 F.2d 516, 517 (4th Cir. 1990).

194. 40 C.F.R. § 123.46(c).

195. 33 U.S.C. § 1314(1)(3); 40 C.F.R. § 123.46(b); see also St. Mary's, 945 F.2d at 69; Roll Coater, Inc. v. Reilly, 932 F.2d 668, 669 (7th Cir. 1991).

196. 33 U.S.C. § 1314(l)(3); 40 C.F.R. § 123.46(b); see St. Mary's, 945 F.2d at 69.

197. 33 U.S.C. § 1313(e)(1).

appropriate when species inhabiting a given site are more or less sensitive than those used in developing the numeric criteria, or when water chemistry at a site differs significantly from the water chemistry used in developing the criteria. EPA's Water Quality Standards Handbook provides guidance for deriving site-specific ambient criteria.[198]

A state may allow a variance from water quality standards while a permittee investigates the applicability of site-specific criteria. EPA guidance provides that a variance may be based upon any of the grounds outlined in 40 C.F.R. section 131.10(g) for removing a designated use. Further, NPDES permit limitations in effect during the variance period must ensure (i) protection of existing uses of the water body and (ii) compliance with the general section 303(c)(2)(A) requirement of protecting the public health and welfare (even though specific protective criteria may be temporarily exceeded). Because state variance proceedings involve revisions of water quality standards, they must be accompanied by public notice, opportunity for comment, and public hearing. Temporary variances typically extend for a three-year period with the possibility of renewal.[199]

2. Flows

Water quality standards are intended to protect water body uses in critical low-flow conditions. As a result, the critical low-flow condition is used to calculate NPDES permit limitations from applicable criteria. Correspondingly, a state may provide that numeric ambient criteria do not apply below the critical low-flow condition. A state's selection of the critical low-flow condition (for example, 10Q1, 7Q2) can have an impact on NPDES permit limitations for priority pollutants. EPA has allowed states some flexibility in establishing the value or formula for its derivation as long as the state's decision is scientifically defensible.[200]

3. Mixing Zones

A mixing zone is a limited area or volume of water where initial dilution of a discharge takes place. The concept of a mixing zone in the context of water quality standards is that a state may, at its discretion, allow a zone surrounding, or downstream from, a discharge location where numeric ambient criteria are exceeded as long as acutely toxic conditions are prevented. Historically, states have had considerable flexibility in establishing sizes and shapes of mixing zones as long as

---

198. *See* HANDBOOK 4-1 through 4-19. *See* Preamble, National Toxics Rule, 57 Fed. Reg. at 60,865 and Preamble, Proposed Great Lakes Rule, 58 Fed. Reg. at 20,918–21.

199. 40 C.F.R. § 131.13; *see* Preamble, Proposed Great Lakes Rule, 58 Fed. Reg. at 20,921–24.

200. *See* HANDBOOK at 2-10.

the state's determinations are scientifically defensible.[201] In recent years, how-ever, EPA has begun to discourage the use of mixing zones.

4. Schedules of Compliance

States may allow a permittee time to meet permit limitations based upon new or revised water quality standards as long as the state's laws or water quality stan-dards clearly provide for such a compliance schedule.[202] According to a decision by the EPA Environmental Appeals Board, *Star-Kist Caribe, Inc.*, EPA may not provide any compliance schedule where state water quality standards are silent on the issue.[203]

---

201. *See* HANDBOOK at 2-7 to 2-9.

202. 33 U.S.C. § 1313(e)(3)(A) & (F); 40 C.F.R. § 130.5(b)(1) & (6).

203. *In re* Star-Kist Caribe, Inc., NPDES Appeal No.88-5 (U.S. EPA Env'tl. Appeals Bd. May 26, 1992).

CHAPTER 3

NPDES Permit Application and Issuance Procedures

RANDY HILL*

I. Applicability and Scope

The procedures that applicants must follow in applying for a permit under the National Pollutant Discharge Elimination System (NPDES) are contained in 40 C.F.R. part 122. The procedures that the U.S. Environmental Protection Agency (EPA or the Agency) must follow in issuing those permits are contained in 40 C.F.R. part 124. States are required to adopt procedures equivalent to part 124 in order to be authorized to operate the NPDES permit program in lieu of the federal government.[1] Some of the requirements discussed below, however, apply only to EPA-issued permits. Except for those identified as EPA-only requirements, the requirements discussed below apply to both EPA and state programs.

II. Types of NPDES Permits

Permits issued to direct dischargers under the NPDES program can take one of two forms: an individual or a general permit.

---

* The views expressed here are the author's and do not necessarily reflect those of the United States Environmental Protection Agency or the United States Department of Justice.

The author acknowledges the contributions of Karen Wardzinski, Serena P. Wiltshire, and Robin A. Fastenau to the 1994 edition of this chapter.

1. 40 C.F.R. § 123.25(a)(24)–(a)(35).

A. INDIVIDUAL PERMITS

Individual permits, as the name implies, are permits issued to one facility or source[2] based on site-specific information related to it. The NPDES permit application filed by the facility provides most of this.

B. GENERAL PERMITS

In contrast to an individual permit, a general permit covers an entire group or category of similarly situated but separately located facilities. General permits usually are developed at the initiative of the permitting agency before the permit application process. As a result, the agency must rely on information from sources other than the NPDES permit applications gathered about the category of facilities to be covered. Generally the agency does not evaluate site-specific information for any facility in the context of developing a general permit.

In addition, facilities ultimately covered under a general permit do not need to submit a permit application. Instead, facilities wishing to be covered by a general permit need only submit a notice of intent to be covered that requires limited information on who the facility is, where it is located, and why it fits the category covered by the general permit.[3]

General permits are specifically authorized and are being used extensively in the permitting of stormwater discharges.[4] In addition, general permits may be appropriate for nonstormwater discharges from any category of sources within a defined geographic area that

1. involve similar operations;
2. discharge the same types of wastes;
3. require the same effluent limitation, operating conditions, or standards for sewage sludge use or disposal;
4. require the same or similar monitoring; and
5. are more appropriately controlled under a general than an individual permit.[5]

---

2. An individual permit could also be issued to a number of sources that are all part of the same discharge system, such as a permit issued to a privately owned treatment works that also includes some or all of its users as co-permittees. Although such permits include more than a single source, one permit is issued to the entire system and is still based on site-specific information obtained through the application process. 40 C.F.R. § 122.44(m).

3. 40 C.F.R. § 122.28(b)(2).

4. 40 C.F.R. § 122.28(a)(2)(i). Indeed, the use of general permits was first suggested to EPA by the U.S. District Court for the District of Columbia in response to EPA's attempts to exempt large categories of stormwater discharges from NPDES permit requirements. NRDC v. Train, 396 F. Supp. 1393 (D.D.C. 1975), aff'd, NRDC v. Costle, 568 F.2d 1369 (D.C. Cir. 1977). For more information on stormwater permits, see chapter 8.

5. 40 C.F.R. § 122.28(a)(2)(ii).

As an example, EPA has used general permits successfully in the permitting of offshore oil and gas operations, where the movement of mobile drilling rigs makes individual permit issuance quite burdensome.[6]

Substantively, a general permit is no different from an individual permit; it must include all the same types of permit limitations required to be included in individual permits. General permits are simply an administrative mechanism developed by EPA through procedures similar to APA rulemaking[7] to permit efficiently large numbers of similarly situated sources in the least burdensome manner for both the Agency and the permittees.[8]

The permit authority, however, can require any discharger covered by a general permit to obtain an individual permit whenever the circumstances of the discharge have changed so that individual control is required or whenever new regulations affecting the discharge are put into effect. For EPA-issued general permits only, EPA is required to notify the discharger in writing that an application for an individual permit is required and to provide the discharger with an application form and a deadline for filing it. The general permit will automatically terminate when the individual permit becomes effective.[9]

Authorized NPDES states that wish to issue general permits must demonstrate to EPA the authority to issue such permits. EPA must approve this authority as part of the state's basic NPDES program.[10]

III. Application Requirements

A. WHO MUST APPLY?

Any person who discharges or proposes to discharge pollutants from a point source to waters of the United States must apply for an NPDES permit.[11] If a facility or activity is owned by one person but operated by another, it is the operator's duty to apply for the permit.[12]

---

6. *See* 40 C.F.R. § 122.28(c).

7. EPA does not, however, follow all of the requirements associated with promulgation of rules, particularly compliance with the Regulatory Flexibility Act, 5 U.S.C. § 601 *et. seq.* In EPA's view, general permits are, like individual permits, "licenses" under the APA, and are therefore issued by adjudication, not rulemaking. *See, e.g.,* 63 Fed. Reg. 52,430, 52,462 (explaining EPA's position in the context of a stormwater general permit).

8. 40 C.F.R. § 124.10(c)(2)(i).

9. 40 C.F.R. § 122.28(b)(2).

10. 40 C.F.R. § 123.25(a)(6). All but two of the states/territories approved to issue NPDES permits have authority also to issue general permits. *See* 65 Fed. Reg. 50,528, 50,529 (Aug. 18, 2000).

11. EPA has construed the phrase "proposes to discharge" to include facilities that have the "potential to discharge," for example, because of wet weather runoff, even if there is not a specific plan to do so. 66 Fed. Reg. 2,960, 3,007 (Jan. 12, 2001).

12. 40 C.F.R. §§ 122.21(a) and (b).

B. TIMING OF APPLICATION

In general, applicants must submit complete applications to the permit authority (either EPA or the authorized state) on the form provided by that authority at least 180 days prior to commencing the discharge.[13] For industrial stormwater discharges, the applicant must apply 180 days before commencing the activity that may result in a stormwater discharge (90 days for construction activity).[14] In the case of permit renewal, the application must be submitted at least 180 days before the expiration of the existing permit.[15] Besides the fact that EPA generally needs at least this amount of time to issue a permit, this timing is especially important in the case of permit renewal because it will affect whether an expired permit will be administratively extended under the Administrative Procedures Act (APA) while permit reissuance is pending.[16]

C. CONTENT OF APPLICATION

The following information is required to be submitted in application Form 1 required of all NPDES permit applicants:

1. the activities requiring an NPDES permit;
2. the name, mailing address, and location of the facility requiring the permits;
3. the Standard Industrial Classification (SIC) codes[17] that best describe the products or services provided by the facility;
4. the operator's name, address, telephone number, ownership status, and status as a federal, state, private, public, or other entity;
5. whether the facility is located on Indian lands;
6. a list of all other environmental permits or construction approvals received or applied for by the facility;
7. a topographic map of the facility; and
8. a brief description of the nature of the facility's business.[18]

Applicants for an NPDES permit must also submit an additional form that varies according to the type of discharger. Form 2C must be filed by existing

---

13. 40 C.F.R. § 122.21(c)(1).

14. *Id.*

15. 40 C.F.R. § 122.21(d).

16. See section VII, below, for a discussion of APA extensions of permit time.

17. The SIC code system has been replaced by the North American Industrial Classification System (NAICS). See http://www.census.gov/epcd/www/naics.html for information. EPA has not yet updated its regulations at 40 C.F.R. § 122.21(f)(3) to conform, but one can assume that the permit applicant should use NAICS codes instead.

18. 40 C.F.R. § 122.21(f).

manufacturing, commercial mining, and silvicultural dischargers. Similarly, new sources and new dischargers (discussed below) must submit a specific form (Form 2D), as must concentrated animal feeding operations (Form 2B), publicly owned treatment works (Form 2A), and dischargers of stormwater associated with industrial activity (Form 2F). The information required on these forms includes a detailed description of the discharge and the factors that may influence the discharge.[19]

D. SIGNATURE REQUIREMENTS

The signature requirements for applications vary depending on the type of entity that is applying. For a corporation, the application must be signed by a "responsible" corporate officer.[20] For a partnership or sole proprietorship, the application must be signed by a general partner or the sole proprietor, respectively. Finally, for a municipality or other public entity, the signatory must be either a principal executive officer or a ranking elected official. In each case the signatory must certify as to the accuracy and completeness of the application.[21]

IV. Permit Issuance Process

A. REVIEW FOR COMPLETENESS

Upon receipt, EPA is required to review each permit application to make sure it is complete and notify the applicant in writing of its completeness or deficiencies.[22] If the application is deficient, EPA is required to provide the applicant with a list of the information required to make it complete and to specify the date for submitting the necessary information. State programs are not required to contain such completeness-review provisions (although many state programs do contain such requirements.)[23]

---

19. *See* 40 C.F.R. §§ 122.21(g)–(k).

20. "A responsible corporate officer" is defined in 40 C.F.R. § 122.22(a)(1) as "(i) a president, secretary, treasurer, or vice-president of the corporation in charge of a principal business function, or any other person who performs similar policy- or decision-making functions for the corporation, or (ii) the manager of one or more manufacturing, production, or operating facilities, provided, the manager is authorized to make management decisions which govern the operation of the regulated facility . . . and where authority to sign documents has been assigned or delegated to the manager in accordance with corporate procedures."

21. *See* 40 C.F.R. § 122.22(d).

22. 40 C.F.R. § 124.3(c).

23. *Id.*

B. EFFECTIVE DATE OF APPLICATION

The effective date of the application is the date upon which EPA notifies the applicant that the application is complete. At that time, in the case of major new source or major new discharger applications, EPA must provide the applicant with a "project decision schedule"—a schedule of target dates for issuing the draft permit, giving the public notice, completing the public comment period, and issuing the final permit. States are not required to issue such a schedule.[24] The effective date of application where a state is the permitting authority is defined by state law or regulation.

C. TENTATIVE PERMIT DECISION, ISSUANCE OF A DRAFT PERMIT, AND PUBLIC NOTICE

After an application is complete, the permitting authority is required to decide tentatively either to prepare a draft permit or to deny the application. If EPA tentatively denies a permit, it must issue notice (both to the applicant and to the public) of its intent to deny. However, state permit authorities are only required to do so if required by state law.[25]

If the permitting authority decides tentatively to issue a permit, it must prepare a draft permit and a fact sheet that "sets forth the principal facts and the significant factual, legal, methodological and policy questions considered in preparing the draft permit."[26] The permit authority must then mail notice that a draft permit has been prepared along with a copy of the draft permit, the fact sheet, and the permit application to the applicant; all appropriate federal, state, and local agencies; all users of any POTW applying for a permit; and all persons included on a specially developed mailing list.[27] The permit authority also must give notice to all other persons potentially affected by the permit through whatever medium can be used to elicit public participation. In state-administered programs, notice must be given in whatever manner constitutes legal notice under state law.[28]

The notice shall allow at least 30 days for review of and comment on the draft permit. If a public hearing is to be held, the permit authority must give notice of that hearing at least 30 days in advance of the hearing date.[29] The permit authority can extend the 30-day comment period to accommodate requested hearings or

---

24. 40 C.F.R. §§ 124.3(f) and (g).

25. 40 C.F.R. §§ 124.6(a) and (b).

26. 40 C.F.R. § 124.6(c) and (e), and § 124.8(a). If a fact sheet is not required under § 124.8(a), EPA is required to prepare a "statement of basis," which briefly describes the derivation of the reasons for the conditions of the permit. *See* 40 C.F.R. § 124.7. States are not subject to this requirement.

27. 40 C.F.R. § 124.10(c).

28. *Id.*

29. 40 C.F.R. § 124.10(b).

other requests for additional comment time. The public-comment period is automatically extended to the close of the public hearing if any hearing is held.[30]

D. PUBLIC COMMENT/HEARING

During the public-comment period, all interested parties may comment on the draft permit and may request a hearing if one has not already been scheduled by the permit authority. A party requesting a hearing must do so in writing and must state the issues it proposes to raise at the hearing.[31]

Also during the public-comment period, all "reasonably ascertainable issues" must be raised by interested parties in order to preserve those issues for evidentiary hearing on appeal.[32] While all detailed technical documents supporting these issues do not need to be submitted at this time, an interested party's failure to present these documents may affect the permit authority's ability to consider them in making its decision on the permit. EPA may require parties to submit such documentation where it appears likely that issuance of the permit will be contested.[33]

EPA can, however, choose to reopen a comment period and require parties to submit all "reasonably available" factual information (including all supporting material) during the comment period. Parties must be given at least 60 days after the notice of reopening to submit such information. In addition, any interested person may file a response to information submitted by any other person within 20 days of the date EPA set for filing of such material.[34]

If any of the issues raised or the information submitted during the public-comment period raises substantial new questions about a permit, EPA may prepare a new draft permit, prepare a revised fact sheet or statement of basis, or reopen the comment period. Comments filed during the reopened comment period must be limited to the issues giving rise to the substantial new questions. (The reopening provisions discussed above may differ under state-administered programs.)[35]

E. FINAL PERMIT DECISION

After the close of the comment period, EPA is required to issue a final permit decision by notifying the applicant and each person who has submitted written

---

30. 40 C.F.R. § 124.12(c).
31. 40 C.F.R. § 124.11.
32. 40 C.F.R. § 124.13.
33. *Id.*
34. 40 C.F.R. § 124.12(a).
35. 40 C.F.R. §§ 124.14(b) and (c).

comments or requested notice of the final permit decision. The notice shall include a reference to the procedures required for contesting a decision.[36] EPA also is required to issue a response to comments when the final permit decision is issued and must specify in that document which provisions in the draft permit, if any, were changed in response to comments.[37]

EPA's final permit decision becomes effective 30 days after the date notice is served unless otherwise specified or unless an appeal is filed with EPA's Environmental Appeals Board (EAB).[38] If no changes to the draft permit were requested by commenters, the permit becomes effective immediately upon issuance of the notice of final permit decision.[39]

V. State Certification of EPA-Issued Permits and EPA Review of State-Issued Permits

A. STATE CERTIFICATION

EPA cannot issue an NPDES permit until the state in which the discharge originates or will originate either certifies that the discharge, as permitted, will comply with the relevant sections of the CWA and all applicable state laws and regulations, or waives certification.[40] The applicant may obtain the state's certification and submit it to EPA with its permit application, although it is not specifically required to do so at that time. As a practical matter, state certification may be difficult to obtain at the application stage, because the state will not know at that point what conditions and limitations will be imposed by EPA in the permit.

If the applicant does not submit the certification with its application, EPA will request certification from the state. If the state has not responded by the time EPA is ready to issue a draft permit, EPA will send a copy of the draft permit to the state and notify the state that unless it responds within a reasonable time (not to exceed 60 days) the state will be deemed to have waived certification.[41]

A state may either deny certification, grant certification unconditionally, or grant certification on condition that the permit be revised to include additional or more-stringent provisions. EPA is prohibited from issuing a permit where the state denies certification.[42] Where the state conditionally grants certification,

---

36. 40 C.F.R. § 124.15(a).

37. 40 C.F.R. § 124.17.

38. 40 C.F.R. § 124.15(b).

39. *Id.*

40. CWA § 401(a)(1), 33 U.S.C. § 1341(a)(1); 40 C.F.R. § 124.53.

41. 40 C.F.R. §§ 124.53(b) and (c). EPA, may, however, in its discretion accept a late-submitted certification. Puerto Rico Sun Oil Co. v. EPA, 8 F.3d 73 (1st Cir. 1993).

42. 40 C.F.R. § 124.55(a)(1).

EPA must include in the final permit those conditions that the state finds necessary to comply with applicable law.[43]

B. EPA REVIEW

1. Statutory Authority to Review

Pursuant to section 402(b) of the CWA, EPA may authorize a state to administer NPDES permits within the jurisdictional waters of that state. In order for states to be granted such authority, the state must submit, and EPA must approve, a full and complete description of the program it proposes to establish.[44] At a minimum, the state program must contain adequate authority for the state to issue permits, ensure that the public and any affected state receive notice for each application, provide an opportunity for public comment and hearing on permit decision, abate permit violations, and provide for appropriate civil and criminal penalties for enforcement purposes.[45]

Although a state, having been granted permitting authority, is the primary issuer of NPDES permits, EPA retains oversight authority over state permitting. As discussed in more detail below, under certain conditions a state-issued NPDES permit cannot be issued if the EPA Administrator objects.[46] Sections 402(b)(5) and (d)(1) of the CWA provide that states shall forward a copy of every permit application and notice of every permit action to EPA. However, rather than reviewing all permit actions, EPA and an authorized state generally identify those categories of permits EPA will review in the Memorandum of Agreement (MOA), as discussed below. A state NPDES permit cannot be issued if the Administrator within 90 days of receiving notice of the proposed permit objects in writing to its issuance as being outside the guidelines and requirements of the CWA.[47]

2. Regulatory Standard/MOA Agreement as to What Is Reviewed

Any state that seeks to administer its NPDES program under section 402(b) of the CWA must prepare a Memorandum of Agreement (MOA) to be executed by the state director and approved by the EPA Regional Administrator.[48] The MOA

---

43. 40 C.F.R. § 124.55.

44. 40 C.F.R. § 123.21.

45. CWA § 402(b)(1), 33 U.S.C. § 1342(b)(1); 40 C.F.R. § 123.25. EPA may withdraw a state's NPDES program authority based upon circumstances set forth in 40 C.F.R. § 123.63(a). A state may voluntarily withdraw its NPDES program authority or that authority may be ordered to withdraw by the Administrator. 40 C.F.R. § 123.64.

46. CWA § 402(d)(2), 33 U.S.C. § 1342(d)(2).

47. CWA § 402(d)(2), 33 U.S.C. § 1342(d)(2).

48. 40 C.F.R. § 123.21(a)(4).

must include such terms, conditions, or agreements, consistent with the NPDES regulations, as are relevant to the administration and enforcement of the state's regulatory NPDES program.[49] The MOA must specify classes and categories of permits that the state will send to the Regional Administrator for review and the procedures that will be followed for such review.[50] The Administrator may not approve any MOA that contains provisions that restrict EPA's statutory oversight responsibilities.[51]

The MOA may include provisions waiving EPA review of certain "classes and categories" of permits. However, the following categories may not be waived: discharges into the territorial sea; discharges that may affect the waters of a state other than the one in which the discharge originates; discharges proposed to be regulated by general permits; discharges from POTWs with average discharges exceeding 1 million gallons per day; discharges of uncontaminated cooling water exceeding 500 million gallons per day; discharges from any major discharger within the 21 industrial categories in appendix A to part 122; and discharges from other sources with a daily average discharge exceeding 0.5 million gallons per day.[52]

Each state agency administering an NPDES permit program shall transmit copies of permit program forms and any other relevant information agreed to by the state director in the MOA to the Regional Administrator.[53] At a minimum, the MOA shall provide for the transmittal of a copy of all complete permit applications, notice of any agency action relating to the application or to a general permit,[54] and copies of any significant comments received on the permit.[55]

The MOA shall provide a period of time, up to 90 days from receipt of proposed permits, in which the Regional Administrator may make general comments upon, objections to, or recommendations with respect to proposed permits.[56]

3. Veto of State-Issued Permits

a. Basis for Veto. If the Regional Administrator objects to a proposed permit, he or she must set forth in writing and submit to the state director, within 90 days of receiving the proposed permit, a statement of the reasons for the objection and the actions that must be taken to eliminate the objection, including the effluent limi-

---

49. 40 C.F.R. § 123.24(b).
50. 40 C.F.R. § 123.24(b)(2).
51. 40 C.F.R. § 123.24(a).
52. 40 C.F.R. § 123.24(d).
53. 40 C.F.R. § 123.43(a).
54. Id.
55. 40 C.F.R. § 123.43(c).
56. 40 C.F.R. § 123.44(a)(1).

tations and conditions that the permit would include if issued by EPA.[57] The Regional Administrator may object to a permit based on the following grounds:

1. The permit fails to apply or to ensure compliance with any applicable requirement of 40 C.F.R. part 123;

2. In the case of a proposed permit for which notification to the Administrator is required, the written recommendations of an affected state have not been accepted by the permitting state and the Regional Administrator finds the reasons for rejecting the recommendations inadequate;

3. The procedures followed in formulating the proposed permit failed to comply in a material respect to the terms of the CWA, implementing regulations, or the MOA;

4. State findings made in connection with the proposed permit misinterpret the CWA or any guidelines or regulations under the CWA or misapply them to the facts;

5. Provisions of the proposed permit relating to record maintenance, reporting, monitoring, or sampling are judged by the Regional Administrator to be inadequate to assure compliance with permit conditions;

6. The proposed permit fails to carry out the provisions of the CWA or any applicable regulations, in the case of permits issued in the absence of EPA promulgated effluent limitations guidelines or sewage sludge standards;

7. Issuance of the proposed permit would in any other respect be outside the requirements of the CWA or its regulations;

8. The effluent limits of a permit fail to satisfy the requirements of 40 C.F.R. section 122.44(d) (water quality–based limitations for NPDES permits); or

9. For a permit issued in the Great Lakes region, the permit does not comply with requirements based on EPA's "Great Lakes Initiative" rule at 40 C.F.R. part 132.[58]

In adopting these specific regulations defining when a state-issued permit is outside the guidelines and requirements of the CWA, EPA noted that although many of the listed grounds require consideration of state factual determinations, EPA's review is purely legal and involves consideration of a state's factual determinations only in limited circumstances necessary to ensure compliance with the CWA.[59] In fact, the bases for EPA review and veto are quite broad and provide the Agency with great discretion in making its decisions.

---

57. 40 C.F.R. § 123.44(b)(2).
58. 40 C.F.R. § 123.44(c).
59. 43 Fed. Reg. 22,160, 22,161 (May 23, 1978).

b. Procedures for Veto. Within 90 days of receipt of a proposed permit to which the EPA Administrator has objected, the Administrator must notify the state in writing of EPA's objection to the issuance of the permit.[60] The Administrator must include in the written notification a statement of the reasons for such objection and the effluent conditions and limitations that must be included within the permit if it is to be issued by the Regional Administrator. The state director or any interested person may request that a public hearing be held.[61]

If requested by the state or if warranted by significant public interest, the Regional Administrator shall expeditiously conduct a public hearing in accordance with the procedures set forth in 40 C.F.R. part 124.[62] Following the hearing, the Regional Administrator shall reaffirm the original objection, modify the terms of the objection, or withdraw the objection and notify the state of EPA's decision.[63] If the Regional Administrator does not withdraw the objection and the state does not resubmit a proposed permit revised to meet the objections, exclusive authority to issue the permit passes to EPA.[64]

The normal process for EPA permit issuance (discussed above in section E) applies to permits issued following veto of state-proposed permits. EPA's veto and subsequent issuance or denial of a federal NPDES permit are subject to review in the U.S. Courts of Appeals pursuant to section 509(b)(1)(F) of the CWA.[65]

In 2000, EPA promulgated, as part of a much larger rulemaking package, an amendment to its veto regulations that would allow it to object to and veto state permits that have expired at the end of their five-year terms (and have been administratively continued under the state law equivalent of the APA) (see section VII, *infra*). The objection would otherwise be based on the same criteria and follow the same procedures as described above.[66] EPA has delayed the effective date of these regulations until April 30, 2003, and has solicited comment on potential changes.[67]

---

60. 40 C.F.R. § 123.44(b)(2).

61. 40 C.F.R. § 123.44(e).

62. 40 C.F.R. § 122.10 (public notice requirements) and §§ 122.12(c) and (d) (hearing procedures).

63. 40 C.F.R. § 123.44(g).

64. 40 C.F.R. §§ 123.44(h)(2) and (3).

65. 33 U.S.C. § 1369(b)(1)(F). *See* Champion Int'l Corp. v. EPA, 850 F.2d 182 (4th Cir. 1988); District of Columbia v. Schramm, 631 F.2d 854 (D.C. Cir. 1980).

66. 65 Fed. Reg. 43,586, 43,661 (July 11, 2000) (promulgating 40 C.F.R. § 123.44(k)).

67. 66 Fed. Reg. 53,044 (Oct. 18, 2001).

VI. Effect of Permit Issuance—Permit Shield

With a few exceptions, compliance with a permit during its terms constitutes compliance with the CWA.[68] This is often referred to as the "permit shield." The permit shield is a major benefit to a permittee since it shields the permittee from any obligation to meet more-stringent limitations promulgated by EPA unless and until the permit expires or is appropriately modified or reissued.

Under EPA policy and recent court decisions, the scope of the permit shield is broader than simply allowing the permittee to discharge those pollutants listed in the permit. The CWA prohibits only those discharges expressly limited in a permit. Pollutants not limited in the permit can be discharged without violating the CWA, so long as those pollutants were disclosed by the permittee on its permit application or were previously undetected.[69] This finding is consistent with EPA's written statements on the scope of the permit shield.[70] Of course, an approved NPDES state can adopt a more-stringent shield provision that could prohibit any discharge not expressly authorized by a permit.[71]

The issuance of a permit, however, does not convey any property rights or any exclusive privilege to the permit holder. Nor does it authorize the permit holder to injure persons or property, invade other private rights, or infringe on any state or local laws.[72]

VII. Permit Term, Expiration, and APA Extension

Under CWA Section 402(b)(1)(B), an NPDES permit term cannot exceed five years. Pursuant to the terms of the federal Administrative Procedures Act (APA),

---

68. CWA § 402(k), 33 U.S.C. § 1342(k). Compliance with an NPDES permit is not deemed to be compliance with the standards imposed under CWA § 307 for toxic pollutants that are injurious to human health. *Id.*; Inland Steel Co. v. EPA, 574 F.2d 367, 373 (7th Cir. 1978) (§ 402(k) insulates a permit holder from any change in regulation until the change is incorporated into the permit, but authorizes permit modification to incorporate toxic standards); *See In re* Ketchikan Pulp Co., 7 E.A.D. 605 (EAB 1998) (this is leading case out of the EAB on permit as a shield).

69. Piney Run Preservation Ass'n v. County Comm'nrs. of Carroll County, Md., 268 F.3d 255 (4th Cir. 2001, *cert. denied*, 70 U.S.L.W. 3707 (U.S. May 20, 2002).

70. EPA, "Policy Statement on Scope of Discharge Authorized and Shield Associated with NPDES Permits" (July 1, 1994) (available at http://es.epa.gov/oeca/ore/water/shield.html). *See also* 45 Fed. Reg. 33,516, 33,523 (May 19, 1980) ("a permittee may discharge a . . . pollutant not limited in its permit, and EPA will not be able to take enforcement action against the permittee so long as the permittee complies with the notification requirements of the [regulation].").

71. CWA § 510, 33 U.S.C. § 1370. Such a state law, however, would be "broader in scope" than the federal NPDES program, and thus could not be enforced by a CWA citizen suit. Atlantic States Legal Fdn. v. Eastman Kodak Co., 12 F.3d 353 (2d. Cir. 1993).

72. 40 C.F.R. § 122.5.

however, an NPDES permit will administratively be continued beyond its expiration date pending EPA action on reissuance, provided the permittee has timely submitted a complete application for renewal in accordance with EPA requirements.[73] Permits continued in this manner remain in full force and effect until the effective date of the new permit.[74]

For general permits, EPA takes the view that an NOI constitutes the equivalent of an application for renewal of the general permit. Therefore, persons who have already obtained coverage under a general permit can maintain that coverage by submitting a new NOI prior to the expiration of the old general permit. However, since the permit has expired, new dischargers cannot submit an NOI and obtain coverage until the general permit is reissued.[75]

State-issued permits and EPA permits issued in states that have had their NPDES program approved since the date of issuance cannot be extended unless the state has a comparable administrative continuance law.[76] Most states do have comparable laws.

VIII. Special NPDES Program Requirements for New Sources

The NPDES permit application and issuance procedures discussed above generally apply to dischargers who need to renew an existing permit and to sources who plan to begin discharging but who do not have a permit to do so. There are some deviations from the general requirements, however, in the case of "new sources."

A "new source" is defined in the federal regulations as any building, structure, facility, or installation from which there is or may be a "discharge of pollutants," the construction of which commenced . . . after promulgation of standards of performance under Section 306 of CWA that are applicable to such source,[77] and (1) it is constructed at a site at which no other source exists, (2) it totally

---

73. 5 U.S.C. § 558(c); *see also* 40 C.F.R. § 122.6. In NRDC v. EPA, 859 F.2d 156, 213 (D.C. Cir. 1988), the D.C. Circuit upheld the administrative continuance of NPDES permits containing best practicable technology (BPT) limitations even though the statutory deadline for meeting more stringent best available technology (BAT) limitations had already passed.

74. 40 C.F.R. § 122.6(b).

75. *See, e.g.*, 65 Fed. Reg. 65,000, 65,006 (Nov. 15, 2000).

76. 40 C.F.R. § 122.6(d).

77. 40 C.F.R. § 122.2. A source is also considered a "new source" if the construction of that source begins after the proposal of such standards, but only if the proposed standards are actually promulgated within 120 days of their proposal. *Id.*, CWA § 306(a)(2). EPA rarely, if ever, promulgates final standards within 120 days of proposal. EPA's authority to use the date of promulgation of final regulations, rather than proposed regulations (unless promulgated final within 120 days), to trigger new source characterization was upheld in NRDC v. EPA, 822 F.2d 104 (D.C. Cir. 1987).

replaces the process or production equipment, or (3) its processes are substantially independent of an existing source at the same site.[78]

Only sources constructed or modified after EPA has promulgated national new-source performance standards (NSPS) regulations applicable to the source are "new sources." Modifications to an existing source may make the discharger a new source if construction, after the promulgation of an applicable NSPS, creates a new building, structure, facility, or installation that meets the criteria in (2) and (3) above.[79] Sources that are newly built or planning on discharging for the first time, but for which NSPS have not yet been issued by EPA, are considered "new dischargers."[80]

In terms of characteristics, there is little difference between new sources and new dischargers, and for most NPDES purposes, they are treated the same. The most significant exception to this rule is the application of the National Environmental Policy Act of 1969 (NEPA).[81] Section 511(c)(2) of the CWA states that NEPA applies to the issuance of new source permits.

As a result, EPA must evaluate new sources to determine whether permit issuance constitutes a "major federal action significantly affecting the quality of the human environment,"[82] and, if so, EPA must prepare an environmental impact statement (EIS) prior to permit issuance.[83]

If an EIS is prepared, EPA must include in the EIS a recommendation to either issue or deny the permit. If EPA recommends permit issuance, the EIS shall recommend actions, if any, that should be taken to prevent or minimize any adverse environmental impacts. If EPA recommends permit denial, the EIS shall contain the reasons for the recommendation and list those measures, if any, that the applicant could take to cause the recommendation to be changed.[84] The EIS process significantly increases the time involved in the NPDES permitting process and requires the applicant to submit more information to EPA than otherwise is required.

---

78. 40 C.F.R. § 122.29(b)(1).

79. 40 C.F.R. § 122.29(b)(3).

80. A new discharger is defined as any building, structure, facility, or installation (a) from which there is or may be a discharge of pollutants, (b) that did not commence the discharge at a particular "site" prior to August 13, 1979, (c) that is not a new source, and (d) that never received a final NPDES permit for discharges at the "site." 40 C.F.R. § 122.2.

81. 42 U.S.C. §§ 4321–4370e. The CWA is one of the few EPA-administered programs subject to NEPA. The only other activity under the CWA that is subject to NEPA review is the granting of financial assistance to POTWs under section 201 of the CWA. States with approved programs are not subject to this requirement since the issuance of a permit by a state is not a federal action. 40 C.F.R. §§ 122.21(l) and 122.29(c).

82. *See* 40 C.F.R. §§ 122.21(l) and 122.29(c).

83. *See* 40 C.F.R. § 122.21(k) (special provisions for new source applications) and 40 C.F.R. pt. 6, subpt. F (NEPA environmental review provisions).

84. 40 C.F.R. § 122.29(c).

New sources and new dischargers are subject to a different application of effluent limitations than are existing sources. A new source (or a new discharger, the construction of which started after October 18, 1972) that meets the applicable NSPS before the commencement of its discharge may not be subject to any more stringent NSPS or to any more-stringent technology-based standards under section 301(b)(2) of the CWA for the soonest ending of the following periods:

1. ten years from the date that construction is completed;
2. ten years from the date the source begins to discharge; or
3. the period of depreciation on amortization of the facility.[85]

This so-called ten-year grace period has been restricted by EPA, however. The protection against more-stringent standards does not apply (1) to permit conditions that are not technology-based, such as water quality standards or toxic effluent standards; (2) to additional permit conditions developed pursuant to 40 C.F.R. section 125.3 to control toxic pollutants or hazardous substances not controlled by NSPS; and (3) for an NPDES permit issued within the protection period, to the part of the permit term that will expire on or after the expiration of the protection period.[86]

IX. Permit Appeals

A person seeking to appeal the denial or issuance of an NPDES permit under the EPA permit program generally must file an administrative appeal with EPA and then may seek judicial review in federal court.

Prior to June 2000, EPA provided for two different (and both quite complicated) administrative procedures to appeal an NPDES permit. The first involved an evidentiary hearing in front of an administrative law judge.[87] The second, the "nonadversarial panel proceeding," was a less formal, more technical proceeding, which could be invoked to review the permit issuance procedures either during or after issuance of the final permit.[88] After either process, there was a requirement for a second administrative appeal to EPA's Environmental Appeals Board (EAB).[89] EPA subsequently issued new regulations that eliminated the evidentiary hearing/nonadversary panel process step and provided for a one-step administrative appeal directly to the EAB.[90]

---

85. 40 C.F.R. § 122.29(d)(1).

86. 40 C.F.R. § 122.29(d)(2).

87. 40 C.F.R. pt. 124, subpt. E (1999) (superseded).

88. 40 C.F.R. pt. 124, subpt. F (1999) (superseded).

89. 40 C.F.R. § 124.91 (1999) (superseded).

90. 65 Fed. Reg. 30,886 (May 15, 2000) (codified at 40 C.F.R. § 124.19).

A. EAB HEARING PROCESS

1. Procedure for Requesting and Obtaining EAB Review

A party appealing from the issuance of an NPDES permit by an EPA Regional Administrator must file a petition for review with the EAB within 30 days after receiving notice of the denial or decision.[91] The petition for review must contain the bases for the appeal. In addition, the EAB may, sua sponte, review the permit within 30 days by serving notice of intent to do so on the interested parties.[92] The EAB must either grant or deny the petition for review within a reasonable time after filing.[93]

If the EAB accepts a petition for review, the parties may then file briefs on their positions under a schedule established by the EAB.[94] The regulations thus, by their terms, appear to contemplate a two-step process, that is, that the Board will grant or deny review, and then, if review is granted, will accept briefs and argument before deciding the merits. Yet, as the EAB has made clear, most appeals are decided at the initial stage, that is, when the EAB decides to grant or deny the petition for review. As the Board has explained,

> [a] petition for review under Section 124.19 is not analogous to a notice of appeal that may be supplemented by further briefing. Although briefing may occur after review has been granted, the discretion to grant review is to be sparingly exercised, and therefore, * * * a petition for review must specifically identify disputed permit conditions and demonstrate why review is warranted.[95]

Therefore, it is critical for the petition for review to describe all of the issues being appealed and the factual and legal reasons for the appeal. It is not sufficient for a petitioner to rely on previous statements of its objections, such as prior comments on a draft permit.[96]

> Only those persons who participated in the permit process leading up to the permit decision, either by filing comments on the draft permit or by participating in the public hearing, may appeal a permit decision.[97] Any issues raised

---

91. 40 C.F.R. § 124.19(a).

92. 40 C.F.R. § 124.19(b).

93. 40 C.F.R. § 124.19(c).

94. *Id.*

95. *See* ENVIRONMENTAL APPEALS BOARD PRACTICE MANUAL (hereinafter "EAB Practice Manual") 40 (Feb. 2002) (available at http://www.epa.gov/eab/pmanual.pdf) (quoting *In re* LCP Chemicals-N.Y., 4 E.A.D. 661, 665 n.9 (EAB 1993)).

96. *In re* Town of Ashland Wastewater Treatment Facility, NPDES Appeal No. 00-15, slip op. at 10 (EAB, Feb. 23, 2001).

97. 40 C.F.R. § 124.19(a)

in the petition must have been previously raised by someone (either petitioner or another commenter) during the public comment period (including any public hearing), provided that they were "reasonably ascertainable" at that time.[98]

Although the decisions of the EAB are considered to be the decisions of the Administrator and, therefore, final, the EAB still may refer matters to the Administrator in exceptional cases.[99]

2. Scope of EAB Review

There is no appeal as of right from the Regional Administrator's permit decision.[100] "[T]he petitioner has the burden of demonstrating that review should be granted. In particular, the petition must show that the condition in question is based on 'a finding of fact or conclusion of law which is clearly erroneous,' or 'an exercise of discretion or an important policy consideration which the [EAB] should, in its discretion, review.' "[101] "[T]his power of review should only be sparingly exercised. . . . [M]ost permit conditions should be finally determined [by the EPA Regional Office]."[102]

B. JUDICIAL REVIEW OF FINAL AGENCY PERMIT ACTION

In order to seek judicial review of a decision on an NPDES permit dispute, a party must have exhausted administrative remedies and there must be final agency action on the permit.[103] For purposes of judicial review, EPA action is final (1) when the EAB denies review; (2) when the EAB issues a decision on the merits and does not remand the proceeding; or (3) when the remanded proceeding is completed (including any appeals of the remanded proceeding if the Board explicitly requires a further appeal).[104] Appeals of final EPA action on a permit must be made to the U.S. Court of Appeals within 120 days of final Agency action pursuant to CWA section 509(b)(1).

Note that the administrative appeal procedure described above does not apply to state-administered programs. Appeals of state permit decisions are governed by state administrative law, and EPA does not require any administrative

---

98. 40 C.F.R. § 124.13

99. 57 Fed. Reg. at 5,321 (Feb. 13, 1992).

100. EAB Practice Manual, *supra* note 95, at 44 (citing *In re* Miners Advocacy Council, 4 E.A.D. 40, 42 (EAB, May 29, 1992)).

101. EAB Practice Manual, *supra* note 95, at 44 (quoting 40 C.F.R. § 124.19(a)).

102. 45 Fed. Reg. 33,290, 33,412 (May 19, 1980).

103. 40 C.F.R. § 124.19(e).

104. 40 C.F.R. § 124.19(f)(1).

appeal process. EPA regulations do, however, explicitly require that states provide an opportunity for review in state court of the final approval or denial of permits "sufficient to provide for, encourage, and assist public participation in the permitting process."[105] EPA has explained that states must allow not only the permittee or those with a "property interest" in the waters where the discharge occurs, but other affected citizens.[106] The requirement is satisfied automatically if the state provides access to its courts equivalent to that provided under CWA section 509(b)(1) and Article III of the U.S. Constitution.[107]

C. EFFECT OF APPEAL ON THE ISSUED PERMIT

If a person requests EAB review of a permit decision on a reissued permit, the terms of the reissued permit that are being challenged are stayed and the terms of the preexisting permit remain in effect pending the outcome of the hearing. Uncontested provisions become effective unless they are not separable from the provisions being contested.[108] The Regional Administrator must, as soon as possible after the appeal is filed, notify the EAB, the permittee, and all other interested parties of those conditions that are uncontested; those conditions take effect 30 days after the notification.[109] By contrast, if a person requests review of a permit issued for a discharge for which there is no prior permit, the discharger is without a permit pending final action on the appeal.[110]

D. APPEAL OF GENERAL PERMITS

There is no administrative appeal process, nor an exhaustion requirement, to challenge a federally issued general permit.[111] These permits either must be challenged directly in the U.S. Court of Appeals under CWA section 509(b)(1), or a party subject to a general permit may apply for an individual permit for his or her source and appeal the issuance, denial, or terms of that permit through the process outlined above.[112]

---

105. 40 C.F.R. § 123.30.

106. *Id.*; 61 Fed. Reg. 20,972, 20,973 (May 8, 1996).

107. 61 Fed. Reg. at 20,975.

108. 40 C.F.R. §§ 124.16(a)(1) and (2).

109. 40 C.F.R. §§ 124.16(a)(2)(ii), 124.60(b)(1).

110. 40 C.F.R. § 124.16(a)(1). There is a slight exception to this rule for certain permits for offshore or coastal oil and gas drilling rigs; if the Regional Administrator finds that compliance with certain permit conditions is necessary to avoid irreparable environmental harm during the EAB appeal process, he or she may specify those permit conditions that must be met in the interim. 40 C.F.R. § 124.60(a)(1).

111. 40 C.F.R. § 124.19(a).

112. 40 C.F.R. §§ 122.28(b)(3), 124.19(a).

X. Permit Modification, Revocation, Termination, and Transfer

Once a final permit is issued, there are a number of situations in which the permit must or may be modified, revoked and reissued, terminated, or transferred before its expiration date. The type of changes occurring at the facility will determine which type of alteration must be made to the permit. A request for any of these types of permit changes may be made by the permittee or any other interested person. The regulations require permit changes in some situations and also allow EPA to initiate permit changes.

A. PERMIT MODIFICATION OR REVOCATION AND REISSUANCE

At any time during the term of the permit, the permittee may request that a permit be modified or revoked and reissued for specified causes listed in the regulations. EPA may initiate a modification, or revocation and reissuance, when it receives information, either through facility inspections or the permittee itself, that indicates to the Agency that appropriate cause exists for such a change.[113] When a permit is modified, only the conditions subject to the modification are reopened. If a permit is revoked and reissued, the entire permit is reopened and subject to revision and the permit is reissued for a new term.[114]

1. Permit Modification

There are two types of modifications that can be made to a permit: major and minor. From a procedural standpoint, these differ primarily with respect to the public notice requirements—major permit modifications require public notice and comment, whereas minor modifications do not. From a substantive standpoint, minor modifications are generally more trivial or procedural or make permit conditions more stringent. Major modifications, on the other hand, are appropriate when there are material and substantial changes to a facility or when certain new information becomes available or new regulations are promulgated.

EPA believes that a requirement for public notice and opportunity for a hearing under section 124.5 for major modifications is necessary because the public has a right to know of any permit modifications that may render a permit less stringent and that could therefore adversely affect the environment. Minor modifications that may result in more stringent permit terms are not subject to the decision-making procedures of section 124.5 because the only entity adversely affected by more-stringent permit terms is the permittee, who receives notice and

---

113. 40 C.F.R. § 122.62.
114. *Id.*

retains the right to object to any proposed modifications to a permit that are more stringent.[115]

a. Minor Modifications. As defined in the regulations, minor modifications are nonsubstantive in nature or require imposition of more-stringent permit conditions. Examples of minor modifications include: correction of typographical errors; addition of more frequent monitoring or reporting requirements; modifications of interim compliance dates or construction schedules for new sources; changes to identify new ownership where other changes are not necessary; or shutting down one outfall under circumstances that will not otherwise violate the permit terms.[116] Permit modifications can be processed as minor modifications only if the permittee consents to the modifications.[117] If the permittee does not consent, then the modification must be processed as a major modification requiring compliance with part 124 draft permit requirements and public notice as required in section 122.62.

b. Major Modifications. Virtually all modifications that result in less-stringent permit conditions are treated as major modifications requiring public notice and comment and compliance with the administrative procedures identified in 40 C.F.R. section 124.5. As noted above, major modifications will be implemented only for cause. The regulations currently identify seventeen situations that are considered sufficient cause for a permit modification.[118] Generally, cause for a major modification may be established if there are material and substantial alterations to the permitted facility that occurred after the permit was issued or when new information becomes available, but only if such information was not available and would have justified the application of different standards at the time the permit was issued.[119] The regulations specifically state that in order to form the basis for a permit modification, the term "new information" does not refer to revised regulations, guidance, or test methods.

Cause for a modification can be established if the standards or regulations on which the permit was based have been changed by regulation or judicial decision. However, a modification based on changed regulations can be justified only if the permit condition was based on an effluent limitation guideline, EPA-approved water quality standards, or secondary treatment regulations, and EPA has revised that portion of the regulation, and the permittee has requested modification within

---

115. 44 Fed. Reg. 32,854, 32,869 (June 7, 1979).

116. 40 C.F.R. § 122.63.

117. *Id.*

118. 40 C.F.R. § 122.62(a). These 17 identified and acceptable causes for a modification may also form the basis of a revocation and reissuance of a permit if the permittee agrees or makes such a request.

119. 40 C.F.R. §§ 122.62(a)(1) and (2).

90 days after *Federal Register* notice of the action under 40 C.F.R. section 124.5.[120]

It has been argued that if EPA revises a regulation from which specific permit terms are derived, the permittee should not have to request a permit modification because the older regulations or guidelines are no longer in effect. EPA rejected this argument as having been based on a fundamental misunderstanding of the enforceability of permit terms as written—all permit terms and conditions are fully enforceable unless and until they are modified, revoked, or judicially stayed.[121] Thus, it is essential that a permittee request a modification to its permit if the grounds for such modification are based on a revision of EPA regulations or guidance.

If the requested modification is based on a judicial decision that revises any applicable regulation, the court of competent jurisdiction must have remanded and stayed EPA's promulgated regulations or ELGs and a request for a modification must be filed by the permittee within 90 days of judicial remand.[122]

Finally, cause for a modification based on new regulations can be based upon modified state certifications of NPDES permits, that is, if there is a change in the state law or regulation upon which a certification is based pursuant to section 124.55(b).[123] Under section 124.55(b), if the modified state certification is received before final Agency action on the permit, the permit shall be based on the more-stringent state law identified in the modified permit. If the modified certification is received after final Agency action on the permit, then the EPA Regional Administrator may modify the permit at the request of the permittee only to the extent necessary to delete any conditions invalidated by a court of competent jurisdiction or an appropriate state board or agency.[124]

Additional causes for major permit modifications include circumstances when good cause, such as an act of God, strike, flood, or other event over which the permittee has no control, exists for a modification of a compliance schedule (but in no case may this extend beyond statutory deadlines); when an appropriate request for a variance has been made under sections 301(c), 301(g), 301(h), 301(i), 301(k), or 316(a) of the CWA or for "fundamentally different factors"; to incorporate an applicable section 301(a) toxic effluent standard or prohibition; or to correct technical mistakes such as errors in calculations or mistaken interpre-

---

120. 40 C.F.R. § 122.62(a)(3)(i).

121. 44 Fed. Reg. 32,854, 32,869 (June 7, 1979).

122. 40 C.F.R. § 122.62(a)(3)(ii).

123. 40 C.F.R. § 122.62(a)(3)(iii). If a state court or administrative body stays the effect of a state certification, the state agency responsible for providing the certification must issue a revised certification before EPA will modify the permit. Puerto Rico Sun Oil Co. v. EPA, 8 F.3d 73, 80 (1st Cir. 1993).

124. 40 C.F.R. § 124.55(b).

tations of law.[125] A modification to a permit may also be made when a permittee has installed the treatment technology adopted by the permitting authority in setting effluent limits under section 402(a)(1) of the CWA, and has properly maintained and operated the facilities, but nevertheless is unable to achieve the identified effluent limits. Under these circumstances, the permit may be modified to reflect the level of pollutant control actually achieved; however, such limits may never be less stringent than any subsequently promulgated ELG.[126]

2. Revocation and Reissuance

A permit may be revoked and reissued (as opposed to simply modified) for any of the causes for permit modification identified in 40 C.F.R. section 122.62(a), if the permittee requests or agrees to such relief.[127] A permit also may be revoked and reissued (or modified) if cause exists for termination under section 122.64, but EPA determines that revocation and reissuance are more appropriate. Finally, EPA may revoke and reissue (or modify) a permit to change the permittee's name or to incorporate appropriate permit conditions, where EPA receives notification of a proposed transfer of the permit.[128]

B. PERMIT TERMINATION

EPA may terminate a permit during its term or deny a permit renewal application for any of the following reasons:

1. noncompliance by the permittee with any condition of the permit;
2. the permittee's failure in the application or during the permit issuance process to disclose fully all relevant facts or the permittee's misrepresentation of any relevant fact at any time;
3. a determination that the permitted activity endangers human health or the environment and can only be regulated to acceptable levels by permit modification or termination; or
4. a change in any condition that requires either a temporary or permanent reduction or elimination or any discharge or sludge use or disposal practice controlled by the permit—for example, plant closure or termination of discharge by connection to a POTW.[129]

---

125. *See* 40 C.F.R. § 122.62(a) for a complete listing of all applicable causes for requests for major modifications.

126. 40 C.F.R. § 122.62(a)(16).

127. 40 C.F.R. § 122.62(a).

128. 40 C.F.R. § 122.62(b).

129. 40 C.F.R. § 122.64.

C. PERMIT TRANSFERS

A permit may be transferred automatically if the permittee provides notice of the transfer to EPA at least 30 days in advance of the transfer date; includes with this notice a written agreement between the existing and new permittees for transfer of permit responsibility, coverage, and liability between the parties on a specific date;[130] and EPA does not notify the permittee of its intent to modify or revoke and reissue the permit. An automatic transfer is effective on the date specified in the agreement between the parties and does not require public notice and comment under part 124. Where EPA chooses, or where the permittee missed the deadline for automatic transfer, a permit can be transferred through permit modification (or through revocation or reissuance if the permittee agrees).

D. PROCEDURES FOR MODIFICATION, REVOCATION AND REISSUANCE, OR TERMINATION OF PERMITS

Part 124 contains procedures for EPA decision making for issuing, modifying, revoking and reissuing, or terminating NPDES permits. Permits may be modified, revoked and reissued, or terminated either at the request of the permittee, any other interested person or upon the request of the state director for the reasons identified in section 122.62 (modification or revocation and reissuance) or 122.64 (termination).[131] All requests shall be in written form and shall contain facts and reasons supporting the request.

If EPA rejects the request to modify, revoke, or terminate the permit, EPA must serve the requesting party with a brief written response giving a reason for the decision.[132] Denials of requests are not subject to public notice, comments, or hearings. Denials by the EPA Regional Administrator may be appealed to the EAB by a letter briefly setting forth the relevant facts.[133] The appeal shall be considered denied if the EAB takes no action on the letter within 60 days after receiving it.[134] This informal appeal is a prerequisite to seeking judicial review of EPA action in denying a request for modification, revocation, or termination.[135]

If EPA initially decides to modify or revoke and reissue the permit, then the director must prepare a draft permit under section 124.6 incorporating the proposed changes.[136] EPA may request additional information before granting the

---

130. 40 C.F.R. § 122.61(b).
131. 40 C.F.R. § 124.5.
132. 40 C.F.R. § 124.5(b).
133. *Id.*
134. 40 C.F.R. § 124.5.
135. 5 U.S.C. § 704.
136. 40 C.F.R. § 124.5(c).

request. EPA may, in the case of a modification, and shall, in the case of a reissued permit, require the submission of a new permit application. With respect to a request for a modification, all other aspects of the original permit shall remain in effect for the duration of the unmodified permit. When a permit is revoked and reissued, the entire permit is reopened. However, during the reissuance proceedings the permittee shall comply with all conditions of the existing permit until a new final permit is issued.[137] Minor modifications as defined in section 122.63 are not subject to these provisions.[138]

There are a number of different procedural mechanisms for termination of EPA-issued permits during the term of the permit. If a permit is terminated during its term for any reason specified in section 122.64(a) other than the elimination of the discharge, and the permittee does not request termination, EPA continues to follow formal evidentiary hearing procedures before an ALJ prior to termination; such procedures are specified in 40 CFR part 22.[139] If the permittee requests termination during the term of the permit, EPA issues a "notice of intent to terminate," which is just like a draft permit under section 124.6; EPA then follows the procedures of part 124 as if it were issuing or denying a permit.[140] If a permit is being terminated because of elimination of the discharge, and the permittee objects to termination of the permit, then EPA also issues a notice of intent to terminate.[141] If, however, the permit is being terminated due to elimination of the discharge and the permittee does not object, then EPA does not need to go through any administrative process; rather, the permit terminates automatically 30 days after notice to the permittee. To qualify for this expedited process, there must not be any ongoing state or federal enforcement action or citizen suit pending against the permittee at the time of termination.[142] For state-issued NPDES permits, the procedures are generally the same, except that states are not required by EPA to conduct formal evidentiary hearings before terminating a permit during its term.[143]

When EPA is the permitting authority, all draft permits, including notices of intent to terminate, shall be based on the administrative record as defined in section 124.9.[144] Section 124.9 requires that the administrative record include the application and any supporting data; the draft permit or notice of intent to deny the application or to terminate; the statement of basis or fact sheet; all documents

---

137. 40 C.F.R. § 124.5(c)(2).

138. 40 C.F.R. § 124.5(c)(3).

139. 40 C.F.R. § 124.5(d)(2); *see also* 40 C.F.R. § 22.44.

140. 40 C.F.R. § 124.5(d)(1).

141. *Id.*

142. 40 C.F.R. § 122.64(b).

143. *Id.*

144. 40 C.F.R. § 124.5(e).

cited in the statement of basis or fact sheet; and other documents contained in the supporting file for the draft permit.[145]

E. ANTIBACKSLIDING PROHIBITIONS

As discussed earlier, the CWA controls the discharge of pollutants through the application of technology-based effluent limitations or more-stringent water quality–based limitations. EPA was directed to implement technology-based requirements primarily through the development of national effluent limitation guidelines (ELGs) for categories of point source discharges, which are then incorporated into NPDES permits. In the absence of ELGs, technology-based effluent limits are incorporated into NPDES permits on a case-by-case basis under section 402(a)(1)(B) of the CWA, which authorizes the permitting authority to establish effluent limitations using his or her best professional judgment (BPJ)[146] as to what constitutes the appropriate technology requirements for that facility. The antibacksliding policy was originally adopted by EPA in order to implement the CWA goal of continued further progress toward eliminating pollutant discharges.[147] The policy prohibits the renewal of a permit with effluent limitations or standards less stringent than those in the previous permit, unless the circumstances on which the previous permit were based have materially and substantially changed and would constitute cause for permit modification or revocation and reissuance.[148]

In the case of an NPDES permit in which the initial effluent limitations were developed based on BPJ, a permit may not be renewed, reissued, or modified to incorporate subsequently promulgated less-stringent ELG limitations unless certain conditions are met.[149] These conditions are limited to the following:

1. Material and substantial alterations or additions to the permitted facility occurred after permit issuance that would justify the new limits;
2. a. Information is available that was not available at the time of permit issuance (other than revised regulations, guidance, or test methods) and that would have justified the application of less-stringent standards at the time of permit issuance, or

---

145. 40 C.F.R. § 124.9.

146. In developing permit limits based on BPJ, the permitting authority must consider the same factors used in the development of ELGs as set forth in CWA § 304(b). As a practical matter, however, a BPJ determination is tailored to the relevant circumstances and capabilities of a facility and inherently incorporates any necessary allowances for variations in individual plants.

147. 49 Fed. Reg. 37,898, 38,019 (Sept. 26, 1984).

148. CWA § 402(o) (1987), codified in 40 C.F.R. § 122.44(l)(1).

149. 40 C.F.R. § 122.44(l)(2).

       b.   The Administrator determines that technical mistakes or mistaken interpretations of law were made in issuing the BPJ permit;

3.   A less-stringent effluent limitation is necessary because of events over which the permittee has no control and for which there is no reasonably available remedy;

4.   The permittee has received a permanent modification under sections 301(c), 301(g), 301(h), 301(i), 301(k), 301(n), or 316(a); or

5.   The permittee has installed treatment facilities required to meet the effluent limits and has properly operated and maintained the facilities but has nevertheless been unable to achieve the previous effluent limitations. In this case the limitations in the revised or modified permit may reflect levels of pollutant control actually achieved.[150]

In the Water Quality Act of 1987, Congress statutorily approved the antibacksliding policy adopted by EPA through regulation by adding section 402(o) to the CWA. In fact, section 402(o) goes beyond EPA's initial policy in some cases. For example, it prohibits modifying BPJ permits due to excessive costs.[151] Section 402(o)(1) also prohibits backsliding from water quality–based permit limits under sections 301(b)(1)(C) or 303(d) or (e). Section 303(d)(4) allows effluent limitations based on total maximum daily load or other waste-load allocations to be revised if the revision will assure the attainment of such water quality standard or if the designated use that is not being attained is removed in accordance with established procedures. Such revisions must also be consistent with the antidegradation policy established under the CWA.[152] EPA's regulations prohibiting backsliding have not yet been modified to incorporate this prohibition against backsliding from water quality–based permit limits.[153] EPA's regulations at 40 C.F.R. section 122.44(l)(1) also continue to restrict backsliding in some cases not covered by the Water Quality Act Amendments. EPA has indicated it does not intend to revise its rules to recognize a broader prohibition.[154]

With respect to permits for sludge use and disposal, EPA has stated that the antibacksliding provisions of 40 C.F.R. section 122.44(l) do not apply.[155] This means that if the permit contains requirements developed on a case-by-case basis using BPJ under EPA's interim sludge-permitting strategy that are more stringent than subsequently promulgated part 503 standards, the reissued permit may include the less-stringent part 503 standard rather than the BPJ interim limit. It is

---

150. 40 C.F.R. § 122.44(l)(2)(i).

151. 54 Fed. Reg. 251 (Jan. 4, 1989), deleting prior 40 C.F.R. § 122.62(a)(15) (1980).

152. CWA § 303(d)(4)(B), 33 U.S.C. § 1313(d)(4)(B).

153. 54 Fed. Reg. 252 (Jan. 4, 1989).

154. *Id.*

155. 54 Fed. Reg. 18,716, 18,743 (May 2, 1989).

EPA's position that because part 503 standards must be protective of public health and the environment from reasonably anticipated adverse effects, back-sliding from more-stringent requirements would still not result in significant public health or environmental effects.[156]

.

---

156. *Id.*

CHAPTER 4

Publicly Owned Treatment Works (POTWs)

ALEXANDRA DAPOLITO DUNN*

I. Applicability and Scope

Today, more than 16,000 wastewater treatment plants in the United States treat more than 32 billion gallons of wastewater each day.[1] The Clean Water Act (CWA) contains numerous provisions specific to these publicly owned wastewater treatment works (POTWs). Municipal wastewater is collected in sewers ("the collection system") and transported via gravity and lift stations that pump the water to the POTW for treatment. POTW treatment is classified as primary, secondary, and tertiary. Through these processes, POTWs strive to achieve applicable National Pollutant Discharge Elimination System (NPDES) permit limitations, meet water quality standards in their receiving waters, and generate recyclable sewage sludges.

The CWA's POTW provisions are focused on: (1) ensuring that wastewater in the United States is treated to a minimum of "secondary treatment"; (2) establishing management programs for the use and disposal of sewage sludges (or "biosolids"); and (3) ensuring that POTWs set and enforce specific pretreatment limits on industrial dischargers sending their wastewater to POTWs.

---

*   The author acknowledges the contributions of Dale Murad to the 1994 edition of this chapter.

1. 1996 Clean Water Needs Survey Report to Congress, U.S. EPA; for general wastewater treatment statistics *see also* Progress in Water Quality: An Evaluation of the National Investment in Municipal Wastewater Treatment, EPA Report No. 832-R-00-008 (June 2000).

II. Effluent Limitations Applicable to POTWs

A. TECHNOLOGY-BASED LIMITATIONS

Municipal wastewater consists primarily of domestic wastewater from households and of industrial wastewater from manufacturing and commercial activities within a POTW's service area. The wastewater generally contains organic and inorganic solids, fine suspended solids, dispersed solids, and dissolved organic solids. In geographic areas with "combined sewers," which accept both storm water and sanitary water, the wastewater also will contain sediment and other pollutants carried in stormwater runoff. In areas with "separate" sanitary and storm sewers, infiltration of storm- and groundwater into the sanitary sewer pipes may also contribute additional pollutants to the wastewater.

CWA section 301(e)(3)(A) requires effluent limitations for POTWs to be based upon "secondary treatment." CWA 304(d)(1) directs the Environmental Protection Agency (EPA) to define "the degree of effluent reduction attainable through the application of secondary treatment." Accordingly, at 40 C.F.R. section 133.102, EPA specifies the minimum level of effluent quality for three conventional wastewater pollutants: biochemical oxygen demand (BOD), total suspended solids (TSS), and pH.

To achieve these regulatory treatment levels, POTWs first implement "primary treatment" practices, which include screening, sedimentation, and/or skimming of the wastewater to remove oils, greases, and large solids (such as rags and debris). These practices are followed by "secondary treatment," which uses microorganisms to consume biodegradable organics. Typical secondary treatment technologies include activated sludge systems, trickling filters, and rotating biological contactors. In addition, depending on local effluent discharge requirements, POTWs may perform other advanced treatment such as nitrification, denitrification, physical-chemical treatment to remove dissolved metals or organics, or disinfection to kill pathogens. When treatment is complete, the POTW's effluent generally is discharged to a receiving stream, river, creek, lake, or estuary. Some POTWs apply reclaimed or treated effluent to golf courses, parkland, and cropland.

Although CWA section 301(h) provides for case-by-case review and NPDES permit waivers of secondary treatment requirements for POTWs that discharge into marine waters, very few POTWs discharge effluent directly to the ocean.[2] In 1981, Congress established December 29, 1982, as the cutoff for 301(h) waiver applications.[3] In 1987, Congress added additional requirements and prohibitions

---

2. *See* 40 C.F.R. pt. 125, subpt. G for EPA regulations regarding 301(h) waivers.

3. *See* NRDC v. EPA, 656 F.2d 768 (D.C. Cir. 1981); Municipal Wastewater Treatment Construction Grant Amendments of 1981, Pub. L. No. 97-117, 95 Stat. 1623, § 22 (1981).

to the program.[4] Of the 208 applicants in 1982, only 36 permittees and 9 applicants pending decision remain in the 301(h) program as this book goes to press.[5]

B. WATER QUALITY–BASED LIMITATIONS

Under CWA section 301(b)(1)(C), POTWs also are required to achieve effluent limitations more stringent than those that would be required on the basis of the application of technology-based standards alone. Water quality–based permit limitations are developed for POTWs in the same manner as other point source dischargers. (Water quality–based controls are discussed in chapter 2.)

III. POTW NPDES Permit Requirements

The NPDES permit application requirements for POTWs are outlined at 40 C.F.R. section 122.21(j). POTW NPDES applications must include a variety of information, such as: facility information; population served; whether the municipality owns or maintains the collection system; whether the collection system is separate sanitary or combined storm and sanitary; the wastewater flow rate the plant was built to handle; identification of outfalls; location of surface impoundments; information on wastewater applied to the land or effluent sent to other facilities for treatment prior to discharge; and information on underground injection if applicable. Plants with a design flow greater than or equal to 0.1 million gallons per day (mgd) also must provide: information on average daily volume of inflow and infiltration; topographic maps; process flow diagrams; schedules of improvements or construction; information on effluent discharges, including a description of the outfall and the receiving waters; and a description of the type of treatment provided. All wastewater treatment plants also must provide effluent monitoring information for specific parameters: BOD, fecal coliform, design flow rate, pH, temperature, and TSS.[6] Those with a flow equal to or greater than 0.1 mgd also must monitor for ammonia, chlorine, dissolved oxygen, nitrate/nitrite, Kjeldahl nitrogen, oil and grease, phosphorous, and total dissolved solids.[7] Facilities with a design flow rate equal to or greater than 1 mgd, and those with a pretreatment program, also must monitor for additional toxic pollutants.[8] All facilities must provide any whole effluent toxicity tests conducted during the four and one-half years prior

---

4. Water Quality Act of 1987, § 303, Pub. L. No. 100-4; *see also* 59 Fed. Reg. 40,642 (Aug. 9, 1994).

5. *See* http://www.epa.gov/owow/oceans/discharges/301h.html; *see also* 40 CFR pt. 125, subpt. G; 69 Fed. Reg. 45,831 (Aug. 29, 1996).

6. 40 C.F.R. § 122.21(j)(4)(i); Table 1A to Appendix J to 40 C.F.R. pt. 122.

7. Table 1 to Appendix J to 40 C.F.R. pt. 122.

8. Table 2 to Appendix J to 40 C.F.R. pt. 122.

to the date of the NPDES application.[9] Larger POTWS and those with pretreatment programs must also submit the results of valid WET tests.[10]

Under the NPDES wastewater treatment "bypass" regulations at 40 C.F.R. 122.21(m)(4)(i), bypassing or diverting wastewater from the treatment works is prohibited unless in summary: (1) the bypass was unavoidable to prevent loss of life, personal injury, or severe property damage; (2) there were *no feasible alternatives to the bypass*, such as the use of auxiliary treatment facilities, retention of untreated wastes, or maintenance during normal periods of downtime. . .; and (3) the permittee submitted the required notices. The seminal yet controversial case interpreting EPA's bypass regulations is United States v. City of Toledo, 63 F. Supp. 2d 834 (N.D. Ohio 1999). In *Toledo*, the court found that the term "no feasible alternatives to the bypass" includes the fact that the POTW could have taken preventative steps to increase plant capacity by constructing additional treatment units or storage equipment.

IV. POTW Pretreatment Programs

This chapter contains a brief overview of POTW pretreatment programs. (See chapter 5 for a more detailed discussion of the pretreatment program.) Generally, to address toxic pollutants, POTWs must develop pretreatment programs that meet EPA regulations promulgated under CWA section 307(b). In 2002, more than 1500 POTWs nationwide were implementing pretreatment programs.[11] These federal pretreatment regulations and local pretreatment programs are designed to prevent industrial and other nondomestic wastewater sources from discharging pollutants into a POTW that:

- are not susceptible to treatment;
- will "interfere" with the POTW's operation or its use or disposal of sewage sludge;
- will "pass through" the treatment works; or
- will be otherwise "incompatible" with the treatment works.

Through pretreatment limits, nondomestic and industrial sources must meet federal, state, or local limitations on the amounts of pollutants they discharge to a POTW. Therefore, pretreatment programs also enhance recycling opportunities by minimizing the pollutants remaining in wastewater and sewage sludges.[12]

---

9. 40 C.F.R. § 122.21(j)(5)(1).

10. *Id.* at § 122.21(j)(5)(2).

11. EPA, Pretreatment Frequently Asked Questions, http://www.epa.gov/npdes/faqs.cmf ?program_id=3 (Mar. 2002); *see also* Introduction to the National Pretreatment Program, EPA-B-98-002 (Feb. 1999).

12. *See* 40 C.F.R. § 403.2 (outlining general pretreatment regulation objectives).

A. APPLICABILITY

Under 40 C.F.R. section 403.8(a), POTWs with a total design flow greater than five mgd that receive pollutants from industrial users that pass through or interfere with the POTW's operations must develop a pretreatment program. EPA regions or NPDES delegated states may require smaller POTWs to establish a pretreatment program if necessary to prevent interference with POTW operations or pollutant pass-through.[13]

B. PRETREATMENT STANDARDS

POTWs required to have pretreatment programs must enforce two types of federal pretreatment standards: categorical pretreatment standards and prohibited discharge standards.

1. Categorical Standards

Categorical pretreatment standards are technology-based limitations on pollutant discharges to POTWs, which EPA develops under CWA 307(c) for the specific industrial source categories listed in CWA section 306(b)(1)(A).[14] Categorical standards are promulgated at 40 CFR, chapter I, subchapter N, parts 400 to 471. These categories include dairy products, grain mills, seafood processing, textile mills, electroplating, and iron and steel manufacturing. Under certain conditions, POTWs may grant variances from the pollutant limits specified in categorical standards to industrial users to reflect removal of a pollutant by the POTW.[15] These credits can reduce the extent to which an industrial user must pretreat its discharge.[16] Variances from categorical pretreatment standards also are available for "fundamentally different factors" specific to certain industrial users.[17] These factors can include the nature or quality of pollutants in the industrial user's process wastewater; cost of compliance and energy requirements associated with the treatment technology; and other issues regarding the age, size, and configuration of the industrial user's facility.[18]

---

13. *See* 40 C.F.R. § 403.8(a) (these circumstances include the nature or volume of industrial influent, treatment process upsets, violations of POTW effluent limitations, or contamination of municipal sludge).

14. *See* 40 C.F.R. § 403.6 (categorical standards provisions).

15. *See* 40 C.F.R. § 403.7 (removal credits). For example, the POTW must submit detailed information and certifications that the removal credits will not cause the POTW to violate NPDES permit limits or pertinent sludge requirements. 40 C.F.R. § 403.7(e)(2)(v)–(vi). A POTW granting removal credits must monitor monthly and make annual reports. 40 C.F.R. § 403.7(f)(3).

16. *See* removal credits discussion at chapter 5 for greater detail.

17. 40 C.F.R. § 403.13.

18. *Id.* at § 403.13(d).

2. Prohibited Discharge Standards

Prohibited discharge standards are general prohibitions on the discharge to POTWs of wastes that (1) create a fire or explosion hazard; (2) are corrosive; (3) are solid or viscous pollutants that will obstruct flow; (4) will interfere with POTW operations; (5) are hot enough to interfere with POTW biological processes; (6) contain petroleum and other specific oils; (7) cause toxic gases, vapors, or fumes and pose a threat to worker health and safety at the POTW; and (8) contain any trucked or hauled pollutant.[19]

C. SUBSTANTIVE POTW PRETREATMENT PROGRAM REQUIREMENTS

Key POTW pretreatment program requirements, outlined at 40 C.F.R. section 403.8(f), include:

- the legal authority to control indirect dischargers and to enforce pretreatment requirements in federal, state, or local court;
- procedures to ensure program compliance by identifying and locating all industrial users, identifying the character and volume of pollutants industrial users discharge to the POTW, notifying industrial users of their status under the program and of applicable requirements, receiving self-monitoring reports from industrial users, and randomly sampling effluent from industrial users;
- funding and adequate personnel to implement the program;
- the ability to establish specific local limits; and
- procedures for investigating and responding to noncompliance, including the collection of evidence for use in enforcement proceedings and an enforcement-response plan detailing how it will use its enforcement powers.

POTWs with pretreatment programs must determine at least every two years whether each "significant industrial user"[20] needs a "slug" control plan for non-routine, episodic discharges to the POTW, including accidental spills.[21] Such POTWs also must publish an annual notice of industrial users in "significant non-compliance with pretreatment requirements."[22] Pretreatment POTWs also must comply with detailed reporting and record-keeping requirements, outlined at 40 C.F.R. section 403.12.

---

19. *See* 40 C.F.R. § 403.5(b) (general and specific discharge prohibitions).
20. Defined at 40 C.F.R. § 403.3(t).
21. *Id.* at § 403.8(f)(2)(v).
22. *Id.* at § 403.8(f)(2)(vii).

D. PRETREATMENT PROGRAM SUBMISSION
AND APPROVAL PROCEDURES

The processes for POTWs to receive pretreatment program approval or conditional approval are outlined at 40 C.F.R. sections 403.8 to 403.11. POTWs must submit detailed information to their state or EPA region, such as copies of statutes and ordinances, a description of the POTW's organization, and of funding levels.[23] Within 60 days of receiving a submission, the "approval authority" (the Director in an NPDES state with an approved State Pretreatment Program or the EPA Regional Administrator in a non-NPDES state or state without an approved pretreatment program) makes a preliminary determination on the program.[24] If the submission meets pretreatment program requirements, the approval authority notifies the POTW and public notice begins under 40 C.F.R. section 403.11.[25] Once a pretreatment program is approved, the EPA region or state NPDES Director will reissue or modify the POTW's NPDES permit to incorporate the approved program conditions as enforceable conditions of the NPDES permit.[26] If the submission does not meet requirements, the POTW may supplement the application.[27]

E. POTW PRETREATMENT PROGRAM MODIFICATIONS

The approval authority or the POTW may modify a pretreatment program to reflect changing conditions at the POTW. Modifications are required whenever the POTW's operation of the pretreatment program differs significantly from the POTW's original submission. EPA's regulations define "substantial modifications" and "nonsubstantial modifications" at 40 C.F.R. section 403.18. Substantial modifications, approved under the same procedures as the original approval of a pretreatment program, are those that would:

- significantly impact the program's operation;
- increase POTW pollutant loadings;
- relax requirements imposed on indirect dischargers; or
- fall into other categories listed at section 403.18(c).

For other program modifications, typically considered nonsubstantial modifications, the POTW must notify the approval authority 30 days prior to implementation. Approval will occur by operation of law 90 days after the notification

---

23. *Id.* at § 403.9(b).
24. *Id.* at § 403.9(e).
25. *Id.*
26. *Id.* at § 403.8(e)(4).
27. *Id.* at § 403.9(f).

is submitted, unless the approval authority deems the modification a substantial modification requiring more extensive review.[28]

V. Sewage Sludge Use and Disposal

Sewage sludge is the residual organic material that results from the wastewater treatment process. EPA defines sewage sludge as "any solid, semisolid, or liquid residue removed during the treatment of municipal waste water or domestic sewage."[29] Today, there are four primary methods that POTWs implement to manage and dispose of sewage sludge: (1) application to the land as fertilizer ("biosolids") after additional treatment; (2) placement on a surface disposal site; (3) placement in a municipal solid waste landfill; or (4) firing in a sludge incinerator.[30] EPA estimates that the nation's 16,000 POTWs generate approximately 7 million tons of sewage sludge annually. Approximately 60 percent of all sewage sludge is land applied; 17 percent is landfilled; 20 percent is incinerated; and 3 percent is used as landfill or mine reclamation cover.

CWA section 405 governs the disposal and use of sewage sludge and establishes a comprehensive program to reduce potential environmental risks and to maximize beneficial uses of sewage sludge. In particular, in 1987 Congress added CWA section 405(d) to direct EPA to undertake two rounds of rulemaking to set numeric limits to protect public health and the environment from any reasonably anticipated adverse effects of toxic pollutants in sewage sludge. CWA section 405(e) prohibits any person from disposing of POTW sewage sludge except in compliance with the 405(d) regulations. EPA did not meet the CWA's timetable for the two rounds of 405(d) regulations and was sued under the CWA's citizens' suit provisions in Gearhart v. Reilly, Civ. No. 89-6266-HO (D. Or.). The *Gearhart* consent decree has governed essentially all of EPA's CWA section 405(d) activities since 1990.

A. ROUND ONE SLUDGE REGULATIONS

CWA section 405(d)(2)(A) requires EPA in the first round of sludge regulations to establish numeric limits and management practices for toxic pollutants that, based on "*available information* on their toxicity, persistence, concentration, mobility, or potential for exposure may be present in sewage sludge in concen-

---

28. *Id.* at § 403.19(c)–(d).

29. 40 C.F.R. § 501.2 (sewage sludge includes, but is not limited to, solids removed during primary, secondary, or advanced wastewater treatment, scum, septage, portable toilet pumpings, and sewage sludge products).

30. At one time, the Marine Protection, Research, and Sanctuaries Act regulated ocean and estuary disposal of sewage sludge until the Ocean Dumping Ban Act of 1988 prohibited the practice after 1991. See P.L. 100-688, 33 U.S.C. § 1414(b).

trations which may adversely affect public health or the environment."[31] After analyzing 50 pollutants, conducting a National Sewage Sludge Survey, and gathering data, all pursuant to the *Gearhart* consent decree, EPA in early 1993 published final Round One sewage sludge regulations, which are codified in several subparts of 40 C.F.R. part 503.[32] The regulations have been amended several times to make technical changes and amendments, most recently in 1999.[33]

Forty C.F.R. part 503 subpart B regulates the land application of sewage sludge. These regulations contain pollutant limits for metals in land-applied sludges such as arsenic, cadmium, copper, lead, mercury, nickel, and zinc.[34] There are two types of land applied sludges: Class A biosolids, which cannot contain detectable pathogen levels and must meet vector attraction reduction requirements; and Class B biosolids, which can contain detectable pathogen levels.[35] The regulations also contain management practices, reporting, and record-keeping requirements.[36]

Forty C.F.R. part 503 subpart C regulates the surface disposal of sewage sludge (that which is placed on or applied to a surface disposal site). These regulations contain limits for metals such as arsenic, chromium, and nickel, and also set forth management practices, reporting, and record-keeping requirements.[37]

Forty C.F.R. part 503 subpart E regulates the incineration of sewage sludge. These regulations contain limits for arsenic, cadmium, chromium, lead, nickel, and total hydrocarbons (THC).[38] The regulations also set forth management practices relating to monitoring THC, oxygen, moisture, and temperatures and performance testing, reporting, and record-keeping requirements.[39]

In addition, New Source Performance Standards under Clean Air Act (CAA) section 111 contain sewage sludge incinerator emission limitations for particulate matter and opacity and establish operational, monitoring, testing, and reporting requirements.[40] The CAA National Emission Standards for Hazardous Air Pollutants (NESHAPs) for mercury and beryllium also apply to sludge incineration.[41] Furthermore, CAA section 110 state implementation

31. 33 U.S.C. § 1345(d)(2)(A) (emphasis added).
32. 58 Fed. Reg. 9248 (Feb. 19, 1993). Part 503 subpart A contains general provisions on applicability, permits, exclusions, sampling and analysis, and definitions.
33. 64 Fed. Reg. 42,551 (Aug. 4, 1999).
34. 40 C.F.R. pt. 503.13, Table 1.
35. 40 C.F.R. pt. 503 subpt. D (503.30–503.33).
36. 40 C.F.R. §§ 503.14, 503.16, 503.17.
37. 40 C.F.R. §§ 503.20–503.28.
38. 40 C.F.R. §§ 503.43–503.44.
39. 40 C.F.R. §§ 503.45–503.48.
40. 40 CFR pt. 60, subpt. O.
41. 40 C.F.R. §§ 503.43(a)–(b); 40 C.F.R. pt. 61, subpts. C, E.

plans apply emission limits and other restrictions to criteria pollutant emissions from sewage sludge incinerators.

B. ROUND TWO REGULATIONS

CWA section 405(d)(2)(B) requires EPA in the second round of sludge regulation to identify *additional* toxic pollutants that "may adversely affect public health or the environment."[42] Following a risk assessment, in 1999 EPA determined it would regulate dioxins and coplanar polychlorinated biphenyls (PCBs) in its Round Two regulations.[43] Based on the risk assessment's results, EPA proposed to take, and then finalized, "no regulatory action" for dioxins and PCBs in land-disposed or incinerated sludges by the December 15, 2001, consent decree deadline.[44] For land-applied sludge, however, EPA proposed a limit of 300 parts per trillion (ppt) toxic equivalents (TEQ) for dioxins and coplanar PCBs, as well as monitoring, record-keeping, and reporting requirements.[45] EPA received significant comments on these proposed land application regulations. In May 2002, EPA published a Notice of Data Availability to take additional public comment on a revised risk assessment and additional new data.[46] The parties to the *Gearhart* consent decree amended it in April 2002 to require EPA to finalize the Round Two regulations for land-applied sewage sludge by October 17, 2003. [47]

VI. Sewer Overflows

The CWA's POTW provisions are rooted in the premise that the sewer collection system will carry its wastewater load to the plant for treatment without leaking or discharging untreated wastewater to navigable waters of the United States. Accordingly, any wastewater that reaches surface waters of the United States without secondary treatment is considered a discharge without a permit in violation of the CWA.[48] During periods of heavy rain or snow melt, high volume of stormwater can enter the sewer system either by design (combined sewers) or unintentionally through a multitude of fissures and cracks that form through aging pipes or via illicit connections by homeowners or businesses (separate sanitary sewers). Sanitary sewer overflows (SSOs) are caused by this heavy volume, as well as by root growth, pipe breaks and cracks, oil and grease backups, or other human- or naturally introduced blockages in the collection system. SSOs are and

---

42. 33 U.S.C. § 1345(d)(2)(B).

43. 64 Fed. Reg. 72,045 (Dec. 23, 1999).

44. 66 Fed. Reg. 66,228 (Dec. 21, 2001).

45. 64 Fed. Reg. 72,045 (Dec. 23, 1999).

46. 67 Fed. Reg. 40,554 (June 12, 2002)

47. Gearhart v. Whitman, Civ. Dist. Ct. No. 89-6266-HO (D. Or.).

48. 33 U.S.C. § 1311(a).

have been an enforcement priority for EPA's Office of Enforcement and Compliance Assurance for several years.[49]

A. COMBINED SEWER OVERFLOWS

Combined sewer systems are most common in older urbanized areas. These systems were designed to combine and deliver all storm- and wastewater to the closest treatment plant. Overflow points were strategically placed to protect a treatment plant from being overwhelmed by stormwater during wet weather. Once the volume in the sewer system exceeds its capacity, these combined sewer overflow (CSO) discharge points automatically activate, releasing wastewater directly and without treatment to nearby streams, rivers, lakes, or estuaries. CSOs are point sources subject to NPDES permitting requirements.[50]

EPA published a National CSO Control Strategy in 1989.[51] In 1992, EPA convened a CSO Federal Advisory Committee Act (FACA) work group to assist in the development of a more comprehensive CSO policy. EPA then published a draft CSO policy in 1993 and a final CSO policy in 1994.[52] Under the CSO policy, municipalities are required to immediately implement nine minimum controls, which do not require significant engineering studies or major construction to reduce CSOs and their effects on receiving water quality. The nine minimum controls are:

1. proper operation and regular maintenance;
2. maximum use of the collection system for storage;
3. review and modification of pretreatment requirements;
4. maximization of flow to the POTW for treatment;
5. elimination of dry weather CSOs;
6. control of solid and floatable materials in CSOs;
7. pollution prevention programs;
8. public notification of CSOs; and
9. monitoring to characterize CSO impacts and controls.

The CSO policy also requires CSO permittees to develop long-term control plans for controlling CSOs to a level that would meet state water quality standards (WQS). Permittees may use one of two approaches: (1) demonstrate that their plan is adequate to meet WQS ("demonstration approach"), or (2) implement a minimum level of treatment (for example, primary clarification of at least 85 percent of the collected combined sewage flows) that is presumed to meet

---

49. *See, e.g.,* FY 2002/2003 OECA Memorandum of Agreement Guidance 3 (June 2001).
50. 59 Fed. Reg. 18,689 (Apr. 19, 1994).
51. 54 Fed. Reg. 37,370 (Sept. 8, 1989).
52. 58 Fed. Reg. 4994 (Jan. 19, 1993); 59 Fed. Reg. 18,688 (Apr. 19, 1994).

WQS, unless data indicate otherwise ("presumption approach"). During the CSO long-term planning process, state WQS authorities are to review and revise, as appropriate, their WQS. Permit authorities also are to consider the financial capability of permittees when reviewing CSO control plans.

In 2001, Congress added section 402(q) to the CWA to specifically address CSOs.[53] Section 402(q)(1) codifies the CSO policy by stating that each permit, order, or decree issued after December 21, 2000, must conform to the policy. Section 402(q)(2) requires EPA to issue guidance to facilitate the water quality and designated-use reviews for CSO receiving waters contemplated under the CSO policy. Section 402(q)(3) requires EPA to issue a Report to Congress on the process made by states and municipalities in implementing and enforcing the CSO policy. EPA provided the 402(q)(3) Report on January 29, 2002.[54] The report finds that progress has been made in implementing and enforcing CSO controls as a result of the 1994 CSO Policy and that public health and water quality benefits are being realized.[55]

In 2001, Congress also added section 1301 to the CWA, establishing a two-year sewer overflow control grant program. Congress authorized $750 million in fiscal years 2002 and 2003 for the program. Congress, however, never funded the program. This provision also calls for EPA to prepare a second Report to Congress by December 2003 to summarize the extent of human health and environmental impacts from CSOs and sanitary sewer overflows. EPA is on schedule to complete this second report.

B. SANITARY SEWER OVERFLOWS

Discharges that occur within sewer systems that are designed to carry only sewage to the wastewater plant for treatment are called sanitary sewer overflows (SSOs).[56] In contrast to the engineering designs that provide for CSOs at specified outfalls, SSOs occur in unanticipated locations and can spill into basements, out of manholes, and into surface waters. EPA estimates that there are at least 40,000 SSOs per year. As discussed above, the only authorized discharges from sanitary sewer systems under the CWA are those in compliance with an NPDES permit that contains technology-based effluent limitations based upon secondary treatment, and any needed water quality–based effluent limitations. As SSOs by nature occur in the collection system before secondary treatment, they can never

---

53. *Wet Weather Water Quality Act of 2000,* within the *Consolidated Appropriations Act for Fiscal Year 2001,* P.L. 106-554.

54. *Report to Congress, Implementation and Enforcement of the Combined Sewer Overflow Control Policy,* EPA 833-R-01-033, http://www.epa.gov/npdes.

55. *Id.* at ES-4.

56. *See* EPA Sanitary Sewer Overflows Homepage, http://www.epa.gov/owm/ ssodesc.htm.

comply with the secondary treatment standard and are thus viewed as prohibited by the CWA.[57] EPA recognizes, however, that exceptional wet weather circumstances may make some SSOs unavoidable and thus presently can excuse SSOs through enforcement discretion.

Recognizing the SSO challenges, in December 1994 EPA chartered an SSO FACA Subcommittee to evaluate the need for national policy or guidance on SSOs. The FACA met sporadically with little consensus until President Clinton issued a May 1999 memorandum directing EPA to "improve protection of public health at our Nation's beaches by developing, within one year, a strong national regulation to prevent the 40,000 annual sanitary sewer overflows."[58] The FACA resumed work and by October 1999 recommended that EPA move forward with an SSO proposed rule. On January 3, 2001, EPA Administrator Browner signed an SSO proposed rule for *Federal Register* publication. However, the Bush administration, under its Regulatory Review Plan, withdrew the proposed regulations before they were published in the *Federal Register.*[59]

The proposed regulations would expand NPDES permitting requirements to sanitary sewer collection systems and to SSOs. The regulations would apply standard permit conditions to SSOs regarding collection system capacity, management, operation, and maintenance (CMOM) requirements. The regulations would contain a prohibition on all SSOs, but provide a framework for raising defenses to unavoidable discharges. They also would establish SSO reporting and record-keeping requirements and require public notification of SSOs. The regulations also would apply NPDES permit conditions to municipal satellite collection systems (sewers operated by one municipality that convey the water to a treatment plant owned by another municipality).

The signed but never-proposed SSO regulations remain available on EPA's web site,[60] and stakeholders have provided EPA with extensive comment despite the absence of a formal comment period. In November 2001, EPA committed to proposing the January 3, 2001, proposed regulatory text in fall 2002 with a revised preamble to accept public comment on issues raised over the past months. Until federal regulations provide additional guidance, EPA will continue to deal with SSOs primarily through enforcement actions.[61]

---

57. 33 U.S.C. §§ 1311(a)–(b)(1)(B).

58. Memorandum from President William J. Clinton to Administrator, U.S. EPA (May 29, 1999).

59. *See* 66 Fed. Reg. 7701 (Jan. 24, 2001).

60. http://www.epa.gov/npdes/home.cfm?program_id=4.

61. *See* FY 2002/2003 OECA Memorandum of Agreement Guidance 3 (June 2001).

CHAPTER 5

Pretreatment and Indirect Dischargers

CORINNE A. GOLDSTEIN

I. Overview

A. OBJECTIVES

Section 307(b)(1) of the Clean Water Act (CWA) requires the Environmental Protection Agency (EPA) to establish pretreatment standards for pollutants "which are determined not to be susceptible to treatment" by publicly owned treatment works (POTWs) or "which would interfere with the operation of such treatment works."[1] This statutory mandate has been interpreted by the agency as requiring it to promulgate pretreatment standards for pollutants that

1. will interfere with the operation of a POTW, including interference with its use and disposal of sewage sludge; or
2. pass through the POTW or otherwise would be incompatible with the POTW.[2]

Another objective of the pretreatment program is to improve opportunities for recycling and reclaiming municipal and industrial wastewaters and sludges.[3]

---

1. 33 U.S.C. § 1317(b)(1). *See* United States v. Hartsell, 127 F.3d 343 (4th Cir. 1997), *cert. denied*, 523 U.S. 1030 (1998) (Congress has authority under the Constitution to regulate discharges to POTWs).

2. 40 C.F.R. §§ 403.2(a) and (b).

3. 40 C.F.R. § 403.2(c).

B. DEFINITIONS

"Indirect dischargers" are nondomestic facilities that do not discharge wastewaters directly to U.S. waters, but instead discharge their wastewaters to POTWs.[4]

A "publicly owned treatment works" (POTW) is a treatment works as defined by CWA section 212, which is owned by a state or municipality.[5] POTWs treat domestic and municipal wastes, as well as industrial wastewaters, and discharge these treated wastewaters to U.S. waters pursuant to the National Pollutant Discharge Elimination System (NPDES) permits issued by EPA or by a state having NPDES authority.

"Pretreatment" means the reduction, alteration, or elimination of pollutants in wastewater prior to the discharge of the wastewater to a POTW.[6]

C. APPLICABILITY

The pretreatment program and regulations govern the introduction of pollutants to POTWs by nondomestic sources, regardless of whether the pollutants are introduced to the POTW by sewer pipe, or are transported by truck or rail, or are otherwise introduced into the POTW.[7] The program also applies to POTWs that receive wastewaters from sources subject to National Pretreatment Standards.[8] National Pretreatment Standards are

1. pollutant limits established by EPA for all nondomestic dischargers to POTWs (general pretreatment limits);
2. pollutant limits established by EPA for specific categories of industry (categorical pretreatment standards); and
3. local pollutant limits established by POTWs in accordance with EPA's regulations.[9]

EPA has promulgated general pretreatment regulations that apply to all nondomestic sources of pollutants that discharge wastewaters to POTWs. These general pretreatment regulations prohibit certain discharges altogether and require

---

4. 40 C.F.R. § 403.3(g).

5. 33 U.S.C. § 1292(2); 40 C.F.R. § 403.3(o). 40 C.F.R. § 125.58(u) defines POTW (for purposes of section 301(h) requests) as "a treatment works, as defined in section 212(2) of the [CWA], which is owned by a State, municipality, or intermunicipal or interstate agency." "Municipality" is defined at 40 C.F.R. § 122.2. It should be noted that the definition excludes privately owned treatment works (*see* 40 C.F.R. § 122.44(m)) and federally owned treatment works.

6. 40 C.F.R. § 403.3(q).

7. 40 C.F.R. § 403.1(b)(1).

8. 40 C.F.R. § 403.1(b)(2).

9. *See* 40 C.F.R. §§ 403.3(j) and 403.5(d).

POTWs to establish local pretreatment limits, when necessary, to prevent interference or pass-through.[10]

The agency also promulgates national categorical pretreatment standards. These are technology-based standards that EPA establishes on an industry category-by-category basis and that apply to all facilities in the industrial category, unless a facility obtains a variance from the applicability of the standards.[11]

Nondomestic sources that discharge to POTWs must comply with the general pretreatment regulations, any applicable categorical pretreatment standards, and any more-stringent local limits established by the POTWs into which these sources discharge wastewaters. The requirements for certain sources defined in 40 C.F.R. section 403.3(t) as "significant industrial users" (SIUs), which include all indirect dischargers that are subject to categorical pretreatment standards, must be incorporated in a permit or equivalent individual control mechanism.[12]

II. The General Pretreatment Requirements

A nondomestic source may not discharge to a POTW any pollutant that would cause pass-through or interference.[13] "Pass-through" means a discharge that exits a POTW into U.S. waters in quantities or concentrations that, alone or in combination with other discharges, is a cause of a violation of the POTW's NPDES permit.[14] This includes a discharge that causes an increase in the magnitude or duration of a violation of a POTW's permit.[15]

"Interference" means a discharge that, alone or in conjunction with other discharges, (1) inhibits or disrupts the POTW, its treatment processes or operations, or its sludge processes, use, or disposal; and (2) is a cause of a violation of any requirement of the POTW's NPDES permit or of the prevention of sewage sludge use or disposal in compliance with applicable laws, regulations, and permits.[16] This, too, includes discharges that cause an increase in the magnitude or duration of a violation.[17] A discharge can cause interference or pass through even if it is not the sole cause of a violation, though it must be more than a de minimis cause.[18]

---

10. 40 C.F.R. § 403.5. "Interference" and "pass-through" are terms defined at 40 C.F.R. § 403.3 at paragraphs (i) and (n), respectively. See the interference and pass-through discussion below.
11. *See* 33 U.S.C. §§ 1317(a) and (b). *See* 40 C.F.R. pts. 405–471.
12. 40 C.F.R. § 403.8(f)(1)(iii).
13. 40 C.F.R. § 403.5(a)(1).
14. 40 C.F.R. § 403.3(n).
15. *Id.*
16. 40 C.F.R. § 403.3(i).
17. *Id.*
18. Arkansas Poultry Federation v. EPA, 852 F.2d 324 (8th Cir. 1998).

The general pretreatment regulations also prohibit specific discharges to POTWs, including:

1. pollutants that create a fire or explosion hazard in the POTW, including, but not limited to, wastestreams with a closed-cup flashpoint of less than 140 degrees Fahrenheit or 60 degrees Centigrade, using the test methods in 40 C.F.R. section 261.21;

2. pollutants that will cause corrosive structural damage to the POTW, but in no case discharges with a pH less than 5.0, unless the POTW is specifically designed to accommodate such discharges;

3. solid or viscous pollutants in amounts that will cause obstruction to the flow in the POTW, resulting in interference;

4. any pollutant, including oxygen-demanding pollutants such as biochemical oxygen demand, released in a discharge at a flow rate and/or pollutant concentration that will cause interference with the POTW;

5. heat in amounts that will inhibit biological activity in the POTW resulting in interference, but in no event heat in such quantities that the temperature at the POTW treatment plant exceeds 104 degrees Fahrenheit or 40 degrees Centigrade, unless approved by the state in an NPDES state with an approved pretreatment program or by the EPA Regional Administrator in a non-NPDES state or an NPDES state without an approved pretreatment program;

6. petroleum oil, nonbiodegradable cutting oil, or products of mineral oil origin in amounts that will cause interference or pass-through;

7. pollutants that result in the presence of toxic gases, vapors, or fumes within the POTW in a quantity that may cause acute worker health and safety problems; and

8. any trucked or hauled pollutants, except at discharge points designated by the POTW.[19]

POTWs with pretreatment programs must develop local limits to implement these general and specific prohibitions.[20] All other POTWs must develop local limits where pollutants contributed by nondomestic sources have caused interference or pass-through and the violation is likely to recur.[21]

---

19. 40 C.F.R. § 403.5(b).

20. 40 C.F.R. § 403.5(c)(1). Any POTW with a total design flow greater than 5 million gallons per day and receiving nondomestic discharges that pass through or interfere with the operation of the POTW or are otherwise subject to National Pretreatment Standards is required, with limited exceptions, to develop a pretreatment program. 40 C.F.R. § 403.8(a). Regulators may require POTWs with a design flow less than 5 million gallons per day to develop a pretreatment program. *Id. See In re* City of Yankton, 1993 EPA ALJ LEXIS 288 (Jan. 21, 1993), *aff'd*, 1994 EPA App. LEXIS 44 (July 1994).

21. 40 C.F.R. § 403.5(c)(2).

Local limits are intended to prevent site-specific treatment or compliance problems resulting from discharges to POTWs by nondomestic sources. These limits, together with other appropriate changes in the POTW treatment plant or operations, must be adequate to ensure compliance by the POTW with its permit or sludge use and disposal practices.[22] Local limits may be more or less stringent than EPA's categorical pretreatment standards. A local limit that is less stringent than a categorical standard, however, does not relieve the discharger from having to comply with the categorical standard.[23]

Local limits may not be developed and enforced without individual notice to persons or groups who have requested such notice and an opportunity to respond.[24] Local limits that are developed by POTWs in accordance with EPA's regulations become Pretreatment Standards for purposes of section 307(d) of the CWA.[25] This means that the local limits are enforceable by EPA.[26] A discharger cannot challenge the validity of local limits in an EPA enforcement proceeding.[27]

III. Categorical Pretreatment Standards

A. APPLICABILITY OF AND BASIS FOR THE STANDARDS

Categorical pretreatment standards are established by EPA and specify quantities or concentrations of pollutants or pollutant properties that may be discharged to a POTW by existing or new industrial users in specific categories of industry.[28] Facilities that are uncertain as to whether they fall within a particular category may submit a category determination request to the appropriate regulatory official. Such requests must be submitted within 60 days after the effective date of a categorical pretreatment standard.[29] If a facility disagrees with the category determination, it may file a petition with the EPA Regional Administrator to contest the decision or to request reconsideration. Such a petition must be filed within 30 days following the date of receipt of the category determination.[30] EPA's category determination decision is directly reviewable in the courts of appeal.[31]

---

22. 40 C.F.R. §§ 403.5(c)(1) and (2).

23. 40 C.F.R. § 403.6.

24. 40 C.F.R. § 403.5(c)(3).

25. 40 C.F.R. § 403.5(d); 33 U.S.C. § 1317(d).

26. *In re* Jehovah-Jireh Corp., 2001 EPA ALJ LEXIS 42 (July 25, 2001). Also available at: http://www.epa.gov/oalj/orders/jehov725.pdf.

27. *In re* Advanced Electronics, 2000 EPA ALJ LEXIS 64, (Aug. 15, 2000) (also available at: http://www.epa.gov/oalj/orders/advanced.pdf); *see also* United States v. Hartsell, 127 F.3d 343 4th Cir. 1997), *cert. denied*, 523 U.S. 1030 (1998).

28. 40 C.F.R. § 403.6.

29. 40 C.F.R. § 403.6(a)(1).

30. 40 C.F.R. § 403.6(a)(5).

31. Modine Mfg. Corp. v. Kay, 791 F.2d 267 (3rd Cir. 1986).

Categorical pretreatment standards are based upon the toxic and nonconventional pollutant removals that can be achieved by the regulated industry using the best available technology (BAT).[32] The pollutants for which EPA establishes categorical pretreatment limits are those pollutants that EPA determines will interfere with or pass through POTWs. The pass-through test that EPA uses to determine which pollutants to regulate compares the pollutant removal rates that POTWs achieve with the removal rates that industry could achieve using BAT.[33]

The categorical pretreatment standards for existing sources are referred to as "PSES" or pretreatment standards for existing sources. PSES are based upon application of BAT to the regulated wastestreams. While the discharge limits that apply to industrial facilities that discharge wastewaters directly to U.S. waters are also based upon the application of BAT, the technologies on which the direct and indirect discharge limits are based may differ within an industrial category to take into account differences among such dischargers, such as the amount of land that is available to install treatment technology.[34]

EPA establishes "PSNS," or pretreatment standards for new sources, as a set of separate categorical pretreatment standards.[35] A "new source" is any building, structure, facility, or installation from which there is a discharge of pollutants, the "construction" of which began after the publication of proposed categorical PSNS that will be applicable to the source if the standards are thereafter promulgated, if

1. the building, structure, facility, or installation is constructed at a site at which no other source is located; or
2. the building, structure, facility, or installation totally replaces the process or production equipment that causes the discharge of pollutants at an existing source; or
3. the new production or wastewater-generating processes are substantially independent of an existing source at the same site.[36]

The pretreatment standards for new sources (PSNS) are similar to the new source performance standards applicable to direct dischargers under section 306

---

32. H.R. Rep. No. 830, 95th Cong., 1st Sess. at 87 (1977). *See* the BAT discussion in chapter 2.

33. Preamble, Organic Chemicals and Plastics and Synthetic Fibers Category Effluent Limitations Guidelines, Pretreatment Standards, and New Source Performance Standards; Final Rule (OCPSF Final Rule), 52 Fed. Reg. 42,522, 42,545 (Nov. 5, 1987).

34. *See* Preamble, OCPSF Final Rule, 52 Fed. Reg. at 42,548.

35. 33 U.S.C. § 1317(c).

36. *See* 33 U.S.C. § 1316(a); 40 C.F.R. §§ 122.2, 112.29.

of the CWA and are based upon the best available demonstrated control technology, processes, operating methods, or other alternatives.[37]

Because POTWs are designed to treat conventional pollutants (for example, biological oxygen demand and total suspended solids), EPA has not established categorical pretreatment standards for conventional pollutants. Indeed, if a POTW is not complying with its NPDES permit as a result of inadequate design or operation of the POTW, the agency cannot require pretreatment of conventional pollutants except to ensure compliance with categorical pretreatment standards.[38] POTWs, however, may establish local limits on conventional pollutants, and often do so. Typical reasons for a POTW to establish local limits on conventional pollutants are (1) to address a local problem if the POTW is overloaded, or (2) to raise revenues.

Categorical pretreatment standards apply to regulated process streams at all facilities within the regulated categories of industry regardless of the size of the POTW to which they discharge and regardless of whether the POTW is specifically designed to handle industrial wastes.[39] This ensures that facilities within a regulated industry achieve a nationally uniform degree of pollution control.[40] Categorical pretreatment standards apply to requested facilities even if a POTW fails to include them in a permit it issues to a regulated industrial user; a POTW cannot waive the applicability of such standards to its users.[41] Dischargers are strictly liable for violations of categorical pretreatment standards (and local limits). There is no need for the government or a citizen to show that a discharger's violation of a categorical pretreatment standard caused a POTW to violate an applicable requirement.[42]

---

37. Preamble, OCPSF Final Rule, 52 Fed. Reg. at 42,525. *See* South Holland Metal Finishing Co. v. Browner, 97 F.3d 932 (7th Cir. 1996) (court of appeals does not have jurisdiction to hear challenge to EPA opinion that discharger is a new source). *See also* the new source discussion as it relates to NPDES permits for direct dischargers in chapter 2.

38. 33 U.S.C. § 1342(m).

39. Cerro Copper Products Co. v. Ruckelshaus, 766 F.2d 1060 (7th Cir. 1985), *transferred to* Natural Resources Defense Council v. EPA, 790 F.2d 289 (3rd Cir. 1986), *cert. denied sub nom.* Chemical Manufacturers Ass'n v. Natural Resources Defense Council, 479 U.S. 1084 (1987). It is important for a user in a regulated industrial category to understand which of its wastestreams is subject to the categorical pretreatment standards. *See, e.g.*, United States v. Clark Equip. Co., 1996 WL 363050, 42 ERC 1734 (D.N.D 1996) (wastewater from a testing operation covered by metal finishing standards); *In re* B.J. Carney Industries, 1997 EPA App. LEXIS 7 (June 9, 1997) (contaminated groundwater pumped from an equipment vault of a wood treatment facility is a regulated process wastewater in the timber products processing category).

40. 40 C.F.R. § 403.6.

41. International Union v. Amerace Corp., 740 F. Supp. 1072 (D.N.J. 1990).

42. *Id.; see also* United States v. Alley, 755 F. Supp. 771 (N.D. Ill. 1990).

B. THE COMBINED WASTESTREAM FORMULA

Where wastewaters from a categorical industrial user's regulated process are combined prior to treatment with wastewaters regulated by another categorical pretreatment standard or with unregulated wastewaters (for example, utility or stormwaters) and such combination would result in a reduction of the concentration of the regulated pollutant in the mixed waters, compliance with categorical pretreatment requirements must be determined by application of EPA's combined wastestream formula. The calculated alternative limits are applied to the mixed effluent and are substituted for the categorical pretreatment standard. The purpose of the formula is to ensure that an industrial discharger does not substitute dilution for treatment to comply with applicable categorical pretreatment standards. If the user monitors the segregated-process wastestream, then compliance is measured against the categorical pretreatment standard; if the user monitors the combined stream, then compliance is measured against the alternative limit calculated by application of the combined wastestream formula.[43]

The combined wastestream formula may be used to calculate both alternative concentration limits and alternative mass limits.[44] It is also used to calculate both daily maximum discharge limits and average discharge limits. The formula may not be used if the alternative limit is below the analytical detection limit for the regulated pollutant.[45]

C. DEADLINES

Facilities that are subject to categorical pretreatment standards must comply with the standards by the deadlines EPA establishes when it promulgates the standards. The compliance date may not exceed three years after the promulgation of such standards.[46]

D. INNOVATIVE TECHNOLOGY DEADLINE EXTENSIONS

An existing facility may comply with a categorical pretreatment standard by (1) replacing existing production capacity with an innovative production process that will result in an effluent reduction significantly greater than that required by the applicable standards, or (2) installing an innovative control technique that will enable the facility either to achieve a significantly greater effluent reduction than required by the standard or to achieve the reduction required by the standard, but at significantly lower cost than estimated by EPA. A facility that so intends to

---

43. International Union v. Amerace Corp., 740 F. Supp. 1072 (D.N.J. 1990).
44. 40 C.F.R. § 403.6(e)(1).
45. 40 C.F.R. § 403.6(e)(2).
46. 33 U.S.C. § 1317(b)(1).

comply with the pretreatment standards may apply for and obtain from the POTW to which it discharges (with the concurrence of EPA) a two-year extension of the date by which compliance with an applicable categorical pretreatment standard is required.[47]

In order to be considered "innovative," the production process or pollution control technique cannot have been commercially demonstrated in the industry of which the facility requesting the extension is a part.[48] An extension of the deadline may be granted only if the innovative system has the potential for industry-wide application.[49]

IV. Modifications of and Variances from Categorical Pretreatment Standards

A. REMOVAL CREDITS

A POTW that receives wastewaters from dischargers subject to categorical pretreatment standards may, with the approval of EPA, modify the categorical pretreatment standards to take into account the pollutant removal that the POTW consistently achieves. These modifications of categorical pretreatment standards are known as "removal credits." Removal credits cannot cause a POTW to violate local, state, or federal sludge requirements.[50]

The U.S. Court of Appeals held in *Natural Resources Defense Council v. EPA*[51] that POTWs could not grant removal credits until EPA promulgated regulations under section 405 of the CWA governing the disposal of municipal sludge. The Third Circuit decision was codified by Congress in section 406(e) of the Water Quality Act of 1987.[52]

Sludge regulations are codified at 40 C.F.R. part 503,[53] and 40 C.F.R. part 403 provides for removal credits for those pollutants covered by the sludge rules. In particular, 40 C.F.R. section 403.7(a)(3)(iv) provides that removal credits may be granted for certain pollutants, based upon the particular sludge disposal method used by the POTW. Some pollutants are eligible for removal credits dependent simply on the method of sludge disposal used.[54] Other pollutants are

---

47. 33 U.S.C. § 1317(e). *See* 33 U.S.C. § 1311(k).

48. *See, e.g.*, 40 C.F.R. § 125.22.

49. 33 U.S.C. § 1317(e)(1).

50. 33 U.S.C. § 1317(b)(1).

51. 790 F.2d 289 (3d Cir. 1986).

52. Pub. L. No. 100-4, § 406(e), 101 Stat. 7, 73 (1987), 33 U.S.C. § 1345.

53. *See* the chapter 4 discussion of the part 503 sludge regulations.

54. 40 C.F.R. § 403.7(a)(3)(iv)(A).

eligible for removal credits if a particular sludge disposal method is used and if the sludge does not exceed the concentrations listed for those pollutants.[55]

New appendix G to part 403 lists the specific pollutants, and concentrations, if applicable, that are eligible for removal credits.[56] Finally, removal credits may be granted for any pollutant in sewage sludge when the POTW disposes all of its sewage sludge in a municipal solid waste landfill unit that meets the criteria in 40 C.F.R. part 258.[57]

While the POTW is the entity that grants removal credits, it may do so only if it has received EPA authorization. To obtain EPA approval to grant removal credits, a POTW must demonstrate that it consistently removes the pollutants for which it is seeking to grant credits. The requirements for demonstrating consistent removal are set forth in 40 C.F.R. section 403.7(b). The requirements include data collected throughout one full year demonstrating the level of pollutant removal the POTW achieves.[58] POTWs that at least once annually experience overflows in which untreated wastewaters are discharged to receiving waters must take such overflows into consideration when calculating removal credits.[59]

If removal credits are issued, the POTW must demonstrate (at least once annually) that it is continuing to achieve the same level of removal on which the credits were based. If the POTW's removal rate declines, then the removal credits must be modified or withdrawn. This cannot be done, however, until the POTW and all industrial dischargers who have received removal credits are given notice of the proposed modification or withdrawal and there has been an opportunity for a hearing.[60]

B. FUNDAMENTALLY DIFFERENT FACTORS VARIANCES

Facilities also may obtain a variance from the application of categorical pretreatment standards if they can demonstrate that they are fundamentally different from the facilities that EPA evaluated when it developed the categorical pretreatment standards at issue.[61]

An application for a fundamentally different factors (FDF) variance must be submitted to EPA within 180 days after the date on which the relevant categorical pretreatment standard was promulgated.[62] The application, which may seek

---

55. 40 C.F.R. § 403.7(a)(3)(iv)(B).
56. 40 C.F.R. pt. 403 App. G.
57. 40 C.F.R. § 403.7(a)(3)(iv)(C).
58. 40 C.F.R. § 403.7(b)(2)(iii)(B)(1).
59. *See* 40 C.F.R. § 403.7(h).
60. 40 C.F.R. § 403.7(f)(4)(iii).
61. 33 U.S.C. § 1311(n). *See* 40 C.F.R. § 403.13.
62. 33 U.S.C. § 1311(n)(2).

a modification of one or more of the pollutant limits established by the categorical pretreatment standard, must be based solely on information and data submitted to EPA during the rulemaking proceeding concerning the standards, unless the applicant did not have a reasonable opportunity to submit the information or data during the rulemaking.[63] An application for an FDF variance does not stay the applicant's obligation to comply with the standard that is the subject of the application.[64]

If an FDF variance is granted, the alternative limit or limits may not be less stringent than justified by the fundamental difference. The limit also may not result in a nonwater quality environmental impact that is markedly more adverse than considered by EPA in establishing the standards.[65]

C. Net/Gross Calculation

Categorical pretreatment standards may be adjusted to reflect the presence of pollutants in the industrial user's intake water.[66] An industrial user wishing to obtain credit for intake pollutants must make application to the appropriate authority and meet the criteria set out at 40 C.F.R. section 403.15(b). Further, categorical pretreatment standards can be adjusted only if the applicable standards in 40 C.F.R. subchapter N specifically provide that they shall be applied on a net basis.[67]

V. Reporting, Monitoring, and Record Maintenance Obligations

A. INDUSTRIAL USERS SUBJECT TO CATEGORICAL STANDARDS

1. Baseline Monitoring Reports

Within 180 days after the effective date of a categorical pretreatment standard, facilities subject to the standard must submit a "baseline monitoring report."[68] The report must describe the operations of the facility and provide information on flow rates and pollutants discharged by the facility.[69] If the facility is not already in compliance with the categorical pretreatment standards, the report also must include a schedule for the facility to come into compliance with the standards. The completion date in the schedule cannot be later than the date EPA established for compliance with the standards.[70]

---

63. 33 U.S.C. § 1311(n)(1)(B).
64. 33 U.S.C. § 1311(n)(6).
65. 33 U.S.C. § 1311(n)(2)(C) and (D).
66. 40 C.F.R. § 403.15.
67. 40 C.F.R. § 403.15(c).
68. 40 C.F.R. § 403.12(b).
69. *Id.*
70. 40 C.F.R. § 403.12(b)(7).

2. Compliance Reports

Within 90 days following the date for final compliance with applicable categorical pretreatment standards or, in the case of new sources, following commencement of the discharge to a POTW, facilities subject to the standards must submit a report indicating whether they are in compliance with the standards.[71] A discharger cannot question its own reports in an enforcement action; they are considered admissions of liability.[72]

3. Periodic Reports

Facilities subject to categorical pretreatment standards also must submit reports during June and December of each year, unless required more frequently by the applicable standards or by regulatory authorities.[73] These reports must contain data on the nature and concentration of pollutants being discharged, including the results of sampling and analysis of the discharge, and the effluent flow. If the discharge is subject to mass limits, information must also be submitted concerning the mass of pollutants discharged and, when requested, the facility's production rate.[74] All pollutant analyses must be performed in accordance with procedures in 40 C.F.R. part 136 or alternative procedures approved by EPA.[75]

If the sampling indicates a violation, the facility must notify the regulatory authorities within 24 hours of becoming aware of the violation. The facility then must submit the results of repeat analyses within 30 days after becoming aware of the violation, unless the regulatory authority samples the facility at least monthly or the regulatory authority sampled the facility between the time of the original sample and the time the facility received the results of the sample.[76]

If a facility monitors any pollutant more frequently than required by the regulators using approved sampling and analytical procedures, the results of that monitoring must also be included in the semiannual reports.[77]

B. INDUSTRIAL USERS NOT SUBJECT TO CATEGORICAL STANDARDS

Industrial facilities that are not subject to categorical pretreatment standards must submit reports as required by the regulatory authorities. For those facilities that

---

71. 40 C.F.R. § 403.12(d).

72. United States v. Sheyenne Tooling & Manufacturing Co., 952 F. Supp. 1414 (D.N.D. 1996), aff'd, 162 F.3d 1166 (8th Cir. 1998).

73. 40 C.F.R. § 403.12(e).

74. Id.; 40 C.F.R. § 403.12(g). See RSR Corp. v. Browner, 924 F. Supp. 504 (S.D.N.Y. 1996), aff'd, 1997 U.S. App. LEXIS 5523 (2d Cir. 1997) (upholding EPA decision that production data are effluent data subject to disclosure when pretreatment standards are production-based).

75. 40 C.F.R. § 403.12(g)(4).

76. 40 C.F.R. § 403.12(g)(2).

77. 40 C.F.R. § 403.12(g)(5).

are classified as significant industrial users but are not subject to categorical standards,[78] reports must be submitted at least once every six months on dates established by the regulators.[79]

C. REPORTING OBLIGATIONS APPLICABLE
TO ALL INDUSTRIAL USERS

1. Slug Load Notification

All industrial users must notify the POTW immediately of all discharges that could cause problems at the POTW, including any slug loadings.[80] A slug discharge is any discharge of a nonroutine, episodic nature, including but not limited to an accidental spill or a noncustomary batch discharge.[81]

2. Notification of Hazardous Waste Discharges

Industrial users must notify regulatory authorities in writing of any discharge into a POTW of a substance that, if otherwise disposed, would be a hazardous waste under 40 C.F.R. part 261.[82] These notices were required to be submitted by existing facilities in early 1991. New sources must submit the notices within 180 days after the discharge to the POTW of any waste that would be hazardous under 40 C.F.R. part 261. The notice must include a certification that the facility has a program in place to reduce the volume and toxicity of hazardous wastes to the degree it has determined to be economically practical.[83] The notification requirement does not apply to pollutants already reported under the self-monitoring requirements.[84] Small-quantity dischargers are exempt from the notification requirement.[85]

Whenever hazardous wastes are newly identified or listed under the Resource Conservation and Recovery Act, facilities discharging such wastes to POTWs must provide notice of the discharge within 90 days of the effective date of the regulation identifying or listing the waste.[86]

3. Notification of Changed Discharge

All industrial users are to promptly notify the POTW in advance of any substantial change in the volume or character of pollutants in their discharge, including

---

78. *See* 40 C.F.R. § 403.3(t) for definition of "significant industrial user."

79. 40 C.F.R. § 403.12(h); *see Amerace Corp.*, 740 F. Supp. 1072 (holding that data must be submitted even for unregulated pollutants).

80. 40 C.F.R. § 403.12(f).

81. 40 C.F.R. § 403.8(f)(2)(v).

82. 40 C.F.R. § 403.12(p)(1).

83. 40 C.F.R. § 403.12(p)(4).

84. 40 C.F.R. § 403.12(p)(1).

85. 40 C.F.R. § 403.12(p)(2).

86. 40 C.F.R. § 403.12(p)(3).

the listed or characteristic wastes for which the industrial user has submitted initial notification as discussed above.[87]

D. RECORDS MAINTENANCE

Records of monitoring activities must be kept at least three years and must be made available for inspection upon request by regulatory authorities.[88]

VI. Enforcement of Pretreatment Standards

Section 307(d) of the CWA states that after the effective date of a pretreatment standard promulgated under this section, it shall be unlawful for any owner or operator of any source to operate any source in violation of such standard. Pretreatment standards include EPA's general and specific discharge prohibitions, categorical pretreatment standards, and local limits.[89]

Pursuant to section 309(f) of the act, EPA may, after 30 days' notice to the POTW and the state, commence an enforcement action against an indirect discharger for a violation of section 307(d) of the act. EPA may seek appropriate relief in district court, including a permanent or temporary injunction and civil or criminal penalties.[90]

Pursuant to 40 C.F.R. section 403.8(f)(1), a POTW with a pretreatment program must also have legal authority to require compliance with pretreatment standards, to halt any discharge of pollutants, and to seek judicial relief. A citizen suit also may be brought against an indirect discharger for violation of a pretreatment standard, pursuant to section 505(f)(4) of the CWA.[91]

Enforcement actions may be brought not only against the indirect discharger, but also against a "responsible corporate officer" of the discharger. This includes individuals who do not have any formal title and who do not themselves exercise control over the activity causing the discharge, so long as the individual has the authority to exercise such control.[92] See chapter 11 for a more detailed description of the enforcement provisions of the CWA.

---

87. 40 C.F.R. § 403.12(j).
88. 40 C.F.R. §§ 403.12(o)(2) and (3).
89. 33 U.S.C. § 1317(d).
90. 33 U.S.C. § 1319(f). *See* 40 C.F.R. § 403.5(e).
91. 33 U.S.C. § 1365(f)(4).
92. United States v. Iverson, 162 F.3d 1015 (9th Cir. 1998); United States v. Hong, 242 F.3d 528 (4th Cir. 2001), *cert. denied*, 122 S.Ct. 60 (2001).

CHAPTER 6

Wetlands: Section 404

SYLVIA QUAST*
STEVEN T. MIANO**

I. Introduction and Scope

The regulation of wetlands under the Clean Water Act (CWA) has been evolving rapidly over the course of the last few decades and, in particular, over the last several years. The recognition of the need to protect against further loss of wetlands habitat, fostered by the increased recognition of the important functions and values of wetlands, has been tempered by recent judicial decisions that arguably decrease the extent of federal jurisdiction over these important resources. The next several years may well prove to be a turning point in the future of wetlands protection at both the federal and state levels.

Section 404 of the CWA requires permits for the discharge of "dredged or fill material" into "waters of the United States."[1] The term "waters of the United States" has historically been viewed expansively including every conceivable surface water body and wetland. As discussed further in this chapter, recent court decisions have, in some instances, altered this expansive view. This chapter will cover all aspects of the 404 program, including the scope of the Army Corps of Engineers' (the Corps) and the Environmental Protection Agency's

The authors acknowledge the contributions of Lawrence R. Liebesman to the 1994 edition of this chapter.

* Ms. Quast would like to acknowledge the assistance of Hugh Barroll and Lisa Clay in writing her portions of this chapter. She notes that the views expressed herein do not necessarily represent the views of the United States Environmental Protection Agency or the United States Department of Justice.

** Mr. Miano would like to acknowledge the able assistance of Nicholas T. Saidel, an associate at Wolf, Block.

1. 33 U.S.C. § 1344(a).

(EPA) jurisdiction, their respective roles in permitting and enforcement, and the relatively new issue of takings. While implementation of section 404 can be delegated to states, as this book goes to press only two states, Michigan and New Jersey, have delegated programs. For that reason, the bulk of this chapter will focus on regulation of wetlands under federal law. However, because most states do have independent regulatory programs addressing wetlands, the issue of state regulation is covered to some extent.

II. The Scope of Jurisdiction under Section 404

The scope of jurisdiction under the section 404 program has fluctuated over the course of the CWA's history. This fluctuation has largely resulted from differing definitions of "navigable waters of the United States," the statutory language defining the scope of authority for both the EPA and the Corps under section 404 of the CWA. Section 404(a) grants authority to the Corps to issue permits "for the discharge of dredged or fill material into the navigable waters at specified disposal sites."[2] Judicial and regulatory interpretations of this phrase have dictated whether particular wetlands and particular activities fall within the reach of these government agencies.

Aside from the broad authority granting language encapsulated in the term "navigable waters," there are other elements that come into play when evaluating the Corps's jurisdictional reach with respect to wetlands. The definition of wetlands, the regulatory language and practices embodying the evolution of that definition, and the wetlands delineation process all are issues relevant to determining the scope of jurisdiction under the section 404 program.

A. THE DEFINITION OF WETLANDS

The definition of wetlands is dependent on the definition of the term "navigable waters" under the CWA. The act defines "navigable waters" as "waters of the United States, including the territorial seas."[3] Notwithstanding this seemingly broad definition, the determination of what constitutes a "water of the United States" is often difficult and contentious. The Corps has issued regulations defining the term "waters of the United States" to include, inter alia,

> waters such as intrastate lakes, rivers, streams (including intermittent streams), mudflats, sandflats, wetlands, sloughs, prairie potholes, wet meadows, playa lakes, or natural ponds, the use, degradation or destruction of which could affect interstate or foreign commerce. . . .[4]

---

2. *Id.*

3. 33 U.S.C. § 1362(7).

4. 33 C.F.R. 328.3(a)(3)(2001).

The Corps's regulations give examples of the kinds of activities that "could affect" interstate commerce sufficiently to bring such waters within the regulatory program.[5] These include:

1. waters used by interstate or foreign travelers or for recreational purposes;
2. waters from which fish or shellfish are taken and are later sold in interstate or foreign commerce; and
3. waters that are used or could be used for industrial purposes by industries in interstate commerce.

However, at least one court has struck down this definition. In *United States v. Wilson*, the 4th Circuit declared that the language of Corps's regulations went beyond the congressional intent for Corps's jurisdiction over bodies of water. The Court stated that "the regulation requires neither that the regulated activity have a substantial effect on interstate commerce, nor that the covered waters have any sort of nexus with navigable, or even interstate, waters."[6] The court relied on *United States v. Lopez,*[7] in which the Supreme Court ruled that Congress could only regulate those things that had a "substantial effect on interstate commerce."

Notwithstanding the *Wilson* court ruling, the Corps's regulations have not yet been changed and are at least hypothetically enforceable in other jurisdictions. However, the effect on this definition from the Supreme Court's recent *SWANCC* decision, discussed later in this chapter, remains unclear.

The Corps's regulations also define "waters of the United States" to include, inter alia:

1. All interstate waters including interstate wetlands; and
2. Wetlands adjacent to waters otherwise defined as "waters of the United States."[8]

Both the Corps's and EPA's regulations define "wetlands" to include:

[T]hose areas that are inundated or saturated by surface water or groundwater at a frequency and duration sufficient to support, and that under normal circumstances do support, a prevalence of vegetation typically adapted for life in saturated soil conditions. Wetlands generally include swamps, marshes, bogs, and similar areas.[9]

---

5. 33 C.F.R. 328.3.
6. United States v. Wilson, 133 F.3d 251, 257 (4th Cir. 1997).
7. United States v. Lopez, 514 U.S. 549 (1995).
8. 33 C.F.R. § 328.3(a).
9. 33 C.F.R. § 328.3(b); 40 C.F.R. § 230.3(t).

As discussed further in the section of this chapter on the Corps's wetlands delineation manual, wetlands are typically determined based on the presence of three parameters: (1) soils, (2) hydrology, and (3) vegetation.

Historically, the courts have liberally construed the term "navigable waters of the United States," thus providing the Corps and EPA with wide latitude over regulatory implementation of the section 404 program. Judicial review of wetlands determinations often has been based entirely on the Corps's administrative record.[10] This has given much weight to the Corps's and EPA's regulatory definition of wetlands. Nevertheless, as explained in subsequent sections of this chapter, the United States Supreme Court's *SWANCC* decision recently struck down one part of the regulatory definition of wetlands, the Migratory Bird Rule.

B. ADJACENT WETLANDS

The Corps's definition of "waters of the United States" includes wetlands adjacent to such waters.[11] The Corps's regulations define "adjacent" to mean "bordering, contiguous, or neighboring. Wetlands separated from other waters of the United States by manmade dikes or barriers, natural river berms, beach dunes and the like are adjacent wetlands."[12] The Corps's regulation of adjacent wetlands was reviewed by the Supreme Court in *United States v. Riverside Bayview Homes.* In that case, the Supreme Court unanimously upheld the Corps's more expansive 1975 definition of "navigable waters" to include "adjacent wetlands," noting that it was consistent with the "breadth of congressional concern for protection of water quality and aquatic ecosystems" underlying the 1972 CWA.[13] The Court also based its ruling on the fact that a Congressional bill was defeated that would have restricted the Corps's jurisdiction from reaching the wetlands at issue. Finally, the Court declared that Congress intended to regulate at least some waters that could not be deemed "navigable" under the classical understanding of the term. Therefore, the Corps properly extended its jurisdiction to include nonnavigable wetlands that were adjacent to navigable waters. However, the Court explicitly left open the issue of whether the Corps could extend its authority to isolated, intrastate, nonnavigable wetlands.

Courts have further defined the question of what will be considered "adjacency" for purposes of jurisdiction within the section 404 program. Most recently, in *United States v. Buday*, the court held that Clean Water Act jurisdiction extends

---

10. *See* National Wildlife Federation v Hanson, 623 F. Supp. 1539 (E.D.N.C. 1985).

11. 33 C.F.R. § 328.3(a)(7).

12. 33 C.F.R. § 328.3(c).

13. 474 U.S. 121, 133 (1985).

to wetlands adjacent to a tributary of a navigable-in-fact body of water.[14] In *United States v. Banks*, the court concluded that a wetland is adjacent to navigable waters where a hydrological connection existed primarily through groundwater, and secondarily through surface water during storms.[15] In a case decided prior to *Riverside Bayview Homes*, the 11th Circuit held that a wetland separated from a river by a 30-foot-wide manmade berm is considered "adjacent."[16]

However, once this adjacency becomes too attenuated geographically, some courts have not considered the wetlands adjacent. In *United States v. Sargent County Water*, the seven-mile distance between sloughs and the Wild Rice River was too great for the court to find adjacency even though there was a surface water connection.[17] Also, in *United States v. Wilson*, where the wetlands involved were more than ten miles from the Chesapeake Bay, more than six miles from the Potomac River, and hundreds of yards from the nearest creeks, the court felt that this distance rendered the wetlands beyond the scope of the Corps's jurisdiction.[18]

C. ISOLATED WETLANDS AND THE MIGRATORY BIRD RULE

In 1977, the Corps amended its regulations to define "waters of the United States" to include "isolated wetlands and lakes, intermittent streams, prairie potholes, and other waters that are not part of a tributary system to interstate waters or to navigable waters of the United States, the degradation or destruction of which could affect interstate commerce." The Corps pointed to the 1975 decision in *NRDC v. Callaway* for support of its extension of authority. In *Callaway*, the district court for the District of Columbia declared that Congress passed the Clean Water Act with the notion of asserting federal jurisdiction over the nation's waters to the maximum extent possible under the commerce clause of the Constitution.[19] Subsequent to the issuance of these regulations, at least one circuit court upheld the notion of regulating isolated wetlands. In *Leslie Salt Co. v. United States*, the Court of Appeals for the Ninth Circuit ruled that the Corps had jurisdiction over isolated waters and wetlands near San Francisco. The court held that man-made wetlands are subject to CWA jurisdiction even though the activities of state and other federal agencies created conditions resulting in the wetlands. In addition, the seasonal nature of ponding on the site was held not to be an obstacle to Corps jurisdiction.[20]

---

14. 138 F. Supp. 2d 1282 (D. Mont. 2001).
15. 115 F.3d 916 (11th Cir. 1997).
16. United States v. Tilton 705 F.2d 429 (11th Cir. 1983).
17. United States v. Sargent County Water, 876 F. Supp. 1090 (D.N.D. Apr. 6, 1992).
18. United States v. Wilson, 133 F.3d 251 (4th Cir. 1997).
19. 392 F. Supp. 685 (D.D.C. 1975).
20. 896 F.2d 354 (9th Cir. 1990); *See also* United States v. Southern Inv. Co., 876 F.2d 606 (8th Cir. 1989) holding that man-made wetlands are subject to CWA jurisdiction.

With the promulgation of the Migratory Bird Rule in 1986, the Corps attempted to extend its authority even further with respect to wetlands. The new regulations broadened wetlands jurisdiction to include isolated, nonnavigable, and wholly intrastate wetlands used by migratory birds. The Migratory Bird Rule was challenged in the landmark case of *Solid Waste Agency of Northern Cook County v. United States Army Corps of Engineers (SWANCC)*.[21] In a sharply divided 5-to-4 decision, the Supreme Court in *SWANCC* invalidated the Migratory Bird Rule, thereby cutting back the Corps's jurisdiction over wetlands for the first time.

In reaching its conclusion in *SWANCC*, the Court first distinguished its unanimous ruling in *Riverside Bayview Homes*. As in *Riverside*, the Court recognized that the term "navigable" was of "limited import" and that Congress intended to "regulate at least some waters that would not be deemed 'navigable' under the classical understanding of the term."[22] The Court refused, however, to take the next step and hold that section 404(a) extended to isolated wetlands frequented by migratory birds. The Court's opinion distinguished *Riverside* because its holding there was based upon "Congress's unequivocal acquiescence to, and approval of, the Corps' regulations interpreting the CWA to cover wetlands adjacent to navigable waters."[23] Furthermore, the majority found that Congress's affirmation of the Corps's jurisdiction in *Riverside* was based on the significant nexus between the wetlands at issue and navigable waters, commenting that the wetlands in *Riverside* were "inseparably bound up with the 'waters of the United States.' "[24]

The *SWANCC* opinion highlighted the fact that while the legislative history regarding the 1978 amendments to the CWA made it clear that Congress had acquiesced to the Corps's assertion of jurisdiction over wetlands adjacent to navigable waters, similar legislative history was absent regarding Congressional approval of the Migratory Bird Rule. While conceding that in *Riverside* the Court had de-emphasized the importance of the term "navigable" in the CWA, the Court stated that adoption of the Corps's interpretation here would inappropriately assign no meaning to the term. The Court concluded that "it is one thing to give a word limited effect and quite another to give it no effect whatever."[25]

In response to the *SWANCC* decision, prior to leaving office, President Clinton issued an executive order requiring federal agencies to develop memoranda of understanding with the Fish and Wildlife Service, within two years, to promote

---

21. 531 U.S. 159, 167 (2001).
22. *Id.* (citing *Riverside Bayview Homes*, 474 U.S. at 133).
23. *Id.*
24. *Id.*
25. *Id.* at 172.

the conservation of migratory bird populations if their actions might have a "measurable negative effect on migratory bird populations."[26]

There has been some confusion left by the Supreme Court's holding in *SWANCC*. The ambiguity lies in how broad or narrow the holding should be interpreted. Under a narrow reading, the Corps will only lose jurisdiction when the wetland is completely isolated, nonnavigable, intrastate, and the sole basis of jurisdiction is the presence of migratory birds.[27] Notably, the court did not expressly invalidate any of the definitions of "waters of the United States" in 33 C.F.R. part 328. It only invalidated the Migratory Bird Rule as an extension of 33 C.F.R. part 328. Therefore, a valid argument exists that the *SWANCC* decision only prohibits the assertion of jurisdiction based solely on the presence of migratory birds.

On the other hand, *SWANCC* could be read broadly in light of the Court's discussion of *Riverside Bayview Homes* and its reliance on "navigability."[28] A broad reading of *SWANCC* would mean that the Corps only has jurisdiction over waters that are either navigable in fact, or have a "substantial nexus" to navigable waters, such as those directly adjacent to navigable waters. A broad reading would require the Corps to establish more substantial connections to traditionally navigable waterways to gain jurisdiction over a wetland.

There is some case law being developed by the lower courts as to how to apply the precedent created by *SWANCC*. For instance, some courts have taken a narrow view of the holding in *SWANCC*. The Court in *United States v. Interstate General Co.*, in its decision to find Corps jurisdiction proper over wetlands adjacent to headwaters of two creeks, comprised of intermittent streams and drainage ditches that averaged two feet in width and depth (held to be navigable, not isolated), opined that *SWANCC* was limited to an invalidation of the Migratory Bird Rule.[29] However, the Court in *United States v. Newdunn Associates* reached a different conclusion. In response to a motion for a preliminary injunction to stop filling wetlands that were connected to a stream by a culvert underneath a highway, the court held that *SWANCC* has significantly altered the contours of the CWA's jurisdiction beyond the demise of the Migratory Bird Rule.[30]

While the total implications of the ruling are not yet clear, a few key points are clear. First, it seems as if the U.S. Army Corps will be cautious in asserting jurisdiction over nonnavigable isolated waters. Second, it will be more commonplace

---

26. Executive Order No. 13186 (1/10/01), section 3; 66 Fed. Reg. 3853 (Jan. 17, 2001).

27. *See generally* Note, "Clearing the Muddy Waters? An Examination of *SWANCC* and the Implications for Wetlands Protection and the Administrative State, 36 Wake Forest L. Rev. 845 (Fall 2001).

28. *Id.*

29. United States v. Interstate General Co., 152 F. Supp. 2d 843 (D. Md. 2001).

30. United States v. Newdunn Associates, 195 F. Supp. 2d. 751 (E.D. Va.. 2002).

that developers and others wishing to work in or fill such isolated waters will only need to obtain permits from state agencies. Third, state governments will now be looking to fill the current gaps in their wetland legislation, as there is now less federal overlap. Fourth, there is likely to be initial confusion and delays in determining which waters remain subject to federal jurisdiction. Finally, those considering projects in such waters are well advised to carefully evaluate all potential issues prior to proceeding.

D. WETLANDS DELINEATION MANUALS

Notwithstanding the use of identical regulatory definitions, the Corps and EPA often do not agree upon whether a given area is a wetland. Historically, these different methodologies for assessing whether an area is "wetlands" resulted in the proliferation of numerous delineation manuals among various governmental agencies, including the Corps, EPA, the U.S. Fish and Wildlife Service (FWS), and the Soil Conservation Service (SCS). Generally speaking, all of the manuals set out the process and steps to determine whether or not an area is a wetland. They focus on the presence of three parameters: (1) the presence of hydric soils; (2) the presence of certain hydrology; and (3) the presence of hydrophytic vegetation (species that typically grow in wetlands environments). The process by which the Corps determines the presence of wetlands at a particular site is known as a Jurisdictional Determination. The manual issued in 1987 by the Corps (the 1987 manual) eventually became the standard presently used by most federal and state agencies. Manuals issued in 1989 and 1991, which offered different tests for determining the presence of wetlands, proved controversial and were never put into widespread use.[31]

First, the 1987 manual stresses the need to verify that all three parameters (hydrology, vegetation, and soil type) exist prior to classifying an area as wetlands. Second, the 1987 manual focuses on hydrology. Where hydrology is questionable, the 1987 manual requires stronger evidence that the vegetation is hydrophytic. Third, the 1987 manual gives less weight to facultative species (species that do not grow exclusively in wetlands) as positive indicators of existence of a wetlands. Finally, the 1987 manual stresses the need to use sound professional judgment in making wetlands determinations, thereby allowing trained

---

31. The Energy and Water Development Appropriations Act of 1991 invalidated the 1989 manual. *See* H.R. 2427, 102 Cong., First Sess. (1991). The 1993 Energy and Water Appropriations Act continued the 1992 act's mandate requiring the use of the 1987 manual until a final manual is adopted. EPA-funded wetlands studies are intended to establish a solid scientific basis for wetlands identification. *See generally* Independent Agencies Appropriations Act of 1993, Pub. L. No. 102-389. In the meantime, the Corps will continue to use the 1987 manual. *See* Army Corps Baltimore District Public Notice, Special Notice #89-13.

wetland consultants to take into careful consideration the evidence of all three parameters to evaluate the existence of a wetland.

Such professional judgment was taken into account in the case of *In re* Condor Land Co., where a wetlands determination was upheld on the grounds that EPA and Corps experts identified necessary hydrophytic vegetation, hydric soils, and hydrology to establish the existence of jurisdictional wetlands.[32] This case also brought to light the issue of whether the manual or the field personnel have the final say in making a wetlands determination. The judge in *In re* Condor Land Co. held that the specific observations of the field personnel regarding the physical characteristics of the subject property are key in determining whether such property meets the regulatory definition of wetlands. The manual, according to the court, is only an aide to reaching that determination.[33]

In some instances, the determination of soil characteristics under the manual can be complicated where the soils have been disturbed. "Prior converted cropland" is an example of one of those disturbed soil types. Such prior converted cropland is not considered wetlands because the water regime in the soils has been substantially altered and is therefore considered to be of low ecological value.[34] If, however, the prior converted cropland is abandoned for five years and the wetland characteristics return, the Corps jurisdiction is restored.

E. LONGEVITY OF WETLANDS DELINEATIONS

On August 14, 1990, the Corps issued a regulatory guidance letter (RGL) entitled "Expiration Dates for Wetlands Jurisdictional Delineations." This RGL establishes the length of time a wetlands delineation remains valid.[35] The RGL establishes that:

1. written delineations made before August 14, 1990, and that do not specify a time limit are valid for two years from the effective date;
2. written delineations made before August 14, 1990, and that specify a time limit are valid until the date specified;
3. oral delineations no longer are valid; (in rare cases, the Corps may honor a previous oral wetlands delineation, however there is a presumption that oral delineations are not valid);

---

32. *In re* Condor Land Co., No. CWA-404-95-106 (ALJ Charneski Dec. 8, 1998).

33. *Id.*

34. Regulatory Guidance Letter (RGL) 90-7 (Sept. 27, 1990). The Corps regulations also state that waters of the United States do not include prior converted cropland. 33 C.F.R. § 328.3(a)(8).

35. RGL No. 90-6.

4. written wetland delineations made after August 14, 1990, generally are valid for three years, and validity may be extended for up to five additional years; and

5. the time limits for delineations made before August 14, 1990, do not apply if a wetlands application has been completed or where the applicant can fully demonstrate that substantial resources were expended or committed in reliance upon the prior delineation. (Substantial resource commitment generally includes final engineering design work, contractual commitments for construction, and purchasing or long-term leasing of property.)

III. State Authority in Light of *SWANCC*

The *SWANCC* decision has left a gap in the regulation of isolated wetlands throughout the country. Many states had framed their wetlands regulations based on the notion that primary authority rested with the Corps, oftentimes only establishing jurisdiction through the CWA's section 401 state water quality certification authority. Even in states with extensive wetlands-permitting programs, most mirror the federal regulatory program. Therefore, many states left isolated wetlands without specific state protection. This has left isolated wetlands in many states with no regulatory protection whatsoever.

This issue has prompted states to enact new legislation with the purpose of closing the potential loopholes created by the *SWANCC* decision. The process has proven to be a difficult one for many states, as new programs require funding, expertise, and personnel that are currently unavailable. At present, there is no federal funding for states to establish newer, more-inclusive wetlands programs. It is expected by some that without outside funds many states will not be able to develop and implement new wetlands programs, as state legislatures will not support enactment of wetlands programs that require additional resources. Added to this dilemma is the fear of many state officials that, by barring federal jurisdiction over large tracts of wetlands, the states will no longer be able to maintain federal water quality standards.

Several states, including Wisconsin[36] and Virginia, have responded with new regulation. North Carolina and Ohio have also taken steps to preserve isolated wetlands. Other states, including Delaware, have committed to ensuring that their isolated wetlands will be protected in light of the *SWANCC* decision. Many expect that most states will follow suit. In some cases, states that are addressing isolated wetlands in new legislation are also addressing the issue of incidental fallback, which will be discussed in the next section.

---

36. Wis. Stat. Ann. § 281.36.

IV. The Section 404 Permit Program

A. ACTIVITIES COVERED

CWA section 301(a) prohibits the discharge of any pollutant by any person into waters of the United States unless such discharge is made in compliance with various CWA sections, including section 404.[37] Section 404 focuses on the discharge of dredged or fill material into waters of the United States, including wetlands, and establishes the permit program that is overseen by the Corps of Engineers.[38]

Although the words "dredged and fill material" are often spoken in one breath, "dredged material" and "fill material" are two separate concepts. "Fill material" means "material placed in waters of the United States where the material has the effect of . . . [r]eplacing any portion of a water of the United States with dry land; or [c]hanging the bottom elevation of any portion of a water of the United States."[39] Roughly speaking, it may be thought of as material that comes from outside the waterbody or wetland in question. Examples of fill material include rock, sand, soil, clay, plastics, construction debris, wood chips, overburden from mining, or other excavation activities—but the term does not include trash or garbage.[40] The term "discharge of fill material" is defined as "the addition of fill material into waters of the United States" and includes a broad range of activities ranging from the placement of fill necessary for the construction of any structure in a water of the United States to the creation of artificial reefs.[41] Placement of pilings in waters of the United States is also considered to be a discharge of fill material.[42]

"Dredged material," on the other hand, means "material that is excavated or dredged from waters of the United States."[43] In contrast to fill material, it generally refers to material that comes from the waterbody or wetland in question, and does not require that the material change the bottom elevation or destroy waters of the United States. The term "discharge of dredged material" means "any addition of dredged material into, including redeposit of dredged material other than incidental fallback within, waters of the United States."[44] Section 404 authorization is not required for "any incidental addition, including redeposit, of dredged material associated with any activity that does not have or would not have the

---

37. 33 U.S.C. § 1311(a).

38. 33 U.S.C. § 1344.

39. 67 Fed. Reg. 31,129 at 31,142–43 (May 9, 2002), to be codified at 33 U.S.C. § 323.2(e) and 40 C.F.R. § 232.2.

40. *Id.*

41. 33 U.S.C. § 323.2(f) and 40 C.F.R. § 232.2.

42. 33 U.S.C. § 323.3(c) and 40 C.F.R. § 232.2.

43. 33 U.S.C. § 323.2(c) and 40 C.F.R. § 232.2.

44. 33 U.S.C. § 323.2(d) and 40 C.F.R. § 232.2.

effect of destroying or degrading an area of waters of the United States," except in the context of mechanized land-clearing, ditching, channelization, and other excavation activity, unless it can be demonstrated that such activities would not destroy or degrade waters of the United States.[45]

One reason that the distinction between the two concepts is important is that discharges of dredged material, in contrast to discharges of fill material, specifically exclude "incidental fallback" or discharges with de minimis effects from coverage. The term "incidental fallback" describes de minimis redeposits of soil during dredging operations, such as "when a bucket used to excavate material from the bottom of a river, stream, or wetland is raised and soils or sediment fall from the bucket back into the water."[46] Although what this means in terms of whether a particular activity requires authorization is still being fought out, it is clear that the exclusion of "incidental fallback" from regulation does not mean that redeposit of material into a wetland is never regulated.[47] Instead, the courts will look carefully to the effects of the redeposit on the wetland, and activities that destroy the ecology of the wetland will be covered even if they do not involve the introduction of material from somewhere else.[48]

Courts will often look to the more general definition of what constitutes a regulated activity under the CWA, that is, an addition of a pollutant from a point source into waters of the United States, rather than focusing on the definitions of dredged and fill material in order to determine whether a particular activity requires section 404 authorization.[49] In this context, they have determined that a wide variety of activities require 404 authorization when they occur in waters of the United States, including: land-clearing;[50] movement of cobbles in a streambed;[51] operation of a bulldozer in a stream channel;[52] construction of dams and the placement of riprap;[53] the use of indigenous bog vegetation and clays to create roads and windrows in a peat bog;[54] boats churning up and redepositing

---

45. 33 U.S.C. § 323.2(d)(3) and 40 C.F.R. § 232.2.

46. National Mining Ass'n v. United States Army Corps of Engineers, 145 F.3d 1399, 1403 (D.C. Cir. 1998).

47. Id. at 1405 ("we do not hold that the Corps may not legally regulate some forms of redeposit under its section 404 permitting authority").

48. See Borden Ranch Partnership v. United States Army Corps of Engineers, 261 F.3d 810, 814–15 (9th Cir. 2001), aff'd per curium, 123 S. Ct. 599 (2002).

49. See, e.g., id.; United States v. Deaton, 209 F.3d 331, 334–37 (4th Cir. 2000).

50. Avoyelles Sportsmen's League v. Marsh, 715 F.2d 897 (5th Cir. 1983).

51. United States v. Sinclair, 767 F. Supp. 200 (D. Mont. 1990).

52. United States v. Larkins, 657 F. Supp. 2d 76 (W.D. Ky. 1987).

53. Minnehaha Creek Watershed Dist. v. Hoffman, 597 F.2d 617 (8th Cir. 1979).

54. United States v. Bay Houston Towing Co., 33 F. Supp. 2d 596 (E.D. Mich. 1999).

vegetation and sediment;[55] sidecasting from ditches;[56] deep ripping (a form of plowing that drags shanks 4 to 7 feet deep through the earth);[57] and farming activities such as plowing, disking, and seeding that were not eligible for the exemption in section 404(f).[58]

Activities the courts have held do not require 404 authorization include: release of impounded sediment from a deactivated dam;[59] release of lead shot from shotguns;[60] refuse to be deposited in a proposed landfill in a wetland;[61] mining overburden deposited in a stream;[62] draining of wetlands where there is not an accompanying discharge of dredged or fill material;[63] flooding;[64] and erosion of soil as a result of releases of water.[65]

B. TYPES OF PERMITS

The Corps has a variety of means through which it can authorize discharges of dredged or fill material. Procedures for modifying, suspending, or revoking permits may be found at 33 C.F.R. section 325.7.

1. Nationwide Permits

The Corps has authority to issue general permits under CWA section 404(e) for categories of discharges that will cause only minimal adverse environmental effects when performed separately and will have only minimal adverse cumulative effects.[66] One such type of general permit is a nationwide permit (NWP), which is issued by the Chief of Engineers and is designed to regulate activities with little, if any, delay or paperwork.[67] Examples of activities covered by NWPs include: utility line activities, outfall structures and maintenance, construction or

---

55. United States v. M.C.C. of Florida, Inc., 772 F.3d 1501 (11th Cir.1985).

56. United States v. Deaton, 209 F.3d 331, 334–37 (4th Cir. 2000).

57. Borden Ranch Partnership v. United States Army Corps of Engineers, 261 F.3d 810 (9th Cir. 2001), *aff'd per curium*, 123 S. Ct. 599 (2002).

58. United States v. Akers, 785 F.2d 814 (9th Cir. 1985).

59. Froebel v. Meyer, 13 F. Supp. 2d 843 (E.D. Wis. 1998).

60. Long Island Soundkeeper Fund v. New York Athletic Club, 42 ERC 1421 (S.D.N.Y. 1995). Note, however, that the court held that a section 402 permit was required for such a discharge.

61. Resource Investments Inc. v. United States Army Corps of Engineers, 151 F.3d 1162 (9th Cir. 1998).

62. West Virginia Coal Ass'n v. EPA, 932 F.2d 934 (4th Cir. 1991).

63. Save Our Community v. EPA, 971 F.2d 1155 (5th Cir. 1992).

64. Abenaki Nation of Mississquoi v. Hughes, 805 F. Supp. 234, 248 (D. Vt. 1992).

65. State of Missouri *ex rel.* Ashcroft v. Department of the Army Corps of Engineers, 526 F. Supp. 660 (W.D. Mich. 1980).

66. 33 U.S.C. § 1344(e).

67. 33 C.F.R. § 330.1(b).

expansion of a single-family housing, cranberry production activities, completed enforcement actions, stream and wetland restoration, and cleanup of hazardous and toxic waste.[68] Two or more NWPs may be combined or an NWP may be combined with an individual permit to authorize an activity.[69] NWPs require the issuance of a state water quality certification under CWA section 401.[70]

As a general matter, if an activity and permittee satisfy all of a NWP's conditions (including the general conditions placed on all NWPs), the permittee is authorized to proceed with the activity without notifying the Corps.[71] However, some NWPs require a predischarge notification (PDN) to be provided before the activity may be undertaken.[72] Some NWPs that involve a discharge into wetlands also require a wetland delineation as part of the PDN.[73] The Corps's District Engineer has 30 days from receipt of a complete PDN to notify the applicant that the activity does not qualify for a NWP; otherwise, the applicant may proceed with the activity.[74] Mitigation can be required if, after review of the PDN, the District Engineer determines the impacts are more than minimal.[75] Mitigation then will be necessary to allow the project to go forward under the NWP regulations. Moreover, the Corps retains discretionary authority to suspend, modify, or revoke any NWP authorization based on concerns for the aquatic environment as expressed in EPA's section 404(b)(1) guidelines or for reasons of public interest.[76] If a District Engineer determines that the proposed activity would have more than minimal individual or cumulative net adverse effects on the environment or would be otherwise contrary to the public interest, the District Engineer may modify the NWP to minimize or eliminate those effects or require an individual permit.[77]

2. Regional Permits

Regional permits are another type of general permit, but are issued by a Division or a District Engineer of the Corps, rather than on a nationwide basis.[78] Availability of regional permit authorization may require case-by-case reporting and acknowledgment, but no other separate applications or other authorization docu-

---

68. 67 Fed. Reg. 2020, 2077 (Jan. 15, 2002).
69. 33 C.F.R. § 330.6(c) and (d).
70. 33 C.F.R. § 330.4(c).
71. 33 C.F.R. § 330.1(c).
72. 33 C.F.R. § 330.1(e).
73. 33 C.F.R. § 330.1(e)(3).
74. 33 C.F.R. § 330.1(e).
75. 33 C.F.R. § 330.1(d).
76. *Id.*
77. *Id.*
78. 33 C.F.R. § 325.2(e)(2).

ments are required.[79] In addition, the issuing authority retains discretionary authority to suspend, modify, or revoke any regional permit authorization based on concerns for the aquatic environment or the public interest.[80]

In some rapidly developing areas, EPA and the Corps have been developing Special Area Management Plans (SAMPs) to address compliance with section 404 permitting requirements on a regional basis. In a SAMP, a regional plan defines areas where development will be permitted, what mitigation will be required for development, and what areas will be protected from development.

3. Programmatic Permits

These are another type of general permit and are founded on an existing state, local, or other federal agency program and are designed to avoid duplication with such programs.[81]

4. Letters of Permission

A letter of permission is a type of individual permit issued through the use of an abbreviated processing procedure that includes coordination with federal and state fish and wildlife agencies and a public interest evaluation, but does not require publishing of an individual public notice.[82] Letters of permission are seldom used since they are available only in limited circumstances.

5. Individual Permits

In the section 404 context, the term "individual permit" typically refers to a permit granted on an individualized, case-by-case basis through the standard review process. This process is described in more detail in section C below.

6. Emergency Procedures

Division engineers are authorized to approve expedited processing procedures in emergency situations, which are defined as situations that would result in an unacceptable hazard to life, a significant loss of property, or an immediate, unforeseen, and significant economic hardship if corrective action requiring a permit is not undertaken within a time period less than the normal time needed to process an application.[83] Even in such situations, the Corps is required to make

---

79. 33 C.F.R. § 325.6(c)(1).
80. 33 C.F.R. § 325.7.
81. 33 C.F.R. § 325.5(c)(3).
82. 33 C.F.R. § 325.2(e)(1).
83. 33 C.F.R. § 325.2(e)(4).

reasonable efforts to receive comments from interested agencies and the public and to publish as soon as practicable notice of the special procedures.[84]

7. After-the-Fact Permits

If the Corps discovers that an unauthorized discharge of dredged or fill material has taken place, it may nevertheless accept and process a permit application for that discharge provided that the violator has completed initial corrective measures, as required by the Corps.[85] The application is processed in the same manner as an individual permit.[86] However, an "after-the-fact" permit will not be processed if: restoration of the waters of the United States that eliminates current and future detrimental impacts is complete, the District Engineer determines legal action is appropriate or has already denied legal authorization, or where enforcement litigation has already been initiated by another agency (unless the District Engineer determines that processing of the application is clearly appropriate.)[87] Because after-the-fact permits are considered to be an enforcement response, the decision to process such a permit application is discretionary and section 404 violators should not assume that they will necessarily be available.[88]

C. THE INDIVIDUAL PERMIT PROCESS

The individual permit process under section 404 consists of a series of steps: submission of an application; public notice (and in some cases public hearing) for the proposed project; compliance with a variety of legal provisions outside of section 404 (such as CWA section 401 state water quality certification, the National Environmental Policy Act, the Endangered Species Act, the Coastal Zone Management Act, and historical preservation laws); and the issuance of a record of decision/statement of findings and permit, as appropriate. The decision of whether to grant a permit is based on the Corps's public interest review process and the factors identified in EPA's guidelines developed pursuant to CWA section 404(b)(1).

1. The Permitting Process

Although applicants have the option of consulting with the Corps prior to submitting an application for a 404 permit in order to learn what information they

---

84. *Id.*

85. 33 C.F.R. § 326.3(e).

86. *Id.*

87. *Id.*

88. United States v. Cumberland Farms of Connecticut, 647 F. Supp. 1166, 1183 (D. Mass. 1986), *aff'd*, 826 F.2d 1151, 1157 (1st Cir. 1987).

will have to supply in order to obtain a permit,[89] the first formal step of the permitting process is submitting a permit application.[90] The application consists of a standard form plus any drawings, sketches, or plans sufficient for purposes of providing public notice of the proposed activity and must include the information described in 33 C.F.R. section 325.1(d).

Within 15 days of receipt of a permit application, the District Engineer must determine either that the application is complete and issue a public notice or that it is incomplete and notify the applicant of what additional information is necessary.[91] The public notice must include sufficient information so as to give interested parties a clear understanding of the nature and magnitude of the activity in question.[92] The public will typically be given 30 days to comment on the application.[93] The District Engineer must consider all comments received in response to the public notice, and may also give the applicant an opportunity to respond to the comments received.[94] Although not required,[95] the District Engineer will also evaluate the application to determine the need for a public hearing pursuant to 33 C.F.R. part 327.[96]

As part of the permitting process, the Corps is required to ensure compliance with a variety of provisions outside of section 404; for example:

- The District Engineer is to follow the Corps' regulations pertaining to the National Environmental Policy Act of 1969 (NEPA), and a permit decision will require either an environmental assessment or an environmental impact statement, unless the proposed activity is categorically excluded.[97]
- Pursuant to the Coastal Zone Management Act, the District Engineer is also required to obtain a certification from the applicant that a proposed activity affecting the coastal zone is consistent with an approved state coastal zone management program.[98]
- The District Engineer will also follow Corps regulations pursuant to the National Historic Preservation Act if the proposed activity would

---

89. 33 C.F.R. § 325.1(b).

90. 33 C.F.R. § 325.1(c).

91. 33 C.F.R. § 325.2(a)(2).

92. 33 C.F.R. § 325.3(a).

93. 33 C.F.R. § 325.2(d)(2).

94. 33 C.F.R. § 325.2(a)(3).

95. Water Works and Sewer Board City of Birmingham v. U.S. Army Corps of Engineers, 983 F. Supp. 1052 (N.D. Ala. 1997).

96. 33 C.F.R. § 325.2(a)(5).

97. 33 C.F.R. § 325.2(a)(4).

98. 33 C.F.R. § 325.2(b)(2).

involve any property listed or eligible for listing on the National Regis-ter of Historic Places.[99]

• Applications must be reviewed for potential impacts on threatened or endangered species pursuant to section 7 of the Endangered Species Act. If the proposed activity will affect such a species or its critical habitat, the District Engineer must initiate formal consultation procedures with the relevant agency, whether the federal Fish and Wildlife Service or the National Marine Fisheries Service.[100]

• An applicant must also apply for a water quality certification (WQC) pursuant to section 401(a) of the CWA from the state in which the dis-charge originates.[101] A permit cannot be granted unless a section 401 certification is obtained or waived. A waiver may be explicit or will be deemed to occur if the certifying agency fails or refuses to act on a request for certification within 60 days after receipt of such request unless the Corps's District Engineer determines that the state is to have a shorter or longer time period to act.[102] The certification may contain conditions imposed by the state.

This requires a significant amount of interagency coordination on permit applications. Moreover, "full consideration and appropriate weight" must be given to comments from federal, state, and local agencies on matters within their expertise.[103] To deal with situations involving disputes over permit decisions, the Corps entered into MOAs pursuant to CWA section 404(q) with EPA, the Department of Commerce (National Marine Fisheries Service), and the Depart-ment of Interior (Fish and Wildlife Service) that established a formal process for timely elevation of such disputes. Elevation for individual permit cases may occur where the permit would have unacceptable adverse effects to "aquatic resources of national importance" (ARNIs). The MOAs also provide for eleva-tion of broader policy-level issues. Nevertheless, invocation of the formal section 404(q) process and elevation to the headquarters level is relatively rare.

After completing the foregoing actions, the District Engineer will determine whether a permit should be granted, based on the record and the regulations dis-cussed below in section C.2.[104] The District Engineer will prepare either a State-ment of Findings or, if an environmental impact statement has been prepared, a

---

99. 33 C.F.R. § 325.2(b)(3).
100. 33 C.F.R. § 325.2(b)(5).
101. 33 C.F.R. § 325.2(b)
102. 33 C.F.R. § 325.2(b)(1)(ii).
103. 33 C.F.R. §§ 320.4(a)(3), (c) and (d).
104. 33 C.F.R. § 325.2(a)(6).

Record of Decision.[105] If the final decision is to deny the permit, the applicant will be advised in writing[106] and may avail itself of the Corps's administrative appeal process.[107] If the final decision is to grant the permit, the permit will be forwarded to the applicant for signature but will not be valid until signed by the issuing official.[108] The permit may include special conditions as necessary to satisfy legal requirements or the public interest,[109] and it will specify time limits for completing the work or activity.[110] In principle, District Engineers are supposed to decide all applications not later than 60 days after receipt of a complete application,[111] but, for a variety of reasons, it is seldom the case that the individual permit process takes only 60 days from submission of an application to final decision on a permit.

Section 404(c) of the CWA grants EPA the power to veto or place restrictions on a section 404 individual permit after notice and opportunity for public hearing if the discharge would have an unacceptable adverse effect on municipal water supplies, shellfish beds and fishing areas, wildlife, or recreational areas.[112] Under this same provision, EPA has the authority to prohibit or restrict use of sites for discharges even if no permit application is pending. Although EPA rarely exercises its 404(c) authority, the courts have given it substantial deference when its vetoes have been challenged.[113]

2. Permitting Decision Considerations

a. Public Interest Review. The decision of whether to issue a permit depends on an evaluation of the probable impacts, including cumulative impacts, of the proposed activity and its intended use on the public interest.[114] The "public interest review" required for all Corps permits involves a case-specific weighing of a cornucopia of factors, which may include considerations of conservation, economics, aesthetics, general environmental concerns, historic values, fish and wildlife values, flood damage prevention, water supply and conservation, water quality,

---

105. *Id.*

106. 33 C.F.R. § 325.2(a)(7).

107. 33 C.F.R. Part 331.

108. 33 C.F.R. § 325.2(a)(7).

109. 33 C.F.R. § 325.4.

110. 33 C.F.R. § 325.6(c).

111. 33 C.F.R. § 325.2(d)(3).

112. 33 U.S.C. § 1344(c).

113. James City County v. EPA, 12 F.3d 1330 (4th Cir. 1993); Bersani v. EPA, 850 F.2d 36 (2d Cir. 1988); City of Alma v. United States, 744 F. Supp. 1546 (S.D. Ga. 1990); Newport Galleria Group v. Deland, 618 F. Supp. 1179 (D.D.C. 1985).

114. 33 C.F.R. § 320.4(a).

and energy, among others.[115] Some courts have held that the Corps should not consider areas outside of waters of the United States in evaluating a proposed activity,[116] but others have held that the Corps may reasonably interpret the CWA to consider cumulative impacts on an entire ecosystem, not just those on the water receiving the discharge.[117] The Corps regulations give special deference to state and local planning decisions in considering the public interest.[118]

The courts have given considerable deference to Corps permitting decisions with regard to the general balancing of all public interest review factors. For example, the Corps's decision to deny a permit for a proposed landfill because its environmental impacts outweighed the public benefits of the project was upheld as having a rational basis in the record.[119]

b. EPA's Section 404(b)(1) Guidelines. Central to the permit decision process is whether the proposed discharge activity would comply with the guidelines promulgated by the EPA pursuant to CWA section 404(b)(1), set forth in 40 C.F.R. part 230. If it does not, a permit for the activity will be denied.[120] If it does, a permit will be granted "unless issuance would be contrary to the public interest."[121]

The guidelines provide that, except as provided in CWA section 404(b)(2), the discharge of dredged or fill material will not be permitted if there is a practicable alternative to the proposed discharge that would have less adverse impact on the aquatic ecosystem, so long as the alternative does not present other significant environmental consequences.[122] An alternative is "practicable" if it is available and capable of being done after taking into account cost, existing technology, and logistics in light of overall project purposes.[123] If otherwise practicable, an area not owned by the project applicant that could be reasonably obtained to fill the basic purpose of the proposed activity may be considered as an alternative.[124] Unless clearly demonstrated otherwise, it will be presumed that there are practicable alternatives to discharge activity that occurs in, but is not dependent

---

115. *Id.*

116. *See, e.g.,* Wetlands Action Network v. U.S. Army Corps of Engineers, 222 F.3d 1105 (9th Cir. 2000).

117. *See, e.g.,* United States v. Mango, 199 F.3d 85 (2d Cir. 1999).

118. 33 C.F.R. § 320.4(j)(2).

119. B&B Partnership v. United States, 133 F.3d 913 (4th Cir. 1997).

120. 33 C.F.R. § 320.4(a)(1); Fox Bay Partners v. U.S. Army Corps of Engineers, 831 F. Supp. 605 (N.D. Ill. 1993).

121. 33 C.F.R. § 323.6(a).

122. 40 C.F.R. § 230.10(a).

123. 40 C.F.R. § 230.10(a)(2).

124. *Id.*

on being in or having access to, a wetland or other "special aquatic site."[125] (The various types of special aquatic sites are discussed in 40 C.F.R. section 230.4.) The presumption of practicable alternatives is very strong.[126] Moreover, all such practicable alternatives that do not involve a discharge into a special aquatic site are presumed to have less adverse impact, unless clearly demonstrated otherwise.[127] The section 404(b)(1) alternatives analysis may overlap significantly with the alternatives analysis required by NEPA and must include alternatives evaluated under a coastal zone management or other planning process.[128]

The definition of the project's purpose plays a key role in developing an alternatives analysis and in the public interest review process more generally. As the courts have pointed out, "Obviously, an applicant cannot define a project in order to preclude the existence of any alternative sites and thus make what is practicable appear impossible."[129] On the other hand, "under the guidelines, not only is it permissible for the Corps to consider the applicant's objectives; the Corps has a duty to take into account the objectives of the applicant's project. Indeed, it would be bizarre if the Corps were to ignore the purpose for which the applicant seeks a permit and to substitute a purpose it deems more suitable."[130] Thus, for example, a court upheld the Corps's decision to consider only alternatives within the city limits to a proposed golf course because an out-of-town golf course would have thwarted the city's purpose in building it.[131]

The 404(b)(1) guidelines further state that, except as provided in CWA section 404(b)(2), the discharge of dredged or fill material shall not be permitted if it will cause or contribute to significant degradation of waters of the United States, including significant adverse effects on human health or welfare, aquatic ecosystems, and recreational, aesthetic, and economic values.[132] Findings of significant degradation will be based upon detailed chemical, biological, and physical evaluations and testing procedures for judging the impact of dredged and fill material disposal on the aquatic ecosystem and human use.[133]

---

125. 40 C.F.R. § 230.10(a)(3). Friends of the Earth v. Hintz, 800 F.2d 822 (9th Cir. 1986), involved the issuance of an after-the-fact permit to fill 17 acres of wetlands on Washington's Pacific coast for a combined log storage and export facility, and provides an example of a "water-dependent" project. In that case, the court agreed that no practicable alternative existed because the alternatives were too costly or logistically infeasible.

126. Buttrey v. United States, 690 F.2d 1170, 1180 (5th Cir. 1982).

127. *Id.*

128. 40 C.F.R. § 230.10(a)(4) and (5).

129. Sylvester v. U.S. Army Corps of Engineers, 882 F.2d 407, 409 (9th Cir. 1989).

130. Louisiana Wildlife Fed'n v. York, 761 F.2d 1044, 1048 (5th Cir. 1985).

131. Stewart v. Potts, 996 F. Supp. 668 (S.D. Tex. 1998).

132. 40 C.F.R. § 230.10(c).

133. *Id.*

Also, except as provided in CWA section 404(b)(2), the discharge of dredged or fill material shall not be permitted unless appropriate and practicable steps have been taken to minimize adverse effects on the aquatic ecosystem.[134] A variety of mitigation measures is identified at 40 C.F.R. section 230.70 through 230.77. Sufficient mitigation can avoid a finding a significant degradation of waters for which insufficient mitigation measures have been held to be grounds for denying a permit.[135]

Finally, no permit will be given for the discharge of dredged or fill material if the discharge would cause or contribute to violation of any applicable state water quality standard, violate toxic effluent standards or prohibitions in CWA section 307, jeopardize the continued existence of a species protected under the Endangered Species Act or adversely affect that species' critical habitat, or violate certain protections applying to marine sanctuaries.[136]

D. MITIGATION POLICY AND BANKING

As already noted, the section 404(b)(1) guidelines require that applicants take all practicable steps to minimize the adverse effects of proposed filling activities. A great deal of scientific uncertainty exists regarding wetland evaluation methods and success possibilities for various types of mitigation. In 1990, the Corps and EPA signed a mitigation MOA designed to set a uniform mitigation policy. The MOA:

- endorses a national goal of no overall net loss of the nation's remaining wetlands base;
- requires sequencing of mitigation, that is, the Corps must first determine that potential impacts have been avoided to the maximum extent practicable, then determine whether any remaining impacts have been minimized, and only then allow compensation for unavoidable wetlands losses;
- allows deviation from strict sequencing where EPA and the Corps agree that the proposed discharge can reasonably be expected to result in environmental gain or insignificant environmental losses and where discharge is necessary to avoid environmental harm;
- establishes a minimum requirement of one-to-one (1:1) acreage replacement of wetlands to achieve a "no net loss" of values, which ratio may be higher or lower depending upon the functional values of the area sub-

---

134. 40 C.F.R. § 230.10(d).
135. Town of Norfolk v. U.S. Army Corps of Engineers, 968 F.2d 1438 (1st Cir. 1992).
136. 40 C.F.R. § 230.10(b).

ject to impact, the type of wetlands on the site, and availability of mitigation technology;

- establishes that compensatory mitigation (such as restoration of existing degraded wetlands or creation of man-made wetlands) should be undertaken, when practicable, on-site or in the same geographical area (for example, same watershed), and should be of the same type of wetlands as the wetlands affected (in-kind) rather than a different type of wetlands (out-of-kind);
- calls for careful consideration of likelihood of success in determining the nature and extent of compensatory mitigation, with restoration being preferred because it is more likely to be successful; and
- states that mitigation banking may be an acceptable form of compensatory mitigation under specific criteria designed to ensure an environmentally successful bank.

With regard to the last point, the Corps and EPA have developed section 404 guidance that provides procedures and guidelines for establishing, evaluating, and withdrawing credits from a wetland mitigation bank.[137] The guidance emphasizes the importance of legal and financial assurances that the bank will be in place in perpetuity is important, such as providing conservation easements or transfers to a state resource agency or other appropriate entity and providing financial assurances for startup and endowment of the bank. Also important under the guidance is that adequate monitoring be in place to ensure that the bank is achieving its goals so that credit is awarded only for actual environmental benefits that have been achieved.

V. Enforcement: Potential Liabilities for Violating Section 404

As is the case for other violations of the CWA, discharges of dredged or fill material into waters of the United States without a permit (if not otherwise exempted) or in violation of a section 404 permit may subject the violator to administrative, civil, and/or criminal enforcement action. It may also subject the violator to citizen suit liability under section 505 of the CWA. Rather than repeat the more general discussion in chapter 11 of this book regarding CWA enforcement, this section will focus on issues peculiar to section 404 enforcement cases.

A. AGENCY ROLES AND ADMINISTRATIVE ENFORCEMENT

One of the most fundamental differences between enforcement of section 404 and enforcement of other provisions in the CWA is that the EPA shares enforcement

---

137. The guidance on wetlands banking is available at http://www.epa.gov/owow/wetlands/mitbankn.html.

responsibilities with the Corps. Thus, in addition to the authorities given to EPA in section 308 to request information from an alleged violator and to have a right-of-entry onto property and in section 309 to issue administrative compliance orders and assess administrative penalties, the Corps may also take administrative action against section 404 violators. For example, the Corps can issue orders (commonly known as "cease and desist orders") finding a violation of the CWA and requiring all illegal activity to stop.[138] Refusal to comply carries no administrative penalty but may be a factor in a future civil action for injunctive relief and penalties. Section 309(g) also gives the Corps the power to levy administrative penalties. The Corps has the option of resolving violations through the use of "after-the-fact" permits, which authorize illegal fill activities that have already occurred and allow fill to remain in place.[139] Violations that have subsequently been authorized through an after-the-fact permit may nonetheless be subject to administrative penalties.

Persons running afoul of section 404's requirements will typically hear first from the Corps simply because it has more field personnel, but the Corps and EPA formalized their division of enforcement responsibilities in a 1989 MOA between the two agencies. That MOA provides (1) that the Corps will be the lead enforcement agency for all Corps-issued permits and for unpermitted discharge violations that are not forwarded to EPA; and (2) that EPA will be the lead (a) on all unpermitted discharge violations involving repeat and flagrant violators, and (b) where EPA requests lead-agency status for a particular case or where the Corps recommends that the EPA take the lead on an action.

B. CIVIL ENFORCEMENT

In accordance with the Corps's and EPA's shared responsibility for implementing section 404, both agencies may refer violations of section 404 to the U.S. Department of Justice for filing of a civil enforcement action. Although judicial actions to enforce section 404 have many commonalities with actions to enforce other violations of the CWA, this subsection will focus on differences that arise in the section 404 context.

1. Affirmative Defenses

a. Statute of Limitations. The statute of limitations for 404 violations is the same as for any other CWA violation, but one issue that is unique to 404 violations is when the limitations period begins to run. Defendants will typically argue that the limitations period begins when the illegal discharge of dredged or fill material

---

138. 33 C.F.R. § 326.3(c).
139. 33 C.F.R. § 326.3(e).

occurred, but the government has met with some success in arguing that when the illegal discharge has been left in place, there is a continuing violation.[140] Citizen suit plaintiffs have attempted to use a similar theory to avoid arguments that wetlands violations are wholly past.[141]

b. Section 404(f) Exemptions. One category of affirmative defenses that is unique to section 404 enforcement actions is found in section 404(f), which provides that the discharge of dredged and fill material in connection with certain activities is exempt from permitting requirements.[142] These activities include: normal farming, silviculture, and ranching activities; maintenance of structures such as dikes, dams, levees, breakwaters, and transportation structures; construction or maintenance of farm or stock ponds or irrigation ditches, or maintenance of drainage ditches; construction of temporary sedimentation basins on construction sites; construction or maintenance of farm or forest roads using best management practices; or certain areawide waste treatment programs.[143]

However, the exemption from regulation for these types of activities is subject to a significant qualifying provision in section 404(f)(2), known as the "recapture provision," which states that:

> Any discharge of dredged or fill material into the navigable waters incidental to any activity having as its purpose bringing an area of the navigable waters into a use to which it was not previously subject, where the flow or circulation of navigable waters may be impaired or the reach of such waters be reduced, shall be required to have a permit under [section 404].[144]

Thus, for example, courts have held that converting from silviculture to soybean production and even from wetlands farming to dryland farming can subject the activities in question to recapture under section 404(f)(2), particularly if it involves hydrological alterations, such as loss of wetlands.[145]

In keeping with the broad remedial purposes of the CWA, the section 404(f) exemptions are to be construed narrowly and the burden of proving that an activity

---

140. *See, e.g.,* United States v. Hallmark Construction Co., 14 F. Supp. 2d 1069 (N.D. Ill. 1998).

141. Informed Citizens United, Inc. v. USX Corp., 36 F. Supp. 2d 375 (S.D. Tex. 1999); North Carolina Wildlife Ass'n v. Woodbury, 29 ERC [BNA] 1941 (E.D.N.C. 1989).

142. 33 U.S.C. § 1344(f).

143. *Id.*

144. 33 U.S.C. § 1344(f)(2).

145. Borden Ranch Partnership v. United States Army Corps of Engineers, 261 F.3d 810 (9th Cir. 2001), *aff'd per curiam,* 123 S. Ct. 599 (2002). ; United States v. Brace, 41 F.3d 117 (3d Cir. 1994); United States v. Akers, 785 F.2d 814 (9th Cir. 1985); United States v. Huebner, 752 F.2d 1235, 1240 (7th Cir. 1985); Avoyelles Sportsmen's League v. Marsh, 715 F.2d 897 (5th Cir. 1983).

is exempt falls on the party claiming the exemption.[146] The exemption for normal farming activities in section 404(f)(1) has been very narrowly construed to apply only in areas that were part of an established, ongoing farming operation at the time of the filling in question.[147]

c. Nationwide Permits. Possession of a nationwide permit is also an affirmative defense to an enforcement action, the burden of proof for which falls on the defendant.[148]

2. Remedies

a. Injunctive Relief. In addition to the negative injunction often ordered in CWA, courts in 404 cases will typically order restoration of the waters in question,[149] or where that is not possible, mitigation or the creation of new wetlands to replace those lost.[150] Related injunctive relief includes orders requiring the removal of fill material, breaching of levees, and filling in of ditches that served to drain wetlands.[151] Sometimes courts will give defendants the option of reducing penalties by undertaking restoration.[152] In evaluating proposed restoration plans, courts will consider whether the plan will: confer maximum environmental benefits; be achievable as a practical matter; and bear an equitable relationship to the degree and kind of the wrong it is intended to remedy.[153]

b. Civil Penalties. Calculation of civil penalties in the 404 context is in most respects no different from calculation of civil penalties for any other CWA vio-

---

146. United States v. Brace, 41 F.3d 117 (3d Cir. 1994); United States v. Akers, 785 F.2d 814 (9th Cir. 1985); United States v. Huebner, 752 F.2d 1235, 1240 (7th Cir. 1985); Avoyelles Sportsmen's League v. Marsh, 715 F.2d 897 (5th Cir. 1983).

147. *See* United States v. Larkins, 852 F.2d 189 (6th Cir. 1988); United States v. Akers, 785 F.2d 814 (9th Cir.); United States v. Huebner, 752 F.2d 1235 (7th Cir. 1985); United States v. Cumberland Farms of Conn., 647 F. Supp. 1166 (D. Mass. 1986), *aff'd*, 826 F.2d 1151 (1st Cir. 1987).

148. United States v. Cumberland Farms of Connecticut, 826 F.2d 1151, 1157 (1st Cir. 1987).

149. *See, e.g.,* United States v. Parks Banks, 115 F.3d 916 (11th Cir. 1997); United States v. Cumberland Farms of Connecticut, 826 F.2d 1151, 1164 (1st Cir. 1987); United States v. Van Leuzen, 816 F. Supp. 1171 (S.D. Tex. 1993); United States v. Edwards, 667 F. Supp. 1204 (W.D. Tenn. 1987); United States v. Ciampitti, 615 F. Supp. 116 (D.N.J. 1984).

150. *See, e.g.,* Borden Ranch Partnership v. United States Army Corps of Engineers, 261 F.3d 810 (9th Cir. 2001), *aff'd per curium*, 123 S. Ct. 599 (2002).

151. *See, e.g.,* United States v. Larkins, 657 F. Supp. 76 (W.D. Ky. 1987), *aff'd* 852 F.2d 189 (6th Cir. 1988).

152. *See, e.g.,* Borden Ranch Partnership v. United States Army Corps of Engineers, 261 F.3d 810 (9th Cir. 2001), *aff'd per curium*, 123 S. Ct. 599 (2002).; United States v. Cumberland Farms of Connecticut, 826 F.2d 1151, 1164 (1st Cir. 1987).

153. United States v. Cumberland Farms of Connecticut, 647 F. Supp. 1166 (D. Mass. 1986), *aff'd*, 826 F.2d 1151 (1st Cir. 1987).

lation. One issue that is unique to the 404 context is how to count the number of days of violation for illegal dredged or fill material that has been left in place. Some courts have held that each day that the dredged or fill material is left in place counts as a separate day of violation for purposes of calculating the maximum penalty, while others have rejected what is known as the "continuing violation" theory.[154] Although the courts have been equivocal on this issue, defendants in 404 cases should assume that the government will rely on a continuing violation theory in calculating the maximum penalty in any case.

Defendants should also assume that the government will insist that a consent decree to resolve violations contain a provision requiring them to pay stipulated penalties—typically a certain sum per day—in the event of violation or nonperformance of the decree's terms. Stipulated penalties can be substantial and even dwarf the civil penalty originally agreed to in the decree.[155]

3. Preenforcement Review

The courts have generally held that they do not have jurisdiction over challenges to EPA administrative orders, Corps cease-and-desist orders, and wetlands determinations until a judicial enforcement action is brought.[156]

VI. The Takings Issue

The Fifth Amendment to the Constitution states that "No person shall . . . be deprived of . . . property without due process of law, nor shall private property be taken for public use, without just compensation." The Supreme Court and lower courts have established a body of law used to determine when government actions affecting private property amount to a "taking" of that property by the government. When private property is "taken" by the government, the property owner must be fairly compensated.

Initially, the courts recognized takings claims based on government actions that resulted in a physical seizure or occupation of private property. The courts subsequently ruled that, in certain limited circumstances, government regulation affecting private property also may amount to a taking.

---

154. United States v. Cumberland Farms of Connecticut, 647 F. Supp. 1166 (D. Mass. 1986) (accepting continuing violation theory), *aff'd,* 826 F.2d 1151 (1st Cir. 1987); Borden Ranch Partnership v. United States Army Corps of Engineers, 1999 U.S. Dist LEXIS 21389 (E.D. Cal. 1999) (rejecting continuing violation theory), *aff'd,* 261 F.3d 810 (9th Cir. 2001), *aff'd per curium,* 123 S. Ct. 599 (2002).

155. *See, e.g.,* United States v. Krilich, 126 F.3d 1035 (7th Cir. 1997).

156. Rueth v. EPA, 13 F.3d 227 (7th Cir. 1993) (compliance order); Howell v. Army Corps of Engineers, 794 F. Supp. 1072 (D. N.M. 1992); Leslie Salt Co. v. United States, 789 F. Supp. 1030 (N.D. Cal. 1991) (cease and desist order); Mulberry Hills Development Corp. v. United States, 772 F. Supp. 1553 (D. Md. 1991) (same).

Wetlands regulation has been subject to takings challenges similar to other land use, regulatory, and planning programs. If the Corps denies a section 404 permit application, the applicant may either challenge the permit denial in federal district court or show that the denial of the section 404 permit constituted a taking of private property under the Fifth Amendment to the Constitution for which the federal government must compensate the landowner. This type of taking is also known as "inverse condemnation."

There is a strong presumption of constitutionality of government environmental regulation. The factors considered by courts in determining whether a "taking" has occurred have been construed differently within the court system, but usually include some combination of the following:

1.   whether there was a denial of economically viable use of the property as a result of the regulatory imposition;

2.   whether the property owner had distinct investment-backed expectations; and

3.   whether it was an interest vested in the owner, as a matter of state property law, and not within the power of the state to regulate under common law nuisance doctrine.

The Federal Circuit has held that if the analysis of the first prong concludes that a regulatory action "categorically" prohibits all economically viable use of the land at issue, then the only remaining issue is under the third prong, whether regulation would be permitted under common law nuisance doctrine. Therefore, in the first instance, the analysis depends upon whether there has been a total or partial deprivation of economically viable use.[157]

Executive Order 12630 requires federal agencies to consider the takings implications of their activities, unless exempt. The CWA section 404 permit program is included under the order. The attorney general has issued guidelines to implement the order in the *Federal Register*.[158]

The *Penn Central Co. v. New York City* case was the first to consider investment-backed expectations as a significant factor in determining whether a regulatory action has taken private property in violation of the Fifth Amendment of the Constitution.[159] However, this concept has been deemed so poorly defined that even today there lacks clarity among the courts as to how it should be interpreted.

The landmark 6-to-3 Supreme Court opinion in *Lucas v. South Carolina Coastal Council*, authored by Justice Scalia, was the next Supreme Court case to

---

157. Florida Rock Industries. v. United States, 18 F.3d 1560 (Fed. Cir. 1994).
158. 53 Fed. Reg. 8859 (March 15, 1988).
159. 438 U.S. 104 (1978).

have a significant impact on regulatory takings law. In this case, the Supreme Court held that a regulation denying a property owner all economically viable use of his land requires compensation under the "takings" clause of the Fifth and Fourteenth amendments to the Constitution.[160] In the past, courts have found no taking to have occurred when the underlying state law is designed to further a valid public purpose. The Supreme Court reversed and remanded a ruling by the South Carolina supreme court that the state's 1988 Beachfront Management Act was a legitimate exercise of the state's police power that did not require compensation, despite the fact that the property owner was unable to develop valuable beachfront property.[161]

The action began in 1986 when the petitioner, Lucas, purchased two beachfront lots for development. In 1988, the South Carolina legislature passed the Beachfront Management Act, a statute designed to preserve the state's beaches by expanding the "critical area" where development could not occur. Lucas was awarded a $1.2-million judgment by the trial court. The state supreme court reversed, holding that it was bound by the legislature's findings that the law was necessary to prevent serious public harm and to further other public purposes such as aesthetics and tourism.

In reversing the state supreme court, the Supreme Court placed heavy emphasis on the economic loss. It found that where a regulation denies a property owner all economically viable use of his or her land, there is a presumption that a compensable taking has occurred. The legislature's mere declaration that the state law was intended to confer a public benefit and to prevent harm was not sufficient to defeat a takings claim where total deprivation of all economically viable use had occurred. The Court further clarified, however, that a regulation is not a taking if it is consistent with restrictions that background principles of the state's law of property and nuisance already placed upon ownership. As an example, the Court referred to the right of government to prevent flooding of others' property.[162]

The *Lucas* case has fostered a vast array of interpretations from the lower courts, ones that oftentimes do not seem consistent with one another. Some lower courts interpreted *Lucas* as clarifying that newly enacted regulations may restrict the use of property, but not eliminate it altogether, without compensation. Yet other courts have interpreted *Lucas* as requiring an analysis of whether there was an investment-backed expectation. For example, some decisions simply adopt the *Lucas* inquiry into "background principles of state law" and apply it as a proxy for *Penn Central's* investment-backed expectations standard. There are also a

---

160. 505 U.S. 1003, 112 S. Ct. 2886 (1992).

161. *Id.*

162. *Id.*

number of cases that find *Lucas* to require that the denial of all economic use is a taking only so long as such a denial also extinguishes the owner's reasonable expectations.[163]

A 1993 case worth noting is *Tabb Lakes v. United States*.[164] This case dealt with both the issue of "temporary takings" and the question of whether takings jurisprudence allows the division of a single parcel into discrete segments to determine whether rights in a particular segment have been abrogated. The case involved a property that was divided up into five subdivisions, three of which were wetlands. The Corps issued a cease-and-desist order from filling the wetlands until the property owners obtained a permit under section 404 of the Clean Water Act. This cease-and-desist order lasted for about three years, until it was finally adjudicated that the Corps lacked jurisdiction over these particular wetlands. Following the litigation, Tabb Lakes proceeded to fill the wetlands and develop all of its property as originally planned. All the subdivisions were eventually sold. Tabb Lakes then filed a complaint in the court of federal claims, alleging a "temporary taking" had occurred from the date of the cease-and-desist order till it was finally quashed three years later. The trial court granted a motion of summary judgment for the government, finding no taking had occurred.

The federal circuit court first disclaimed any discrepancy between a "temporary" versus a "permanent" taking. The court found the relevant takings analysis to be the same. The court then held that "a taking by regulatory action is recognized only if it goes 'too far.' "[165] The court then opined that the *Lucas* precedent supported the argument that the government interference in this case did not go "too far." The court stated that "the cease and desist order, while stopping the filling of wetlands, specifically left the door open to development by obtaining a permit."[166] Utilizing *Riverside* as support, the court stated that the "mere assertion of regulatory jurisdiction by a governmental body does not constitute a regulatory taking."[167]

The court then tackled the issue of whether a takings analysis should assess the "parcel as a whole" for economic loss, or rather those subdivisions that were burdened by the governmental regulation.[168] Relying on *Penn Central Transportation Co. v. New York City*, the court in *Tabb Lakes* declared that the "quantum of land to be considered is not each individual lot containing wetlands or even the combined area of wetlands. . . . If that were true, the Corps' protection of wetlands via a permit system would, ipso factor, constitute a taking in every

---

163. *See Great Expectations: Will* Palazzolo v. Rhode Island *Clarify the Murky Doctrine of Investment-Backed Expectations in Regulatory Takings Law?* 9 N.Y.U. Env'tl. L.J. 449 (2001).

164. 10 F.3d 796 (Fed. Cir. 1993).

165. *Id.* at 800 (citing Lucas v. South Carolina Coastal Council, 112 S. Ct. 2886, 2893 (1992)).

166. *Id.* at 801.

167. *Id.*

168. *Id.* at 802.

case where it exercises its statutory authority."[169] However, because the court previously found that the cease-and-desist order did not amount to a taking, it did not need to apply that analysis in this case.

In *Florida Rock Industries v. United States*, the Federal Circuit vacated an award of just compensation, holding that the lower court had incorrectly found that there was only a nominal residual value in wetlands that the owner was not permitted to mine.[170] The court noted that the question of when a regulatory taking occurs "cannot be answered as a matter of absolute doctrine, but instead requires case-by-case adjudication," including a balancing of landowner's rights and the government's right to regulate.[171] On remand, the lower court held that the 1980 wetlands permit denial was a partial regulatory taking compensable under the Fifth Amendment and awarded $752,444, plus interest, as a result of the claimant's not being able to mine the limestone on the property purchased. The court held that the denial of the section 404 permit frustrated the company's reasonable investment-backed expectations that it would be able to extract limestone from 98 acres of its own land.[172]

Three months after the decision in *Florida Industries*, the case of *Loveladies Harbor v. United States* came before the U.S. Court of Claims. This case involved a 12.5-acre parcel of land, 11.5 acres of which were wetlands. The 12.5 acres were part of a larger 51-acre parcel owned by Loveladies, which in turn was part of an original 250-acre tract that Loveladies had acquired in 1958. The balance of the 250 acres, 199 acres, had been developed before 1972 and before the enactment of section 404 of the Clean Water Act. The New Jersey Department for Environmental Protection (NJDEP), after lengthy negotiations, issued a permit for development of 12.5 acres of the 51-acre parcel. Loveladies applied for a section 404 permit from the Corps and was denied. The lower court held in favor of Loveladies and the government appealed.[173]

The federal circuit replaced the traditional balancing of interests with an analysis of whether, as a matter of state property law, the interest alleged to have been taken is vested in the owner or within the power of the state to regulate under common law nuisance doctrine. The court affirmed the award of just compensation, finding that the evidence before the lower court supported its determination that the landowner had been deprived of all economically viable uses of the property, and that the state nuisance law would not prevent the desired

---

169. *Id.*
170. 18 F.3d 1560 (Fed. Cir. 1994).
171. *Id.* at 1570, 1571.
172. 45 Fed. Cl. 21 (1999).
173. 28 F.3d 1171 (Fed. Cir. 1994).

construction in the wetlands.[174] In deciding the issue, the court declined to consider the entire 250-acre parcel originally purchased since it determined that it would be manifestly unfair to include within the takings analysis the land that has been developed or sold before the enactment of section 404.[175]

Interestingly, several recent cases have shown some courts' unwillingness to find a regulatory taking. In *Good v. United States*,[176] the property owner sought to develop property containing wetlands, and the court concluded that the property owner's expectations that he would be able to develop the property were not reasonable in light of wetlands protection constraints and Endangered Species Act concerns. *Good* may therefore stand for the proposition that if a property owner is aware of restrictive regulations prior to purchase and during investment in the property, there is no reasonable investment-based expectation and therefore no compensable taking. In *Forest Properties v. United States*, the court found that the permit denial did not significantly interfere with investment-backed expectations, in part because the property owner still was able to profitably develop a majority of the 62-acre property.[177] In *Broadwater Farms Joint Venture v. United States*, the court found no taking where the developer was precluded from developing 12 of 27 lots because the developer's investment-backed expectations were not reasonable where it had both constructive and actual knowledge of wetlands laws at the time it purchased the property.[178]

On the other hand, in *Palm Beach Isles Associates v. United States*,[179] the court found that a categorical taking occurred as a result of the Corps's refusal to grant a section 404 permit authorizing the fill of approximately 50 acres of shoreline wetlands and submerged land lying below the mean high-water mark in the bed of Lake Worth. The court then held that, in a categorical takings case, the property owner's reasonable expectations should not be part of a takings analysis. The court equated a categorical regulatory taking with a physical taking and noted that in "a physical takings context, the question is not why the owner acquired the property taken, but only did she own it at the time of the taking."[180] The court distinguished the *Good* case by citing that it did not involve a categorical taking. The court also noted that "ever since *Penn Central*, it has been understood that having reasonable investment-backed expectations is, generally speaking, a part of a successful claim of regulatory taking, claims that typically involve something less than a total wipeout. . . ."[181]

---

174. *Id.*
175. *Id.* at 1181.
176. 189 F.3d 1355 (Fed. Cir. 1999).
177. 177 F.3d 1360 (Fed. Cir. 1999).
178. 45 Fed. Cl. 154 (Ct. Cl. 1999).
179. 231 F.3d at 1357 (Fed. Cir. 2000).
180. *Id.*
181. *Id.* at 1360.

Recently, the Supreme Court attempted to offer additional guidance with respect to regulatory takings within the context of wetlands permits. The case *Palazzolo v. Rhode Island*[182] involved a tract of land containing, in part, salt marshes. The landowner, a sole shareholder of a corporation whose charter was revoked, was passed title upon the charter's revocation. Preceding this passing of title, the Resource Management Council of Rhode Island promulgated regulations designating salt marshes as protected coastal wetlands. The landowner applied for a permit to fill the property. His application was denied, and he filed a takings action, which was initially rejected in the lower courts. The Supreme Court affirmed in part and reversed in part.

The Court refuted the state court's holding that a postregulation acquisition of title was fatal to the claim for deprivation of all economic use because the landowner was constructively on notice. While conceding that the right to improve property is subject to the reasonable exercise of state authority (including zoning and land-use restrictions), the Court held that the Takings Clause of the Constitution allows a landowner to "to assert that a particular exercise of the State's regulatory power is so unreasonable or onerous to compel compensation."[183] To hold otherwise, the Court stated, would give carte blanche to the state with respect to even the most unreasonable land-use restrictions, so long as the title passed post-enactment. The Court held that, to adopt the state court's interpretation would effectively "put an expiration date on the Takings Clause."[184]

The court in *Palazzolo* failed to specifically set out the circumstances under which a legislative enactment would be deemed a background principle of state law, except to say that a law does not become a background principle for subsequent owners by enactment itself. It further suggested that only objective factors, such as the nature of the land use proscribed, should be taken into account. Finally, a background principles analysis should be made in terms of common understanding of permissible limitations derived from a state's legal tradition.

Interestingly, the court in *Palazzolo* did agree with the state court's conclusion that all economically beneficial use was not deprived because the uplands portion of the property could still be improved. Also, while the court expressed some discomfort with the logic of some of its prior cases indicating that the extent of deprivation effected by a regulatory action is measured against the value of the parcel as a whole, it declined to address the "parcel issue" because the landowner failed to raise it.[185]

---

182. 533 U.S. 606 (2001).

183. *Id.* at 613.

184. *Id.*

185. *Id.* at 616.

Ripeness is an issue that often comes up in wetlands takings cases. However, most courts have held that a takings claim is not ripe for review until the owners actually file for a section 404 permit.[186] Finally, in a case in which local zoning laws would have prohibited development even if the Corps had granted the section 404 permit, one court has held that there is no taking. In *City National Bank of Miami v. United States*, the court held that the mere fact that the federal government shares a common goal with states and localities is not sufficient to open the federal government to liability for the effects of state actions.[187]

VII. State Authority to Implement a Section 404 Permit Program

Under section 404(g) through (l) of the CWA, a state may apply to assume the section 404 program, except for waters that traditionally have been used for navigation by interstate and foreign commerce, over which the Corps retains jurisdiction.[188] EPA is given authority to approve any state application for assuming the program, and has issued very detailed guidelines for reviewing state program applications,[189] including allowing a state to have more stringent or extensive requirements than provided under the regulations.[190] However, only two states, Michigan and New Jersey, have taken over the section 404 program. EPA retains authority to review state-issued permits and may transfer permitting authority to the Corps if the state permit is not satisfactory to EPA.[191] In some cases, the Corps has used statewide programmatic general permits that provide for expedited joint federal/state processing of permit applications, giving primary authority to the state permitting agency and effectively delegating the 404 program to the states in question.

VIII. "No Net Loss" Policy

George Bush, Sr., during his administration, articulated a goal of "no net loss" of wetlands. To this end, he established an interagency task force under the Domestic Policy Council in order to study how this goal could be achieved. While this task force did author a comprehensive plan, it was not fully implemented by the

---

186. *Palazzolo*, 533 U.S. 606 (2001); Robbins v. United States, 46 ERC 1505 (Ct. Cl. 1998); Lakewood Associates v. United States, 45 Fed. Cl. 320 (Ct. Cl. 1999); Heck and Associates v. United States, 37 Fed. Cl. 245 (Ct. Cl. 1997). In *Cristina Investment Corp. v. United States*, a takings claim was denied based on a statute of limitations rationale. *See* 40 Fed. Cl. 571 (Ct. Cl. 1998).

187. 33 Fed. Cl. 759 (Ct. Cl. 1995).

188. 33 U.S.C. § 1344(g)–(l).

189. 40 C.F.R. pt. 233. A-4.

190. 40 C.F.R. § 233.1(c).

191. 40 C.F.R. § 233.50.

end of the Bush presidency. Bill Clinton affirmed his commitment to the "no net loss" policy when he took office in 1992, convening his own interagency working group to set forth the principles that would guide this policy. While wetlands degradation has slowed over the past ten years, it is widely accepted that the "no net loss" objective has not been met. The National Research Council issued a report on June 26, 2001, entitled *Compensating for Wetlands Losses Under the Clean Water Act*, which concluded that "mitigation" programs were not meeting the goal of "no net loss" for wetlands.[192] The report stated that the literature on compensatory mitigation suggests that required mitigation projects often are not undertaken or fail to meet permit conditions. Also, it determined that the performance expectations in the section 404 permitting program regarding mitigation have been unclear, and compliance has often not been assured. Finally, it argued that, even in cases where permit conditions were satisfied, required compensation actions were poorly designed or carelessly implemented. The Corps issued a regulatory guidance letter (01-1) on November 1, 2001, in response to the National Research Council report, pledging its continued support of the "no net loss" policy, as well as outlining new measures to achieve that goal.[193] It remains to be seen how the policy will be implemented in the future.

IX. Practical Suggestions for Addressing Section 404

The following suggestions are offered in the context of a section 404 proceeding:

1. As part of due diligence when acquiring property, include an assessment of the presence of wetlands and waters of the United States more generally on the property.
2. Hire experts who understand section 404.
3. Contact the relevant federal and state agencies early in the process, taking advantage of the Corps's preapplication consultation process. Also, in matters involving agricultural land, consult the Natural Resource Conservation Service to avoid problems such as loss of crop subsidies.
4. Ensure that your application package is complete and persuasive.
5. Deal positively with the agencies.
6. Develop a strong negotiating strategy that stresses the merits of the project and wetlands avoidance and mitigation efforts.
7. In the context of mitigation, if you are unable to find someone else to do mitigation for you (such as a mitigation bank), expect that you will have ongoing responsibilities, including compliance oversight.

---

192. Daily Env't Rep. (BNA), at A-4 (June 27, 2001).
193. Daily Env't Rep. (BNA), at A-2 (Dec. 10, 2001).

8. Carefully monitor construction activities post–permit issuance, to avoid violations.
9. Consider the effect of *SWANCC* on your project as well as any new state laws enacted in response to that decision.
10. Respond quickly and effectively if an enforcement action is initiated.

CHAPTER 7

Oil and Hazardous Substances Spills: Section 311

DAVID G. DICKMAN*

I. Introduction and Scope

Section 311 of the Clean Water Act (CWA) (as amended by the Oil Pollution Act of 1990)[1] governs prevention of, and response to, accidental releases and spills of oil and hazardous substances to waters of the United States. Section 311 complements section 402 of the CWA.[2] Section 402 regulates discharges of pollutants that are anticipated and relatively routine, and thus appropriately addressed through a permit program. Alternatively, the provisions of section 311 address discharges resulting from accidental releases and spills of a limited category of pollutants, which are oil and hazardous substances. Section 311 provides for spill prevention requirements, spill reporting obligations, and spill response planning and authorities. Regulatory implementation and enforcement of section 311 are the dual responsibility of the Coast Guard and the EPA. The Coast Guard is primarily responsible for regulation and enforcement related to vessels and marine transportation–related facilities[3] while the EPA is responsible for nontransportation-related facilities.[4]

---

* The author acknowledges the contributions of Karen Wardzinski to the 1994 edition of this chapter.
  1. 33 U.S.C. § 1321.
  2. 33 U.S.C. § 1342.
  3. A marine transportation–related facility includes a deepwater port.
  4. The president has delegated to the EPA the authority to regulate nontransportation-related onshore facilities under CWA, §§ 311(j)(1)(A) and (C) and 311(j)(5). The president delegated this authority to the Department of Transportation for transportation-related onshore facilities, deepwater ports, and vessels. Executive Order No. 12777 (56 Fed Reg. 54757-70 (Oct. 22, 1991)). A Memorandum of Understanding (MOU) between the Department of Transportation and the EPA establishes

A. THE COMPREHENSIVE ENVIRONMENTAL RESPONSE, COMPENSATION, AND LIABILITY ACT (CERCLA)

Section 311 addresses the discharge of oil *and hazardous* substances. The Comprehensive Environmental Response, Compensation, and Liability Act (CERCLA)[5] addresses releases of hazardous substances to all environmental media, including water. Thus, two federal environmental statutes come into play with respect to discharges of hazardous substances to waters of the United States. "Hazardous substances" as that term is defined by CERCLA is broader than the narrow category of hazardous substances covered by section 311.[6] Although CERCLA does not supersede section 311, releases of hazardous chemicals to the water are comprehensively addressed under the CERCLA. As a result, federal response and enforcement efforts under section 311 tend to focus primarily on discharges of oil to waters of the United States rather than on discharges of hazardous substances. The EPA can

---

the definitions of nontransportation-related facilities and transportation-related facilities. These definitions are reprinted at 40 C.F.R. part 112, Appendix A.

For purposes of determining the applicability of EPA or Coast Guard regulations, a nontransportation-related facility includes the nontransportation-related portion of a complex. A complex is a facility with a combination of transportation-related and nontransportation-related components. An example would be a marine transfer facility with aboveground storage tanks. *See, e.g.,* 33 C.F.R. § 154.1020 (defining "marine transportation-related facility" regulated by the Coast Guard for purposes of response planning to be that portion of a complex that extends from the facility oil transfer system's connection with the vessel to the first valve inside the secondary containment surrounding tanks in the nontransportation-related portion of the facility).

Further, it should also be noted that, on November 26, 2002, the president signed the Homeland Security Act of 2002 (H.R. 5005, 108th Cong.), which transfers the Coast Guard to the newly created Department of Homeland Security. Under section 888 of the act, the Coast Guard is maintained as a distinct entity within the new department, and the secretary of the new department is prohibited from substantially or significantly reducing the missions of the Coast Guard or the Coast Guard's ability to perform those missions, including environmental protection. Therefore, while the Coast Guard will remain responsible for regulation and enforcement under section 311 for marine transportation–related facilities and vessels, the Executive Orders and Memoranda of Understanding that currently delineate responsibilities under section 311 between the EPA and the Department of Transportation will likely require amendment in light of the transfer of the Coast Guard out of the Department of Transportation.

5. 42 U.S.C. § 9601 *et seq.*

6. *See Id.* § 9601(14). Under this section, the term "hazardous substance" is defined for purposes of CERCLA to include any "hazardous substance" designated under section 311 of the CWA as well as any CERCLA–designated substance, any RCRA hazardous waste, any CWA toxic pollutant, any hazardous air pollutant, and any imminently hazardous chemical substance under the Toxic Substances Control Act. Petroleum oil is specifically excluded from the definition of "hazardous substance" under CERCLA as is natural gas and liquefied natural gas (LNG).

nevertheless assess penalties for spills of hazardous substances to waters of the United States. (See section VI below.)

B. THE OIL POLLUTION ACT (OPA)

In reaction to the Exxon Valdez oil spill and the inadequacy of existing controls to prevent or minimize the damage it caused, Congress enacted the Oil Pollution Act of 1990 (OPA).[7] The OPA was enacted to expand prevention and preparedness requirements for oil spills, improve response capabilities, increase the limits of liability for discharges of oil, and establish expanded research and development funds. The OPA also established a new Oil Spill Liability Trust Fund (OSTLF). Subtitles B and C of Title IV of the OPA extensively amended section 311. For purposes of this book, discussion of the OPA is limited to those provisions that directly affect section 311.

C. DEFINITIONS

"Discharge" is defined broadly in section 311 to include any spilling, leaking, pumping, pouring, emitting, emptying, or dumping of oil or hazardous substances.[8] "Oil" also is defined broadly in section 311 to include oil of any kind including petroleum, fuel oil, oil refuse, sludge, and oil mixed with wastes other than dredged spoil.[12] This definition is not limited to petroleum products and thus encompasses oils such as mineral or vegetable oils. Oil for purposes of discharge liability under the OPA is defined to exclude any kind of oil that is considered a hazardous substance subject to the CERCLA.[9]

The EPA identifies "hazardous substances" by specific listings in implementing regulations. To date, the EPA has designated approximately 300 chemicals as hazardous substances.[10]

D. THE GENERAL DISCHARGE PROHIBITION IN CWA SECTION 311

Section 311 prohibits the discharge of oil or hazardous substances into or upon designated waters of the United States and adjoining shorelines in such quantities as are determined by EPA to be harmful.[11]

---

7. Pub. L. No. 101–380 (Aug. 18, 1990) (hereinafter OPA).

8. 33 U.S.C. § 1321(a)(2).

9. 33 U.S.C. § 2704.

10. Hazardous substances for purposes of section 311 are listed at 40 C.F.R. part 116.

11. 33 U.S.C. § 1321(b)(3).

The "designated waters" to which this prohibition applies include navigable waters of the United States (including the territorial seas) and adjoining shorelines and the contiguous zone. The general prohibition in section 311 also applies to waters beyond the contiguous zone that contain or support natural resources under the exclusive management of the United States (the Exclusive Economic Zone (EEZ)) or where the discharge results from activities regulated by the Outer Continental Shelf Lands Act or the Deepwater Ports Act of 1974.[12]

The EPA has determined that a "harmful quantity" of oil is an amount that, when discharged, violates applicable water quality standards, or causes a film or sheen upon or discoloration of the surface of the water or adjoining shorelines, or causes a sludge or emulsion to be deposited beneath the surface of the water or on the adjoining shoreline.[13]

The discharge of a hazardous substance is determined to be "harmful" if the amount meets or exceeds the designated "reportable quantity" for the substance as determined by the EPA. Reportable quantities range from 1 to 5,000 pounds discharged, depending on factors such as the toxicity of the substance.[14]

E. EXEMPTIONS FROM THE GENERAL DISCHARGE PROHIBITION OF SECTION 311

Over the years there had been much confusion about the relationship between discharges requiring a National Pollutant Discharge Elimination System (NPDES) permit under section 402 of the CWA and discharges prohibited under section 311. In 1978 Congress amended section 311 to clarify this issue and to ensure that section 311 will be applied primarily to "classic spill" situations. Section 311 now provides that the following discharges are *not* prohibited:

1. Discharges in compliance with an NPDES permit, where the discharge is subject to a pollutant-specific effluent limitation or a limitation on an indicator parameter intended to address the pollutant in question;
2. Discharges identified in the NPDES permit process, made a part of the public record, and subject to a condition in the permit; and

---

12. *Id.*

13. 40 C.F.R. § 110.3. The sheen test was challenged in Orgulf Transp. Co. v. United States, 711 F. Supp. 344 (W.D. Ky. 1989). The *Orgulf* court held that the EPA regulation determining that the discharge of oil, which creates a sheen on the water, "may be harmful" within the meaning of section 311 of the CWA is valid, though most spills, even if de minimis, will cause a sheen.

14. Reportable quantities of hazardous substances are established by EPA regulation at 40 C.F.R. part 117.

3. Continuous or anticipated intermittent discharges from a point source, identified in a permit or permit application, that are caused by events occurring within the scope of relevant operating or treatment systems.[15]

The latter two exemptions apply to discharges of hazardous substances regardless of whether the discharge is in compliance with the permit.[16]

Discharges of hazardous substances from industrial facilities to publicly owned treatment works (POTW) are not subject to regulation under section 311. However, section 311 does apply to discharges of hazardous substances to a POTW from a mobile source, such as a truck, unless the discharger has authorization from the POTW to discharge and the discharge is pretreated to comply with CWA requirements.[17]

Discharges of oil from vessels into the contiguous zone or that may affect natural resources under the exclusive management of the United States that comply with the International Convention for the Prevention of Pollution from Ships (MARPOL 73/78)[18] are excluded from the prohibition in section 311.[19] Section 311 also exempts discharges in quantities and at times and locations or under circumstances and conditions deemed not to be harmful by regulation.[20]

---

15. 33 U.S.C. § 1321(a)(2).

16. 40 C.F.R. §§ 117.12(c) and (d).

17. *Id.*

18. International Convention for the Prevention of Pollution From Ships, Nov. 2, 1973, 12 I.L.M. 1319, *as amended by* Protocol, *adopted* Feb. 17, 1978, 17 I.L.M. 546 (MARPOL 73/78). The 1973 Convention was never ratified by the United States or by the required number of states to allow it to come into force by itself. *See* H.R. Rep. No. 96-1224 (1980), reprinted in 1980 U.S.C.C.A.N. 4849, 4850. The original Convention was modified and incorporated into the 1978 Protocol, which was adopted on February 17, 1978, and ratified by the U.S. Senate on July 2, 1980. *See id.* The provisions of the Convention were enacted in the United States through the Act to Prevent Pollution from Ships, Pub. L. No. 96-478, 1980 U.S.C.C.A.N. (96 Stat.) 2297 (*codified at* 33 U.S.C. §§ 1901 *et seq.*).

19. 33 U.S.C. § 1321(b)(3). *See also* 40 C.F.R. § 110.5(b). Operational discharges of oil from ships at sea are regulated under Annex I of MARPOL 73/78. Unlike oil under section 311, oil for purposes of Annex I of MARPOL 73/78 is limited to petroleum oils. Discharges of some other non-petroleum oils from ships that are considered oil for purposes of section 311 are regulated under Annex II of MARPOL 73/78 as "noxious liquid substances." MARPOL 73/78 and APPS establish operational, monitoring, and record-keeping requirements for the discharges of both oil and noxious liquid substances that must be complied with before such discharges would be exempted from coverage under section 311.

20. 33 U.S.C. § 1321(b)(3).

In this regard, the EPA has exempted certain discharges, including discharges of oil from properly functioning vessel engines and discharges of oil accumulated in the bilge of a vessel that comply with the requirements of MARPOL 73/78.[21]

F. SPILL NOTIFICATION REQUIREMENT

The person in charge of the vessel or facility discharging harmful quantities of oil or a hazardous substance in violation of the discharge prohibition in section 311 must report the discharge to the appropriate federal agency as soon as that person has knowledge of the discharge.[22] The United States has established a National Response Center (NRC), run by the Coast Guard, to receive such reports and determine the response action, if any, that is necessary.[23] In turn, the NRC is required to notify the affected state.[24] Reports filed with the NRC cannot be used as the basis for any criminal action against the person reporting, except in a prosecution for giving false statements or for perjury.[25]

II. Spill Prevention

Section 311 mandates that the President issue regulations establishing procedures, methods, equipment, and other requirements to prevent discharges of oil and hazardous substances from vessels and facilities and to contain such discharges.[26] By Executive Order, the President delegated authority to the EPA to regulate non-transportation-related onshore facilities,[27] and has delegated to the Department of

---

21. 40 C.F.R. § 110.5(a).

22. 33 U.S.C. § 1321(b)(5). *See also* 40 C.F.R. § 110.6 (EPA regulations regarding notification); 33 C.F.R. § 153.203 (Coast Guard regulations regarding notification). In addition to the CWA notification requirements, the release of a hazardous substance identified under section 101 of CERCLA to any environmental medium, including water, in an amount at or greater than the reportable quantity for the substance during a 24-hour period, must also reported immediately. 42 U.S.C. § 9603.

23. The NRC telephone number to report discharges of oil and hazardous substances (as well as terrorist actions) is 1-800-424-8802.

24. 33 U.S.C. § 1321(b)(5).

25. *Id.*

26. *Id.* § 1321(j)(1)(C).

27. Executive Order No. 12777 (56 Fed. Reg. 54757-70 (Oct. 22, 1991)), § 2(b)(1).

Transportation the authority to regulate tank vessels, transportation-related facilities and offshore facilities.[28]

A. SPCC PLANS: NONTRANSPORTATION-RELATED FACILITIES[29]

For nontransportation-related facilities, the EPA in 1973 promulgated regulations requiring facilities[30] that drill, produce, gather, store, process, refine, transfer, distribute, or consume oil to have a fully prepared and implemented Spill Prevention, Control, and Countermeasures (SPCC) Plan.[31] The regulation applies to nontransportation-related facilities that:

1. Have an aggregate aboveground oil storage capacity of greater than 1,320 gallons, or greater than 660 gallons capacity in a single aboveground

---

28. *Id.* § 2(b)(2).

29. The EPA issued a final rule on July 17, 2002, significantly amending the SPCC requirements. 67 Fed. Reg. 47041–47152. This final rule was effective on August 16, 2002. The final rule called for a two-part phase-in of the revised SPCC planning requirements. If the facility was in operation on or before August 16, 2002, the final rule requires that the SPCC plan be amended to comply with the new regulatory requirements on or before February 17, 2003, and that the amended plan be implemented not later than August 18, 2003. Facilities subject to the regulations that become operational between August 16, 2002, and August 18, 2003, must prepare and implement a SPCC plan compliant with the new regulations before August 18, 2003. *Id.* at 47143 (to be codified at 40 C.F.R. § 112.3(a)).

However, the deadlines in the regulations have been the subject of significant comment by various industry groups. As a consequence, the EPA has indicated that it will propose a temporary suspension of the deadline for submission and implementation of the revised plans. Further, some industry groups have filed suit, seeking either to limit the scope of the revised regulations or challenging the administrative rulemaking process followed by the EPA. Therefore, in light of the uncertainty regarding the implementation of the revised regulations, the text reflects the preexisting regulations. The changes in the July 17, 2002, final rule are discussed in the applicable footnotes.

30. The July 17, 2002, final rule defines the term "facility," which had not been defined in the pre-existing regulations. A facility is defined as "any mobile or fixed, onshore or offshore building, structure, installation, equipment, pipe, or pipeline (other than a vessel or public vessel) used in oil well drilling operations, oil production, oil distribution, and waste treatment, or in which oil is used. . . ." 67 Fed. Reg. 47142 (to be codified at 40 C.F.R. § 112.2). Inclusion of equipment in the definition means that facilities must take into account the oil containment capacity of equipment in determining their facility's oil storage capacity and the applicability of the SPCC regulations.

31. 40 C.F.R. § 112.1(b). This section has been revised in the July 17, 2002, final rule to make owners or operators of facilities that use oil, such as electrical substations and facilities containing electrical transformers, subject to the applicability of the SPCC regulations if they meet the requisite criteria. 67 Fed. Reg. 47142.

container, or an aggregate underground oil storage capacity greater than 42,000 gallons,[32] and;

2.   Could reasonably be expected to discharge oil in harmful quantities into navigable waters of the United States.[33]

An SPCC Plan must contain the following information in the enumerated sequence:[34]

1.   For a facility that had experienced one or more spills within the past year, a written description of each spill, the corrective action taken, and plans for preventing recurrence;

---

32. 40 C.F.R. § 112.1(d)(2). This section has been revised in the July 17, 2002, final rule to raise the threshold for aboveground storage capacity by eliminating the requirement to prepare and implement a SPCC plan if any single container has a capacity greater than 660 gallons. 67 Fed. Reg. 47140.

Additionally, the final rule further limits the potential applicability of the regulations by providing new exemptions in calculating the capacity of both underground and aboveground storage tanks. In calculating a facility's underground tank storage capacity, the final rule excludes completely buried tanks that are subject to the EPA's (40 C.F.R. part 280) or an approved state's (40 C.F.R. part 281) underground storage tank (UST) regulations. *Id.* (to be codified at 40 C.F.R. § 112.1(d)(2)(i)). In calculating the aboveground storage capacity, the final rule provides that only containers with a capacity of 55 gallons or greater be counted and also states that permanently closed containers need not be counted. *Id.* (to be codified at 40 C.F.R. § 112.1(d)(2)(ii)).

Finally, the final rule provides other exemptions not in the preexisting regulations. There is an exemption provided for facilities or parts thereof that are used exclusively for wastewater treatment. *Id.* at 47141 (to be codified at 40 C.F.R. § 112.1(d)(6)). There is also an exemption provided for off-shore oil drilling, production, or workover facilities that are subject to the notices and regulations of the U.S. Minerals Management Service (MMS). *Id.* (to be codified at 40 C.F.R. § 112.1(d)(3)).

33. 40 C.F.R. § 112.1(b). The July 17, 2002, final rule expands the applicability of the SPCC regulations to also cover facilities that may discharge harmful quantities of oil "into or upon waters of the contiguous zone, or in connection with activities under the Outer Continental Shelf Lands Act or Deepwater Port Act, or affecting natural resources belonging to, appertaining to, or under exclusive management authority of the United States (including resources under the Magnuson Fishery Conservation and Management Act. . . ." 67 Fed. Reg. 47140 (amending 40 C.F.R. § 112.1(b)).

In addition to the specific criteria enumerated to determine which facilities must prepare and submit a SPCC plan, the final rule added a provision that authorizes EPA Regional Administrators to require, on a case-by-case basis, that a facility subject to the jurisdiction of the EPA under section 311(j) of the Clean Water Act prepare and implement a SPCC plan, even if the facility is otherwise exempt from the SPCC requirements. *Id.* at 47141 (to be codified at 40 C.F.R. § 112.1(f).

34. The July 17, 2002, final rule allows differing formats for the SPCC plan other than the one format specified in the pre-existing rule. The final rule also allows the use of other formats such as state plans, Integrated Contingency Plans, and other formats acceptable to the EPA Regional Administrator. If another format is used, there must be a cross-reference in the plan to the requirements listed in the SPCC rule. Also, if another format is used, the plan must still include all applicable SPCC requirements, either in the plan or a supplement. 67 Fed. Reg. 47145 (amending 40 C.F.R. § 112.7).

2. A prediction of the direction, rate of flow, and total quantity of oil that could be discharged where experience indicates a potential for equipment failure;

3. A description of containment and/or diversionary structures or equipment to prevent discharged oil from reaching navigable waters;

4. When it is determined that containment and/or diversionary structures are not practicable, a demonstration of the impracticability accompanied by a practical oil spill contingency plan and a written commitment of manpower, equipment, and materials to quickly control and remove spilled oil; and

5. A complete discussion of the spill prevention and control measures applicable in the regulations to the type of facility and/or its operations.[35]

Each plan must be reviewed and certified by a professional engineer.[36] For facilities that newly meet the criteria for submission of the SPCC Plan, the plan must be submitted within six months after the facility becomes operational, and

---

35. 40 C.F.R. § 112.7. The July 17, 2002, final rule has substantially revised the substantive requirements for the preparation and implementation of the SPCC plan. Among other things, the final rule:

1. Removes the requirement to describe each spill during the past 12-month period, requiring instead a discussion of the facility's conformance with the SPCC rules. 67 Fed. Reg. 47145 (to be codified at 40 C.F.R. § 112.7(a)(1)).

2. Adds a provision explicitly allowing deviations from most of the rule's substantive requirements (except secondary containment requirements) provided that the reasons for the nonconformance are explained and an equivalent environmental protection is provided through an alternate measure. *Id.* (to be codified at 40 C.F.R. § 112.7(a)(2)).

3. Adds a requirement to describe the physical layout of the facility, including a facility diagram. *Id.* (to be codified at 40 C.F.R. § 112.7(a)(3)).

4. Adds a requirement for facilities on which it is not practicable to install secondary containment equipment, in addition to providing a strong oil spill contingency plan and a written commitment to provide adequate response manpower and materials as was required under the preexisting rule, to perform periodic integrity testing of containers and periodic leak-testing of valves and piping. *Id.* at 47146 (to be codified at 40 C.F.R. § 112.7(d)).

In addition, the requirements in the pre-existing 40 C.F.R. § 112.7 have been substantially reorganized in the July 17, 2002, final rule into new sections 112.7 through 112.15 based on the type of facility and the type of oil stored.

36. 40 C.F.R. § 112.3(d). The July 17, 2002, final rule adds specificity to the Professional Engineer's certification by requiring that the PE consider applicable industry standards and certify that the Plan has been prepared in accordance with the requirements of 40 C.F.R. part 112.

must be implemented as soon as possible—but in no case later than one year after the facility begins operations.[37] A complete copy of the plan must be kept at the facility.[38]

SPCC plans can be amended either upon order of the EPA Regional Administrator or based on periodic required review of the plan by the owner or operator of the facility. Whenever a facility covered by an SPCC plan discharges more than 1,000 gallons of oil into navigable waters or onto adjoining shorelines in a single incident, or discharges harmful quantities of oil on two occasions in the prior 12-month period, the facility is required to submit specific information regarding the incident(s) and the facility to the EPA Regional Administrator and the applicable state agency, along with a copy of the SPCC Plan. Based on review of the SPCC Plan by the EPA, taking into account any recommendations of the state, the EPA can require amendment of the plan.[39] Any amendment required by the Regional Administrator can be appealed to the Administrator of the EPA.[40]

Further, the SPCC Plan is required to be reviewed by the facility owner or operator at least once every three years,[41] or whenever there is a change in facility design, construction, operation, or maintenance that materially affects the facility's potential for the discharge of oil into the navigable waters or adjoining shorelines.[42] After such review, the owner or operator must amend the SPCC Plan within six months to include more-effective prevention and control technology if such technology will significantly reduce the likelihood of a spill and the technology has been field-proven at the time of the review.[43]

---

37. Id. § 112.3(b). The July 17, 2002, final rule requires that, for facilities that become operational after August 18, 2003, the SPCC plan must be prepared and implemented before the facility begins operations. 67 Fed. Reg. 47143 (amending 40 C.F.R. § 112.3(b)).

38. 40 C.F.R. § 112.3(e).

39. Id. § 112.4. Under the July 17, 2002, final rule, the geographic area for the type of discharges that must be reported has been revised to reflect the changes to the geographic area in the revised § 112.1(b). See note 33 supra. In addition, while the 1,000-gallon threshold for a single discharge remains unchanged, the threshold for reporting two discharges has been raised from a discharge of a "reportable quantity" to a threshold of more than 42 gallons (1 barrel) for each of the discharges. 67 Fed. Reg. 47144 (amending 40 C.F.R. § 112.4(a)). Finally, the final rule provides that, in addition to allowing the Regional Administrator to require changes to the SPPC plan after initial review of the submitted plan, the RA can also require changes after an on-site review of the plan. Id. (amending 40 C.F.R. § 112.4(d)).

40. 40 C.F.R. § 112.4(f).

41. Id. § 112.5(b). The July 17, 2002, final rule provides for review by the facility operator every five (5) years in lieu of every three (3) years under the preexisting rule. 67 Fed. Reg. 47145 (amending 40 C.F.R. § 112.5(b)).

42. 40 C.F.R. § 112.5(a).

43. Id. § 112.5(b).

B. MARINE FACILITIES AND VESSELS

The Coast Guard has been delegated the authority to issue regulations for the prevention of pollution from marine terminals and vessels.[44] Under this authority, the Coast Guard has promulgated specific requirements for marine facilities, vessels, and the transfer of oil and other cargoes between vessels and facilities.

Coast Guard pollution prevention regulations apply to facilities, including mobile facilities,[45] that are capable of transferring oil or hazardous materials,[46] in bulk, to or from a vessel where the vessel has a total capacity, from a combination of all bulk products carried, of 250 barrels or more.[47] Certain other facilities that transfer oil or hazardous materials in bulk only to vessels with a capacity of less than 250 barrels may also be required to comply with the regulations upon written notice if such compliance is determined by the Coast Guard to be necessary for the safety of the facility, its personnel, or the public.[48]

The operator of a facility that meets the regulatory criteria must submit a letter of intent to operate a facility or to conduct mobile facility operations with the Coast Guard not less than 60 days before operations begin.[49] The facility operator must also submit an Operations Manual along with the letter of intent.[50] The Operations Manual must comply with very specific content requirements[51] and must be approved by the Coast Guard.[52] All operations on the facility must comply with the procedures established in the operations manual.[53] Facilities must also comply with equipment, containment, and operations requirements related to the transfer of oil and hazardous materials.[54] This includes the designation and training of persons in charge of transfer operations.[55]

---

44. 49 C.F.R. § 1.46.

45. A mobile facility is any facility that can readily change location, such as a tank truck or tank car, other than a vessel. 33 C.F.R. § 154.105.

46. Hazardous materials include hazardous substances designated under section 311 of the CWA. *See* 33 C.F.R. § 154.105; 46 C.F.R. § 153.2.

47. 33 C.F.R. § 154.100(a).

48. *Id.* § 154.100(b).

49. *Id.* § 154.110.

50. *Id.* § 154.300(a).

51. *Id.* § 154.310.

52. *Id.* § 154.325.

53. *Id.* § 154.750.

54. Equipment and containment requirements are in 33 C.F.R. part 154, subpart C, and operations requirements are in 33 C.F.R. part 154, subpart D.

55. 33 C.F.R. § 154.710.

The Coast Guard has issued separate equipment and operational pollution prevention requirements for vessels. These requirements apply to vessels that operate under the authority of the United States wherever they are located. They also apply to vessels that operate under the authority of a country other than the United States while they are in the navigable waters of the United States or at a port or terminal subject to the jurisdiction of the United States.[56] As with facilities, the operator of any vessel with a capacity of 250 or more barrels of oil or hazardous materials must designate and train a person in charge of each transfer to or from the vessel.[57] In addition, the operator of the vessel must provide transfer procedures for the vessel for any transfer to or from the vessel or from tank to tank within the vessel,[58] and comply with the transfer procedures for any transfer that occurs.[59] Equipment and containment requirements specifically for vessels are also established.[60]

In addition to specific marine facility and vessel pollution prevention requirements, the Coast Guard also regulates transfers of oil and hazardous material cargoes that occur in the navigable waters or contiguous zone of the United States to, from, or within each vessel with a capacity of 250 or more barrels of oil or hazardous materials.[61] The regulations provide that the Coast Guard can issue suspension orders to suspend any transfer operations when a condition is found that requires action to prevent a discharge or the threat of a discharge.[62] The regulations also have specific requirements for any transfer, including the completion of inspection forms by persons in charge prior to transfer.[63] Finally, the Coast Guard regulates the lightering of oil or hazardous materials between vessels that occur in the navigable waters of the United States, on waters over which the United States asserts exclusive fishery management authority (the EEZ), and on waters superjacent to the Outer Continental Shelf of the United States.[64]

III. Removal and Response Authority

Major criticisms of section 311 authority for response and removal of oil and hazardous substance spills arising from the handling of the Exxon Valdez oil spill

---

56. 33 C.F.R. § 155.100.
57. *Id.* §§ 155.700–155.710.
58. *Id.* §§ 155.720–155.750.
59. *Id.* § 155.730.
60. 33 C.F.R. part 155, subpart B.
61. 33 C.F.R. § 156.100.
62. *Id.* §§ 156.112–156.113.
63. *Id.* § 156.150.
64. 33 C.F.R. part 156, subpart B.

included unclear federal removal authority and inadequate and dilatory federal removal efforts.[65] The OPA amended the federal authority in section 311 to respond to oil and hazardous substance spills into designated waters.

A. AUTHORITY TO ACT

Prior to OPA, section 311 authorized the president to respond to discharges of oil and hazardous substances, but largely a great deal of latitude was provided to private cleanup efforts by the discharger. OPA amended section 311 to mandate the president to take action to ensure "effective and immediate removal of a discharge, and mitigation or prevention of a substantial threat of a discharge, of oil or a hazardous substance."[66] Such required action may include direct federal response and removal, directing or monitoring state or local government and responsible-party response and removal efforts, and removal or destruction of a vessel discharging or threatening to discharge by whatever means available.[67] The president has delegated the response and removal authority under section 311 to the Coast Guard and the EPA by Executive Order.[68]

B. SUBSTANTIAL THREATS TO PUBLIC HEALTH OR WELFARE

The responsibility of the government to respond to an oil or hazardous substance discharge is even clearer when the discharge threatens public health. Section 311 now states that the president "shall direct all federal, state and private actions to remove the discharge or to mitigate or prevent the threat of discharge" when the discharge or threat of discharge constitutes a substantial threat to public health or welfare.[69] Section 311 authorizes the president to remove or arrange for the removal of the discharge or to mitigate or prevent the substantial threat of the discharge, and to remove and if necessary destroy a vessel discharging or threatening to discharge by whatever means available. Under this authority, the president may act without regard to any other provision of law governing federal government contracting or employment.[70] Further, the EPA or the Coast Guard may seek appropriate relief in the federal district court necessary to abate any imminent and substantial threat to human health or welfare or to the environment,

---

65. *See,* e.g., S. Rpt. No. 101-94, 101st Cong. 2d Sess. 2–3 (1990), *reprinted in* 1990 U.S.C.C.A.N. 722, 723–24.

66. 33 U.S.C. § 1321(c)(1)(A).

67. *Id.* § 1321(c)(1)(B).

68. § 3, Executive Order No. 12777 (56 Fed. Reg. 54757-70 (Oct. 22, 1991)).

69. 33 U.S.C. § 1321(c)(2)(A).

70. *Id.* § 1321(c)(2)(B).

including public and private property as well as living and nonliving natural resources, presented by a discharge of oil or hazardous substances.[71]

C. FEDERAL RESPONSE UNITS

Section 311 requires the president to establish a National Response Unit under the Coast Guard. This National Response Unit is responsible for administration and maintenance of three strike teams, one for the Atlantic Coast, one for the Gulf Coast, and one for the Pacific Coast, that serve as highly trained and equipped technical advisors to the Federal On-Scene Coordinator (FOSC). The FOSC is the federal official responsible for overseeing spill response efforts in the event of a CWA section 311 or CERCLA discharge. The OPA mandated that the National Response Unit be in charge of the coordination and use of private and public personnel and equipment to remove a worst-case discharge, and to mitigate or prevent a substantial threat of such a discharge, from a vessel or facility.[72]

In addition to the National Response Unit, each Coast Guard District is required to operate a Coast Guard District Response Group that consists of Coast Guard personnel and equipment who are responsible for various ports in these districts and pre-positioned response equipment. These District Response Groups are required to review the various contingency plans that affect their areas of responsibility, and to provide technical assistance to the EPA or Coast Guard FOSC as requested.[73]

D. RESPONDER IMMUNITY

In order to encourage quick and aggressive responses to oil spills, the OPA amends Section 311 of the CWA to provide immunity from liability for persons undertaking voluntary response actions or response actions without knowing for certain that they are the responsible party.[74] This immunity does not apply, however, to the responsible party, to response actions taken under the CERCLA, to personal injury or wrongful death, or to actions that are grossly negligent or occur due to willful misconduct.[75] The responsible party for the spill becomes liable for removal costs or damages attributable to a person immunized from liability under this section.[76]

---

71. *Id.* § 1321(e).

72. *Id.* § 1321(j)(2).

73. *Id.* § 1321(j)(3).

74. *Id.* § 1321(c)(4)(A). A responsible party for purposes of section 311 has the same meaning as that term is given under the OPA liability provisions. *Id.* § 1321(c)(6).

75. *Id.* § 1321(c)(4)(B).

76. *Id.* § 1321(c)(4)(C).

IV. Response Planning

Another criticism of the cleanup of the Exxon Valdez oil spill was the lack of coordination at the scene and the overlapping nature of then-existing oil spill contingency plans. The OPA significantly revised the contingency planning and response requirements from the national to the local level.

A. FEDERAL RESPONSE CONTINGENCY PLANS

Section 311 establishes the National Contingency Plan (NCP) as the primary contingency planning vehicle to provide for the efficient, coordinated, and effective response to oil and hazardous substance discharges. Under section 311, the president must prepare and publish the NCP.[77] The president has delegated this responsibility to the EPA by Executive Order.[78] Section 311 requires that removal of oil and hazardous substances and actions taken to minimize damage from discharges of oil and hazardous substances be done, to the greatest extent possible, in accordance with the NCP.[79]

The NCP has been promulgated by the EPA[80] and is required by section 311 to include the following:

1. Assignment of duties and responsibilities among federal departments, in consultation with state and local agencies, for water pollution control and conservation and trusteeship of natural resources.

2. Identification, procurement, maintenance, and storage of response equipment and supplies.

3. Establishment of Coast Guard spill response strike teams.

4. A system of surveillance and notice to safeguard against discharges or imminent threats of discharges of oil and hazardous substances and to ensure earliest possible notice for response.

5. Procedures and techniques to employ in identifying, containing, dispersing, and removing oil and hazardous substances.

6. A schedule, prepared in cooperation with states, that identifies dispersants and other chemicals that may be used to respond to oil and hazardous substance discharges, and the waters where they may be used.

7. A system whereby an affected state or states may act to remove a discharge of oil or a hazardous substance and the state(s) may be reimbursed

---

77. *Id.* § 1321(d)(1).

78. § 1(a), Executive Order No. 12777 (56 Fed Reg. 54757-70 (Oct. 22, 1991)) (amending Section 1(b)(1) of Executive Order No. 12580 (52 Fed. Reg. 2923 (Jan. 23, 1987)).

79. 33 U.S.C. § 1321(d)(4).

80. 40 C.F.R. part 300.

for the reasonable costs of such removal from the Oil Spill Liability Trust Fund.

8. Criteria and procedures to respond immediately and effectively to discharges or threats of discharges that pose a substantial threat to the public health or welfare.

9. Procedures and standards for removing a worst-case discharge of oil, and for mitigating or preventing a substantial threat of such a discharge.

10. Designation of the federal official who will be the FOSC.

11. Procedures for coordinating response actions among the various federal response entities.

12. A fish and wildlife response plan, developed in consultation with the U.S. Fish and Wildlife Service, the National Oceanographic and Atmospheric Administration, and other interested parties, including state fish and wildlife officials, for the protection, rescue, and rehabilitation of fish and wildlife resources and their habitat.[81]

Section 311 also requires, for areas designated by the president, the establishment of Area Committees composed of qualified personnel, appointed by the president, from federal, state, and local agencies.[82] The Area Committee, under the direction of the FOSC for its area, is required to prepare an Area Contingency Plan (ACP). They are also required to work with state and local officials to ensure preplanning of joint response efforts and to expedite decisions for use of dispersants and other mitigating substances and devices.[83] The ACP supplements the NCP by including more-specific resource and response information for the specific area covered. The ACP must be approved by the president and periodically reviewed after initial approval.[84] The authority related to designation of areas, establishment of Area Committees, and preparation, approval, and review of ACPs has been delegated by Executive Order to the EPA for the inland zone and to the Coast Guard for the coastal zone, as those terms are defined in the NCP.[85]

B. FACILITY AND VESSEL RESPONSE PLANS

1. Section 311 Requirements

The OPA significantly strengthened section 311's requirements for preparing spill prevention and response plans by owners and operators of vessels and facilities. The OPA amended section 311 to require the submission of plans that

---

81. 33 U.S.C. § 1321(d)(2).

82. *Id.* § 1321(j)(4).

83. *Id.* § 1321(j)(4)(B).

84. *Id.* § 1321(j)(4)(D).

85. Executive Order No. 12777 (56 Fed Reg. 54757-70 (Oct. 22, 1991)), § 1(b).

respond, "to the maximum extent possible, to a worst-case discharge, and to a substantial threat of such a discharge, of oil or a hazardous substance."[86]

Section 311 sets minimum requirements for such plans. Vessels, offshore facilities, and onshore facilities that, because of their location, can reasonably be expected to cause substantial harm to the environment by discharging into or on the navigable waters, adjoining shorelines, or the exclusive economic zone, must prepare plans that:

1. are consistent with the requirements of the NCP and area contingency plans;
2. identify a qualified individual with responsibility for implementing removal actions;
3. identify and ensure, by contract or other means, the availability of private personnel and equipment adequate to remove, to the maximum extent practicable, a worst-case discharge or to prevent a threat of such a discharge;
4. require training, equipment testing, personnel drills, and the response actions that will be carried out by facility personnel;
5. are updated periodically; and
6. are resubmitted for approval of each significant change.[87]

Further, section 311 requires that unannounced drills be periodically conducted in areas covered by the ACP that exercise the tank vessel and facility response plans. Such drills may include participation by federal, state, and local agencies, owners, and operators of vessels and facilities, and private industry.[88]

Section 311 provides that the owner or operator of a tank vessel or facility can not claim as a defense to liability under the OPA that the owner or operator was acting in accordance with a required response plan.[89] Further, section 311 provides that the U.S. Government is not liable for any damages arising from actions or omissions relating to any required response plan.[90]

2. Nontransportation-Related Facility Response Plans

The EPA has promulgated response planning regulations for nontransportation-related facilities that, because of their location, could reasonably be expected to cause substantial harm to the environment by discharging oil into the navigable

---

86. 33 U.S.C. § 1321(j)(5)(A).
87. *Id.* § 1321(j)(5)(C).
88. *Id.* § 1321(j)(7).
89. *Id.* § 1321(j)(5)(G).
90. *Id.* § 1321(j)(8).

waters or the adjoining shorelines.[91] Under these regulations, only owners or operators of "substantial harm facilities" are required to prepare and submit oil spill response plans.[92]

There are two methods by which a facility could be determined to be a "substantial harm facility." The first is through the use of substantial harm criteria by which owners and operators of facilities identify whether their facilities are "substantial harm facilities."[93] The second is through identification made by an EPA Regional Administrator based on the specific criteria identified for owners and operators or on other relevant site-specific characteristics and environmental factors identified in the regulations.[94]

Owners or operators of "substantial harm facilities" must submit response plans to respond to a worst-case discharge.[95] Under section 311 as amended by the OPA, a worst-case discharge for a facility is defined as the largest foreseeable discharge in adverse weather conditions.[96] The EPA has interpreted this to mean an amount based on the capacity of the largest single tank within a secondary containment area, or the combined capacity of a group of aboveground tanks permanently connected via a manifold system in a common secondary containment area, whichever is greater.[97] In addition to worst-case discharges, owners or operators must also plan for responding to a small spill and a medium spill. A small spill is defined as any spill less than or equal to 2,100 gallons.[98] A medium spill is defined as any spill greater than 2,100 gallons and less than 36,000 gallons or 10 percent of the capacity of the largest tank, whichever is less, provided that these amounts are less than the worst-case discharge amount.[99]

The regulations also establish requirements mandating that facilities have the response equipment necessary to respond to the maximum extent practicable to a worst-case discharge and to other discharges as appropriate.[100] The plan must identify and ensure the availability of this required equipment by contracts or other approved means.[101] The regulations also require the owner or operator of

---

91. 59 Fed. Reg. 34070-136 (July 1, 1994) (codified at 40 C.F.R. §§ 112.20–112.21)

92. A model facility response plan is located at 40 C.F.R. part 112, appendix F.

93. 40 C.F.R. § 112.20(f)(1); 40 C.F.R. pt. 112, app. C.

94. Id. §§ 112.20(f)(2), (f)(3).

95. Id. § 112.20 (h)(5).

96. 33 U.S.C. § 1321(a)(24).

97. 40 C.F.R. pt. 112, app. D.

98. 40 C.F.R. § 112.20(h)(5)(ii).

99. Id. § 112.20(h)(5)(iii).

100. Id. § 112.20(h)(3). Required equipment is determined by guidance provided at 40 C.F.R. pt. 112, app. E.

101. Id. § 112.20(h)(3)(ii). "Contract or other approved means" is defined at 40 C.F.R. § 112.2.

any facility that is required to have a response plan to implement a response training and drill/exercise program as part of the response plan.[102]

3. Marine Transportation–Related Facility Response Plans

The Coast Guard has promulgated regulations requiring response plans for marine transportation–related (MTR) facilities. An MTR facility is any onshore facility, or that part of an onshore facility complex, subject to regulation by two or more federal agencies, used or intended to be used to transfer oil to or from a vessel.[103] The Coast Guard has determined that a "substantial harm facility" is any fixed or mobile MTR facility that is used, or is intended to be used, to transfer oil to or from a vessel with a capacity of 250 barrels or more. A "substantial harm facility" also includes a deepwater port or any MTR facility so designated by the Coast Guard. [104]

The Coast Guard has also identified more stringent response planning requirements for a "significant and substantial harm facility." A "significant and substantial harm facility" includes a fixed MTR onshore facility capable of transferring oil to or from a vessel with a capacity of 250 barrels or more, except a facility that is part of a nontransportation-related fixed onshore facility with a storage capacity of less than 42,000 gallons. It also includes a deepwater port and any MTR facility so designated by the Coast Guard.[105] Response plans for a "significant and substantial harm facility" must be submitted and must receive approval by the Coast Guard.[106]

As with the EPA regulations for nontransportation-related facilities, the owner or operator of an MTR facility to which the response plan requirements are applicable must plan for the worst-case discharge. However, the worst-case discharge criteria for an MTR facility response plan are different than for a nontransportation-related facility under EPA regulations. For a fixed onshore MTR facility, a worst-case discharge is calculated based on the loss of the entire capacity of all in-line and breakout tanks needed for continuous operation of transfer pipelines plus the discharge from all piping carrying oil between the marine transfer manifold and the nontransportation-related portion of the facility.[107] For a mobile MTR facility, a worst-case discharge would be the loss of the entire contents of the container in which oil is stored or transported.[108]

---

102. *Id.* § 112.21.

103. 33 C.F.R. § 154.1020.

104. *Id.* § 154.1015(b).

105. *Id.* § 154.1015(c).

106. *Id.* § 154.1017(b).

107. *Id.* § 154.1029(b).

108. *Id.* § 154.1029(c).

As with mandated planning for medium and small discharges required under the EPA regulations for nontransportation-related facilities, Coast Guard regulations require the response plan to also address response requirements for a "maximum most probable discharge" and an "average most probable discharge." [109] A "maximum most probable discharge" is a discharge of the lesser of 1,200 barrels of oil or 10 percent of the volume of a worst-case discharge.[110] An "average most probable discharge" is a discharge of the lesser of 50 barrels or one percent of the volume of the worst-case discharge.[111]

Similar to the EPA regulations, Coast Guard regulations require equipment necessary to respond to a worst-case discharge, which must be assured by contract or other approved means,[112] and for training[113] and drills/exercises[114] for MTR facilities. However, unlike EPA regulations, plan development and equipment requirements are based heavily on the persistency characteristics of the oil handled by the facility.[115]

4. Vessel Response Plans

Similar but separate response plan requirements have been promulgated by the Coast Guard for vessels. These response plan requirements apply to every vessel that operates on the navigable waters of the United States or that transfers oil in a port or place subject to the jurisdiction of the United States.[116] While the general criteria for response planning requirements in section 311 apply to both vessels and facilities, the mobile nature of vessels has resulted in a significantly different methodology for developing and evaluating vessel response plans.

As with MTR facilities, the Coast Guard generally requires that vessel owners and operators plan for a worst-case discharge, a maximum most-probable discharge, and an average most-probable discharge. The "worst-case discharge" means a discharge in adverse weather conditions of a vessel's entire oil cargo.[117] The "maximum most-probable discharge" means a discharge of 2,500 barrels of oil for vessels with an oil cargo capacity equal to or greater than 25,000 barrels, or 10 percent of the vessel's oil capacity for vessels with a capacity greater than

---

109. Requirements for a "significant and substantial harm facility" are at *Id.* § 154.1035(b)(2) and for a "substantial harm facility" at *Id.* § 154.1040(b).

110. *Id.* § 154.1020.

111. *Id.*

112. Means for ensuring the availability of resources by contract or other approved means are identified at *id.* § 154.1028.

113. *Id.* § 154.1050.

114. *Id.* § 154.1055.

115. *Id.* §§ 154.1045, 154.1047.

116. 33 C.F.R. § 155.1015(a).

117. *Id.* § 155.1020.

25,000 barrels.[118] The "average most-probable discharge" means a discharge of the lesser of 50 barrels of oil or one percent of the cargo from the vessel during cargo oil transfer operations to or from the vessel.[119]

The individual requirements for vessel response plans are dependent upon the type of vessel or whether oil is carried as either a primary or secondary cargo or for use by the vessel.[120] Of note, the vessel must identify all of the U.S. ports or places in which it will be operating and have a separate appendix in place to cover the plan requirements, particularly as they relate to response equipment, for each port or place.[121] As with MTR facilities, vessel plan development and equipment requirements are based significantly on the persistency characteristics of the oil being carried.[122] The contract or other means by which the availability of the required equipment is ensured is defined similarly for vessels as it is for MTR facilities, but there are some variances based on the need to account for the fact that the vessel will be operating in various geographic areas.[123] As with facilities, there are also training[124] and drill/exercise requirements[125] for vessels.

5. Response Planning Requirements for Edible Oils

While oil of all kinds is covered under section 311, in 1995 Congress enacted the Edible Oil Regulatory Reform Act,[126] which has had an impact on the response planning regulations issued under section 311 of the CWA. This act requires most federal agencies, when issuing or enforcing any regulation, or establishing any interpretation or guideline, relating to the transportation, storage, discharge, release, emission, or disposal of a fat, oil, or grease, to differentiate among and establish separate classes for: animal fats, oils and greases; fish and marine mammal oils; and, oils of vegetable origin. The federal agency must consider the differences in the physical, chemical, biological, and other properties, and in the

---

118. *Id.*

119. *Id.*

120. *Compare id.* § 155.1035 (establishing response plan requirements for manned vessels carrying oil as a primary cargo) *with id.* § 155.1040 (establishing response plan requirements for unmanned tank barges carrying oil as a primary cargo) *and id.* § 155.1045 (establishing response plan requirements for vessels carrying oil as a secondary cargo).

121. *See, e.g. id.* § 155.1035(i) (requirements for geographic-specific appendices for each Coast Guard zone in which manned vessels carrying oil as a primary cargo will be operating).

122. *Id.* §§ 155.1050, 155.1052.

123. *See id.* § 155.1020.

124. *Id.* § 155.1055.

125. *Id.* § 155.1060.

126. Pub. L. No. 104-55, § 2, *reprinted in* 1995 U.S.C.C.A.N. (109 Stat.) 546 (currently codified at 33 U.S.C. § 2720).

environmental effects, of the classes. As a result of this act, both the EPA and the Coast Guard have issued regulations specifically addressing spill response planning requirements for facilities and vessels that handle, store, and transport edible oils.[127]

V. Liability for Response Costs and Damages

The owner and operator of a facility or vessel that discharges oil into the navigable waters is liable to the United States for actual costs incurred in removing a discharge. Section 311 originally established the liability and the limits of liability for discharges of oil and hazardous substances, and financial responsibility requirements for facilities and vessels to ensure that this liability could be met. Section 311 placed limits on liability for oil or hazardous substance discharges based upon the type of vessel or facility involved. In the case of an inland oil barge, liability was capped at $125 per gross ton of the barge or $125,000, whichever was greater.[128] For any other vessel the limit was the greater of $150 per gross ton or $150,000, except for vessels carrying oil or hazardous substances as a cargo, in which case the limit was the greater of $150 per gross ton or $250,000.[129] Onshore and offshore oil storage facilities had a maximum liability of $50 million.[130] Under section 311, if a discharge proved to be due to willful misconduct within the privity and knowledge of the owner, the owner or operator of a vessel or facility would be liable for the full amount of the recovery and removal costs.[131]

As stated above, liability for discharges of hazardous substances is primarily addressed now under the CERCLA. The OPA significantly revised the liability provisions and other requirements for spills of oil from vessels or facilities, and required that these provisions be applied in lieu of those in section 311.[132] Thus,

---

127. The EPA regulations amending the nontransportation-related facility response plan requirements in 40 C.F.R. part 112 were promulgated at 65 Fed. Reg. 40776 (June 30, 2000). The Coast Guard regulations amending the marine facility response plan regulations in 33 C.F.R. part 154 were promulgated at 61 Fed. Reg. 7931(Feb. 29, 1996) and amending the vessel response plan requirements in 33 C.F.R. Part 155 were promulgated at 61 Fed. Reg. 1098 (Jan. 12, 1996).

128. 33 U.S.C. § 1321(f)(1).

129. *Id.*

130. *Id.* §§ 1321(f)(2), 1321(f)(3).

131. *Id.* §§ 1321(f)(1)–1321(f)(3).

132. OPA § 2002 states that the limitation of liability provisions in subsection (f) of section 311 of the Clean Water Act "shall not apply with respect to any incident for which liability is established" under the OPA.

despite the fact that liability provisions remain in section 311, they are in reality no longer applicable to discharges of oil and hazardous substances.

A. LIABILITY FOR OIL DISCHARGES UNDER THE OPA

The OPA establishes liability for responsible parties for vessels or facilities from which oil is discharged, or that pose a substantial threat of discharge, into or upon the navigable waters[133] or adjacent shoreline or into the U.S. EEZ.[134]

While section 311 made the owner or operator of a vessel or facility from which oil was discharged liable solely for the actual costs of removal and recovery,[135] under the OPA responsible parties are liable for these costs and for damages arising from the discharge.[136] Recoverable damages under the OPA[137] include:

1. damages for injury to, destruction of, loss of, or loss of use of natural resources;[138]

---

133. *See* Rice v. Harken Exploration Co., 250 F.3d 264 (5th Cir. 2001) (holding that the term "navigable waters" as used in the OPA does not cover spills into groundwater). A few courts have stated that the term "navigable waters" for purposes of the OPA is narrower than the term for purposes of the CWA. *See, e.g.,* Sun Pipe Line Co. v. Conewago Contractors, Inc., No. 4: CV-93-1995, 1994 WL 539326 (M.D. Pa. Aug. 22, 1994).

134. 33 U.S.C. § 2702(a).

135. *See* 33 U.S.C.A. § 1321(f) (West 1986).

136. 33 U.S.C. § 2702(b). Response costs include the costs of monitoring of the cleanup by federal agencies. *See* United States v. Hyundai Merchant Marine Co., 172 F.3d 1187 (9th Cir. 1999) (holding that shipowner was liable for Coast Guard monitoring costs of $1.7 million resulting from potential oil spill from grounding of ship even though no major oil spill occurred. Court reasoned that grounding "contained the seeds of a major ecological disaster" and "it was only prudent for the government to rush personnel and equipment to the scene and maintain them there until the threat was over."). *See also* United States v. Conoco, 916 F. Supp. 581 (E.D. La. 1996); United States v. Murphy Exploration and Production Co., 939 F. Supp. 489 (E.D. La. 1996).

137. 33 U.S.C. § 2702(b)(2).

138. The National Oceanographic and Atmospheric Administration (NOAA) issued regulations in 1996 for the assessment of natural resource damages. 15 C.F.R. §§ 990.10–990.66. These regulations provide that natural resource trustees can consider both "active-use" and "passive-use" losses in assessing natural resource damages. Active use is the loss of actual use of the resource while passive use is the loss suffered by those who have never used or intended to use the resource, but value its availability. These regulations were challenged in General Electric Co. v. United States Dept. of Commerce, 128 F.3d 767 (D.C. Cir. 1997) (holding that the issue was not ripe for review, but that the administrative record supported NOAA's inclusion of both types of losses).

2. damages for injury to, or economic losses resulting from destruction of, real or personal property;[139]
3. damages for loss of subsistence use of natural resources, recoverable by any claimant who so uses natural resources regardless of ownership or management of the resources;
4. damages for net loss of revenues such as rents and royalties due to injury or destruction of real or personal property or natural resources;
5. damages due to loss of profits or impairment of earning capacity; and
6. damages for net costs of providing increased or additional public services during or after removal activities.

Under the OPA, any claims for damages must initially be presented to the responsible party prior to the institution of any legal action in order to encourage early settlement.[140] Some courts have determined this to be a jurisdictional requirement.[141]

B. OPA LIMITS OF LIABILITY FOR RESPONSE COSTS AND DAMAGES

The OPA also established much higher limits for spills of oil than were previously established in section 311. In the case of a tank vessel, the OPA establishes caps for the total limit of liability based on the size of the vessel. For a tank vessel, liability is the greater of $1,200 per gross ton or, in the case of a vessel greater than 3,000 gross tons, $10 million, or in the case of a vessel of 3,000 gross tons or less, $2 million.[142] Any other vessel is limited to the higher of $600 per gross ton or $500,000.[143] In the case of an offshore facility that is not a deepwater port, the limit is the total of all removal costs plus $75,000.[144] For any onshore facility

---

139. *See* South Port Marine, L.L.C. v. Gulf Oil Ltd. Partnership, 73 F. Supp. 2d 17 (D. Me. 1999) (upholding jury award to marina of damages for loss of goodwill or business stress caused by gasoline spill that dissolved Styrofoam floats and marina dock), *aff'd in part, rev'd in part on other grounds, remanded,* 2000 U.S. App. LEXIS 31178 (1st Cir. Dec. 7, 2000). *But see* Sekco Energy, Inc. v. M/V Margaret Chouest, 820 F. Supp. 1008 (E.D. La. 1993) (denying economic damages resulting from shutdown of offshore drilling platform while cause of oil spill investigated because losses did not result from damage to real or personal property as required by the OPA).

140. 33 U.S.C. § 2713.

141. *See* Boca Ciega Hotel v. Bouchard Transp. Co., 51 F.3d 235 (11th Cir. 1995); Johnson v. Colonial Pipeline Co., 830 F. Supp. 309 (E.D. Va. 1993).

142. 33 U.S.C. § 2704(a)(1).

143. *Id.* § 2704(a)(2).

144. *Id.* § 2704(a)(3).

or a deepwater port, the limit is $350 million.[145] The president is authorized to lower the limit for onshore facilities by regulation, but to not less than $8 million.

The limits of liability do not apply if it is shown that the discharge was proximately caused by the gross negligence or willful misconduct of, or a violation of a federal safety, construction, or operating regulation by the responsible party, an agent of the responsible party, or a person acting pursuant to a contractual relationship with the responsible party.[146] However, similar to the liability provisions in section 311, the OPA provides that states may enact laws establishing liability for oil spills in excess of the OPA limits of liability.[147]

C. DEFENSES AND EXCLUSIONS TO LIABILITY UNDER THE OPA

Liability under the OPA is strict and absolute, although the act does recognize several standard defenses to liability. However, these are generally more restrictive than those provided under the liability provisions in section 311. Under the OPA, an otherwise responsible party will not be liable if it can demonstrate by a preponderance of the evidence that the discharge was the result of an act of God, an act of war, or an act or omission of a third party, regardless of whether such act or omission was negligent.[148] The third-party defense is contingent upon the responsible party being able to prove, by a preponderance of the evidence, that due care was exercised regarding the nature of the oil discharged and that precautions were taken against foreseeable acts or omissions by the third party.[149] Under the OPA, third parties found to be ultimately liable for costs or damages from an oil spill are entitled to the limitations of liability that apply to any responsible party.[150]

---

145. *Id.* § 2704(a)(4).

146. *Id.* § 2704(c)(1).

147. *Id.* § 2718. In United States v. Locke, 529 U.S. 89 (2000), a unanimous Supreme Court held that the nonpreemption language in the OPA applied only to state laws involving oil spill liability and financial requirements. In *Locke*, an international organization of tank vessel owners and the federal government challenged the state of Washington, which had implemented a number of regulations for oil tankers that supplemented and, in some cases, exceeded federal safety and pollution prevention laws and regulations. The Court held that the nonpreemption language in the OPA did not change the traditional federal preemption of state laws enacted under state police powers seeking to regulate foreign and domestic vessels involved in foreign and interstate commerce.

148. 33 U.S.C. § 2703. The OPA omits one section 311 defense, which states that "negligence on the part of the United States" is a complete defense. 33 U.S.C. § 1321 (f)(1)(C).

149. 33 U.S.C. § 2703(a)(3).

150. *Id.* § 2702(d).

The OPA also excludes from liability discharges (1) allowed by a permit issued under federal, state, or local law; (2) from a public vessel; and (3) from an onshore facility that is subject to the Trans-Alaska Pipeline Authorization Act.[151]

D. FINANCIAL RESPONSIBILITY REQUIREMENTS UNDER THE OPA

The OPA repealed the financial responsibility provisions formerly in section 311(p). Financial responsibility requirements under the OPA ensure that the responsible party is able to meet the liability limits. Under the OPA, all vessels over 300 gross tons (except barges not carrying oil as cargo or fuel) operating in any place subject to the jurisdiction of the United States, or operating in the U.S. EEZ to transship or lighter oil to a port or place in the United States, must provide evidence of financial responsibility.[152] If an owner or operator has a fleet of vessels, evidence of financial responsibility to meet the limit of liability from the largest vessel is required.[153] Failure to provide the required evidence of financial responsibility can result in seizure and forfeiture of the vessel, denial of entry to United States ports or navigable waters, detention of the vessel, or refusal of Customs clearance to depart a United States port.[154]

The OPA requires evidence of financial responsibility for offshore facilities and deepwater ports of $150 million. As with vessels, when a person is responsible for more than one offshore facility under the requirements, evidence of financial responsibility is only required to meet the maximum liability of the facility with the greatest maximum liability.[155]

Evidence of financial responsibility can be proof of insurance, surety bond, guarantee, letter of credit, or qualification as a self-insurer.[156] A major aspect of the financial responsibility provisions is the requirement that any guarantor be subject to United States jurisdiction[157] and subject to direct claims for response

---

151. *Id.* § 2702(c).
152. *Id.* § 2716(a).
153. *Id.*
154. *Id.* § 2716(b).
155. *Id.* § 2716(c).
156. *Id.* § 2716(e).
157. *Id.*

costs and damages.[158] An administrative civil penalty of up to $25,000 per day of violation may be assessed for violations of the financial responsibility requirements.[159]

E. OIL SPILL LIABILITY TRUST FUND (OSLTF)

While the responsible party remains strictly liable for response costs and damages up to the limits of liability, the OPA establishes the OSLTF as an alternate source of fund to pay response costs and damages in certain circumstances.[160] The fund is available, generally subject to appropriation by Congress, for payment of:

1. removal costs incurred by federal authorities consistent with the NCP;
2. to a state for removal costs consistent with the NCP up to $250,000 for immediate response to a discharge or threat of discharge of oil;
3. costs incurred by a natural resource trustee consistent with the NCP;
4. removal costs consistent with the NCP for discharges from a foreign offshore source;
5. uncompensated claims for removal costs determined to be consistent with the NCP;
6. otherwise uncompensated damages;
7. federal administrative, operational, and personnel costs reasonably necessary for the implementation of the OPA;
8. expenses authorized under the Intervention on the High Seas Act to deal with pollution incidents on the high seas that threaten U.S. waters and shorelines;
9. costs to carry out section 311 of the CWA; and
10. liabilities incurred by other federal oil spill trust funds.[161]

Claims against the OSLTF can be made by the responsible party for a discharge for such costs and damages when costs exceed the limits of liability

---

158. *Id.* § 2716(f)(f1).

159. *Id.* § 2716a.

160. The Fund was initially capitalized by a five-cent-per-barrel tax on oil, *see* 26 U.S.C. § 4611(c)(2)(B), and by amounts transferred in part from the former CWA § 311(k) fund. Other sources of funding include excess natural resource damages recovered by trustees, 33 U.S.C. § 2706(f); amounts recovered by the Fund through subrogation, *id.* § 2715; and civil penalties and fines collected for violation of section 311, 33 U.S.C. § 1321(s).

161. 33 U.S.C. § 2712(a).

established for the responsible party, or the responsible party has a valid defense to liability under the OPA.[162]

There is a $1-billion-per-incident cap on payments from the OSLTF. Of this $1 billion, no more than $500 million can be paid for natural resource damages.[163] Under the OPA, anyone paying response costs and damages, including the OSLTF, is subrogated to all rights, claims, and causes of action held by claimants under any other law.[164]

VI. Enforcement of Penalties

Section 311 has historically contained enforcement and civil penalty provisions separate from those applicable to other sections of the CWA. The OPA significantly revised the administrative, civil, and criminal penalties applicable to violations of section 311's discharge prohibition, oil pollution prevention regulations, and spill reporting requirements. Additionally, the OPA amended the administrative enforcement provisions of section 311 to clarify federal search, entry, and inspection authority applicable to vessels and facilities.

A. ENFORCEMENT PROVISIONS

Section 311 establishes federal authority to enforce its provisions on vessels. It states that authorized enforcement personnel may (1) board and inspect vessels in the navigable waters of the United States and the waters of the contiguous zone, (2) with or without a warrant, arrest any person who in the presence of an authorized enforcement person violates the discharge prohibition, and (3) execute any warrant or other process issued by an officer or court of competent jurisdiction.[165]

For facilities, the EPA or the Coast Guard is authorized to require owners and operators of facilities to maintain records; make reports; install, use, and

---

162. *Id.* § 2708(a). In Gatlin Oil Co. v. United States, 169 F.3d 207 (4th Cir. 1999), Gatlin appealed the Fund's determination that it could not recover all of its response costs from the OSLTF despite the fact that the company was entitled to a third-party defense based on the fact that the spill occurred when a vandal opened valves on an oil storage tank. Approximately ten gallons of oil had reached navigable waters, out of the approximate 20,000 to 30,000 gallons that were discharged from the tank. Gatlin presented a claim to the OSLTF of $850,000 to cover all of its removal costs, including those imposed by state officials to protect soil and groundwater. The government stated that only those costs incurred to protect navigable waters from discharge or threat of discharge could be recovered, which was only approximately $7,000. The government based its denial of additional recovery on the language of 33 U.S.C. § 2702(a). The Fourth Circuit held that the government interpretation to be correct based both on the statutory language and congressional intent.

163. OPA § 9001(b) (amending 26 U.S.C. § 9509(c)(2)).

164. 33 U.S.C. § 2715.

165. *Id.* § 1321(m)(1).

maintain monitoring equipment and methods; and provide other information necessary to carry out the objectives of section 311. Further, personnel authorized to enforce section 311 may enter and inspect any facility to which section 311 is applicable and, at reasonable times, have access to and copy any records, take samples, and inspect any required monitoring equipment. Additionally, enforcement personnel may (1) with or without a warrant, arrest any person who violates the provisions of section 311 in the presence or view of such enforcement personnel; and (2) execute any warrant or process issued by an officer or court of competent jurisdiction.[166]

B. CIVIL PENALTIES

The OPA amended section 311 to provide for two classes of administrative civil penalties for violation of the discharge prohibition or regulations issued under the authority of section 311. OPA also amended section 311 so that different administrative due-process requirements are required for the two classes of penalties.[167]

Class I penalties can be assessed up to $11,000 per violation to a maximum of $27,500. Respondents of class I penalty assessments are given a reasonable opportunity to be heard and to present evidence. However, their hearing need not meet the requirements of the Administrative Procedure Act (APA) for formal adjudications.[168]

Class II penalties can be assessed up to $11,000 per day of violation, with a maximum assessment of $137,500. Class II hearings must be on the record and comply with the due-process requirements of the APA.[169]

The OPA also increased the penalties available in a civil action brought in federal district court for violations of section 311 requirements. Any owner, operator, or person in charge of any onshore or offshore facility or vessel may be fined up to $27,500 per day per violation, or $1,100 per barrel of oil or unit of reportable quantity of hazardous substances discharged.[170] The latter provision is unique in terms of authorizing a quantity-based penalty assessment and may potentially result in very large penalties in the event of large-scale spills. Any person who without good cause fails to properly remove a discharge in accordance with directions of an FOSC or who fails to comply with an administrative order issued to protect public health may be liable for a civil penalty of up to $27,500

---

166. *Id.* § 1321(m)(2).
167. OPA § 4301(b).
168. 33 U.S.C. § 1321(b)(6)(B)(i) as amended by the Debt Collection Act of 1997. *See* 40 C.F.R. pt. 19. For a discussion of administrative procedure for EPA enforcement actions, see chapter 11.
169. *Id.* § 1321(b)(6)(B)(ii) as amended by the Debt Collection Act of 1997. *See* 40 C.F.R. pt. 19.
170. *Id.* § 1321(b)(7)(A) as amended by the Debt Collection Act of 1997. *See* 40 C.F.R. pt. 19.

per day of violation or an amount treble the costs incurred by the OSLTF as a result of such failure.[171] Additionally, persons may be liable for a penalty of up to $27,500 per day of violation for failure to comply with pollution prevention regulations issued under the authority of section 311.[172] When the government can demonstrate that the discharge resulted from willful negligence or misconduct, persons may be liable for civil penalties of not less than $110,000 and no more than $3,300 per barrel of oil or unit of reportable quantity discharged.[173]

The OPA also specified criteria to be considered in determining the amount of civil penalty appropriate for a given violation. The person imposing the penalty is to consider the seriousness of the violation, the possible economic benefit to the violator from the violation, past violations, the degree of culpability, efforts to minimize any damage caused by the violation and the degree of success of such efforts, and the impact of the penalty on the violator.[174]

C. CRIMINAL SANCTIONS

The OPA amended the CWA to make criminal sanctions that had been applicable to other provisions of the CWA applicable to violations of the discharge prohibition in section 311.[175] Criminal penalties are authorized for negligent or knowing discharges in violation of the discharge prohibition of section 311. A person who negligently discharges oil or hazardous substances is subject to a fine of up to $25,000 per day of violation, up to one-year imprisonment, or both for a first violation. In the event of a second conviction, the fine may increase to $50,000 per day or two years' imprisonment.[176] "Knowing" violations are liable for a fine of up to $50,000 or three years in prison, or $100,000 or six years' imprisonment for a second conviction.[177]

In addition, criminal sanctions are applicable to any person who knowingly violates the discharge prohibition in section 311 and who knows at the time that the discharge places another person in imminent danger of death or bodily injury. In such case, a person is subject to a fine of $250,000 and/or imprisonment of not more than 15 years. An organization is subject to a fine of up to $1 million. If the conviction is for a violation committed after a first conviction for knowing endangerment, the maximum punishment is doubled.[178]

---

171. *Id.* § 1321(b)(7)(B) as amended by the Debt Collection Act of 1997. *See* 40 C.F.R. pt. 19.
172. *Id.* § 1321(b)(7)(C) as amended by the Debt Collection Act of 1997. *See* 40 C.F.R. pt. 19.
173. *Id.* § 1321(b)(7)(D) as amended by the Debt Collection Act of 1997. *See* 40 C.F.R. pt. 19.
174. *Id.* § 1321(b)(8) as amended by the Debt Collection Act of 1997. *See* 40 C.F.R. pt. 19.
175. OPA § 4301(c).
176. 33 U.S.C. § 1319(c)(2).
177. *Id.* § 1319(c)(2).
178. *Id.* § 1319(c)(3).

CHAPTER 8

"Wet Weather" Regulations:

Control of Stormwater and Discharges From Concentrated Animal Feeding Operations and Other Facilities

RANDY HILL*

DAVID ALLNUTT*

For many years, EPA's efforts to regulate water pollution through the National Pollutant Discharge Elimination System (NPDES) program focused almost exclusively on controlling the discharge of process wastewater from industrial plants and the discharge of sewage from municipal treatment works. Since the late 1980s, however, EPA's NPDES permitting and enforcement programs have placed increasing emphasis on efforts to control "wet weather" discharges such as those from combined sewer overflows, industrial and municipal stormwater systems, and concentrated animal feeding operations. This chapter summarizes the Clean Water Act (CWA) authorities that govern these point source wet weather discharges. A related topic, sewer overflows, is covered in chapter 4.

I. Stormwater

The primary focus of the NPDES program's efforts to improve water quality traditionally has been on controlling the discharge of industrial process wastewater and municipal sewage. Stormwater runoff in the early days of the NPDES program was treated as a diffuse source of nonpoint source pollution. This may have seemed logical because most runoff cannot efficiently be controlled using the strict end-of-pipe effluent limitations that are effective in regulating traditional industrial and municipal discharges.

---

* The views expressed here are the author's and do not necessarily reflect those of the United States Environmental Protection Agency or the United States Department of Justice.

However, many sources of stormwater runoff are discharged through discrete conveyances or separate storm sewers, and thus legally meet the definition of a "point source." As a result, EPA was directed by court order to require NPDES permits for the discharge of stormwater runoff. Since that time, the appropriate means of regulating point source discharges of stormwater has been a matter of serious concern and controversy. EPA promulgated NPDES stormwater regulations in 1973,[1] 1976,[2] 1979,[3] and 1984,[4] most of which resulted in extensive litigation but little, if any, real control of stormwater discharges.

In 1987, however, Congress added section 402(p) to the Clean Water Act,[5] which established a comprehensive new scheme for regulation of stormwater. Section 402(p) provided that, except for five categories of stormwater discharges specified in section 402(p)(2), the EPA (or an approved NPDES state) could not require an NPDES permit for discharges composed entirely of stormwater until after October 1, 1994.[6] The five categories for which permits could be required before October 1, 1994, were:

1.   a discharge with respect to which a permit has been issued prior to February 4, 1987;
2.   a discharge associated with industrial activity;
3.   a discharge from a municipal separate storm sewer system serving a population of 250,000 or more;
4.   a discharge from a municipal separate storm sewer serving a population of 100,000 or more, but less than 250,000; and
5.   a discharge for which the EPA Administrator or the state, as the case may be, determines to contribute to a violation of a water quality standard or is a significant contributor of pollutants to the waters of the United States.[7]

Section 402(p) thus established a phased and tiered approach to permitting stormwater discharges. The five categories identified above comprise what EPA refers to as Phase I of its stormwater permit program. All stormwater discharges

---

1.   38 Fed. Reg. 13,530 *et seq.* (May 22, 1973).
2.   41 Fed. Reg. 11,303 (Mar. 18, 1976).
3.   44 Fed. Reg. 32,854 *et seq.* (June 7, 1979).
4.   49 Fed. Reg. 37,998 *et seq.* (Sept. 26, 1984).
5.   Pub. L. 100-4, § 405, 101 Stat. 69 (Feb. 4, 1987).
6.   As originally adopted, § 402(p)(1) specified that the moratorium on permitting stormwater discharges other than the five categories specified in the statute would expire on October 1, 1992. Congress later extended the deadline to October 1, 1994. Pub. L. 102-580, § 364, 106 Stat. 4862 (Oct. 31, 1992).
7.   33 U.S.C. §§ 1342(p)(1) and (2).

not included in these five categories are covered in Phase II of the program, discussed below.

Stormwater is defined in EPA regulations to include stormwater runoff, snow melt runoff, and surface runoff and drainage.[8] Specifically excluded by statute from the definition of point source are agricultural stormwater discharges.[9]

A. PHASE I STORMWATER DISCHARGES

1. Discharges Associated With Industrial Activity

The term "discharge associated with industrial activity" has been defined by EPA[10] to mean a discharge from any conveyance that is used for collecting and conveying stormwater and that is directly related to manufacturing, processing, or raw material storage areas at an industrial plant in one of the following eleven industrial categories:[11]

1. facilities subject to stormwater effluent limitation guidelines, new source performance standards, or toxic pollutant effluent standards (except such toxic standards as are specifically exempted);

2. facilities in SIC codes 24 (except 2434), 26 (except 265 and 267), 28 (except 283), 29, 31, 32 (except 323), 33, 344, or 373;

3. facilities in SIC codes 10 through 14 (mineral industry) including active or inactive mining operations (except for certain postreclamation activities),[12] and oil and gas exploration, production, processing, or treatment operations, or transmission facilities that discharge stormwater contaminated through contact with overburden, raw materials, intermediate products, finished products, byproducts, or products located on the site of such operations;

4. hazardous waste treatment, storage, or disposal facilities, including those operating under interim status or pursuant to a Resource Conservation and Recovery Act (RCRA) Subtitle C permit;

5. landfills, land application sites, and open dumps that receive or have received any industrial wastes, including facilities subject to RCRA Subtitle D;

---

8. 40 C.F.R. § 122.26(b)(13).

9. 33 U.S.C. § 1362(14).

10. 40 C.F.R. § 122.26(b)(14).

11. 40 C.F.R. §§ 122.26(b)(14)(i)–(xi).

12. The regulation of stormwater discharges from inactive mining operations under CWA section 402(p) was specifically upheld in American Mining Congress v. EPA, 965 F.2d 759 (9th Cir. 1992).

6. recycling facilities, including metal scrap yards, battery reclaimers, salvage yards, and automobile junkyards, including SIC codes 5015 and 5093;

7. steam electric power generating facilities, including coal handling sites;

8. transportation facilities classified under SIC codes 40, 41, 42 (except 4221–4225), 43, 44, 45, and 5171 that have vehicle maintenance shops, equipment cleaning operations, or airport de-icing operations;

9. treatment works treating domestic sewage or any other sewage sludge or wastewater treatment devices or systems used in the storage, treatment, recycling, or reclamation of municipal or domestic sewage. Excluded are farmlands, domestic gardens, lands used for the beneficial application of sludge, or areas in compliance with CWA section 405;

10. construction activity including clearing, grading, and excavation activities, except operations that result in the disturbance of less than five acres of land; and

11. facilities covered under SIC codes 20, 21, 22, 23, 2434, 25, 265, 267, 27, 283, 285, 30, 31 (except 311), 323, 34 (except 3441), 35, 36, 37 (except 373), 38, 39, and 4221–4225.[13]

EPA's definition of stormwater discharge associated with industrial activity includes, but is not limited to, discharges from industrial plant yards; immediate access roads; rail lines used to carry materials and products; material handling sites; refuse sites; sites used for the application or disposal of process wastewater; sites used for the storage and maintenance of material handling equipment; sites used for residual treatment, storage, or disposal; shipping and receiving areas; manufacturing buildings; storage areas (including tank farms) for raw materials and products; and areas where industrial activity has occurred in the past and significant materials remain and are exposed to stormwater.[14]

---

13. Under EPA's original regulations, facilities in this category 11 were required to obtain permits only if there was actual exposure of significant materials to stormwater. 55 Fed. Reg. 47,990, 48,063 (Nov. 16, 1990) (promulgating § 122.26(b)(14)(xi)). In Natural Resources Defense Council v. EPA, 966 F.2d 1292 (9th Cir. 1992), the Ninth Circuit struck down the exclusions recognized by categories 10 (construction areas that disturb less than five acres) and 11 (light industries without actual exposure), remanding both for further agency proceedings. The court found that EPA's rule-making record did not support these exclusions. EPA subsequently announced the position that the Ninth Circuit's decision did not have the effect of automatically subjecting stormwater discharges in the two affected categories to immediate permit application and issuance requirements, and that further rule making would be necessary to bring them into the permit program. 57 Fed. Reg. 60,444, 60,446 (Dec. 18, 1992). These sources remained unregulated until EPA promulgated its phase II regulations in 1999. *See* 64 Fed. Reg. 68,722, 68,783 (Dec. 8, 1999).

14. 40 C.F.R. § 122.26(b)(12).

a. Industrial Stormwater Discharges to Storm Sewer Systems. Dischargers of stormwater associated with industrial activity that is discharged through a municipal separate storm sewer to a water of the United States are required to obtain their own NPDES permit, separate from that issued to the municipality.[15] Such discharges are classified as discharges "associated with industrial activity." As such, they are subject to the best-available technology/best conventional technology (BAT/BCT) requirements of section 301(b)(2) and are subject to additional limitations to protect water quality imposed under CWA section 301(b)(1)(C).

Similarly, all operators of stormwater discharges associated with industrial activity that discharge into a privately or federally owned stormwater conveyance are required to be covered by an NPDES permit (individual, general, or as a co-permittee to a permit issued to the portion of the system that discharges directly to a water of the United States).[16]

b. Exclusions. The term "discharges associated with industrial activity" excludes discharges from facilities or activities that are already excluded from the NPDES program under 40 C.F.R. part 122.[17]

In particular, section 402(1)(2) of the CWA[18] exempts from NPDES permitting requirements stormwater discharges that are not contaminated by contact with any overburden raw material, intermediate products, finished products, byproducts, or waste products located on the site of oil, gas, or mining operations. Congress recognized that in the mining and oil and gas industries, stormwater often is channeled around plants and operations in order to prevent stormwater from becoming contaminated. Conveyances at such operations used to collect stormwater located at the plant or directly related to manufacturing, processing, or raw-material storage are required to obtain an NPDES permit.[19]

c. Conditional Exclusion for "No Exposure" of Industrial Activities and Materials in Stormwater. EPA regulations exclude from coverage as "industrial activity" discharges composed entirely of stormwater (other than construction sites) where there is "no exposure" of industrial materials to stormwater.[20] To qualify for the exclusion, the operator of the discharge must provide a storm-resistant shelter to protect industrial materials from exposure to stormwater, certify once every five years that there are no contaminated stormwater discharges from the entire facility, and allow for inspection of the facility by the permit-issuing

---

15. 40 C.F.R. § 122.26(a)(4); 55 Fed. Reg. 48,006 (Nov. 16, 1990).

16. 40 C.F.R. § 122.26(a)(5).

17. 40 C.F.R. § 122.26(b)(14); *see also* 40 C.F.R. § 122.3 and discussion above for exclusions from NPDES program.

18. 33 U.S.C. § 1342(l)(2).

19. *See* 40 C.F.R. § 122.26(b)(14)(iii).

20. 40 C.F.R. § 122.26(g).

authority and by the municipal separate storm sewer systems (often referred to as "MS4s"), if the discharge is through an MS4.[21] The certification requirement is very detailed. The facility must provide its name, address, phone number, and geographical information, and must further indicate that none of these materials or activities are, or will be exposed to, precipitation: areas for use, storage, or cleaning of industrial equipment; materials on the ground from spills or leaks; materials or products from past industrial activity; material handling equipment (other than adequately maintained vehicles); materials or products during loading/ unloading or transporting activities; materials or products stored outside (except for final products intended for outside use, such as cars); materials in open, dete- riorated, or leaking drums, barrels, tanks, or containers; materials or products handled/stored on roads or railways owned/maintained by the discharge; waste material; application or disposal of process wastewater (unless otherwise permit- ted); and particulate matter or residuals from roof stacks/vents (unless otherwise regulated).[22]

A facility that qualifies for the exclusion and submits the required certifica- tion does not need to obtain an NPDES permit for its stormwater discharges, unless it is subsequently designated for permit coverage by the permit-issuing authority as contributing to a water quality standards violation or as a "significant contributor" of pollutants.[23]

d. Types of Permit Applications for Discharges Associated With Industrial Activity. Operators of discharges of stormwater associated with industrial activity, like all others in need of permit, are required to obtain an NPDES permit in one of two ways: (1) an individual NPDES permit or (2) a general NPDES permit.

(i) Individual Permits. Facilities required to, or choosing to, obtain an individual permit must submit Form 2F—the NPDES application form applicable to dis- charges composed entirely of stormwater. (All permit applicants must also sub- mit Form 1 when seeking an NPDES permit.)

Form 2F requires facility-specific information including: (1) a detailed site topographic map, (2) the identification of significant materials treated or stored on site and associated management and disposal practices, (3) the location and description of structural and nonstructural controls to reduce pollutants in the stormwater runoff, (4) an estimate of impervious surface areas, (5) a detailed nar- rative description of facility activities, (6) a certification that stormwater outfalls have been tested or evaluated for the presence of unpermitted nonstormwater dis- charges, and (7) any existing information on significant leaks and spills to toxic

---

21. 40 C.F.R. § 122.26(g)(1).
22. 40 C.F.R. § 122.26(g)(4).
23. 40 C.F.R. § 122.26(g)(3)(iv).

or hazardous pollutants occurring within three years of application submittal.[24] In addition, an individual applicant must submit quantitative analytical data from stormwater outfalls collected during storm events.[25]

(ii) General Permit. A general permit application is the other basic alternative available to dischargers of stormwater associated with industrial activity, and the one that most dischargers, as well as EPA and authorized states, appear to prefer. Where EPA has issued a general permit for a group of dischargers, an eligible facility need only submit a "notice of intent" (NOI) to be covered by the permit. The information requirements imposed in an NOI usually are established in the general permit and generally are far less burdensome than those imposed by an individual or group application. At a minimum, the NOI must request information on the legal name and address of the owner or operator, the facility name and address, the type of facility or discharge, and the receiving stream.[26]

In 1992, EPA issued its first general permits covering stormwater discharges associated with industrial activity, except for discharges from construction activity.[27] These general permits, which EPA later referred to collectively as the "Baseline General Permit,"[28] were applicable in numerous states and territories (and in Indian country) where EPA has permit-issuing authority. Among other things, these general permits required facilities covered to develop and implement stormwater pollution prevention plans (SWPPPs) and to undertake limited monitoring that varies according to the type of industrial activity. These permits also imposed a numeric effluent limitation on discharges of coal pile runoff. These permits served as a model to be used in whole or in part by states issuing stormwater permits. The Baseline General Permits were later replaced by the "Multi-Sector General Permit" discussed below.

For discharges associated with construction activity, EPA issued a similar "Baseline Construction General Permit" in 1992,[29] and reissued the permit in 1998.[30] Similar to the baseline permit for nonconstruction industrial facilities, the Baseline Construction General Permit contained requirements to submit a "Notice of Intent" to be covered (at least 48 hours prior to commencing construction), a prohibition on discharging sources of nonstormwater, requirements for releases of hazardous substances or oil in excess of reporting quantities, requirements for developing and implementing stormwater pollution prevention plans, and requirements for site inspections. The centerpiece of the permits is the

---

24. 40 C.F.R. §§ 122.26(c)(1)(i)(A)–(D).

25. 40 C.F.R. § 122.26(e)(1).

26. 40 C.F.R. § 122.21(a).

27. 57 Fed. Reg. 41,237 (Sept. 9, 1992).

28. 60 Fed. Reg. 50,804, 50,808 (Sept. 29, 1995).

29. 57 Fed. Reg. 41,176 (Sept. 9, 1992); 57 Fed. Reg. 44,412 (Sept. 25, 1992).

pollution prevention plan, which is required to include: (1) a site description; (2) a description of controls to be used at the site (for example, erosion and sediment controls to prevent contaminated runoff during construction, and stormwater management measures, which are structural features built into the site during construction but which are designed primarily to control postconstruction pollution); (3) a description of maintenance and inspection procedures; and (4) a description of pollution prevention measures for any nonstormwater discharges that exist. The construction general permits, in essence, "federalize" existing state or local erosion and sediment control programs, in that the permittee must provide a certification that its stormwater pollution prevention plan reflects requirements related to protecting water resources that are specified in state or local sediment and erosion plans or stormwater management plans.[31]

(iii) Group Permit Application. Under the original 1990 phase I stormwater regulations, EPA recognized a third way that operators of stormwater discharges associated with industrial activity (other than construction activity) could apply for and obtain an NPDES permit: the group application process. Under the "group application" regulation, a group of similar facilities could submit a single group application for their stormwater discharges. Group applications were appropriate for facilities that have the same or similar operations, discharge the same types of wastes, are subject to the same CWA effluent limitation guideline (ELG) or the same discharge permit limitations, and are subject to the same or similar monitoring requirements.[32]

Under EPA regulations, industrial facilities had a one-time opportunity to submit a group application, in two parts. Part 1 required that the group identify the member of the group and describe the industrial activities of the group, submit a list of significant materials exposed to precipitation and the management practices used to prevent contact with stormwater, and identify which of the group's participants would submit quantitative data.[33] Part 2 of the group application contained the quantitative data. Facilities rejected from the group by EPA generally were given a year to submit an individual permit application or obtain coverage under a general permit.[34]

---

30. 63 Fed. Reg 7,858 (Feb. 17, 1998); *see also* 63 Fed. Reg. 15,622 (Mar. 31, 1998) (EPA Region 4); 63 Fed. Reg. 36,490 (July 6, 1998) (EPA Region 6).

31. 40 C.F.R. § 122.44(s) (requiring construction stormwater permits to include qualifying state, tribal, or local erosion and sediment control requirements).

32. 40 C.F.R. § 122.28(a)(2)(ii).

33. 40 C.F.R. § 122.26(c)(2)(i).

34. 40 C.F.R. § 122.26(e)(2)(iv).

The group application process resulted in the issuance of the "Multi-Sector General Permit" (MSGP), which EPA first issued in 1995,[35] and subsequently reissued in 2000.[36] EPA received over 1,200 group applications representing over 60,000 different industrial facilities.[37] EPA organized these facilities into 29 different industrial sectors, representing nearly all of the types of facilities (except construction sites) regulated by the phase I industrial stormwater regulations, including, for example, lumber and wood products facilities; paper manufacturing facilities; chemical manufacturing facilities; asphalt paving and roofing materials manufacturers; stone, clay, glass, and concrete products facilities; primary metals facilities; metal mines; coal mines; oil and gas extraction facilities; quarries; hazardous waste treatment, storage, or disposal facilities; landfills; automobile salvage yards; scrap and waste material processing and recycling facilities; steam electric power generating facilities; transportation facilities, including bus terminals or airports; wastewater treatment plants; and many others.[38] EPA later expanded the scope of the MSGP to a number of additional industrial categories and terminated the earlier Baseline General Permit.[39]

The MSGP is similar to the Baseline General Permit in its reliance on SWPPPs as the primary form of effluent limitations and standards controlling industrial stormwater discharges. Yet, since the MSGP was developed in consideration of the detailed industry-specific qualitative and quantitative information provided through the group application process, the MSGP refined the Baseline permit by including industry-specific management practices and other requirements for inclusion in the industry's SWPPP. The MSGP also provides tailored SWPPP requirements for facilities that manage hazardous substances in amounts that trigger section 313 of the Emergency Planning and Community Right-to-know Act (EPCRA)[40] and for salt storage facilities.[41] The MSGP added numeric effluent limitations for certain industrial categories based on previously promulgated effluent guidelines: discharges from phosphate fertilizer manufacturing (40 C.F.R. part 418), asphalt paving and roofing emulsions (40 C.F.R. part 443), cement manufacturing materials storage pile runoff (40 C.F.R. part 411), and discharges resulting from the spray-down of lumber and wood products storage yards (wet decking) (40 C.F.R. part 429).[42] Finally, the MSGP includes analytical pollutant monitoring requirements which are tailored for each industry based

35. 60 Fed. Reg. 50,804 (Sept. 29, 1995).

36. 65 Fed. Reg. 64,746 (Oct. 30, 2000).

37. 60 Fed. Reg. 50,804, 50,807 (Sept. 25, 1995).

38. *Id.* at 50,804.

39. 63 Fed. Reg. 52,430 (Sept. 30, 1998).

40. 42 U.S.C. § 11023.

41. 65 Fed. Reg. 64,746, 64,766 (Oct. 30, 2000).

42. *Id.* at 64,761.

on the data received in the group application process (and, for the 2000 permit, monitoring data reported to comply with the 1995 permit).[43]

2. Discharges from Large and Medium Municipal Separate
Storm Sewer Systems

The other major part of the EPA phase I program regulates MS4s.[44] EPA regulations define "municipal separate storm sewer" to include any conveyance or system of conveyances that is owned or operated by a state or local government entity, that is designed or used for collecting and conveying stormwater, that is not a combined sewer,[45] and that is not part of a publicly owned treatment works (POTW).[46]

Systems serving 250,000 or more residents are "large" MS4s; systems serving between 100,000 and 250,000 are "medium" MS4s.[47] EPA's regulations identify over 200 cities and counties as having either large or medium MS4s.[48] The permit-issuing authority also may designate a municipal system as a large or medium system on a site-specific basis due to its interrelationship to a system that otherwise meets the definition of a large or medium system.[49]

a. Application Requirements for Large and Medium Municipal Separate Storm Sewer Systems. EPA established a detailed two-part application process for large and medium MS4s. Part 1 of the application was a form requiring general information about the MS4, qualitative and quantitative data regarding the quality of the system's stormwater discharges, and a description of existing structural and nonstructural controls to reduce discharges from the system.[50] Part 2 of the application form was designed to supplement information obtained in part 1 and to provide municipalities with the opportunity to propose a comprehensive stormwater management plan to control, to the maximum extent possible, discharges from municipal separate storm sewers. The stormwater management plan needed to address four types of pollutant sources: (1) runoff from commercial and residential areas, (2) runoff from industrial areas, (3) runoff from construction sites, and (4) nonstormwater discharges resulting primarily from illicit connections to the

---

43. *Id.* at 64,768.

44. 40 C.F.R. § 122.26(b)(19).

45. A combined sewer system is one that combines municipal sewage with stormwater runoff. It is a point source that must be permitted in accordance with normal permit issuance procedures. 40 C.F.R. § 122.26(a)(7).

46. 40 C.F.R. § 122.26(b)(8).

47. 40 C.F.R. §§ 122.26(b)(4) and (7).

48. *Id.*

49. *Id.*

50. 40 C.F.R. § 122.26(d)(1).

system and improper disposal practices.[51] All phase I MS4 permit applications were due no later than 1993,[52] and the permit-issuing authority had one year to issue or deny the permit after both parts of the application had been submitted.[53]

Permits must be obtained for all discharges from both large and medium municipal separate storm sewers. NPDES permits are required for point source discharges through the municipal storm sewers to the waters of the United States. One system-wide permit may be issued to cover all dischargers, either as permittees or co-permittees[54] with the municipality, or distinct permits may be issued for any discharge or category of discharges into the system.[55]

b. NPDES Permit Conditions for Municipal Separate Storm Sewer Systems.

Section 402(p)(3)(B) of the CWA provides that permits for discharges from municipal separate storm sewers

1. may be issued on a system- or jurisdiction-wide basis;
2. shall include a requirement to effectively prohibit nonstormwater discharges into the storm sewers; and
3. shall require controls to reduce the discharge of pollutants to the maximum extent practicable, including management practices, control techniques and system, design and engineering methods, and such other provisions as the EPA Administrator or the state determines appropriate for the control of such pollutants.

Through section 402(p)(3)(B), Congress modified the substantive requirements that must be met by municipal stormwater discharges. Such discharges need not meet the technology-based requirements of section 301 of the CWA (either BAT/BCT controls or secondary treatment). Instead, municipal separate storm sewers simply are required to "require controls to reduce the discharge of stormwater to the maximum extent practicable."

One key issue unanswered by section 402(p)(3)(B), however, is whether phase I municipal stormwater permits must assure compliance with water quality standards, as required for other NPDES permits pursuant to section 301(b)(1)(C) of the CWA.[56] EPA had interpreted the answer to this question to be "yes." In a

---

51. 40 C.F.R. §§ 122.26(d)(2)(i) and (iv).

52. 40 C.F.R. §§ 122.26(e)(3) and (4).

53. 40 C.F.R. §§ 122.26(e)(7)(ii) and (iii).

54. Co-permittees are only responsible for compliance with permit conditions relating to the discharge from the municipal system for which they are considered operators. 40 C.F.R. § 122.26(a)(3)(vi).

55. 40 C.F.R. § 122.26(a)(3)(ii).

56. 33 U.S.C. § 1311(b)(1)(C). *See* chapter 2, *infra* for further discussion of effluent limitations to meet water quality standards.

1991 legal opinion issued by EPA's General Counsel, the agency explained that the MEP standard was designed to modify the technology-based requirements of section 301, but not the water quality–based requirements.[57] In 1996, EPA issued its "Interim Permitting Approach for Water Quality–Based Effluent Limitations in Stormwater Permits,"[58] which implicitly reaffirmed the 1991 opinion, but further noted that EPA intended to use "best management practices" in lieu of numeric effluent limits as the primary means of ensuring compliance with water quality standards in municipal stormwater permits. As EPA explained,

> The interim permitting approach uses best management practices (BMPs) in first-round stormwater permits, and expanded or better-tailored BMPs in subsequent permits, where necessary, to provide for the attainment of water quality standards. In cases where adequate information exists to develop more specific conditions or limitations to meet water quality standards, these conditions or limitations are to be incorporated into stormwater permits, as necessary and appropriate.[59]

The agency's interpretation of section 402(p)(3)(B) and the Interim Permitting Approach were reviewed by the U.S. Court of Appeals for the Ninth Circuit in the 1999 decision, *Defenders of Wildlife v. Browner.*[60] The Ninth Circuit disagreed with the agency's interpretation that section 301(b)(1)(C) applied to municipal stormwater permits, saying that the structure of section 402(p)(3)(B) made it clear that Congress intended to *"replace[]"* the requirements of section 301 with a new standard.[61] The court then went on to rule, nonetheless, that EPA had authority under section 402(p)(3)(B), itself, to "require strict compliance with state water quality standards, through numerical limits or otherwise."[62] The court noted that section 402(p)(3)(B)(iii) states that "[p]ermits for discharges from municipal storm sewers . . . shall require . . . *such other provisions as the Administrator . . . determine appropriate for the control of such pollutants."*[63] In light of the discretion in that statutory language, the court noted that EPA could require strict compliance with water quality standards or less-than-strict compliance, and

57. "Compliance with Water Quality Standards in NPDES Permits Issued to Municipal Separate Storm Sewer Systems," Memorandum from E. Donald Elliott, Assistant Administrator and General Counsel, to Nancy J. Marvel, Regional Counsel, Region IX (Jan. 9, 1991) (available on LEXIS, ENVIRN library, CASES file).

58. 61 Fed.. Reg. 43,761 (Aug. 26, 1996). *See also* 61 Fed. Reg. 57,425 (Nov. 6, 1996) (question-and-answer document regarding implementation of the interim permitting approach).

59. 61 Fed. Reg. at 43,761. (Aug. 26, 1996).

60. 191 F.3d 1159 (9th Cir. 1999).

61. *Id.* at 1165 (emphasis in original).

62. *Id.* at 1166.

63. *Id.* (quoting 33 U.S.C. § 1342(p)(3)(B)(iii)) (emphasis added by quoting opinion).

could do so through numeric effluent limitations or best management practices, as the agency saw fit.[64] In light of the Ninth Circuit's decision, EPA subsequently announced that it will continue to follow the interim permitting approach and include effluent limitations, primarily in the form of best management practices, to meet water quality standards.[65]

3. Compliance Deadlines

Section 402(p)(4) provides that all phase I discharges must comply with permit conditions as expeditiously as practicable, but in no event later than three years from the date of permit issuance.[66]

B. PHASE II STORMWATER DISCHARGES

Phase II of the stormwater program covers all stormwater discharges not addressed under the five phase I categories described above. Section 402(p)(5) of the CWA required EPA to conduct two studies of phase II stormwater discharges, identifying additional stormwater sources for possible control and procedures or methods for controlling such sources. Section 402(p)(6) of the CWA further required EPA to issue regulations, by 1993, and based on the (p)(5) studies, that designated additional stormwater discharges that should be regulated to protect water quality and established a comprehensive program to regulate such designated discharges. EPA finally issued its regulations under 402(p)(6) in 1999,[67] extending NPDES permit requirements to discharges from "small" construction sites and "small" MS4s. All other phase II discharges are excluded from NPDES requirements, unless specifically designated as contributing to a violation of water quality standards or as a "significant contributor" of pollutants.

1. Discharges From "Small" Construction Activity

EPA expanded the coverage of the stormwater permit program to cover construction sites that disturb greater than one acre of land (or are part of a larger common plan of development that will disturb greater than one acre).[68] Unlike sites greater than 5 acres, however, EPA regulations provide that sites 1 to 5 acres in size may qualify for a waiver from permitting requirements if the operator of the site certifies to the permit-issuance authority that (a) the construction site is in a region with a "rainfall erosivity factor" of less than 5 (as determined by the 1997 USDA handbook *Predicting Soil Erosion by Water: A Guide to Conservation*

---

64. *Id.*

65. 64 Fed. Reg. 68,722, 68,788 (Dec. 8, 1999).

66. 40 C.F.R. § 122.42(d).

67. 64 Fed. Reg. 68,722 (Dec. 8, 1999).

68. 40 C.F.R. § 122.26(b)(15).

Planning with the Revised Universal Soil Loss Equation (RUSLE),[69] or (b) the activity will occur in an area where controls are not needed to protect water quality (based on a TMDL or equivalent water quality analysis).[70] Sites below one acre can be designated for permitting by EPA or an authorized state where the discharge has the potential to contribute to a violation of water quality standards or to be a significant contributor of pollutants.[71]

As with larger construction sites, EPA anticipates that most discharges from small construction activity will be regulated through general permits.[72] EPA has relaxed the requirement for small construction facilities to submit an NOI to be covered under a general permit, leaving it to the discretion of the permit-issuance authority whether to require small construction sites to submit NOIs.[73] For small construction sites that do not obtain coverage under a general permit, the operator must submit the same individual permit application that larger construction sites submit.[74] As with larger construction sites, permits for small construction sites must incorporate appropriate requirements from state, tribal, or local erosion and sediment control programs.[75]

2. Discharges From "Small Municipal Separate Storm Sewer Systems"
EPA expanded the municipal stormwater program to all MS4s located within a census-determined "urbanized area,"[76] which the Census Bureau defines generally as a place that is densely settled and contains a minimum population of 50,000.[77] All municipal storm sewers within urbanized areas thus are required to obtain an NPDES permit, although EPA provided a possibility for waiver of requirements for municipalities with populations below 10,000 persons. For an MS4 serving a population below 1,000, the municipality must show that its municipal storm sewers are not contributing substantially to the pollutant loadings of any larger MS4 to which its sewers are connected, and that, if that smaller MS4 is discharging any pollutant of concern to an impaired water body, no additional stormwater controls are needed based on an existing TMDL for that water body.[78] For an MS4 serving a population of 1,000 to 10,000, there is a slightly higher showing: The permit-issuance authority must evaluate all waters to which

69. 40 C.F.R. § 122.26(b)(15)(i)(A).
70. 40 C.F.R. § 122.26(b)(15)(i)(B).
71. 40 C.F.R. § 122.26(b)(15)(ii).
72. 64 Fed. Reg. 68,777 (Dec. 8, 1999).
73. 40 C.F.R. § 122.28(b)(2)(v).
74. 40 C.F.R. § 122.26(c)(1)(ii).
75. 40 C.F.R. § 122.44(s)(1).
76. 40 C.F.R. § 122.32(a)(1).
77. 64 Fed. Reg. 68,751 (Dec. 8, 1999).
78. 40 C.F.R. § 122.32(d).

the MS4 discharges and determine that the MS4 is not discharging pollutants at levels requiring additional stormwater controls (nor will the MS4 have the future potential to cause a violation of water quality standards).[79] Similar to the industrial stormwater program, EPA or an authorized state can designate otherwise unregulated MS4s for permitting[80] where (1) the MS4 has the potential for significant water quality impacts,[81] (2) the state determines a permit is necessary to implement a comprehensive watershed plan,[82] (3) the MS4 contributes substantially to the pollutant loadings of another regulated MS4,[83] or (4) in response to a citizen petition.[84]

Like the phase I program, EPA has based phase II NPDES permit requirements on development of comprehensive stormwater management plans. Phase II permits will require, at a minimum, that the MS4 develop, implement, and enforce a stormwater management program designed to reduce the discharge of pollutants to the MEP standard and to "satisfy the water quality requirements of the Clean Water Act."[85] The small MS4 permit must contain six minimum control measures addressing:

1. public education and outreach on stormwater impacts,
2. public involvement/participation,
3. illicit discharge detection and elimination,
4. construction site stormwater runoff control,
5. postconstruction stormwater management in development and redevelopment, and
6. pollution prevention/good housekeeping for municipal operations.[86]

The MS4 is required to identify the BMPs that the MS4 or another entity will implement for each of the six minimum measures, as well as "measurable goals" to demonstrate the effectiveness of those BMPs; the MS4 can select BMPs from a list provided by EPA or the authorized state.[87] The permit must also include more-stringent effluent limitations that modify or add to the six minimum controls based on an approved TMDL or equivalent analysis, as needed to protect water quality.[88] Finally, the phase II permit must contain conditions requiring

79. 40 C.F.R. § 122.32(e).
80. 40 C.F.R. § 122.32(a)(2).
81. 40 C.F.R. § 123.35(b)(1).
82. 40 C.F.R. § 123.35(b)(3).
83. 40 C.F.R. § 123.35(b)(4).
84. 40 C.F.R. § 122.26(f).
85. 40 C.F.R. § 122.34(a).
86. 40 C.F.R. § 122.34(b).
87. 40 C.F.R. § 122.34(d).
88. 40 C.F.R. § 122.34(e)(1).

evaluation of the effectiveness of BMPs in meeting the measurable goals, as well as monitoring, reporting, and record-keeping requirements.[89]

One change from the phase I program is that small MS4s do not necessarily need to apply for and obtain individual NPDES permits covering just their own municipal systems. EPA's phase II regulations authorize issuance of general permits for small MS4s, and the MS4 may seek coverage under such a general permit once issued by EPA or the authorized state, as long as the MS4 submits a "Notice of Intent" that includes information on best management practices and measurable goals the MS4 intends to employ to meet the six minimum measures.[90]

3. Phase II Permit Application Deadlines

EPA generally has allowed small construction sites and small MS4s three years from designation to obtain NPDES permit coverage. Thus, small construction sites initially had to obtain permit authorization by March 10, 2003,[91] unless the site is earlier designated as contributing to a water quality standards violation or otherwise as a "significant contributor of pollutants," in which case the site must submit a permit application (or seek coverage under an existing general permit) within 180 days of designation; the 180-day deadline also applies to sites smaller than 1 acre that are designated.[92] The deadlines for small MS4s are essentially the same: March 10, 2003, was the deadline for most MS4s.[93] For MS4s serving populations less than 10,000, the permit-issuance authority has the discretion to phase in permit requirements on a 5-year schedule through March 8, 2007.[94] Small MS4s that are designated for permit coverage must submit a permit application within 180 days of designation.[95]

II. Concentrated Animal Feeding Operations

When it passed the 1972 Federal Water Pollution Control Act (Clean Water Act), Congress included within the definition of "point sources" subject to NPDES regulation any "concentrated animal feeding operation . . . from which pollutants are or may be discharged."[96] The CWA does not define "concentrated animal feeding operation" (CAFO) or offer any specific guidance as to how discharges from

---

89. 40 C.F.R. § 122.34(e).

90. 40 C.F.R. § 122.33(b)(1).

91. 40 C.F.R. § 122.26(e)(8).

92. 40 C.F.R. §§ 122.26(e)(5), 124.52(c).

93. 40 C.F.R. § 122.26(e)(9)(i).

94. 40 C.F.R. § 123.35(d)(3).

95. 40 C.F.R. § 122.26(e)(9)(ii).

96. 33 U.S.C. § 502(14).

this type of point source are to be controlled as compared to other point sources. In the intervening 30 years, however, EPA regulations and interpretive guidance and court decisions have served to define the universe of regulated CAFOs and to prescribe the standards that these facilities must meet under the CWA.

A. DEFINITION OF CAFO

EPA's earliest efforts to regulate wastewater and manure generated at CAFOs date to the 1970s. Since 1976, EPA regulations have defined "concentrated animal feeding operation" to include any "animal feeding operation" that confines more than a specified number of "animal units" or that is designated a "significant contributor of pollutants" by the NPDES permitting authority. Determining whether any particular livestock operation is a CAFO involves a two-part analysis. One must first determine whether the facility is an "animal feeding operation" and then inquire into whether it confines the requisite number and type of animals to be considered a CAFO by definition and, if not, whether it has been designated a CAFO by the NPDES permitting authority.

EPA and the U.S. Department of Agriculture (USDA) have estimated that approximately 450,000 of the 1.1 million livestock and poultry operations in the United States raise or house animals in confinement and qualify as animal feeding operations (AFOs).[97] EPA and USDA estimate that no more than 5 percent of these 450,000 AFOs qualify as CAFOs subject to regulation under the Clean Water Act.[98] For the remaining 95 percent of AFOs, state-specific regulatory or voluntary efforts are used to assist owners and operators in reducing water pollution and public health risks. These state-specific measures are beyond the scope of this chapter.

1. Which Facilities Qualify as AFOs?

EPA's CAFO regulations define "animal feeding operation" as any "lot or facility" where the following conditions are met:

1. Animals (other than aquatic animals) have been, are, or will be stabled or confined and fed or maintained for a total of 45 days or more in any 12-month period, and

---

97. U.S. Department of Agriculture & U.S. EPA, "Unified National Strategy for Animal Feeding Operations," http://www.epa.gov/owm/finafost.htm (Mar. 9, 1999); *see also* GENERAL ACCOUNTING OFFICE, ANIMAL AGRICULTURE: INFORMATION ON WASTE MANAGEMENT AND WATER QUALITY ISSUES (June 1995).

98. U.S. Department of Agriculture & U.S. EPA, "Unified National Strategy for Animal Feeding Operations," http://www.epa.gov/owm/finafost.htm (March 9, 1999). In January 2001, EPA estimated that there were 13,000 CAFOs subject to regulation under existing CWA regulations. 66 Fed. Reg. 2,960, 2,968–2,969 (Jan. 12, 2001) (preamble to proposed revisions to CAFO regulations).

2.   Crops, vegetation, forage growth, or post harvest residues are not sustained in the normal growing season over any portion of the lot or facility.[99]

The first part of this definition makes clear that AFOs are not limited to facilities that confine any particular type of animal (except that fish or other aquatic animals are excluded), and thus may encompass zoos, kennels, ostrich farms, and so forth, in addition to the more traditional dairy farms, cattle feedlots, and swine farms. If an animal is on a facility for any portion of a day, EPA considers it to be on the facility for a full day for purposes of counting the 45-day period.[100] The 45 days need not be consecutive to qualify the facility as an AFO, and the 12-month period need not correspond to the calendar year.[101] Finally, EPA interprets "maintained" to mean that animals are confined in an area where waste is generated; animals need not be fed or otherwise sustained in a lot or facility to be considered "maintained" there.[102]

The so-called "vegetation" exemption found in the second part of EPA's AFO definition is subject to varying interpretations, but has been interpreted quite narrowly by EPA. Most issues surrounding this second prong of this definition center on whether facilities are excluded from regulation by virtue of having: (1) de minimis vegetation in the confinement area; or (2) seasonal confinement lots that support vegetation during periods when animals are not present. The regulatory history surrounding this provision is, at best, murky.[103] In its Jan-

---

99. 40 C.F.R. § 122.23(b)(1).

100. 66 Fed. Reg. 2,960, 3,004 (Jan. 12, 2001) (preamble to proposed revisions to CAFO regulations); U.S. EPA Office of Water, "Guidance Manual and Sample NPDES Permit for Concentrated Animal Feeding Operations," Final Internal Review Draft, http://www.epa.gov/npdes/pubs/dman_afo-2000.pdf, p. 5 (Sept. 21, 2000).

101. *Id.*

102. U.S. EPA Office of Water, "Guidance Manual and Sample NPDES Permit for Concentrated Animal Feeding Operations," Final Internal Review Draft, http://www.epa.gov/npdes/pubs/dman_afo-2000.pdf, p. 5 (Sept. 21, 2000).

103. As originally proposed in 1975, the AFO definition would have read: "The term 'animal feeding operation' means a lot or facility . . . within which animals have been or will be stabled or confined and fed . . . and crops, vegetation or forage growth are not sustained in the area of confinement." 40 Fed. Reg. 54,182, 54,185 (Nov. 20, 1975). The phrase "normal growing season" appeared nowhere in this proposal. According to the preamble to the final rule, the proposed language led several commenters to "point[] out that a clarification of this definition was necessary, particularly as to the intent of the vegetation criterion." 41 Fed. Reg. 11,458, 11,458 (Mar. 18, 1976). In response to these comments, EPA stated that it was revising the final rule "to include post-harvest residues and to make clear that only confined areas which lack vegetation, crops, etc. in every part or portion of the lot or facility are included within the term 'animal feeding operation.'" 41 Fed. Reg. 11,458, 11,458 (Mar. 18, 1976). Although not discussed in this response to comments, the phrase "normal growing season" was also added to the AFO definition at this point. 41 Fed. Reg. 11,458, 11,460 (Mar. 18, 1976).

uary 2001 proposal to revise the NPDES CAFO regulations, EPA sought to "clarify" the existing regulations, stating that the AFO definition

> was not intended to exclude . . . those confinement areas that have growth over only a small portion of the facility or that have growth only a portion of the time that the animals are present. The definition is intended to exclude pastures and rangeland that are largely covered with vegetation that can absorb nutrients in the manure.[104]

This narrow interpretation of the existing vegetation language appears consistent with earlier interpretations by EPA[105] and at least one court.[106]

2. Which AFOs Are CAFOs by Definition?

EPA's CAFO regulations contain a specific definition used to determine whether a particular AFO qualifies as a CAFO. The regulations contain a formula for calculating "animal units" that involves adding the number of animals multiplied by various factors (for example, "slaughter and feeder cattle multiplied by 1.0 plus the number of mature dairy cattle multiplied by 1.4 . . ."").[107] The regulations then divide the AFO universe into three "tiers." AFOs that confine 300 or fewer animal units (or that confine animals of a type not specifically addressed in 40 C.F.R. part 122, appendix B) are considered CAFOs only if they are designated by the permitting authority (*see* Section II.A.3, *infra*). AFOs confining between 301 and 1,000 animal units (so-called "middle-tier" AFOs) are defined as CAFOs only if, in addition to confining the requisite number of animals: "[1] pollutants are discharged into navigable waters through a man-made ditch, flushing system or other similar man-made device; or [2] pollutants are discharged directly into waters of the United States which originate outside of and pass over, across, or through the facility or otherwise come into direct contact with the animals confined in the operation."[108] While the exact contours of these two additional criteria for middle-tier AFOs may be unclear, the regulations do appear to require that

---

104. 66 Fed. Reg. 2,960, 3,004 (Jan. 12, 2001).

105. 60 Fed. Reg. 44489, 44490–91 (Aug. 28, 1995) (fact sheet to general NPDES permit for CAFOs in Idaho); U.S. EPA Office of Water, Guide Manual on NPDES Regulations for Concentrated Animal Feeding Operations at 4 (Dec. 1995).

106. Concerned Area Residents for the Environment v. Southview Farm (*Southview Farm*), 34 F.3d 114, 123 (2d Cir. 1994) (stating that the vegetation exemption was meant to exclude only those lots that have: (1) enough vegetation to absorb excess nutrients; and (2) too few animals to eat or trample the grass), *cert. denied,* 514 U.S. 1082 (1995).

107. 40 C.F.R. pt. 122, app. B. In addition to the formula, Appendix B also contains tables establishing threshold numbers of animals by animal type to meet the CAFO definition. For example, although there are no animal unit multipliers for turkeys or for ducks, the tables make clear that 55,000 turkeys or 5,000 ducks are equivalent to 1,000 animal units.

108. 40 C.F.R. pt .122, app. B(b).

such a facility actually discharge (either through a man-made device or as a result of direct contact between animals and surface water) in order for the facility to qualify as a CAFO. On the other hand, all AFOs confining more than 1,000 animal units (so-called "upper-tier" AFOs) are defined as CAFOs without reference to method (or existence) of discharge.

EPA's regulations provide an exclusion from the CAFO definition for facilities that discharge only in the event of a 25-year, 24-hour storm event.[109] It is important to distinguish this CAFO definition exclusion from the 25-year, 24-hour design criterion contained in the CAFO effluent guideline (*see* Section II.B.3, *infra*). Even a facility that is designed, constructed, and operated to meet the 25-year, 24-hour design criterion may discharge in events less severe than a 25-year storm; for example, when melting snow combines with several days of 10-year storms to exceed the 25-year storm capacity. As a result, even properly constructed and operated facilities may run afoul of the CWA if they remain unpermitted.[110] In addition, EPA has interpreted the 25-year storm event exclusion quite narrowly, stating that it refers not only to direct discharges from the facility's production area, but also to discharges to surface water resulting from land application or from production area seepage to groundwater with a direct hydrological connection.[111] In light of this interpretation, EPA has said that it "believes that all or virtually all large CAFOs have had a discharge in the past, have a current discharge, or have the potential to discharge in the future" and are therefore point sources.[112]

Finally, it is worth mentioning here that the CAFO definition includes chicken operations only to the extent that they have "continuous overflow watering" or a "liquid manure system."[113] As a result, most chicken operations that employ a dry manure handling system would qualify as a CAFO only if the permitting authority designated it as such. However, EPA interprets the term "liquid manure system" to include poultry operations where dry waste or litter is stacked in areas exposed to rainfall or an adjacent watercourse.[114] Thus, a poorly operated

---

109. 40 C.F.R. pt .122, app. B. The "25-year, 24-hour" precipitation event for a given location may be determined with reference to the National Weather Service's "Technical Paper Number 40, Rainfall Frequency Atlas of the United States," May 1961, as amended. *See* 40 C.F.R. § 412.11(e).

110. *See, e.g.,* Carr v. Alta Verde Industries, 931 F.2d 1055, 1059-60 (5th Cir. 1991).

111. 66 Fed. Reg. 2,960, 3,007 (Jan. 12, 2001).

112. *Id.*

113. 40 C.F.R. pt .122, app. B(a)(7-8), (b)(7-8).

114. U.S. EPA Office of Water, "Guidance Manual and Sample NPDES Permit for Concentrated Animal Feeding Operations," Final Internal Review Draft, http://www.epa.gov/npdes/pubs/dman_afo-2000.pdf, p. 11 (Sept. 21, 2000); U.S. EPA OFFICE OF WATER, GUIDE MANUAL ON NPDES REGULATIONS FOR CONCENTRATED ANIMAL FEEDING OPERATIONS at 6, n.1 (Dec. 1995).

chicken AFO may meet the regulatory definition of CAFO by stacking wastes outdoors and thereby inadvertently establishing a crude liquid manure system.

3. Which AFOs May Be Designated CAFOs?

EPA's regulations set forth a process by which the NPDES permitting authority may, on a case-by-case basis, designate as a CAFO any AFO that it determines is a "significant contributor of pollution to the waters of the United States."[115] The regulations require that any CAFO designation be preceded by an on-site inspection and that the determination to designate be based on the five factors listed in 40 C.F.R. section 122.23(c). No AFO with 300 or fewer animal units may be designated a CAFO unless it also meets the "method of discharge" ("manmade device" or "direct contact") criteria applicable to middle-tier AFOs.[116] A livestock operation that does not qualify as AFO may not be designated as a CAFO, even if it is a significant contributor of pollution.

B. CWA REQUIREMENTS APPLICABLE TO CAFOS

1. Prohibition on Unpermitted Discharges

As "point sources," CAFOs may not discharge pollutants to waters of the United States except in compliance with an NPDES permit.[117] As a result, a discharge of manure, process wastewater, or other pollutants from the confinement area of an unpermitted CAFO would clearly violate section 301(a) of the CWA. Unpermitted discharges from the CAFO's waste storage lagoons, slurry pipes, and other waste handling appurtenances would also seem to be clearly prohibited by section 301(a) of the CWA. In addition, a number of court decisions have held that a discharge of CAFO-generated wastewater from a CAFO's land application area may also violate the CWA.[118] Often, controversies over whether a discharge from

---

115. 40 C.F.R. § 122.23(c).

116. 40 C.F.R. § 122.23(c)(2). Operations that are CAFOs by virtue of designation are not eligible for the 25-year, 24-hour storm event exemption applicable to CAFOs by definition. *See* 66 Fed. Reg. 2,960, 3,006 (Jan. 12, 2001).

117. 33 U.S.C. § 1311(a).

118. *Southview Farm*, 34 F.3d at 121 (holding that runoff from a CAFO's land application area that is "primarily caused by over-saturation of the fields rather than the rain" violates the CWA); Community Ass'n for Restoration of the Env't v. Sid Koopman Dairy, 54 F. Supp.2d 976, 981 (E.D. Wash. 1999) (holding that discharges from land application area violate the CWA because "CAFOs include not only the ground where the animals are confined but also the lagoons and systems used to transfer the animal wastes to the lagoons as well as equipment which distributes and/or applies the animal wastes produced at the confinement area to fields outside the animal confinement area."); Community Ass'n for Restoration of the Env't v. Henry Bosma Dairy, 65 F. Supp.2d 1129, 1155-56 (E.D. Wash. 1999); Waterkeeper Alliance v. Smithfield Foods, 2001 U.S. Dist. LEXIS 21314, *11 (E.D.N.C. Sept. 20, 2001) ("sprayfield areas are a vital part of [the CAFO's] operations and cannot be separated from the confinement areas merely because the waste has been moved from one area of the farm to another").

a CAFO's land application area violate the CWA boil down to a dispute over whether the discharge constitutes "agricultural stormwater" that is exempt from NPDES permitting requirements. The CWA's definition of "point source" excludes "agricultural stormwater discharges and return flows from irrigated agriculture."[119] Some court decisions hold that discharges of CAFO waste are flatly not entitled to the agricultural stormwater exemption.[120] EPA, on the other hand, has interpreted the agricultural stormwater exemption to apply to runoff from CAFOs' land application fields, but only to the extent that the wastewater has been applied in accordance with "proper agricultural practices."[121] Under this interpretation, dry-weather discharges and discharges of CAFO waste that result from excessive or improperly timed application (that is, not made at agronomic rates) violate the CWA. This interpretation is consistent with the Second Circuit's *Southview Farm* opinion.

2. Duty to Apply for NPDES Permit

EPA's NPDES regulations impose a duty to apply for an NPDES permit on any person who "discharges or proposes to discharge pollutants."[122] In the CAFO context, EPA has interpreted this application requirement to encompass any facility that has discharged, is discharging, or has a potential to discharge in the future. EPA has announced that "all or virtually all" CAFOs with more than 1,000 animal units have at least a potential to discharge and are therefore subject to the duty to apply.[123] What little case law exists on this point appears to support EPA's position.[124]

---

119. 33 U.S.C. § 1362(14).

120. *E.g., Waterkeeper Alliance*, 2001 U.S. Dist. LEXIS 21314, *11 ("sprayfields can qualify as point sources when they are part of CAFOs. It is clear that point sources are not subject to the stormwater exemption").

121. 66 Fed. Reg. 2,960, 3,029–3,030 (Jan. 12, 2001); U.S. EPA Office of Water, "Guidance Manual and Sample NPDES Permit for Concentrated Animal Feeding Operations," Final Internal Review Draft, http://www.epa.gov/npdes/pubs/dman_afo-2000.pdf, p. 15 (Sept. 21, 2000).

122. 40 C.F.R. § 122.21(a).

123. 66 Fed. Reg. 2,960, 3,007 (Jan. 12, 2001); U.S. EPA Office of Water, "Guidance Manual and Sample NPDES Permit for Concentrated Animal Feeding Operations," Final Internal Review Draft, http://www.epa.gov/npdes/pubs/dman_afo-2000.pdf, p. 14 (Sept. 21, 2000).

124. Carr v. Alta Verde Industries, 931 F.2d at 1060; Waterkeeper Alliance, 2001 U.S. Dist. LEXIS 21314, *4 ("The court is unpersuaded by defendants' argument that the CWA does not create a cause of action for operating without a required permit"); *Murphy Farms*, 1998 U.S. Dist. LEXIS 21402, *4, (E.D.N.C., Dec. 22, 1998), *remanded on other grounds*, 2000 U.S. App. LEXIS 5460 (4th Cir. N.C. Mar. 29, 2000).

3. Effluent Limitations Applicable to CAFOs

The CWA requires that all NPDES point sources achieve compliance with "technology-based" effluent limits,[125] and EPA has promulgated effluent limitation guidelines (ELGs) to define the technology-based limits for a broad range of industry groups. The ELG for feedlots published at 40 C.F.R. part 412 establishes the technology-based effluent limitations that are to be applied in the NPDES permits issued to most large CAFOs. The Feedlot ELG contains an applicability section that defines the subcategories to which the ELG applies—a universe that differs in many respects from the universe of facilities that qualify as CAFOs. The Feedlot ELG does not apply to CAFOs with fewer than 1,000 animal units or to many facilities with more than 1,000 animal units. For example, a recreational riding stable confining more than 500 horses would qualify as an upper-tier CAFO, but would not be subject to the Feedlot ELG, which covers only race-track-related horse stables. For a CAFO that confines fewer than 1,000 animal units or that does not otherwise satisfy the ELG's applicability criteria, the NPDES permit's technology-based effluent limitations may be based on the permit writer's best professional judgment (BPJ) on a case-by-case basis.[126]

In general, the Feedlot ELG prohibits all discharges of "process wastewater" (including precipitation, wash water, and drinking water that comes into contact with the animals, their feed, and their waste) to waters of the United States, except when rainfall events, either chronic or catastrophic, cause an overflow of process wastewater from a facility designed, constructed, and operated to contain all process-generated wastewater plus the runoff from a 25-year, 24-hour rainfall event.[127] Of course, where these technology-based effluent limits are not sufficient to meet water quality standards, the NPDES permit for a CAFO (as for any NPDES permit) must contain any more stringent requirements necessary to meet these standards.[128]

In September 2000, EPA's Office of Water issued a "final internal review draft" of CAFO permitting guidance. This guidance has been posted on EPA's external web site since early 2001, but was never finalized. The guidance sets forth a number of "special conditions that EPA expects NPDES permits for CAFOs will contain," including requirements to develop and implement a comprehensive nutrient management plan (CNMP) achieving independently enforceable minimum standards and other requirements necessary to protect

---

125. 33 U.S.C. § 1311(b).
126. 33 U.S.C. § 1342(a)(1)(B).
127. 40 C.F.R. § 412.13(b).
128. 33 U.S.C. § 1311(b)(1)(C).

water quality.[129] In at least one instance, an EPA regional office has issued an NPDES CAFO general permit that closely tracks this permitting approach.[130]

C. PROPOSED REVISIONS TO THE CAFO REGULATIONS

In January 2001, EPA proposed the first significant revisions to its CAFO permitting regulations (40 C.F.R. section 122.23) and the Feedlot ELG (40 C.F.R. part 412) in nearly 25 years.[131] Pursuant to the CWA section 304(m) consent decree entered in NRDC v. Reilly, Civ. No. 89-2980 (D.D.C. Jan. 30, 1992), the ELG portions of this proposal must be finalized no later than December 15, 2002. As proposed, these revisions to the permitting and effluent limitations regulations would substantially alter the CAFO regulation landscape. Among other things, the revisions to the NPDES regulations would (1) change the definitions of AFO and CAFO by, for example, revising the vegetation exemption; altering animal thresholds, including dry poultry operations; and changing designation criteria; (2) explicitly impose a "duty to apply" on CAFO operators; (3) clearly require entities (such as meat processors) that exercise "substantial operational control" over CAFOs to be co-permitted; (4) require permit coverage to continue until proper closure of the CAFO; and (5) impose various requirements of the off-site shipment of CAFO wastes. The proposed ELG revisions would require NPDES permits to contain enforceable nutrient management planning requirements and other provisions designed to reduce discharges from CAFO land application sites. As this book goes to press, it remains to be seen which of these proposed revisions to the CAFO regulations will be finalized.

III. Other "Wet Weather" Discharges

A. SILVICULTURE

EPA has adopted special regulations to govern NPDES permitting of "silvicultural activities,"[132] that is, tree farming or forestry.[133] EPA regulations define the

---

129. U.S. EPA Office of Water, "Guidance Manual and Sample NPDES Permit for Concentrated Animal Feeding Operations," Final Internal Review Draft, http://www.epa.gov/npdes/pubs/dman_afo-2000.pdf, p. 25 (Sept. 21, 2000).

130. 66 Fed. Reg. 38,266–38,277 (July 23, 2001) (NPDES General Permit No. AZG800000 for the State of Arizona). A complete copy of this permit is available at http://www.epa.gov/region09/water/npdes/azcafo.html.

131. 66 Fed. Reg. 2,960–3,145 (Jan. 12, 2001). In November 2001, EPA published a "notice of data availability" for this proposed rule which offered additional information and alternatives that EPA was considering in revising the CAFO rules. 66 Fed. Reg. 58,556–58,607 (Nov. 21, 2001).

132. 40 C.F.R. § 122.27.

133. The dictionary definition of "silviculture" is "[t]he care and cultivation of forest trees; forestry." AMERICAN HERITAGE DICTIONARY (New College Edition, William Morris ed. 1976).

term "silvicultural point source" to mean "any discernible, confined, and discrete conveyance related to rock crushing, gravel washing, log sorting, or log storage facilities which are operated in connection with silvicultural activities."[134] The regulations define the terms "rock crushing and gravel washing facilities"[135] and "log sorting and log storage facilities"[136] primarily by reference to the effluent guidelines that regulate such operations.[137]

The regulations go on to exclude from NPDES permitting "nonpoint source activities such as nursery operations, site preparation, reforestation and subsequent cultural treatment, thinning, prescribed burning, pest and fire control, harvesting operations, surface drainage, or road construction and maintenance from which there is natural runoff."[138] In essence, this regulation attempts to define what constitutes a "nonpoint source" excluded from NPDES permitting in the context of silvicultural activities, and the regulation categorically exempts discharges from such activities from the permitting requirement.[139]

As EPA noted in 1999, however, many silvicultural activities, particularly road construction and maintenance, may result in the discharge of pollutants from a "confined, discernible and discrete conveyance," and thus should properly be characterized as "point sources" under the CWA.[140] EPA therefore proposed to remove the sentence quoted above from the existing regulation, which would have had the effect of making most silvicultural discharges phase II stormwater discharges, subject to regulation if designated by EPA or an authorized state.[141] This proposal, however, generated what can only be called a firestorm of adverse

---

134. 40 C.F.R. § 122.27(b)(1).

135. 40 C.F.R. § 122.27(b)(2).

136. 40 C.F.R. § 122.27(b)(3). *See also* 55 Fed. Reg. 20,521 (May 17, 1990) (clarifying scope of this regulation).

137. 40 C.F.R. pt. 436, subpt. B; 40 C.F.R. pt. 429, subpt. I.

138. 40 C.F.R. § 122.27(b)(1). Note that in League of Wilderness Defenders v. Forsgren, 309 F.3d 1181 (9th Cir. 2002) the Ninth Circuit held that aerial pesticide application to forest lands for moth control was a point source discharge subject to NPDES permitting requirements. The court rejected the Forest Service's argument that the silviculture exemption in 40 C.F.R. § 122.27 applies to discharges from aerial applicators.

139. *See* 41 Fed. Reg. 24,709, 24710 (June 18, 1976) (describing the criteria for determining what constitutes a "nonpoint source" for purposes of the regulation now codified at 40 C.F.R. § 122.27).

140. 64 Fed. Reg. 46,012, 46,077–78 (Aug. 23, 1999).

141. *Id.* As EPA explained in its preamble, a number of these discharges would, even after the regulation change, still be exempt from NPDES permit requirements under section 404(f)(1) of the Clean Water Act, 33 U.S.C. § 1344(f)(1). Discharges of dredge or fill materials for the purpose of construction or maintenance of farm roads or forest roads, in particular, are exempt under 33 U.S.C. § 1344(f)(1)(E). For more information on the section 404(f) exemptions, see chapter 6.

reaction.[142] As a result, EPA withdrew the proposal and left the existing regulation in place.[143]

B. AQUATIC ANIMAL PRODUCTION OR AQUACULTURE

Discharges from facilities growing aquatic animals or plants within waters of the United States or that discharge to waters of the United States are not really "wet weather discharges" in that such discharges do not occur solely in wet weather or as a result of stormwater runoff. Yet EPA regulates these facilities as another special class of discharges and with regulatory structures similar to those for the wet weather discharges described above. Therefore, they are dealt with here.

1. Aquatic Animal Production Facilities

EPA regulates discharges from facilities that are engaged in "fish hatching" or similar types of aquatic animal production through special NPDES requirements that parallel those for CAFOs or silvicultural discharges. That is to say, EPA automatically regulates as point sources only a subset of the universe of facilities engaged in aquatic animal production; the remainder are outside the NPDES permitting requirement unless specifically designated by EPA or an authorized state.

EPA defines as a point source a "concentrated aquatic animal production facility" (CAAPF).[144] A CAAPF is a "hatchery, fish farm or other facility"[145] that "contains, grows or holds aquatic animals"[146] in either of the following categories:

(a) cold water fish species in ponds, raceways, or other similar structures which discharge at least 30 days per year and which (1) produce at least 9,090 kg (approximately 20,000 pounds) harvest weight of aquatic animals per year; or (2) feed at least 2,272 kg (approximately 5,000 pounds) of food during the calendar month of maximum feeding;

(b) warm-water fish species in ponds, raceways, or other similar structures that discharge at least 30 days per year and that (1) are not closed ponds that discharge only during periods of excess runoff, and (2) produce at

---

142. *See, e.g., Next Up in TMDL Bashing Order: House Agriculture Committee,* ENVIRONMENT AND ENERGY DAILY, June 26, 2000 (available on LEXIS, ENVIRN library, ALLNWS file) (describing pending legislation to prohibit EPA from finalizing proposed regulation and EPA's announcement to withdraw the change to the silviculture regulation); *Farm and Forestry Groups Swat at EPA Regulatory Authority,* ENVIRONMENT AND ENERGY DAILY, Feb. 15, 2000 (available on LEXIS, ENVIRN library, ALLNWS file) (describing earlier legislative hearings on EPA proposal).

143. 65 Fed. Reg. 43,586, 43,652 (July 13, 2000).

144. 40 C.F.R. § 122.24(a).

145. 40 C.F.R. § 122.24(b).

146. 40 C.F.R. pt. 122, app. C.

least 45,454 kg (approximately 100,000 pounds) harvest weight of aquatic animals per year.[147]

As with the CAFO regulations,[148] aquatic animal production facilities that do not meet these size/operational criteria may be designated by the NPDES permitting authority as a CAAPF, and thus as a point source subject to permitting, if the facility is a "significant contributor of pollution to waters of the United States."[149] EPA or the authorized state is required to conduct an on-site inspection of the facility before designating it for permitting.[150]

2. Aquaculture Projects

Aquaculture projects, as that term is used in the CWA and EPA regulations, are similar to, but distinct from, CAAPFs. In the 1970s, there was interest in reuse of industrial or municipal effluent to grow aquatic organisms,[151] and Congress added section 318[152] to the Clean Water Act to promote such practices, subject to EPA procedures and guidelines.[153]

EPA has issued implementing regulations for section 318.[154] "Aquaculture project" refers to a "defined managed water area which uses discharges of pollutants into that designated area for the maintenance or production of harvestable freshwater, estuarine, or marine plans or animals."[155] EPA or an authorized state may issue a permit for an aquaculture project if it determines, generally, that the project will have significant commercial value,[156] that the discharge of pollutants will increase the harvest from the project,[157] and that the project will not pose a potential human health hazard or cause or contribute to a violation of water quality standards.[158] Permits for aquaculture projects do not need to include technology-based effluent limitations, except for control of toxic pollutants.[159] Aquatic animal production facilities that do not use discharge of wastes from a separate industrial point source for the maintenance, propagation, and/or production of

---

147. *Id.*

148. See section II of this chapter for a thorough discussion of concentrate animal feeding operations (CAFOs).

149. 40 C.F.R. § 122.24(c).

150. 40 C.F.R. § 122.24(c)(2).

151. *See* 65 Fed. Reg. 43,586, 43,649 (July 13, 2000) (describing regulatory history).

152. 33 U.S.C. § 1328.

153. 33 U.S.C. § 1328(b).

154. 40 C.F.R. §§ 122.25, 125.10, 125.11.

155. 40 C.F.R. § 122.25(b)(2).

156. 40 C.F.R. § 125.11(a)(1)(i).

157. 40 C.F.R. § 125.11(a)(2).

158. 40 C.F.R. § 125.11(a)(4)–(a)(5).

159. 40 C.F.R. § 125.10(c).

harvestable organisms are not regulated under the "aquaculture" provisions of section 318 and EPA regulations; rather, they are regulated if they meet the definition of a CAAPF discussed above.[160]

C. COMBINED SEWER OVERFLOWS AND SANITARY SEWER OVERFLOWS

Wet weather discharges of sanitary waste and stormwater from sewers serving publicly owned treatment works, so-called "CSO" and "SSO" discharges, are discussed in detail in chapter 4.

---

160. 65 Fed. Reg. 43,586, 43,649 (July 13, 2000) (quoting 43 Fed. Reg. at 37,132 (Aug. 21, 1978)).

CHAPTER 9

Nonpoint Source Pollution Control

EDWARD B. WITTE*
DAVID P. ROSS

[I]t is the national policy that programs for the control of nonpoint sources of pollution be developed and implemented in an expeditious manner so as to enable the goals of this Act to be met through the control of both point and nonpoint sources of pollution.[1]

I. Introduction

In 1987, Congress added the foregoing national policy on nonpoint source pollution control to the Clean Water Act (CWA). Despite this declaration, a large percentage of our nation's waters have yet to attain their designated uses. The goals of the Clean Water Act, that of eliminating pollutant discharges and providing fishable and swimmable waters, remain elusive targets. In fact, 35 percent of the rivers and streams, 45 percent of the lakes, and 47 percent of the estuaries are impaired. Another 10 percent of the nation's waters are in good, but threatened, condition.[2]

Much of the improvement in our nation's waters is attributable to the control of traditional point sources. A majority of the remaining water quality impairments, however, are largely caused by sources that are not directly controlled

---

* The authors acknowledge the contributions of Serena P. Wiltshire to the 1994 edition of this chapter.

1. 33 U.S.C.A. § 1251(a)(7) (West 2001).

2. U.S. ENVIRONMENTAL PROTECTION AGENCY, THE QUALITY OF OUR NATION'S WATERS: A SUMMARY OF THE NATIONAL WATER QUALITY INVENTORY: 1998 REPORT TO CONGRESS 1 (EPA841-S-00-001) (2000). A copy of the full report is available at http://www.epa.gov/305b/98report.

under the Clean Water Act. Controlling pollution from diffuse runoff is the next great challenge facing our nation's water regulators. As recognized by the Clinton administration in the 1998 *Clean Water Action Plan*, the current regulatory framework does not adequately provide for the control of nonpoint source pollution:

> Implementation of the existing programs will not stop serious new threats to public health, living resources, and the nation's waterways, particularly from polluted runoff. These programs lack the strength, resources, and framework to finish the job of restoring rivers, lakes, and coastal areas.[3]

Critics of the existing federal nonpoint programs argue that the programs lack enforceable mechanisms. The nonpoint source pollution control program under the Clean Water Act envisions a process of identifying waters impaired by nonpoint sources, planning for control of those sources, implementing programs based on the planning, and providing financial incentives to states to accomplish these tasks. The federal program is carrot-based and lacks a sufficient stick to remedy failure.

This shortcoming is based in part on the mechanisms needed to control diffuse runoff. There are limited technical controls that can be applied to the sources, even if the sources can be easily identified. Instead, diffuse runoff is usually controlled through frequently unenforceable "best management practices," such as those employed on agricultural lands and forests. Stream buffers, crop rotations, harvest limitations, and other practices are typically implemented through land use controls, such as zoning and land use planning. These are powers that are traditionally vested in the states. A successful federal program must work with and within the states' powers and must overcome significant interest group pressures that seek to limit federal regulatory involvement.

The remainder of this chapter covers the federal control of nonpoint source pollution under the Clean Water Act. First, in the absence of a formal definition, it addresses the definition of nonpoint source pollution. Next, an overview of the federal statutory program is provided, with a chronologically based status report on the implementation of the Clean Water Act's primary nonpoint source control provision, section 319. Finally, recognizing that the Clean Water Act program is neither comprehensive nor intended to be, the chapter concludes with an overview of other federal and state programs that exist for the control of nonpoint source pollution.

II. The Definition of Nonpoint Source Pollution

The definition of nonpoint source pollution in the Clean Water Act is symbolic of the act's emphasis on controlling these sources of pollution. It does not exist. Congress defines a point source as "any discernible, confined and discrete con-

---

3. THE CLEAN WATER ACT PLAN, Overview (1998), *at* http://www.cleanwater. gov/action.

veyance . . . from which pollutants are or may be discharged."[4] It stands to follow that anything that is not a point source and yet conveys pollutants to our nation's waters is a nonpoint source. Yet the distinction between the two is somewhat blurred. For example, stormwater runoff from construction sites, industrial facilities, and certain municipal areas, as well as concentrated animal feeding operations, are point sources regulated under the National Pollutant Discharge Elimination System (NPDES) under section 402 of the Clean Water Act. On the other hand, similar diffuse sources such as agricultural stormwater runoff and irrigated agriculture return flows are, by definition, not point sources and fall outside the NPDES program.[5]

Despite these apparent inconsistencies, a point source is generally a discharge from a pipe or similar conveyance.[6] A nonpoint source is diffuse runoff and, as described by the U.S. Environmental Protection Agency (EPA), "is caused by rainfall or snowmelt moving over and through the ground and carrying natural and human-made pollutants into lakes, rivers, streams, wetlands, estuaries, other coastal waters, and ground water. Atmospheric deposition and hydrologic modification are also sources of nonpoint pollution."[7] The major sources of nonpoint pollution are agricultural and silvicultural runoff and increasing urbanization. Typical pollutants transported by diffuse runoff include nutrients, bacteria, metals, and sediments.

III. Original Control Provisions in the Clean Water Act of 1972

Congress initially contemplated the importance of controlling nonpoint source pollution in the Clean Water Act of 1972, and provided financial incentives to the states to implement management programs aimed at addressing and controlling nonpoint sources.[8] The central provision is found in section 208.

---

4. 33 U.S.C. § 1362(14).

5. *Id.*

6. There is a significant body of case law regarding what is and is not a point source. *See, e.g.*, Miccosukee Tribe of Indians of Florida v. S. Florida Water Mgmt Dist., 280 F.3d 1364 (11th Cir. 2002) (pump station is a point source); Oregon Natural Desert Ass'n v. Dombeck, 151 F.3d 945 (9th Cir. 1998) (cows not a point source); United States v. West Indies Transport Co., 127 F.3d 299 (3d Cir. 1997) (barge that broke up during a hurricane and its wreckage purposefully sunk considered a point source discharge); Concerned Area Residents for the Environment v. Southview Farm, 34 F.3d 114 (2d Cir. 1994), *cert. denied*, 514 U.S. 1082 (1995) (held that the runoff from the fields to which manure from 700 cattle was applied was not nonpoint source runoff).

7. U.S. ENVIRONMENTAL PROTECTION AGENCY, NONPOINT SOURCE PROGRAM AND GRANTS GUIDANCE FOR FISCAL YEAR 1997 AND FUTURE YEARS, Executive Summary (1996), *at* http://www.epa.gov/owow/nps/guide.html.

8. "It has become clearly established that the waters of the Nation cannot be restored and their quality maintained unless the very complex and difficult problem of nonpoint sources is addressed." S. REP. No. 92-414 (1972), *reprinted in* 1972 U.S.C.C.A.N. 3668, 3705.

A. CLEAN WATER ACT SECTION 208

Section 208 of the Clean Water Act of 1972 set forth a program whereby state and local planning agencies analyzed nonpoint source pollution and developed water quality management programs aimed at controlling those sources.

Ultimately, section 208 is a planning provision. It required the governor of each state to identify, based on published EPA guidelines, the boundaries of each area of the state subject to substantial water quality control problems and to designate a planning agency to develop an area-wide waste management plan for each area.[9] The designated agency was to then implement a continuous planning process that identified, at a minimum, sources of pollution from agriculture, silviculture, mining, and construction, as well as potential saltwater intrusions into freshwater bodies resulting from human influence.[10] Federal grants were made available to designated agencies to assist in the planning process.[11]

B. CLEAN WATER ACT SECTION 303(E)

In addition to the area-wide waste management planning provisions of section 208, each state was also required, under section 303 of the 1972 Clean Water Act, to implement a continuous planning process for each navigable water within the state. Section 303(e) required the state to incorporate the elements of all area-wide management plans into an overall continuing planning process.[12] Thus, area-wide management plans were subject to continuous planning requirements under section 208 and the results of that planning process were to be incorporated into an overall statewide planning process.

C. DEVELOPMENT OF WATER QUALITY MANAGEMENT PLANS UNDER SECTIONS 208 AND 303(E)

The results of the continuous planning process under sections 208 and 303(e) are to be incorporated into an overall Water Quality Management Plan under regulations promulgated by the EPA.[13] At the heart of the Water Quality Management Plan is the development of best management practices aimed at controlling the sources of nonpoint pollution that have been identified under section 208(b) as significant sources of concern.[14]

---

9. 33 U.S.C. § 1288(a).
10. *Id.* § 1288(b).
11. *Id.* § 1288(f).
12. *Id.* § 1313(e)(3)(B).
13. *See* 40 C.F.R. pt. 130 (2001).
14. *See* 40 C.F.R. § 130.6(c)(4).

IV. Enactment of Section 319 in the Water Quality Act of 1987

Recognizing the growing awareness that nonpoint sources of pollution were limiting the ability of the Clean Water Act to restore and maintain the quality of our nation's waters through the NPDES program, Congress added section 319 of the Clean Water Act in 1987. This section specifically addressed the creation of nonpoint source management programs through a three-stage process. First, states were to address nonpoint source pollution by developing nonpoint source assessment reports. Second, the states were to adopt nonpoint source management programs. Finally, the states were to phase in those programs, and could do so with the assistance of federal funds. Essentially, Congress created another planning provision.

A. STATE ASSESSMENT REPORTS UNDER CLEAN WATER ACT SECTION 319(A)

Under section 319(a), each state must submit to the EPA an assessment report that identifies any navigable waters within the state that will not meet applicable water quality standards without additional controls for nonpoint sources of pollution. The state must identify the categories, subcategories, and individual nonpoint sources that significantly contribute to water quality impairment, and must describe a program for the development of best management practices and other measures to control the identified sources of nonpoint pollution.[15] These assessment reports were due to the EPA 18 months after the enactment of the section 319—by August 1998. Failure to meet that deadline meant that the EPA must prepare the report.[16]

B. STATE MANAGEMENT PROGRAMS UNDER CLEAN WATER ACT SECTION 319(B)

Also, by a date 18 months after the enactment of section 319 (by August 1998) the states were to develop state management programs and submit them to the EPA for review and approval.[17] The management programs must identify the best management practices and measures that the state will utilize to reduce pollutant loading from each nonpoint source category, subcategory, and specific source identified in the assessment reports. The program plan must identify the regulatory and nonregulatory programs that implement the best management practices.

---

15. 33 U.S.C. § 1329(a).
16. *Id.* § 1329(c)(2).
17. *Id.*

In addition, a schedule must be developed that includes identifiable and measurable milestones targeting best management practice implementation at the earliest practicable date. At a minimum, the state must implement the program within the first four fiscal years after the date the program is submitted to the EPA.[18] EPA approval of the management program is necessary if the state is to receive federal funding under section 319(h).

C. FEDERAL GRANTS FOR STATE MANAGEMENT PROGRAM IMPLEMENTATION UNDER SECTION 319(H) OF THE CLEAN WATER ACT

Section 319(h) authorizes the EPA to issue grants to states, territories, and tribes on an annual basis, provided certain conditions are met. The conditions effectively set up a competitive process by which states receive federal funding under section 319. The federal share for financing a management program shall not exceed 60 percent. A state must make satisfactory progress in the prior fiscal year towards implementation of its management program, and must at a minimum maintain funding for its nonpoint source programs at a level equal to or greater than its expenditures in 1985 and 1986.[19]

Section 319(h)(5) also authorizes EPA to prioritize funding for those projects that attempt to address difficult nonpoint source pollution problems. Prioritization also is granted to innovative projects, interstate pollution projects, and to groundwater quality protection activities.[20]

V. Selected Milestones in the Section 319 Program[21]

A. 1987: EPA ISSUES NONPOINT SOURCE GUIDANCE

In December 1987, EPA issued a guidance document to assist the states in preparing their assessment reports and management programs. The document, *Nonpoint Source Guidance*, encouraged states to use the 1988 section 305(b) reports as their assessment reports. The section 305(b) Water Quality Inventory Reports are submitted by the states on a biannual basis and describe the water quality of rivers, lakes, and coastal areas of each state. These reports contain information on

---

18. *Id.* § 1329(b).

19. *Id.* § 1329(h).

20. Section 319(i) authorizes EPA to issue grants for groundwater quality projects, but historically, the EPA has blended the 319(i) funding decisions into the section 319(h) program.

21. The following discussion provides just a snapshot of the available resources relating to section 319. For a general background of the program, historical information, and additional links to other nonpoint source control programs at both the federal and state level, see EPA's Office of Wetlands, Oceans and Watersheds web site at http://www.epa.gov/owow/nps.

the sources of pollution that impair the attainment of designated uses of each waterbody, including specific information on the sources of nonpoint source pollution. The *Nonpoint Source Guidance* encouraged states to expand the scope of the 1988 biannual reports to include details required under section 319.

The guidance also encouraged the states to prioritize their programs for targeted action on impaired waters based on a watershed management perspective. Watershed-based planning was viewed as the most efficient and effective means of achieving improvements in water quality. Finally, EPA provided guidance on other federal funding programs under the Clean Water Act, including set-asides available under the section 201 and 205 construction grant allotments, state revolving loan funds available under section 603, and reserved portions of the Title VI allotments under section 604.

B. 1991: CREATION OF SECTION 319 NATIONAL MONITORING PROGRAM

In 1991, EPA established a national monitoring program aimed at evaluating state nonpoint source pollution control projects in order to monitor the effectiveness of nonpoint source pollution controls and to improve the understanding of nonpoint source pollution.[22] EPA updates Congress on the progress of the Section 319 National Monitoring Program in the national water quality inventory reports and in periodic publications in order to disseminate the lessons learned from successful nonpoint source projects to other state programs.[23]

C. 1992: EPA ISSUES FINAL REPORT TO CONGRESS ON SECTION 319 ACTIVITIES

Under section 319(m), EPA was required to report to Congress on the status of the nonpoint source pollution control programs by January 1, 1990. EPA issued its final report in January 1992. The report, *Managing Nonpoint Source Pollution: Final Report to Congress on Section 319 of the Clean Water Act*, detailed the current status of the state management plans. By the end of 1989, EPA had approved all state assessment reports and had approved in full 44 state management programs. By 1991, all state management programs had been approved.

---

22. U.S. ENVIRONMENTAL PROTECTION AGENCY, THE NONPOINT SOURCE MANAGEMENT PROGRAM, POINTER NO. 4 (EPA841-F-96-004D) (1996), *at* http://www.epa.gov/owow/nps/facts/point4.htm.

23. *See, e.g.*, U.S. ENVIRONMENTAL PROTECTION AGENCY, SECTION 319 NONPOINT SOURCE SUCCESS STORIES: VOLUME I (EPA841-S-94-004) (1994) *and* U.S. ENVIRONMENTAL PROTECTION AGENCY, SECTION 319 NONPOINT SOURCE SUCCESS STORIES: VOLUME II (EPA841-R-97-001) (1997). These reports are available at http://www.epa.gov/owow/nps.

D. 1996: NEW FOCUS FOR SECTION 319 PROGRAM GUIDANCE

In 1995, the EPA and the Association of State and Interstate Water Pollution Control Administrators began a series of negotiations aimed at developing a new national strategy for the implementation of section 319. Building on the experience of states, territories, and tribes, a new strategy was developed to ensure a more predictable annual award of section 319 funds with a specific focus on reducing the competitive nature of grant awards, while creating a more flexible use of grant funds by providing less regulatory oversight and administration. This strategy was published on May 16, 1996, and is entitled *Nonpoint Source Program and Grants Guidance for Fiscal Year 1997 and Future Years.*[24]

In order to enhance the section 319 program and speed achievement of the Clean Water Act's goals, nine key elements were developed that will guide the future of the section 319 grant program. In brief, a successful section 319 management program should include the following elements:

1. Explicit goals, objectives, and strategies designed to protect the nation's waters.
2. Balanced planning that emphasizes statewide nonpoint source programs and targeted individual programs for impaired or threatened waters.
3. Abatement of known water quality impairments from existing nonpoint sources and prevention of significant threats from present or future activities.
4. Identification of impaired or threatened waters and watersheds caused by nonpoint source pollution and plans to progressively improve these waters.
5. A review of all program components of section 319 and establishment of flexible approaches to achieve water quality standards as soon as practicable.
6. Efficient and effective management of the nonpoint source management programs.
7. Strengthened partnerships between all levels of government, citizen groups, and private actors.
8. Identification of federal lands not managed consistently with state program objectives.
9. Continuous planning processes for review and evaluation of nonpoint source management programs at least every five years.

---

24. The document is available at http://www.epa.gov/owow/nps/cwact.html.

E. 1998: CLEAN WATER ACTION PLAN

In 1998, the Clinton administration announced a new Clean Water Initiative that culminated in the publication of the *Clean Water Action Plan*.[25] The plan announced 111 key actions that would focus water quality regulation and planning on strengthening public health protections, providing resources to targeted areas, and implementing a commitment to watershed-based management. One of the central components of the plan was to develop a national strategy for the control of polluted runoff, with a focus on section 319 funding, coastal zones, and stormwater runoff in urban areas. The plan called for, and the next budget bill included, an additional $100 million in grant funding under the section 319 program, doubling the section 319(h) funding pool.

The additional $100 million, deemed the "incremental funds," were only to be made available, however, to those states that have successfully implemented the nine key elements of a successful section 319 program as articulated in the May 16, 1996, policy statement, discussed in section IV.C above.[26]

F. 2002 AND BEYOND: SUPPLEMENT GUIDELINES FOR THE AWARD OF SECTION 319 GRANTS ISSUED

The development of Total Maximum Daily Loads (TMDLs) under section 303(d) of the Clean Water Act has dramatically changed the landscape of water quality regulation. TMDLs are addressed in some detail in chapter10. A brief description of the program is provided here to assist in understanding the role of TMDLs in nonpoint source pollution control.

Under section 303(d), each state is to develop TMDLs for every impaired water. These waters are identified in the state biannual water quality reports submitted to the EPA under section 305(b) of the Clean Water Act, or separate 303(d) lists approved by EPA. A TMDL is the amount of a specific pollutant that may be discharged into an impaired water body from all sources, including point and nonpoint sources, taking into account background levels and a calculated margin of safety. Waste load allocations are then implemented through the NPDES program for each point source. Frequently, point sources will be required to implement more-stringent technological controls to achieve established water quality standards for a particular water body as a result of the TMDL.

The importance of the TMDL program is that nonpoint source pollution will influence the waste load allocations of point sources. Despite the fact that

---

25. A copy of the plan is available at http://www.cleanwater.gov/pubs.html.

26. *See* U.S. ENVIRONMENTAL PROTECTION AGENCY, NATIONAL WATER QUALITY INVENTORY: 1998 REPORT TO CONGRESS 249 (2000), *at* http://www.epa.gov/305b/98report.

nonpoint sources are outside the regulatory reach of the NPDES program,[27] a TMDL may be established for an impaired waterbody based solely on nonpoint sources.[28] Thus, a point source may be prohibited from discharging what otherwise would be permitted levels of pollutants based entirely on impairment caused by unregulated sources.

Recognizing the importance of TMDLs in attaining water quality standards, EPA is shifting the focus of the section 319 grant program to better enable states to use section 319 funding in their efforts to establish TMDLs.[29] Specifically, states may continue to use up to 20 percent of the base grant funding, which was authorized under previous supplemental guidance, for development of TMDLs and related activities and may use up to 20 percent of the incremental funding for similar purposes. A renewed focus on watershed-based planning will also highlight the future of the program.

VI. Related Programs for the Control of Nonpoint Source Pollution

A. COASTAL ZONE ACT REAUTHORIZATION AMENDMENTS OF 1990

Congress established a coastal nonpoint source pollution control program under section 6217 of the Coastal Zone Act Reauthorization Amendments of 1990 (CZARA).[30] Under section 6217, 29 coastal states and territories were to establish specific coastal nonpoint pollution control programs aimed at restoring and protecting the coastal waters of the United States. The new nonpoint source programs were intended to augment CWA section 319 programs as well as the existing voluntary coastal management programs developed under the Coastal Zone Management Act of 1972. Like the section 319 programs, the 1972 coastal management programs were incentive-based planning programs aimed at regulating land and water uses and coastal developments that impeded the attainment of established water quality standards.

CZARA required the coastal states to implement specific nonpoint source control programs in compliance with established EPA guidelines. At the heart of

---

27. *See, e.g.*, Oregon Natural Resources Council v. U.S. Forest Service, 834 F.2d 842 (9th Cir. 1987).

28. *See, e.g.*, Pronsolino v. Marcus, 91 F. Supp. 2d 1337 (N.D. Cal. 2000), *aff'd sub nom* Pronsolino v. Nastri, 291 F.3d 1123 (9th Cir. 2002).

29. *See* Supplement Guidelines for the Award of Section 319 Nonpoint Source Grants to States and Territories in FY 2002 and Subsequent Years, 66 Fed. Reg. 47,653 (2001), *at* http://www.epa.gov/owow/nps/Section319/fy2002.html.

30. *See* 16 U.S.C.A. § 1455b (West 2001).

the program is the requirement that states shall develop management measures necessary to ensure attainment of water quality standards, including, where necessary, enforceable management measures.[31] EPA's technical guidance, published in 1993, set forth management measure criteria for the following sources: agriculture, silviculture, urban runoff, hydromodification, and marinas. At the same time, EPA and the National Oceanic and Atmospheric Administration jointly published guidance for the development and approval of the state programs.[32]

EPA recently published the first comprehensive environmental assessment report on the condition of the nation's coastal waters and estuaries.[33] The report was issued in response to a directive under the 1998 *Clean Water Action Plan* and is intended to be used as an analytical baseline against which the progress of the coastal management programs can be assessed. The overall condition of the coastal waters is reported as fair to poor.

B. UNIFIED FEDERAL POLICY FOR WATERSHED MANAGEMENT ON FEDERAL LANDS

Federal agencies control and manage more than 800 million acres of federal land. Recognizing that the federal government itself has major responsibilities towards controlling nonpoint source water pollution, the *Clean Water Action Plan* called on federal agencies to implement a unified policy for watershed-based planning on federal lands. The unified policy was published on October 18, 2000.[34] The policy focuses on the use of watershed planning to assess and monitor watershed conditions, identify priority watersheds, and develop stakeholder partnerships to improve water quality through polluted runoff reduction and natural resource stewardship.

---

31. For more information regarding the Coastal Nonpoint Pollution Control Programs, see U.S. ENVIRONMENTAL PROTECTION AGENCY, PROTECTING COASTAL WATERS FROM NONPOINT SOURCE POLLUTION, POINTER NO. 5 (EPA841-F-96-004E) (1996), *at* http://www.epa.gov/owow /nps/facts/ point5.htm; U.S. ENVIRONMENTAL PROTECTION AGENCY, NATIONAL WATER QUALITY INVENTORY: 1998 REPORT TO CONGRESS, *supra* note 25, at 254–55.

32. *See* Coastal Nonpoint Source Pollution State Program Guidance Documents, 58 Fed. Reg. 5182 (1993). For more information regarding the guidance documents and the coastal zone program, see EPA's Office of Wetlands, Oceans and Watersheds coastal zone web site at http://www.epa.gov/ owow/nps/czmact.html.

33. *See* U.S. ENVIRONMENTAL PROTECTION AGENCY, NATIONAL COASTAL CONDITION REPORT (EPA620-R-005) (2001). A copy of the report and related fact sheet are available at http://www.epa. gov/owow/oceans/nccr.

34. *See* Unified Federal Policy for a Watershed Approach to Federal Land and Resource Management, 65 Fed. Reg. 62,566 (2000), *at* http://www.cleanwater.gov/ufp.

C. ENFORCEABLE STATE MECHANISMS

The control of nonpoint source pollution is a study in classic federalism. As the previous sections of this chapter demonstrate, the federal government has created a framework by which states may plan for and implement programs for the control of nonpoint sources. The federal government maintains a position of regulatory oversight and encourages the states to implement programs through financial incentives, but the Clean Water Act does not give the federal government explicit authority to regulate nonpoint sources. Instead, the power to regulate these sources through enforceable mechanisms remains in the hands of the states, through traditional land use and similar controls. As each state strives to achieve control over these sources, 50 potential programs are in the process of development, experimentation, and implementation. Eventually, efficient and successful programs will arise out of the experimentation and an overall control strategy may be developed.

Recognizing these principles, the Environmental Law Institute (ELI) undertook a series of studies in the late 1990s aimed at identifying existing enforceable state mechanisms for the control of nonpoint source pollution. An enforceable mechanism is a standard or performance requirement that can be applied to an identifiable entity that carries a sanction through civil, criminal, or administrative penalty or loss of license.[35] While the majority of nonpoint source programs continue to be nonregulatory—area-wide planning, grants, cost-share programs, and best management practices—ELI identified several broad categories of existing enforceable state mechanisms that, when viewed together as a whole, have the potential to significantly control nonpoint runoff.

The ELI warns that due to the diverse nature of programs and laws, the creation of definitive categories of controls is not possible. However, the general sources of state authority include: general discharge prohibitions similar to those found in section 301(a) of the Clean Water Act; agricultural laws that control sedimentation through soil and water conservation districts and concentrated animal feeding operations; forestry laws that require harvesting plans and best management practices; septic tank controls found in health and building codes; hydromodification regulations; pesticide registries; general nuisance laws; and overall watershed-based management protection areas.[36] For an excellent description and analysis of existing state programs, the reader should refer to the ELI series *Enforceable State Mechanisms for the Control of Nonpoint Source Water* (1997), *Almanac of Enforceable State Laws to Control Nonpoint Source Water Pollution*

---

35. ENVIRONMENTAL LAW INSTITUTE, ENFORCEABLE STATE MECHANISMS FOR THE CONTROL OF NONPOINT SOURCE WATER, Executive Summary (1997).

36. *See id.*

(1998), and *Putting the Pieces Together: State Nonpoint Source Enforceable Mechanisms in Context* (2000).[37]

D. EFFLUENT TRADING PROGRAMS

Considering the increasing role TMDLs will play in the future of water quality regulation, federal and state governments are continuing to explore the use of effluent trading programs as an innovative alternative to traditional command and control techniques as they search for ways of establishing meaningful incentives that have the ultimate effect of attaining designated uses and water quality standards. Effluent trading contemplates the establishment of pollutant discharges as fungible commodities that can be traded between regulated and nonregulated entities in order to achieve water quality standards for particular water bodies. Effluent trading is seen as an efficient alternative to traditional permitting schemes that has the potential to achieve environmental and social benefits at lower economic costs.

EPA published a basic effluent trading system policy in 1996 that called for the active promotion of effluent trading within watersheds in order to achieve water quality objectives and standards.[38] At the time, the EPA identified several potential forms of trades: intraplant, pretreatment, point/point, point/nonpoint, and nonpoint/nonpoint. The last two identify important potential mechanisms for the control of nonpoint sources of pollution. Where the costs of achieving pollutant reduction in a watershed are more efficiently borne by a nonpoint source, the nonpoint source can implement management measures to achieve a discharge reduction and can market that reduction to other sources in the same watershed. Implementation of effluent trading schemes has immense potential application in the context of TMDL development and implementation.

The current Bush administration recognizes this potential and is actively promoting a water quality trading program that would supersede the basic 1996 policy and, in its place, establish specific program components.[39] However, the eventual application of effluent trading is not without its hurdles. As nonpoint sources are not within the regulatory reach of the federal government under the NPDES program, EPA will need to find some way to incorporate point/nonpoint trades into the NPDES program without exceeding its statutory authority. A key

---

37. Copies of these reports are available at http://www.eli.org/store.

38. *See* Effluent Trading in Watersheds Policy Statement, 61 Fed. Reg. 4994 (1996). More information on EPA's trading policy and proposed framework is available at http://www.epa.gov/owow/watershed/trading.htm.

39. U.S. ENVIRONMENTAL PROTECTION AGENCY, OFFICE OF WATER QUALITY TRADING POLICY, DRAFT EPA PROPOSAL ON WATER QUALITY TRADING PROGRAMS FOR STATES AND TRIBES (Feb. 25, 2002) (proposed policy), *reprinted in* 33 Env't Rep. (BNA) 15, at 828 (Apr. 12, 2002).

component of any trading program will be an enforcement and monitoring provision that ensures actual implementation of contracted trades.

VI. Looking Towards the Future of Nonpoint Source Pollution Control

According to the most recent data from the section 305(b) water quality inventory reports, [40] all states and territories have approved nonpoint source assessments under section 319. EPA has also approved a total of 56 state and territorial nonpoint source management programs. In addition, 20 American Indian tribes have approved assessments and management programs. From 1990 to 1999, $877 million in federal funds were distributed under the section 319 program for nonpoint source control programs. The 1998 *Clean Water Action Plan* called for a renewed focus on watershed management planning and called for an increase in federal funding under various programs, including the section 319 grant program.

However, notwithstanding these efforts, much work remains if the goals of the Clean Water Act are to be attained. The following excerpt from the 2002 Draft EPA Proposal on Water Quality Trading Programs for States and Tribes concisely captures the difficulty of pursuing the enduring goal of water quality improvement through nonpoint pollution control in an increasingly complex financial and ecological environment:

> Times have changed dramatically since the existing regulatory framework was put in place. Today, our nation competes in a highly competitive world market. Population growth and development place greater demands on the environment making it more difficult to maintain environmental standards. These trends will continue. The assimilative capacity of our environment is limited and the technological and economic limitations of our existing regulatory framework are at hand. Finding solutions to complex water quality problems requires innovative strategies that are aligned with core water programs.[41]

The core nonpoint water pollution control programs under the Clean Water Act have been augmented by provisions of the CZARA, continuing development of TMDLs, enforceable state mechanisms, traditional land use planning, and innovative new solutions such as water quality–based trading. The future of water quality control in our nation's waters is dependent on how these programs succeed, independently and cumulatively, in addressing the problem of nonpoint source pollution.

---

40. *See supra* note 25. Chapter 10 of the 1998 Report contains an excellent summary of the nonpoint source programs under the Clean Water Act and other related federal programs.

41. DRAFT EPA PROPOSAL ON WATER QUALITY TRADING PROGRAMS FOR STATES AND TRIBES, *supra* note 38, at 828.

CHAPTER 10

TMDLs: Section 303(d)

LAURIE K. BEALE
KARIN SHELDON

I. Introduction

Section 303(d) of the Clean Water Act (CWA) establishes the Total Maximum Daily Load (TMDL) program, a water quality–based approach to regulating waters that fail to meet water quality standards despite the use of effluent limitations and other pollution control requirements. A TMDL is a calculation of the maximum quantity of a given pollutant that may be added to a waterbody from all sources without exceeding the applicable water quality standard for that pollutant. States[1] (or in some cases, EPA) must establish TMDLs for all pollutants that prevent waters from attaining water quality goals. The TMDL helps regulators devise the limitations necessary to meet water quality standards by identifying and quantifying the individual sources contributing to a particular water quality problem.

Though potentially a powerful regulatory tool, the TMDL program has achieved mixed results since it was enacted in 1972. For many years, both EPA and the states largely ignored the program. Beginning in the mid-1980s, citizen groups were successful in obtaining court orders and consent decrees requiring

---

1. Eligible tribes may also administer the TMDL program for waters within their boundaries. 40 C.F.R. § 130.1 (2001).

states or EPA to establish TMDLs for impaired waterways.[2] More recent litigation has focused on the adequacy and implementation of TMDLs. In 1996, in response to legal challenges and the growing emphasis on TMDLs, EPA undertook a comprehensive evaluation of the TMDL program. In July 2000, the agency promulgated new regulations intended to substantially strengthen the program, particularly emphasizing implementation and control of nonpoint sources. The new regulations, however, generated so much criticism that Congress blocked their implementation, and EPA ultimately postponed their effective date to allow for reconsideration and further public input.[3] A new proposed rule was expected to be issued in draft form in the fall of 2002, but was not yet available at the time of this publication. Although the July 2000 rule never took effect, certain aspects of that rule are discussed below, as they highlight potential future issues regarding EPA's management of the program.

II. TMDL Basics

A. COMPONENTS OF A TMDL

A TMDL is a calculation of the maximum quantity (or "load")[4] of a pollutant that may be added to a waterbody from all sources, including natural background sources, without exceeding the applicable water quality criteria for that pollutant.[5] Although section 303(d) refers to "daily" load, EPA regulations provide that TMDLs may be expressed "in terms of either mass per time, toxicity, or other appropriate measure."[6] A TMDL must take into consideration seasonal variations in water quality conditions and must include a margin of safety to account for any lack of knowledge concerning the relationship between effluent limitations and

---

2. As of April 2002, EPA was under court order or had agreed in consent decrees to establish TMDLs in 22 states if the states failed to act. *See* EPA, TMDL LITIGATION BY STATE, available at http://www.epa.gov/owow/tmdl/lawsuit1.html (last updated Apr. 11, 2002). In July 2002, EPA reported a total of 41,998 impaired water bodies listed for all states and a total of 4,549 approved TMDLs since January 1996. EPA, NATIONAL 303(D) LIST FACT SHEET, available at http://oaspub. epa.gov/waters/national_rept.control (last updated July 15, 2002).

3. Delay of Effective Date of Revisions to the Water Quality Planning and Management Regulation, 66 Fed. Reg. 41,817, 41,818 (2001).

4. 40 C.F.R. § 130.2(e).

5. 33 U.S.C. § 1313(d)(1)(C) (2000); 40 C.F.R. §§ 30.2(e)–(i). TMDLs are generally formulated to meet numeric criteria, but they can also be prepared for narrative water quality standards as long as the narrative standards can be quantified. *See* 40 C.F.R. § 130.7(b)(3); Sierra Club v. Hankinson, 939 F. Supp. 865, 870 (N.D. Ga. 1996).

6. 40 C.F.R. § 130.2(i); *see* National Resources Defense Council v. Muszynski, 268 F.3d 91, 97–99 (2d Cir. 2001) (TMDL need not be expressed as "daily" load if another measure of mass per time best serves the purposes of the CWA).

water quality.[7] A TMDL has two components: a Wasteload Allocation (WLA) and a Load Allocation (LA). The WLA is the portion of a TMDL allocated to existing and future point sources.[8] An LA is the portion of a TMDL attributed to existing and future nonpoint sources, including natural background sources. The LA must be a "best estimate" of loadings from these categories. Where possible, the LA must distinguish between loadings from natural and nonpoint sources.[9] In its simplest form, the sum of the WLAs and LAs, taking into account a margin of safety and seasonal variations, equals the TMDL.[10]

B. THE TMDL PROCESS

1. The Substance of TMDL Submittals

Section 303(d) requires states to identify waters within their boundaries for which technology-based effluent limits and other pollution control requirements "are not stringent enough to implement any water quality standard."[11] In other words, states must identify those waters failing to meet water quality standards in spite of full compliance by dischargers with all conditions and limitations in NPDES permits and all applicable nonpoint source controls. The states must prioritize their impaired waters (also referred to as "water quality limited segments," or WQLSs), based upon the severity of the pollution and the type and use of the waterway.[12] The states' lists of WQLSs and priority rankings are commonly referred to as "303(d) lists."

After identifying and ranking in order or priority their WQLSs, the states must prepare TMDLs for each pollutant impairing each WQLS.[13] The states must submit their section 303(d) lists and TMDLs to EPA, which has 30 days to approve or disapprove them. If EPA disapproves a state's submittals, EPA must prepare its own lists and/or TMDLs for the state's waters within 30 days.[14] States must incorporate approved TMDLs into their continuing planning processes and

---

7. 33 U.S.C. § 1313(d)(1)(C); 40 C.F.R. § 130.7(c)(1).

8. 40 C.F.R. § 130.2(h).

9. 40 C.F.R. § 130.2(g). EPA has issued guidance suggesting that atmospheric deposition of a pollutant also be addressed as part of an LA and attempted to codify this requirement in the July 2000 rule. *See* EPA, NATIONAL CLARIFYING GUIDANCE FOR 1998 STATE AND TERRITORY CLEAN WATER ACT SECTION 303(D) LISTING DECISIONS 5 (Aug. 17, 1997) (hereinafter 1998 GUIDANCE), available at http://www.epa.gov/owow/tmdl/lisgid.html (last updated Feb. 12, 1998); Revisions to the Water Quality Planning and Management Regulation, Final Rule, 65 Fed. Reg. 43,586, 43,662 (July 13, 2000), *effective date delayed for reconsideration*, 66 Fed. Reg. 41,817 (2001).

10. 40 C.F.R. § 130.2(i).

11. 33 U.S.C. § 1313(d)(1)(A); 40 C.F.R. § 130.7(b)(1).

12. 33 U.S.C. § 1313(d)(1)(A); 40 C.F.R. §§ 130.2(j), 130.7(b)(4).

13. 33 U.S.C. § 1313(d)(1)(C); 40 C.F.R. § 130.7(c)(1).

14. 33 U.S.C. § 1313(d)(2); 40 C.F.R. §§ 130.7(d)(1)–(2).

their water quality management plans.[15] States must provide for public review of their TMDL calculations, in accordance with procedures set forth in their continuing planning processes.[16]

2. The Timing of TMDL Submittals

Section 303(d) is unclear as to when states must act to establish TMDLs. The CWA first directed EPA to undertake studies to identify pollutants suitable for TMDL calculation and to publish a list of such pollutants by October 18, 1972.[17] The states then had 180 days to submit to EPA their initial section 303(d) lists and TMDLs. The statute requires states to make additional TMDL submittals to EPA "from time to time."[18] EPA has interpreted the "from time to time" requirement in its regulations by requiring that states submit section 303(d) lists every two years.[19] The lists must identify each WQLS still requiring a TMDL, identify each pollutant impairing each WQLS, establish a priority ranking for each WQLS, and identify the WQLSs targeted for TMDL development within the next two years.[20] EPA has not, however, established a time frame for the submittal of TMDLs.[21] Therefore, although states must identify the TMDLs they intend to prepare within two years, they are not expressly required to submit the so-identified TMDLs at any particular time.

C. TRADING

Neither section 303(d) nor the implementing regulations govern how a state is to allocate a waterbody's loading capacity among the various sources contributing to the load. States need not divide the restrictions in a TMDL equally or in proportion to the load contributions from point and nonpoint sources. States may take a variety of factors into account in setting a TMDL, for example, the relative costs of point and nonpoint source controls, the reliability and effectiveness of such controls, the degree of assurance that the controls will be actually implemented and maintained, and the social and economic benefits of different alloca-

---

15. 33 U.S.C. § 1313(e)(3)(C); 40 C.F.R. §§ 130.5–6, 130.7(d)(2).

16. 40 C.F.R. § 130.7(c)(1)(ii).

17. 33 U.S.C. § 1314(a)(2)(D).

18. 33 U.S.C. § 1313(d)(2).

19. 40 C.F.R. § 130.7(d)(1).

20. 40 C.F.R. § 130.7(b)(1), (b)(4), (d).

21. See San Francisco Baykeeper v. Whitman, No. 01-16111, 2002 WL 1560778, at *5–6 (9th Cir. July 17, 2002). The regulations suggest that states coordinate with the regional EPA administrators to devise comprehensive schedules for TMDL completion. 40 C.F.R. § 130.7(d)(1).

tions.[22] States may implement point/nonpoint source trading and other market-based approaches to water quality improvement.[23]

The current TMDL regulations specifically note that tradeoffs between point and nonpoint sources are permissible, so that where BMPs or other nonpoint source controls are available to absorb the necessary load reductions, a state may make more loading capacity available to point sources.[24] EPA guidance suggests, however, that where a state reduces the WLAs in a TMDL based upon anticipated future reductions in nonpoint source loading, the state provide specific assurances that the reductions will in fact occur.[25] Absent such assurances, the state must allocate the entire load reduction necessary to attain water quality standards to point sources.[26] In making these decisions, states must be mindful of the antibacksliding provisions contained in section 402(o) of the CWA, which may limit the states' flexibility to increase individual WLAs once they are established in a TMDL.[27]

D. MULTISTATE ISSUES

EPA often takes the lead in establishing TMDLs for WQLSs that include the waters of more than one state.[28] The TMDL must meet the most stringent water quality standards applicable to the impaired waterbody. As a practical matter, the TMDL process gives a downstream or neighboring state impacted by pollution from a source state greater ability to protect its water quality standards than would be the case if the affected state simply challenged the source state's violation of the affected state's water quality standards. In the latter circumstance, the downstream state is limited to bringing suit in the source state or seeking redress from the EPA Administrator.[29] With a TMDL in place, the downstream state can

---

22. Proposed Revisions to the Water Quality Planning and Management Regulation, 64 Fed. Reg. 46,012, 46,030 (Aug. 23, 1999).

23. Surface Water Toxics Control Program and Water Quality Planning and Management Program, Final Rule, 57 Fed. Reg. 33,040, 33,048 (July 24, 1992).

24. 40 C.F.R. § 130.2(i).

25. *See* EPA, GUIDANCE FOR WATER QUALITY–BASED DECISIONS: THE TMDL PROCESS, ch. 1 at 3, ch. 2 at 9, ch. 3 at 5–6 (Apr. 1991), available at http://www.epa.gov/owow/tmdl/decisions/dec3.html (last updated July 12, 1999).

26. *Id.* ch. 2 at 9.

27. 33 U.S.C. § 1342(o) (2000). Once TMDL-based effluent limitations are imposed, section 303(d) prohibits revising such restrictions unless: (1) the cumulative effect of all such revised effluent limitations based on the TMDL will assure the attainment of water quality standards, or (2) the designated use that is not being attained is removed. 33 U.S.C. § 1313(d)(4)(A).

28. *See e.g.*, Scott v. City of Hammond, 530 F. Supp. 288 (N.D. Ill. 1981), *aff'd in part, rev'd in part,* 741 F.2d 992 (7th Cir. 1984); *see infra* section III.D.

29. Arkansas v. Oklahoma, 503 U.S. 91 (1992).

rely on the multistate TMDL to protect its water quality rather than being forced to file suit in the upstream state's court or to go to the EPA to seek relief.

III. TMDL Litigation

A. JUDICIAL REVIEW

The actions of state administrative agencies in preparing section 303(d) lists and TMDLs may be reviewed in state courts in accordance with state law.[30] The actions of EPA in approving or disapproving the states' TMDL submissions and, in some cases, in failing to remedy state inaction, are reviewable in the federal district courts.[31] Section 505 of the CWA contains a citizen-suit provision that allows citizens to seek review of EPA's failure to perform any nondiscretionary duty required by the Act.[32] Citizens may thus challenge EPA's failure to approve or disapprove a state's TMDL submittals within the statutory 30-day time period. Where a state completely fails to submit lists or TMDLs, citizens may, in certain circumstances, obtain review of the state's inaction by challenging EPA's failure to address the state's inaction.[33] Courts generally apply the APA arbitrary and capricious standard of review in lawsuits brought pursuant to section 505.[34] The substance of EPA's decision to approve or disapprove a section 303(d) list or a TMDL may be challenged under section 706(2) of the APA as final agency action.[35] Review of the substance of a TMDL prepared by EPA on behalf of a state is also available under section 706(2).[36]

B. THE CONSTRUCTIVE SUBMISSION THEORY

As discussed above, the CWA set an initial deadline of October 18, 1972, for EPA to publish a list of pollutants suitable for TMDL calculation. EPA failed to

---

30. *But see* Monongahela Power Co. v. Chief, Office of Water Resources, No. 30105, 2002 WL 1438541 (W. Va. July 1, 2002) (West Virginia state courts lack jurisdiction to review Department of Environmental Protection's WLAs or § 303(d) lists).

31. Longview Fibre Co. v. Rasmussen, 980 F.2d 1307 (9th Cir. 1992).

32. 33 U.S.C. § 1365(a)(2).

33. *See* section III.B, *infra*. In addition to bringing a citizen suit under the CWA, plaintiffs may be able to challenge EPA's failure to act under section 706(1) of the APA. *See* 5 U.S.C. § 706(1) (allowing court to compel agency action unlawfully withheld or unreasonably delayed); Natural Resources Defense Council, Inc. v. Fox, 30 F. Supp. 2d 369, 377–79 (S.D.N.Y. 1998). *But see* Hayes v. Whitman, 264 F.3d 1017, 1025 (10th Cir. 2001) (dismissing APA failure to act claim where relief was available under section 505 of the CWA, since APA relief is only available where there is "no other adequate remedy") (citing 5 U.S.C. § 704); San Francisco Baykeeper v. Whitman, No. 01-16111, 2002 WL 1560778, at *6 (9th Cir. July 17, 2002).

34. American Canoe Ass'n, Inc. v. EPA, 46 F. Supp. 2d 473, 476–77 (E.D. Va. 1999) (citing National Wildlife Fed'n v. Hanson, 859 F.2d 313, 316 (4th Cir. 1988)).

35. *See, e.g.,* American Canoe Ass'n, Inc. v. EPA, 30 F. Supp. 2d 908, 918-99 (E.D. Va. 1998).

36. *See Longview Fibre*, 980 F.2d at 1313–14.

meet this deadline and did not publish its list until December 1978.[37] Consequently, the states' first section 303(d) lists and TMDLs were due on June 26, 1979. Most states failed not only to meet this deadline, but to make any efforts to submit lists or TMDLs thereafter.[38] EPA's apparent lack of interest in enforcing the program led commentators to suggest and EPA to concede that it was "consciously neglecting" the TMDL requirements.[39] In 1984, in the first successful citizen suit challenging the states' and EPA's failure to implement TMDLs, the plaintiff argued that EPA had a nondiscretionary duty to prepare TMDLs for the states of Indiana and Illinois, which had never submitted a single TMDL. The Seventh Circuit agreed, holding that the states' continued failure to submit TMDLs over a long period of time could amount to the "constructive submission" of no TMDLs.[40] The court of appeals remanded the case to the district court to determine whether the states' inaction "had ripened into a refusal to act."[41] If so, EPA would be required to approve or disapprove the states' determination that no TMDLs were necessary; if EPA disagreed with the states, EPA would have to prepare TMDLs in their stead.[42]

Other courts have adopted the "constructive submission" theory[43] and fleshed out the test for determining when a state's failure to act amounts to a decision not to submit TMDLs, thus triggering EPA's duty to act. The inquiry is factual, and

---

37. EPA finally published the list pursuant to court order. The list identified "all pollutants" as suitable. *See* 43 Fed. Reg. 60,662 (1978).

38. *See, e.g.,* Friends of the Wild Swan, Inc. v. EPA, 130 F. Supp. 2d 1184, 1196 (D. Mont. 1999) (state of Montana, which completed 130 TMDLs in first 19 years of program, will need over 100 years to complete TMDLs for WQLSs listed in 1998); *American Canoe Ass'n,* 30 F. Supp. 2d at 913 (state of Virginia failed to submit any TMDLs during first 20 years of the program); Sierra Club v. Hankinson, 939 F. Supp. 865, 867 (N.D. Ga. 1996) (at its current pace, state of Georgia will take more than 100 years to comply with TMDL requirements).

39. *See* National Resource Defense Council v. Fox, 93 F. Supp. 2d 531, 539 (S.D.N.Y. 2000), *aff'd in part, vacated in part sub nom.* National Resources Defense Council v. Muszynski, 268 F.3d 91 (2nd Cir. 2001). The TMDL program was historically deemed a secondary priority, behind implementation of effluent limitations. *See* Prosolino v. Nastri, 291 F.3d 1123, 1136 & n.15 (9th Cir. 2002).

40. Scott v. City of Hammond, 741 F.2d 992, 996 (7th Cir. 1984).

41. *Id.* at 997–98.

42. *Id.* at 998.

43. *See* Hayes v. Whitman, 264 F.3d 1017, 1024 (10th Cir. 2001); Sierra Club v. EPA, 162 F. Supp. 2d 406, 419 n.18 (D. Md. 2001); Hayes v. Browner, 117 F. Supp. 2d 1182 (N.D. Okla. 2000); *Friends of the Wild Swan,* 130 F. Supp. 2d at 1191; Kingman Park Civic Ass'n v. EPA, 84 F. Supp. 2d 1 (D.D.C. 1999); *American Canoe Ass'n,* 30 F. Supp. 2d at 919–22; Sierra Club v. Hankinson, 939 F. Supp. at 865; Sierra Club v. Browner, 843 F. Supp. 1304 (D. Minn. 1993); Alaska Ctr. for the Env't v. Reilly, 762 F. Supp. 1422, 1429 (W.D. Wash. 1991), *aff'd sub nom.* Alaska Center for the Env't v. Browner, 20 F.3d 981 (9th Cir. 1994). One district court has rejected the theory, finding that the EPA has "at least some discretion" in determining at what point to deem state inaction a refusal to act. Natural Resources Defense Council v. Fox, 30 F. Supp. 2d 369, 376–77 (S.D.N.Y.1998).

most courts have concluded that constructive submission occurs only where the state has not submitted *any* TMDLs, that is, where the state's actions "clearly and unambiguously" express a decision not to submit a TMDL for a particular water-body.[44] The constructive submission theory cannot be used to challenge the time-liness or adequacy of a state's TMDL submissions, as those issues implicate EPA's discretionary duties.[45]

C. CHALLENGES TO THE SUBSTANCE OF TMDLS

EPA's decision to approve or disapprove a state's TMDL submittals is review-able under the APA as final agency action.[46] A court may set aside EPA's approval or disapproval if it determines that EPA's decision was arbitrary, capri-cious, an abuse of discretion, or otherwise contrary to law.[47] Using this theory, plaintiffs have successfully argued that EPA abused its discretion in approving section 303(d) lists where, for example, the lists included only a fraction of the state's impaired waters.[48] Similarly, plaintiffs have successfully challenged EPA's approval of TMDLs where the TMDLs did not include daily limits or account for seasonal variations,[49] and where a state failed to submit a sufficient number of TMDLs for the WQLSs identified on its section 303(d) list.[50] EPA has successfully defended its decisions approving section 303(d) lists where the agency has been able to demonstrate that the states had reasonable explanations

---

44. Hayes v. Whitman, 264 F.3d at 1024 (constructive submission theory did not apply where evidence showed that state of Oklahoma had submitted a small number of TMDLs and had devised a schedule for developing others); *see also* San Francisco Baykeeper v. Whitman, No. 01-16111, 2002 WL 1560778, at *2 (9th Cir. July 17, 2002) (although California failed to submit any TMDLs between 1980 and 1994, no constructive submission found where state subsequently completed 46 TMDLs, established a schedule for completing other TMDLs, and dedicated substantial resources to TMDL program); Sierra Club v. Hankinson, 939 F. Supp. at 872 n.6 (no constructive submission where Geor-gia had made some submission, albeit totally inadequate); *National Resources Defense Council*, 93 F. Supp. 2d at 542 (as long as New York was actively participating in effort to promulgate TMDLs, no constructive submission); Idaho Sportsmen's Coalition v. Browner, 951 F. Supp. 962, 968 (W.D. Wash. 1996) (Idaho had not constructively submitted any TMDLs where state had submitted two); Sierra Club, Northstar Chapter v. Browner, 843 F. Supp. 1304, 1313 n.18 (D. Minn. 1993) (no con-structive submission where state had submitted several § 303(d) lists and EPA had disapproved most recent list).

45. Hayes v. Whitman, 264 F.3d at 1024.

46. *See, e.g.*, Natural Resources Defense Council, Inc. v. Muszynski, 268 F.3d 91, 96–97 (2nd Cir. 2001); Dioxin/Organochlorine Ctr. v. Clarke, 57 F.3d 1517, 1521 (9th Cir. 1995); *cf.* Hayes v. Whitman, 264 F.3d at 1024 (timeliness and adequacy of state's TMDL submissions invoke EPA's discretionary duties).

47. 5 U.S.C. § 706(2)(A) (2000).

48. *Idaho Sportsmen's Coalition*, 951 F. Supp. at 964.

49. Sierra Club v. Hankinson, 939 F. Supp. 865, 871–72 (N.D. Ga. 1996).

50. Friends of the Wild Swan, Inc. v. EPA, 130 F. Supp. 2d 1184, 1195–96 (D. Mont. 1999).

for failing to include waters that plaintiffs alleged were impaired.[51] Likewise, EPA's TMDL approvals have been upheld where courts determined that all of the required elements were included[52] or that EPA's decisions were reasonable and based on credible scientific data.[53]

D. EPA'S EXPANDED AUTHORITY

The statutory language of section 303(d) gives EPA a fairly limited role in the TMDL process—to approve or disapprove a state's TMDL submittals and to prepare section 303(d) lists and TMDLs when a state's submittals are disapproved. EPA's interpretation of its role in the early years of the program led to the lawsuits discussed above, in which courts imposed upon the agency the additional duty of preparing section 303(d) lists and TMDLs for states that fail to do so. EPA has inferred from these rulings and from the broader purposes of the CWA authority to expand its role in overseeing, preparing, and implementing TMDLs. This added oversight has resulted in increasingly detailed regulations and guidance issued by EPA over the past decade.[54] EPA's proposed July 2000 rule attempted to codify many aspects of EPA's expanded authority, including its authority to oversee and ensure TMDL implementation and its authority to prepare TMDLs at a state's request, for interstate or boundary waters, or to implement federal water quality standards.[55]

IV. Sources Subject to TMDL Limitations

A. SOURCES OF HEAT

1. Thermal Discharges

The CWA separately addresses TMDLs for waters impaired by thermal discharges.[56] For such waters, states must establish TMDLs at a level necessary to "assure the protection and propagation of a balanced, indigenous population of

---

51. American Littoral Soc'y v. EPA, 199 F. Supp. 2d 217, 234–36 (D.N.J. 2002); Sierra Club v. EPA, 162 F. Supp. 2d 406, 413–16 (D. Md. 2001); *Friends of the Wild Swan*, 130 F. Supp. 2d at 1193–94. Such challenges may also be rejected on standing, ripeness, or other jurisdictional grounds. *See, e.g.*, Missouri Soybean Ass'n v. EPA, 289 F.3d 509, 512 (8th Cir. 2002) (farmers' association's challenge to approval of § 303(d) list not ripe because harm to farmers from stricter controls that might be imposed when TMDLs were developed was speculative).

52. *Friends of the Wild Swan*, 130 F. Supp. 2d at 1195.

53. Natural Resources Defense Council, Inc. v. Muszynski, 268 F.3d 91, 100–02 (2d Cir. 2001); *cf.* Dioxin/Organochlorine Ctr. v. Clarke, 57 F.3d 1517, 1523, 1525 (9th Cir. 1995).

54. *See* 64 Fed. Reg. 46,012, 46,037–38, 46,040 (Aug. 23, 1999).

55. 65 Fed. Reg. 43,586, 43,669 (July 13, 2000).

56. 33 U.S.C. § 1313(d)(1)(B).

shellfish, fish and wildlife."[57] EPA refers to this standard as "BIP."[58] The BIP standard is generally more flexible than the numeric temperature criterion for a waterway.[59] In calculating thermal TMDLs, states must take into account normal water temperatures, flow rates, seasonal variations, existing sources of heat input, and the dissipative capacity of the water. The thermal TMDL must include a calculation of the maximum heat input that can be made plus a margin of safety.[60]

2. Temperature TMDLs Distinguished from Thermal TMDLs

Section 303(d)'s special treatment of heat was intended to provide relief to large generating plants and prevent costly and unnecessary controls.[61] Based upon this objective and the statutory language, EPA has interpreted the thermal TMDL provision as applying only to waters impaired by point sources of heat. For waters impaired by heat from nonpoint sources, EPA has taken the position that the general TMDL provision applies, meaning that the numeric temperature criterion, rather than the BIP standard, controls the level of allowable heat input.[62] EPA has not expressed a position as to the appropriate standard for waters impaired by a combination of sources.[63] In general, states and EPA have utilized the numeric standard rather than the BIP standard in preparing TMDLs for heat, regardless of the sources of heat input.

B. SOURCES OF POLLUTION

The CWA provides separate definitions of "pollutant" and "pollution." A "pollutant" is any one of a number of listed contaminants (including, for example, dredged spoil, solid waste, chemical waste, biological materials, and industrial, municipal, and agricultural waste) that is "discharged into water."[64] The defini-

---

57. 33 U.S.C. § 1313(d)(1)(D); 40 C.F.R. § 130.7(b)(2) (2001).

58. 64 Fed. Reg. 46,012, 46,017 (1999).

59.   64 Fed. Reg. 46,012, 46,017 (Aug. 23, 1999).

60. 33 U.S.C. § 1313(d)(1)(D); 40 C.F.R. § 130.7(c)(2).

61. 1 ENV'TL POLICY DIV., LIBR. OF CONG., A LEGISLATIVE HISTORY OF THE WATER POLLUTION CONTROL ACT AMENDMENTS OF 1972, at 263–64 (1978); 64 Fed. Reg. at 46,017; see 33 U.S.C. § 1326.

62. 64 Fed. Reg. at 46,017.

63. The CWA is unclear regarding which standard (numeric criteria or BIP) should apply to waters impaired by nonpoint sources or a combination of sources. While section 303(d)(1)(B) expressly references "thermal discharges," that is, point sources, section 303 also contains a provision requiring that water quality standards for heat be consistent with section 316 of the CWA, which sets forth the BIP standard. 33 U.S.C. § 1313(g); see also 33 U.S.C. § 1313(h) (providing that the term "water quality standards" includes thermal standards).

64. 33 U.S.C. § 1362(6); 40 C.F.R. § 122.2.

tion of "pollution" is broader: It comprehends any "man-made or man-induced alteration of the chemical, physical, biological, and radiological integrity of water."[65] Section 303(d) requires TMDLs only for "pollutants."[66] Accordingly, only waters impaired by "pollutants" must be included on section 303(d) lists and be the subject of TMDLs.[67] TMDLs are not required, but may be promulgated, for waters impaired by, for example, flow alterations, habitat alterations, or channelization, since those problems may constitute "pollution," but are not linked to a specific "pollutant."[68] As a practical matter, most types of pollution could not readily be quantified and translated into a "load" for purposes of establishing TMDLs.

V. Implementation of TMDLs

A. POINT SOURCES

Section 303(d) outlines the substance of and process for creating TMDLs but does not expressly provide for their implementation. Section 303(e), however, requires states to have EPA-approved continuing planning processes and water quality management plans, which must include planning and implementation mechanisms for TMDLs.[69] In addition, section 301 requires that NPDES permits include "any more stringent limitation . . . necessary to meet water quality standards."[70] Thus, for waters for which a TMDL has been established, point source discharges must be consistent with the WLA in the TMDL.[71] This requirement is in addition to the applicable technology-based limitation and applies regardless of the costs required to achieve compliance. New or increased discharges are permitted only if the TMDL makes allowance for them, either through specific WLAs or through unallocated capacity.[72] New or increased point source discharges to impaired waters for which a TMDL has not yet been established are

---

65. 33 U.S.C. § 1362(19); 40 C.F.R. § 130.2(c).

66. 33 U.S.C. § 1313(d)(1)(C).

67. 64 Fed. Reg. at 46,020. In the July 2000 rule, EPA proposed requiring states to include on their section 303(d) lists waters impaired by pollution, even though a TMDL would not be required for those waters. 65 Fed. Reg. at 43,665.

68. 64 Fed. Reg. at 46,021; 65 Fed. Reg. at 43,592–93.

69. 33 U.S.C. § 1313(e)(3)(C); 40 C.F.R. §§ 130.5(b)(3), 130.6(c)(1), (6).

70. 33 U.S.C. §§ 1311(b)(1)(C), 1313(e)(3)(A).

71. 40 C.F.R. §§ 122.44(d)(1)(vii)(B), 130.12(a); *see also* Water Quality Planning and Management, Final Rule, 50 Fed. Reg. 1774, 1778 (Jan. 11, 1985).

72. 40 C.F.R. § 122.4(i)(1).

legally problematic, since the permits for those discharges must ensure compliance with water quality standards.[73]

B. NONPOINT SOURCES

Section 303(d) is unclear regarding whether TMDLs apply to nonpoint sources.[74] As discussed above, EPA has interpreted the TMDL requirement as applying to all impaired waters, whether the impairment is caused by point sources, nonpoint sources, or both.[75] In 1999, this interpretation was challenged by landowners and industry groups, who argued that EPA lacked authority to require TMDLs for waters polluted solely by nonpoint sources.[76] The Ninth Circuit upheld EPA's interpretation of the statute.[77] The court found that, although point and nonpoint sources are treated differently in many sections of the CWA, section 303(d) applies regardless of the source of the pollutant at issue. The court noted, however, that because EPA lacked authority to directly regulate nonpoint sources under the CWA, implementation of the load allocations in the TMDL was left to the state's discretion.[78]

---

73. 33 U.S.C. §§ 1311(b)(1)(C), 1313(e)(3)(A); 40 C.F.R. § 122.4(i). For example, in a case brought before the Washington State Pollution Control Hearings Board (PCHB), conservation groups challenged the state's issuance of a general construction stormwater permit on grounds that new discharges into waters listed under section 303(d) would cause water quality standard exceedances, in violation of the CWA. Puget Soundkeeper Alliance Waste Action Project v. Washington Dep't of Ecology, PCHB No. 00-173, 2001 WL 1502152 (Aug. 29, 2001). The PCHB agreed and entered an order prohibiting new discharges into impaired waters unless the discharger affirmatively demonstrated that no water quality violation would occur. Id.; see also Friends of the Wild Swan, Inc. v. EPA, 130 F. Supp. 2d 1207, 1211 (D. Mont. 2000) (enjoining Montana and EPA from issuing new or increased discharge permits pending court-ordered completion of TMDLs). EPA's July 2000 regulation addressed this issue by revising the NPDES program regulations and the federal antidegradation policy to require "reasonable further progress," in the form of additional obligations on point sources, toward attaining water quality standards in impaired waters for which TMDLs had not yet been prepared. See 65 Fed. Reg. at 43,638–43.

74. Section 303(d) requires TMDLs for all waters for which "effluent limitations . . . are not stringent enough to implement any water quality standard," but does not expressly reference nonpoint source pollution. 33 U.S.C. § 1313(a)(1)(A), (C).

75. 40 C.F.R. §§ 130.2(g)–(i), 130.7(b)(1); see also 1998 GUIDANCE, supra note 9, at 8–9.

76. Pronsolino v. Marcus, 91 F.Supp.2d 1337 (N.D. Calif. 2000), aff'd sub nom. Pronsolino v. Nastri, 291 F.3d 1123 (9th Cir. 2002). EPA had prepared a sediment TMDL for the state of California, which the state implemented through restrictions on timber harvesting. The plaintiffs, who stood to lose millions of dollars under the new state guidelines, argued that EPA had exceeded its CWA authority and intruded into the state's traditional control over land use. Pronsolino, 291 F.3d at 1129–30, 1140.

77. Pronsolino, 291 F.3d at 1137.

78. Pronsolino, 291 F.3d at 1140 (noting that states must implement TMDLs only to the extent that they seek to avoid losing federal grant money).

C. SOURCES REQUIRING SECTION 401 CERTIFICATION

Section 401 of the CWA requires that an applicant for a federal license or permit to conduct an activity that "may result in any discharge" to waters regulated by the CWA must obtain from the state where the activity will occur a certification that the discharge will comply with certain enumerated sections of the CWA, including section 303.[79] The certification must include effluent limitations (that is, limitations on point sources)[80] necessary to ensure such compliance.[81] The certification must also include "other limitations" as necessary to ensure that the activity complies with "any other appropriate requirement of State law," including water quality standards.[82] Therefore, for activities requiring section 401 certification, a state could implement WLAs as part of its certification.

VI. TMDLs and the Endangered Species Act

Increasingly, TMDLs are being established for waters that contain species listed as threatened or endangered under the Endangered Species Act (ESA). Section 7 of the ESA requires federal agencies to consult with the Fish and Wildlife Service and/or the National Marine Fisheries Service (Services) to ensure that actions the agencies authorize, fund, or carry out are not likely to jeopardize threatened or endangered species or destroy or adversely modify their critical habitat.[83] Consultations are only required, however, where the agency has discretion to influence the proposed activity for the benefit of the listed species.[84]

EPA has entered into a formal agreement with the Services outlining a process for consulting on certain of EPA's CWA obligations, including approval of state water quality standards and issuance of federal NPDES permits.[85] The agreement does not address whether EPA will consult over its actions approving/disapproving a state's TMDL submittals or preparing TMDLs on a state's behalf.[86] EPA has consulted over these activities in some

79. 33 U.S.C. § 1341(a)(1).

80. *See* Oregon Natural Desert Ass'n v. Dombeck, 172 F.3d 1092, 1095–96 (9th Cir. 1998).

81. 33 U.S.C. § 1341(d).

82. *Id.*; 40 C.F.R. § 121.2(a)(3) (2001); *see* PUD No. 1 of Jefferson County v. Washington Dep't of Ecology, 511 U.S. 700, 711–12 (1994).

83. 16 U.S.C. § 1536(a)(2).

84. Sierra Club v. Babbitt, 65 F.3d 1502, 1508–09 (9th Cir. 1995).

85. *See, e.g.*, 66 Fed. Reg. 11,202, 11,206 (Feb. 22, 2001) (Memorandum of Agreement (MOA) between EPA and Services outlining process for consultations regarding certain of EPA's CWA obligations).

86. *Id.* Region X of EPA issued a draft Regional MOA in 2001 providing for TMDL consultations, but whether this provision will be included in the final MOA is uncertain. *See* EPA, REGION X, FINAL DRAFT: PACIFIC NORTHWEST REGIONAL AGREEMENT BETWEEN THE ENVIRONMENTAL PROTECTION AGENCY, NATIONAL MARINE FISHERIES SERVICE, AND FISH AND WILDLIFE SERVICE 11 (Oct. 24, 2001).

circumstances,[87] and at least one district court has suggested that consultations may be required.[88] To the extent section 303(d) restricts EPA's discretion to base its TMDL decisions on listed species concerns, consultations would not be legally required.[89] EPA's July 2000 rule contained a provision that encouraged, but did not require, states to submit draft 303(d) lists and TMDLs to the Services for comment in order to informally address ESA concerns.[90] Unless EPA formally consults on a TMDL and an incidental take statement is issued, a discharger could be liable under the ESA, despite complying with the terms of the TMDL, if the discharge harmed a listed species or its critical habitat.[91]

VII. The July 2000 TMDL Rule: Future Issues

The July 2000 rule, which was shaped by recommendations of a Federal Advisory Committee Act (FACA) committee convened by EPA in 1996, represented an ambitious overhaul of the current TMDL regulations.[92] The proposed rule began by redefining the TMDL itself—from the sum of WLAs and LAs—to "a written, quantitative plan and analysis," composed of 11 specific elements, for "attaining and maintaining water quality standards."[93] One of the more controversial requirements was that the states prepare comprehensive implementation plans providing "reasonable assurance" that the WLAs and LAs in a TMDL

---

87. *See* American Canoe Ass'n, Inc. v. EPA, 54 F. Supp. 2d 621, 624 (E.D. Va. 1999) (consent decree requiring EPA to consult before approving or establishing § 303(d) lists or TMDLs); American Littoral Soc'y v. EPA, 199 F. Supp. 2d 217, 244–49 (D.N.J. 2002) (claim alleging EPA violated ESA by failing to consult before approving § 303(d) lists and TMDLs moot where EPA initiated consultations after lawsuit was filed).

88. Sierra Club v. EPA, 162 F. Supp. 2d 406, 421–22 (D. Md. 2001).

89. *See* Sierra Club v. Babbitt, 65 F.3d at 1508–09.

90. 64 Fed. Reg. 46,012, 46,038 (Aug. 23, 1999); 65 Fed. Reg. 43,586, 43,633–35 (July 13, 2000).

91. 16 U.S.C. § 1538(a) (2000) (prohibiting "take" of listed species); 16 U.S.C. § 1540(a)–(b) (providing civil and criminal penalties for ESA violations). "Takes" in conformance with a Biological Opinion issued by one of the Services are immune from enforcement. 16 U.S.C. § 1539(a)(1)(B); Ramsey v. Kantor, 96 F.3d 434, 440–42 (9th Cir. 1996). While the Services have stated that they will not actively pursue enforcement against persons operating in compliance with state or federal permits, the ESA contains a citizen-suit provision that could be used by third parties to bring such an action. 16 U.S.C. § 1540(g).

92. 64 Fed. Reg. at 46,013.

93. 65 Fed. Reg. at 43,662. The required elements included, among other things, quantification of the permissible pollutant load and the degree by which the current load exceeds the permissible load; identification of sources and source categories contributing to the load; WLAs and LAs; a margin of safety and seasonal variations; allowance for future growth; and an implementation plan. *Id.*

would actually be implemented.[94] EPA believed this revision was necessary to ensure that TMDLs are not "merely a paper plan to attain water quality standards."[95] EPA has indicated, however, that it may drop this requirement from its forthcoming regulations and will instead focus on implementation through the states' continuing planning processes.[96]

The new rule broadened the TMDL requirements in a number of other respects. For example, the rule enlarged the scope of the section 303(d) list to include all impaired waters, whether or not a TMDL would be legally required for those waters.[97] It further required that states submit comprehensive schedules for the completion of TMDLs for all of their listed waters, and that all TMDLs be established "as expeditiously as practicable," at a minimum within ten years of listing or by 2010.[98] The new rule provided that a state's failure to adhere to its schedule or meet specific TMDL deadlines would trigger EPA's duty to act in the state's place.[99] The rule also attempted to impose more rigorous restrictions on nonpoint sources. Under EPA's currently effective TMDL rules, a load allocation, or LA, is defined as the portion of a TMDL "attributed" to nonpoint sources, that is, the amount of loading that nonpoint sources contribute under the existing scheme of controls.[100] The revised TMDL rules would redefine an LA as an "'allocation' to nonpoint sources, suggesting that nonpoint sources should share in the reductions necessary to meet water quality standards."[101] This change, along with the stricter implementation requirements and the emphasis on addressing waters impaired solely or primarily by nonpoint sources, created a conflict between EPA's duty to oversee the implementation of TMDLs for all waters and the CWA's delegation of nonpoint source control to state and local authorities. How these interests are ultimately balanced remains to be seen.

---

94. 65 Fed. Reg. at 43,663, 668; *see generally* Sierra Club v. Meiburg, No. 01-14587, 2002 WL 1426554 (11th Cir. July 2, 2002) (discussing state of Georgia's failure to implement TMDLs prepared by EPA and EPA's implementation responsibilities under the current regulatory scheme).

95. 65 Fed. Reg. at 43,625; *see also id.* at 43,667–68.

96. *See* EPA, STATUS OF THE TMDL/WATERSHED RULE (June 3, 2002) available at http://www.epa.gov.owow/tmdl/watershedrule/watershedrulefs.html (last updated June 28, 2002).

97. 65 Fed. Reg. at 43,665 (requiring that § 303(d) lists include: waters impaired by pollutants; waters impaired by pollution; waters impaired by atmospheric deposition; and waters impaired by point, nonpoint, or any combination of sources).

98. 65 Fed. Reg. at 43,666.

99. 65 Fed. Reg. at 43,669.

100. 40 C.F.R. § 130.2(g) (2001).

101. 65 Fed. Reg. at 43,662.

CHAPTER 11

Enforcement: Section 309*

I. Civil Judicial Enforcement

BETH S. GINSBERG
JENNIFER E. MERRICK

A. STATUTORY AUTHORITY

Among the various enforcement options available to Environmental Protection Agency (EPA) under Clean Water Act (CWA) section 309 is the ability to commence a civil action in federal district court to redress violations of water pollution control requirements.[1] EPA may seek remedies as appropriate, including injunctive relief and civil penalties up to $27,500 per day for each violation.[2] The statute authorizes EPA to enforce prohibitions on unpermitted discharges;[3]

---

* The authors acknowledge the contributions of Keven McGaffey, Annette L. Hayes, James C. Nicoll, Ann Prezyna, and Martha Fox to the 1994 edition of this chapter.

1. 33 U.S.C.A. § 1319(a)(3), (b) (West 2001).

2. *Id.* §§ 1319(b), (d) (West 2001). Under the Civil Monetary Penalties Adjustment Rule, EPA is permitted to seek a 10-percent increase from the amounts set forth under the CWA as a penalty. *See* 40 C.F.R. pt. 19 (2001). EPA is preparing to issue a revision to the Civil Monetary Penalties Adjustment Rule in the near future. After a new rule-making is completed the maximum penalties available are expected to be as follows: for civil judicial penalties under CWA section 309(d), $30,500 per day per violation; for class I administrative penalties, $12,000 per day per violation, $30,000 maximum; for class II penalties, $12,000 per violation, $152,500 maximum. *See* EPA Clean Water Act section 404 Settlement Penalty Policy § I.C n.10.

3. 33 U.S.C. § 1311(a) (West 2001).

discharges in violation of technology or water quality–based effluent limita-tions,[4] new source performance standards,[5] categorical effluent limitations for toxic pollutants,[6] pretreatment standards,[7] reporting and record-keeping require-ments,[8] discharges in violation of National Pollutant Discharge Elimination Sys-tem (NPDES) permits,[9] aquaculture permits,[10] wetlands permits, permits author-izing dredging or filling activities in navigable waters,[11] and permits authorizing sewage sludge disposal.[12]

B. ENFORCEMENT TRENDS

EPA's enforcement statistics reveal that the most common types of civil enforce-ment actions are those enforcing NPDES permits and preventing unpermitted dis-charges. In 1999, EPA referred nearly 350 civil enforcement actions to the Department of Justice for prosecution (including 87 CWA matters), collected $7.4 million in civil penalties under the CWA, and obtained $577 million in injunctive relief and approximately $8.6 million in Supplemental Environmental Projects.[13] In 2000, EPA collected a $30-million civil penalty—the largest civil penalty ever imposed on a company under the CWA—redressing more than 300 oil spills from pipelines and oil facilities located in six states.[14] In the last few years, EPA has concentrated its enforcement efforts on targeted sectors, includ-ing the concentrated animal-feeding operations in the agricultural sector[15] and combined or sanitary sewer overflows in the municipal sector.[16] Other new devel-

4. *Id.* § 1312 (West 2001).

5. *Id.* § 1316 (West 2001).

6. *Id.* § 1317 (West 2001).

7. *Id.* § 1342(b)(8) (West 2001).

8. *Id.* § 1318 (West 2001).

9. *Id.* § 1342 (West 2001).

10. *Id.* § 1328 (West 2001).

11. *Id.* § 1344 (West 2001).

12. *Id.* § 1345 (West 2001).

13. EPA, ANNUAL REPORT ON ENFORCEMENT AND COMPLIANCE ASSURANCE ACCOMPLISHMENTS IN 1999 at 6–7, Exh. B-1.

14. EPA, OFFICE OF REGULATORY ENFORCEMENT, KOCH INDUSTRIES CIVIL SETTLEMENT, avail-able at http://es.epa.gov/oeca/ore/water/koch/index.html.

15. *See, e.g.,* Community Ass'n for Restoration of the Env't v. Henry Bosma Dairy, 52 Env't Rep. Cas. (BNA) 1167 (E.D. Wash. 2001) (imposing $171,500 in civil penalties for violations in con-nection with discharges from concentrated animal-feeding operation).

16. ANNUAL REPORT ON ENFORCEMENT AND COMPLIANCE ASSURANCE ACCOMPLISHMENTS IN 1999 at A-3.

opments include EPA's aggressive enforcement stance toward stormwater violations[17] as reflected in its 2000 Stormwater Enforcement Strategy.[18]

C. EPA'S ENFORCEMENT JURISDICTION

EPA's enforcement jurisdiction is concurrent with that of the states.[19] Even in those states where EPA has delegated authority to implement the NPDES program, EPA's authority to enforce the mandates of the CWA remains.[20] In those states where EPA has delegated its permitting authority, however, the agency is required to notify such state of a violation and give the state 30 days to bring an enforcement action before EPA may itself commence a civil action.[21]

EPA's enforcement decisions are discretionary; its decision whether to prosecute in a particular circumstance is unreviewable as a matter of law.[22] While EPA's enforcement decisions are discretionary, it cannot prosecute a violation that is being or has been diligently redressed by a comparable state action.[23] EPA's ability to "over-file," or commence a civil enforcement action when a state

---

17. *See, e.g.,* United States v. Wal-Mart Stores, Inc., (W.D. Ark. June 7, 2001) (settlement involving $1-million civil penalty for stormwater violations and establishment of $4.5-million environmental management plan to address stormwater discharges at stores); United States v. Amtrak, No. 01:CV11121 (D. Mass. June 28, 2001) (collecting $1.4-million civil penalty and requiring environmental audits at 51 facilities).

18. These updates and enforcement strategies can be found on EPA's web page at http://es.epa.gov/oeca/ore/water.

19. *See, e.g.,* Citizens Legal Env'tl Action Network, Inc. v. Premium Standard Farms, Inc., 2000 WL 220464, at *15 (W.D. Mo. Feb. 23, 2000). In Southern Ohio Coal Co. v. Office of Surface Mining, 20 F.3d 1418 (1994), the Sixth Circuit similarly found that "U.S. EPA retains independent enforcement authority in primacy states." The Sixth Circuit based that decision on 33 U.S.C. Section 1342(i), or section 402(i) of CWA, which is headed "Federal Enforcement Not Limited" and reads in substance, "Nothing in this section shall be construed to limit the authority of the Administrator to take action pursuant to section 1319 of the title." *Id.* at 1428.

20. 33 U.S.C. § 1342(i).

21. 33 U.S.C. § 1319(a) (West 2001).

22. *See, e.g.,* Sierra Club v. Whitman, 268 F.3d 898 (9th Cir. 2001) (CWA section 309(b) commits to discretion of Administrator option to issue compliance order or to commence civil action, but not to require their use). The Ninth Circuit further emphasized that the "multiplicity of enforcement options presents alternatives with no requirement that one type of enforcement precede another." *Id.* at 905. The circuit courts that reviewed this question concur that agency decisions not to enforce are entirely discretionary and therefore unreviewable. *See also* Dubois v. Thomas, 820 F.2d 943, 947–48 (8th Cir. 1987), Sierra Club v. Train, 557 F.2d 485 (5th Cir. 1977) (same).

23. 33 U.S.C. § 1319(g)(6)(A); *see* United States v. Smithfield Foods, Inc., 191 F.3d 516, 524 (4th Cir. 1999) (allowing EPA enforcement action because state law was not comparable in that it did not provide adequate procedures for notice and public participation and only allowed penalty imposition after permittee's consent).

has taken some action to redress the same violation, is an issue with which the courts will continue to struggle.[24]

D. VENUE AND STATUTES OF LIMITATIONS

The proper venue for civil actions includes the districts where the defendant is located or is doing business.[25] Because the CWA itself does not establish a limitation period within which EPA must commence a civil action, the general five-year statute of limitations applicable to actions concerning civil fines or penalties governs.[26] This five-year limitation period does not, however, bar government actions for injunctive relief.[27]

When an action begins to accrue for statutes of limitations purposes is the subject of frequent litigation. EPA has generally been successful in avoiding strict application of the limitation period provided under 28 U.S.C.A. section 2462 in prosecuting illegal wetlands-fill violations, by arguing that a violation is "continuing" in nature because of the adverse impacts resulting from unremoved fill.[28] The effect of this defense is to preclude the triggering of the limitation period during the time that a violation continues. While some courts have also found "continuing" violations in failures to obtain requisite permits and to complete adequate

---

24. *See, e.g.,* United States v. City of Youngstown, 109 F. Supp. 2d 739, 740 (N.D. Ohio 2000) (fact that state of Ohio is also suing alleged violator does not preclude similar enforcement action by United States). The courts that construed this issue under the CWA have declined to adopt the rationale in Harmon Industries, Inc. v. Browner, 191 F.3d 894 (8th Cir. 1999), precluding EPA overfiling under the Resource Conservation and Recovery Act (RCRA), 42 U.S.C. § 6901 *et seq.* (West 1995 & Supp. 2001). While the operative language in RCRA states that an authorized state program operates "in lieu of" the federal program and that any action taken by the state in such a program has the "same force and effect as taken by the [EPA]" (42 U.S.C. § 6926(b), (d) (West 1995)), the operative language in the CWA omits the "in lieu of" and "same force and effect" language and instead provides that "[n]othing in this section shall be construed to limit the authority of the [EPA] to take action pursuant to section 1319 of this title." 33 U.S.C. § 1342(i) (West 2001); United States v. City of Rock Island, 182 F. Supp. 2d 690 (C.D. Ill. 2001) (allowing overfiling and rejecting Eighth Circuit's *Harmon* analysis).

25. 33 U.S.C. § 1319(b).

26. 28 U.S.C. § 2462 (West 1994).

27. *See, e.g.,* United States v. Telluride Co. 146 F.3d 1241, 1247–48 (10th Cir. 1998) (rejecting concurrent-remedy rule and declining to hold actions seeking restorative injunctions, within scope of limitations bar provided by 28 U.S.C. § 2462); United States v. Banks, 115 F.3d 916, 918 (11th Cir. 1997) (similarly rejecting application of "concurrent remedy rule," which otherwise would bar action at equity if applicable statute of limitations would bar concurrent legal remedy, because plain language of 28 U.S.C.A. section 2462 does not apply to equitable remedies).

28. *See* United States v. Reaves, 923 F. Supp. 1530 (M.D. Fla. 1996); Sasser v. EPA, 990 F.2d 127, 129 (4th Cir. 1993).

submissions,[29] others have been more reluctant to expand the breadth of this doctrine to the point of vitiating the underlying limitation period.[30] Courts have commonly held that the limitation period does not accrue until a defendant files its discharge monitoring reports (DMRs) evidencing the fact of a violation.[31]

E. STANDARDS OF LIABILITY

The CWA is a strict-liability statute.[32] A defendant's good faith or lack of knowledge is irrelevant to establishing civil liability.[33] Negligence or knowledge, however, is expressly required in order to trigger criminal penalties under the statute.[34] The Army Corps of Engineers and EPA share responsibility for administering and enforcing section 404 dredge and fill permits.[35] However, when a defendant is alleged to have illegally filled wetlands in the absence of a section 404 permit, EPA alone has the authority to seek civil penalties for discharge of pollutants into waters of the United States in violation of CWA section 301.[36]

F. ELEMENTS OF PROOF

To commence enforcement under CWA section 309, EPA must prove that a defendant (1) discharged (2) a pollutant (3) into navigable waters (4) from a point source (5) and the discharge was not authorized by one of several specified sections of the CWA.[37] The government commonly establishes an unauthorized discharge by showing that the defendant's actions were not in compliance with the

---

29. *See* Molokai Chamber of Commerce v. Kukui (Molokai), Inc., 891 F. Supp. 1389 (D. Haw. 1995); City of New York v. Anglebrook Ltd. P'ship, 891 F. Supp. 900 (S.D.N.Y. 1995).

30. *See, e.g.,* 3M Co.(Minn. Mining & Mfg.) v. Browner, 17 F.3d 1453 (D.C. Cir. 1994); United States v. Telluride Co., 884 F. Supp. 404, 408 (D. Colo. 1995), *rev'd on other grounds,* 146 F.3d 1241 (10th Cir. 1998) (refusing to apply continuing violation doctrine to defeat statute of limitations in illegal wetlands fill context).

31. *See, e.g.,* Public Interest Research Group of N.J., Inc. v. Powell Duffryn Terminals, Inc., 913 F.2d 64 (3d Cir. 1990) (statute of limitations under CWA did not accrue until defendant filed DMR); United States v. Municipality of Penn Hills, 6 F. Supp. 2d 432 (W.D. Pa. 1998) (same); United States v. Material Serv. Corp., 1996 WL 563462, at *2 (N.D. Ill. Sept. 30, 1996) (same).

32. *See* Kelly v. United States EPA, 203 F.3d 519, 523 (7th Cir. 2000) (citing cases).

33. *Id.*

34. *Id.*; 33 U.S.C. § 1319(c) (West 2001). See section III of this chapter for a more thorough discussion of the standards of criminal conduct under the CWA.

35. 33 U.S.C. §§ 1319(a)(3), 1344.

36. *See* United States v. Appel, 210 F.3d 385 (9th Cir. 2000) (Table) (unpublished); 33 U.S.C. § 1319 (West 2001).

37. *See id.*; Headwaters, Inc. v. Talent Irrigation Dist., 243 F.3d 526, 532 (9th Cir. 2001); 33 U.S.C. § 1311(a) (discharge unlawful except as in compliance with sections 301, 302, 306, 307, 318, 402, and 404).

NPDES permit requirement[38] or the wetlands permitting requirements for dredged or fill material.[39] Liable parties include individuals, corporations, partnerships, associations, states, municipalities, commissions, political subdivisions of a state, or any interstate body.[40] The government may target the named permit holder and any other persons responsible for the discharge.[41]

1. Discharge of a Pollutant

The "discharge of a pollutant" is defined as "any addition of a pollutant to navigable waters from any point source."[42] The CWA defines "pollutant" as "dredged spoil, solid waste, incinerator residue, sewage, garbage, sewage sludge, munitions, chemical wastes, biological materials, radioactive materials, heat, wrecked or discarded equipment, rock, sand, cellar dirt, and industrial, municipal, and agricultural waste discharged into water."[43] These expansive terms have led at least one court to recognize that "the breadth of many of the items in the list of 'pollutants' tends to eviscerate any restrictive effect."[44] Indeed, Congress intentionally defined "pollutant" broadly so as to avoid litigation over whether the discharge of a particular material is subject to control requirements[45] and the courts have consequently construed the term broadly.[46] As a result, while the listing of a specific substance in the definition of "pollutant" can be significant, the fact that a substance is not listed does not remove it from the statute's coverage.[47]

---

38. 33 U.S.C. § 1342.

39. *Id.* § 1344.

40. *Id.* § 1362(5) (West 2001).

41. *See* United States. v. Cooper, 173 F.3d 1192, 1201 (9th Cir. 1999) (for purposes of imposing criminal liability, term "any person" is broad enough to cover permittees and nonpermittees alike); *see also* United States v. Brittain, 931 F.2d 1413, 1418–19 (10th Cir. 1991).

42. 33 U.S.C. § 1362(12) (West 2001); *see also* Miccosukee Tribe of Indians of Fla. v. South Fla. Water Mgmt. Dist., 280 F.3d 1364 (11th Cir. 2002).

43. 33 U.S.C. § 1362(6) (West 2001).

44. Sierra Club, Lone Star Chapter v. Cedar Point Oil Co., 73 F.3d 546, 565 (5th Cir. 1996) (citing Nat'l Wildlife Fed'n v. Gorsuch, 693 F.2d 156, 173 n.52 (D.C. Cir. 1982)).

45. S. Rep. No. 92-414, (1972), *reprinted in* 1972 U.S.C.C.A.N. 3668, 3742.

46. *See, e.g.,* Headwaters, Inc. v. Talent Irrigation Dist., 243 F.3d 526 (9th Cir. 2001) (breakdown product from FIFRA-approved herbicide placed in canals held to be pollutant); Sierra Club v. Sierra Point Oil Co., 73 F.3d 546 (5th Cir. 1996), *cert. denied,* 519 U.S. 811 (1996) (produced water from oil wells held to be a pollutant); United States v. Hamel, 551 F.2d 107 (6th Cir. 1977) (gasoline is a pollutant even though not specifically listed in the statutory definition); United States Public Interest Research Group v. Atlantic Salmon of Main, L.L.C., 2002 WL 242466 (D. Maine 2002) (escaped nonnative fish, feces, feed, copper, and treatment chemicals discharge from Atlantic salmon net pen operation all held to be pollutants); Beartooth Alliance v. Crown Butte Mines, 904 F. Supp. 1168, 26 ELR 20639 (D. Mont. 1995) (acid mine drainage held to be pollutant).

47. *See Sierra Club, Lone Star Chapter,* 73 F.3d at 566 (when necessary, court may determine in citizen suit whether discharged substance is pollutant).

2. Navigable Waters

The CWA defines "navigable waters" as "waters of the United States, including the territorial seas."[48] EPA and the Army Corps of Engineers have promulgated regulations broadly defining "waters of the United States" to include "intrastate lakes, rivers, streams (including intermittent streams), mudflats, sandflats, wetlands, playa lakes, or natural ponds, the use, degradation, or destruction of which could affect interstate or foreign commerce"[49] and "tributaries of [those] waters."[50] While this definition would appear to include all water actually in the United States, the U.S. Supreme Court has recently limited the definition's scope. In 2001, the Court invalidated a 1986 Army Corps of Engineers (Corps) promulgation known as the "Migratory Bird Rule,"[51] which included in the definition of "waters of the United States" those interstate waters that have no connection to any navigable waters but were or would be used as habitat by migratory birds.[52] Because the Supreme Court's *SWANCC* decision is currently spawning a host of lower court decisions further defining and in some cases narrowing the breadth of CWA jurisdiction, as of the date of this publication, it is expected that EPA and the Corps will soon be issuing a new rulemaking re-defining the scope of the government's jurisdiction under the Act to address the significant uncertainties posed by the Supreme Court's decision. For a more thorough discussion of SWANCC and its progeny, see chapter 6.

3. Point Source

A "point source" is defined by the statute as "any discernible, confined, and discrete conveyance, including but not limited to any pipe, ditch, channel, tunnel, conduit, well, discrete fissure, container, rolling stock, concentrated animal feeding operation, or vessel or other floating craft, from which pollutants are or may be discharged."[53] This is an extremely broad definition and has been found to include industrial and municipal discharges as well as bulldozers, backhoes, and the like.[54]

---

48. 33 U.S.C. § 1362(7) (West 2001).

49. 40 C.F.R. § 122.2(c)(e).

50. United States v. Krilich, 209 F.3d 968, 970 (7th Cir. 2000) (quoting 33 C.F.R. § 328.3(a)(2), 40 C.F.R. § 230.3(s)(3)); 40 C.F.R. § 122.2(c)(2001)(e).

51. 51 Fed. Reg. 41206, 41217 (1986).

52. Solid Waste Agency of N. Cook County v. U.S. Army Corps of Eng'rs (hereinafter *SWANCC*), 531 U.S. 159 (2001); *see also* Headwaters, Inc. v. Talen Irrigation Dist., 243 F.3d 526, 533 (9th Cir. 2001) (finding canals to be tributaries and as a result waters regulated under the CWA).

53. 33 U.S.C. § 1362(14).

54. *See* Borden Ranch P'ship v. United States Army Corps of Eng'rs, 261 F.3d 810, 815 (9th Cir. 2001), *aff'd per curiam*, 123 S. Ct. 599 (2002); for discussion of definition's limit *see also* United States v. Plaza Health Laboratories, Inc., 3 F.3d 643, 645–49 (2d Cir. 1993) (human being not a point source subject to criminal liability).

G. TRIAL CONSIDERATIONS

1. THE RIGHT TO A JURY

Defendants in CWA civil enforcement actions are constitutionally guaranteed the right to jury trial to determine liability.[55] The Seventh Amendment to the U.S. Constitution does not, however, guarantee defendants the right to a jury trial to assess the amount of any civil penalty assessed.[56]

2. DMRs as Evidence of Liability

EPA regulations generally require permittees to monitor their discharges, to maintain records of the results of their monitoring, and to report the results to the relevant state or federal agency. Permit holders must certify the accuracy of information contained in the DMRs.[57] Because of the various assurances of reliability inherent in DMRs, courts have readily accepted such records as evidence of liability. [58] The courts have been reluctant to accept claims of inaccurate monitoring as a defense to liability.[59]

3. Prevailing Party Considerations

While section 505 of the CWA expressly authorizes costs of litigation (including reasonable attorneys' fees and expert fees to any prevailing or substantially prevailing party) in a citizen suit, defendants in EPA enforcement actions have unsuccessfully attempted to utilize this provision to seek recovery of litigation costs in EPA enforcement actions.[60]

H. DEFENSES

1. Regulatory Defenses

EPA's NPDES regulations explicitly authorize two affirmative defenses to EPA enforcement actions in the context of an "upset" or "bypass" as defined by regu-

---

55. Tull v. United States, 481 U.S. 412, 427 (1987).

56. *Id.*

57. *Id.* § 122.22(d) (2001). DMRs must contain a complete and accurate record of pollutant monitoring by the permit holders. 40 C.F.R. § 122.41(l)(4)(I). Such accuracy is further encouraged by the availability of criminal penalties for false statements. 33 U.S.C. § 1319 (c)(2) (West 2001).

58. *See, e.g.,* Sierra Club v. Union Oil Co. of Cal., 813 F.2d 1480, 1491, *vacated and remanded on other grounds,* 485 U.S. 931 (1988).

59. *See, e.g.,* Chesapeake Bay Found. v. Bethlehem Steel Corp., 608 F. Supp. 440, 452 (D. Md. 1985).

60. 33 U.S.C. § 1365(d) (West 2001); *see, e.g.,* United States v. Sheyenne Tooling & Mfg. Co., 1998 WL 544413 (8th Cir. Aug. 27, 1998) (unpublished) (denying attorneys' fees to defendant in civil action assessing penalties substantially below those sought by government). Of course, a prevailing defendant may seek fees under the Equal Access to Justice Act (EAJA), 5 U.S.C. Section 504.

lation.[61] If a permit contains an upset provision, a defendant may raise "upset" as an affirmative defense.[62] Only exceptional incidents that are beyond the control of the permittee and that result in temporary noncompliance with permit limitations qualify as an upset.[63]

"Bypass" is defined as the "intentional diversion of wastestreams from any portion of a treatment facility."[64] Bypass is available as a defense only when the action was "unavoidable to prevent loss of life, personal injury, or severe property damage," there were no "feasible alternatives," and the permittee complied with applicable notice requirements.[65] Failure to strictly comply with the substantive and procedural requirements of the upset and bypass defenses may result in waiver of those defenses.[66]

2. Additional Affirmative Defenses

Other, nonregulatory defenses also may be available and should be contemplated as affirmative defenses in EPA enforcement actions. However, since the CWA is a strict liability statute, these defenses are limited. As an initial matter, it is federal law, not state law, that governs which defenses a permittee may raise in the course of a federal proceeding to enforce the terms of a state-issued NPDES permit.[67] While certain affirmative defenses have met with varying success in the courts, a defendant may not collaterally attack the validity of a CWA permit in a federal enforcement action.[68]

a. The Permit Shield. Under most circumstances, a defendant's compliance with the terms of its NPDES permit acts to "shield" the permittee from enforcement attempts associated with its discharge. Section 402 of the CWA provides that compliance with an NPDES permit shall be deemed compliance, for purposes of

---

61. 40 C.F.R. § 122.41(m)(1)(i)(2001).

62. The upset defense is available only if it is specifically authorized by the permit holder's permit. *See* Tobyhanna Conservation Ass'n v. Country Place Waste Treatment Facility, 769 F. Supp. 739, 745 n.15 (M.D. Pa. 1991).

63. *See* United States v. CPS Chem. Co., 779 F. Supp. 437, 454 (E.D. Ark. 1991) (citing cases); *see also* 40 C.F.R. § 122.41(n)(2001).

64. 40 C.F.R. § 122.41(m)(1)(i)(2001).

65. *Id.* § 122.41(m)(4)(2001); *see also* United States v. Weitzenhoff, 35 F.3d 1275, 1286–89 (9th Cir. 1993).

66. *See* Pub. Interest Research Group of N.J. v. United States Metals Ref. Co., 681 F. Supp. 237, 242–43 (D.N.J. 1987); United States v. Town of Lowell, Ind., 637 F. Supp. 254, 258 (N.D. Ind. 1985).

67. *See* Gen. Motors Corp. v. EPA, 168 F.3d 1377, 1380 (D.C. Cir. 1999) (permittee may not attack validity of state permit in federal enforcement action).

68. *Id.* at 1383; *see also* United States v. Gulf States Steel, Inc., 54 F. Supp. 2d 1233 (N.D. Ala.1999).

section 309 and 505 enforcement, with sections 301, 302, 306, 307, and 403 of the CWA.[69] This begs the question, however, of what constitutes "compliance with an NPDES permit."

> EPA's permit shield policy explains that a permit provides authorization and therefore a shield for the following pollutants resulting from facility processes, wastestreams and operations that have been clearly identified in the permit application process. . . (1) pollutants specifically limited in the permit or pollutants which the permit, fact sheet, or administrative record explicitly identify as controlled . . . ; (2) pollutants for which the permit authority has not established limits or other permit conditions, but which are specifically identified as present in facility discharges during the permit application process; and (3) pollutants not identified as present but which are constituents of wastestreams, operations or processes that were clearly identified during the permit application process.[70]

So long as the permit holder complied with the CWA's reporting and disclosure requirements and the discharges were within the reasonable contemplation of the permitting authority, a defendant may invoke the "permit shield defense" even for pollutants not mentioned in the permit.[71]

b. Res Judicata or Claim Preclusion. The doctrine of res judicata is based on the premise that "a final judgment on the merits bars further claims by parties or their privies based on the same cause of action."[72] Res judicata, also known as claim preclusion, has not been widely litigated in the context of the CWA. However, at least one court has held that this doctrine bars EPA from bringing a subsequent Comprehensive Environmental Response Compensation and Liability Act (CERCLA) action when the wrong for which redress is sought is the same as that in a prior CWA action and involved the same underlying facts.[73]

c. Estoppel. In theory, estoppel operates as a bar, preventing a person from denying or asserting anything that contradicts what he or she has established to be true. However, courts have traditionally been reluctant to apply equitable estoppel

---

69. 33 U.S.C. § 1342; EPA OFFICE OF REGULATORY ENFORCEMENT, WATER ENFORCEMENT DIV., POLICY STATEMENT ON SCOPE OF DISCHARGE AUTHORIZED AND SHIELD ASSOCIATED WITH NPDES PERMITS (issued July 1, 1994) (hereinafter DISCHARGE POLICY STATEMENT).

70. DISCHARGE POLICY STATEMENT. *See also In re* Ketchikan Pulp. Co., 7 E.A.D. 605 (EAB 1998) for a thorough discussion of EPA's interpretation of the permit-as-shield defense.

71. See Piney Run Pres. Ass'n v. County Comm'rs of Carroll County, Md., 268 F.3d 255, 268 (4th Cir. 2001); *see also* Atlantic States Legal Found. Inc. v. Eastman Kodak Co., 12 F.3d 353, 357 (2d Cir. 1994).

72. Montana v. United States, 440 U.S. 147, 153, (1979).

73. United States v. Gurley, 43 F.3d 1188, 1195–98 (8th Cir. 1995).

against the government based on acts or representations of its agents. This reluctance has extended to CWA cases in which, in order to mount a successful defense, the defendant must show affirmative misconduct on the part of government employees or agents.[74] The courts have been equally hostile to the defense of collateral estoppel.[75]

d. Mootness. As a general proposition, a case may be mooted by a defendant's voluntary conduct if subsequent events have made it clear that the allegedly wrongful behavior could not reasonably be expected to recur.[76] The U.S. Supreme Court has held open the possibility that an action may be moot if a defendant comes into compliance with its NPDES permit and closes the facility at issue, and if events make clear that permit violations could not reasonably be expected to recur.[77] However, mootness may only preclude issuance of an injunction; civil penalties will not be moot if they were rightfully sought at the time the suit was filed.[78]

e. Laches. The equitable defense of laches bars a claim when the plaintiff has unreasonably and inexcusably delayed proceedings, resulting in prejudice to the defendant.[79] However, courts have generally been reluctant to apply the doctrine of laches to the federal government when it is acting in its sovereign capacity to protect the public welfare.[80] Therefore, while laches has barred CWA claims by citizen groups, defendants have generally not prevailed against EPA in civil enforcement actions.[81]

---

74. *See e.g., In re* Ketchikan Pulp. Co., 7 E.A.D. 605 (EAB 1998); Hobbs v. United States, No. 90-1861, 1991 WL 230202, at *7 (4th Cir. Nov. 8, 1991) (unpublished); *CPS Chem. Co.*, 779 F. Supp. at 452.

75. *See* United States v. City of Erie, Pa., No. 94-281 (W.D. Pa. July 21, 1995); *In re* Marine Shale Processors, Inc., 5 E.A.D. 751, 774–79 (EAB 1995); *but see* United States v. ITT Rayonier, Inc., 627 F.2d 996 (9th Cir. 1980).

76. *See* Friends of the Earth, Inc. v. Laidlaw Env'tl Serv's (TOC), Inc., 528 U.S. 167, 189 (2000) (citing United States v. Concentrated Phosphate Export Ass'n., 393 U.S. 199, 203, (1968)).

77. *Id.* at 193; *see also* Atlantic States Legal Found., Inc. v. Tyson Foods, Inc., 897 F.2d 1128, 1133–34 (11th Cir. 1990).

78. *See* Atlantic States Legal Found., Inc. v. Tyson Foods Inc., 897 F.2d at 1134–36 (violations rightfully sought are those that were ongoing when the suit was filed).

79. *See* Allens Creek/Corbetts Glen Pres. Group, Inc. v. West, 2001 WL 87434 (2d Cir. Jan. 31, 2001) (citing Ivani Contracting Corp. v. City of New York, 103 F.3d 257, 259 (2d Cir. 1997)).

80. *See CPS Chem. Co.*, 779 F. Supp. at 451 (citing cases).

81. *See, e.g., Allens Creek/Corbetts Glen Pres. Group*, 2001 WL 87434 (plaintiffs' delay sufficiently unreasonable and prejudice sufficiently severe to warrant application of laches against residents' group); *CPS Chem. Co.*, 779 F. Supp. at 451 (EPA asserted its claim diligently); *but see* NWF v. Consumers Power, 657 F. Supp. 989, 1011 (D. Mich. 1987) (finding that because "plaintiff is in essence acting as a private attorney general in this matter, it probably is not subject to the doctrine of laches, at least absent a showing of some affirmative misconduct").

f. Impossibility. Because the CWA is a strict liability statute, the impossibility defense has been routinely rejected by courts that have considered it in the context of the CWA.[82] These decisions are consistent with those deciding that the CWA does not recognize the defense of economic or business necessity.[83]

g. Bankruptcy. While bankruptcy is not a defense under the CWA, bankruptcy may impact the government's enforcement abilities. Since CWA civil enforcement actions are exempt from the automatic-stay provisions of bankruptcy, the government may pursue an action for civil penalties outside of bankruptcy.[84] However, any penalty must be collected as part of the bankruptcy proceeding.[85] Therefore, civil penalties may not provide an effective enforcement mechanism in many cases, leaving injunctive relief as an available remedy in these situations.[86]

h. Degree of Harm and Good Faith. As with impossibility, the defense of "no environmental harm" has not fared well. The defense is routinely rejected on the premise that the CWA is a strict-liability statute and, as a result, a defendant must be penalized regardless of the fact that the violation may not have caused any harm (or much harm) to the environment.[87] For the same reason, good faith is not considered a defense, but it may be a factor in determining the size of the penalty.

I. REMEDIES

Section 309 authorizes EPA to seek both civil penalties and injunctive relief to redress violations of the Act.[88]

1. Civil Penalties

The statutory purpose of monetary penalties is to promote environmental compliance, protect public health by deterring future violations, and ensure that violators do not obtain an unfair economic advantage over competitors who have

---

82. *See, e.g.,* United States v. City of Hoboken, 675 F. Supp. 189, 198–99 (D.N.J. 1987).

83. *See, e.g.,* United States v. Boldt, 929 F.2d 35, 41 (1st Cir. 1991).

84. 11 U.S.C. § 362(b)(4)(West); *see, e.g.,* Midatlantic Nat'l Bank v. N.J. Dep't of Env'tl Prot., 474 U.S. 494, 503 (1986); Word v. Commerce Oil Co. *(In re* Commerce Oil Co.*),* 847 F.2d 291, 296–97 (6th Cir. 1988); Penn Terra Ltd. v. Dep't of Env'tl. Res. Pa., 733 F. 2d 267, 278–79 (3d Cir. 1984).

85. *See In re* Commerce Oil Co., 847 F.2d at 296–97.

86. *See, e.g.,* United States v. Jones & Laughlin Steel Corp., 804 F.2d 348, 350–51 (6th Cir. 1986); *Penn Terra Ltd.,* 733 F.2d at 269.

87. *See, e.g., Kelly,* 203 F.3d at 522–23; *see also CPS Chem. Co.,* 779 F. Supp. at 450.

88. 33 U.S.C. §§ 1319(b), (d).

timely performed the necessary compliance.[89] Under CWA section 309(d), violators are subject to a civil penalty not exceeding $27,500 per day for each violation.[90] Once a violation is established, civil penalties are generally considered mandatory (although the amount is discretionary), and the penalty must be paid to the Treasury Department and not some other fund established by public interest or community groups.[91]

In determining the amount of a civil penalty, courts consider six factors: "the seriousness of the violation or violations, the economic benefit (if any) resulting from the violation, any history of such violations, any good-faith efforts to comply with the applicable requirements, the economic impact of the penalty on the violator, and such other matters as justice may require."[92] Courts at times also have been guided by the factors and calculations set forth in EPA's CWA settlement penalty policy.[93]

One of the initial determinations a court must make in calculating an appropriate penalty is the number of violations that have occurred. The statutory phrase "per day for each violation" has been interpreted as meaning that the daily maximum penalty applies separately to each violation of an express limitation.[94] The "single operational upset" (SOU) defense provides that an SOU that leads to simultaneous violations of more than one pollutant parameter will be treated as a single violation.[95] However, the upset must be an unusual or extraordinary event.[96]

---

89. *See* EPA, Interim Clean Water Act Settlement Penalty Policy (Mar. 1, 1995).

90. *See* sources cited *supra* note 2.

91. *See, e.g., Tyson Foods,* 897 F.2d at 1142 (once a violation has been established, penalty is mandatory); Stoddard v. W. Carolina Reg'l Sewer Auth., 784 F.2d 1200, 1208 (4th Cir. 1986) (same); *Powell Duffryn Terminals,* 913 F.2d at 82 (penalties should be paid to Treasury Department rather than to trust fund or similar instrument).

92. 33 U.S.C. § 1319(d).

93. EPA Clean Water Act Section 404 Settlement Penalty Policy; *see also Tyson Foods,* 897 F.2d at 1142 (courts have, however, reduced their reliance on policy since passage of 1987 CWA amendments).

94. *See Borden Ranch P'ship* 261 F.3d at 817 (quoting *Tyson Foods,* 897 F.2d at 1137–38 (11th Cir. 1990)); *see also* United States Env'tl Protection Agency v. City of Green Forest, Ark., 921 F.2d 1394, 1407 (8th Cir. 1990) (violation of monthly average effluent limitation should be counted as 30 separate violations); *Powell Duffryn Terminals,* 913 F. 2d at 78–79 (violations were not "double counted" when district court found that single reported exceedance for pollutant could be counted as a violation of both average concentration limit and maximum concentration limit for that pollutant; nor is it double counting to find that single reported exceedance violated both seven-day discharge limit and 30-day discharge limit for that pollutant).

95. 33 U.S.C. §§ 1319(c)(5), (d), (g)(3) (West 2001).

96. *See Powell Duffryn Terminals,* 913 F.2d at 77.

Once a court determines the number of violations at issue, it then must proceed to consider the six statutory factors listed above. Courts have taken two approaches in applying the six factors: "top-down" and "bottom-up."[97] In the top-down approach, the maximum penalty is first calculated by multiplying the number of violations by the statutory maximum, and that amount is then reduced based on an examination of the six "mitigating" factors.[98] The bottom-up approach, on the other hand, begins with a calculation of the economic benefit a violator gained by noncompliance and is then adjusted upwards using the remaining five statutory factors.[99] The bottom-up approach appears to be the preferred approach of the courts today.[100]

The economic-benefit factor is one that courts scrutinize carefully. One measurement of economic benefit according to EPA is commonly avoided CWA pollution control expenditures, including monitoring and reporting, capital equipment improvements or repairs, operation and maintenance expenses, and one-time acquisitions such as land purchase.[101] Courts have also evaluated economic benefit by looking to the corporate benefit achieved by failing to reduce the volume of pollution created.[102] Regardless of the approach used, a reasonable approximation of economic benefit is sufficient to meet the government's burden with regard to this factor.[103]

2. Injunctions

The CWA authorizes district courts to issue appropriate injunctive relief to redress violations of the CWA.[104] This authority is limited to issuing injunctions to restrain violations or to require future compliance. The government's injunctive authority has been interpreted broadly to enable it to require sediment remediation, wetlands restoration, and the imposition of measures intended to "com-

---

97. *See, e.g.,* United States v. Mun. Auth. of Union Township, 150 F.3d 259, 265 (3d Cir. 1998) (citing cases).

98. *Id.*

99. *Id.*; *see also* INTERIM CLEAN WATER ACT SETTLEMENT PENALTY POLICY, § IV (economic benefit is one crucial factor evaluated by EPA).

100. *See, e.g.,* United States v. Allegheny Ludlum Steel Corp., 187 F. Supp. 2d 426, 444 (W.D. Pa. 2002).

101. *See* INTERIM CLEAN WATER ACT SETTLEMENT PENALTY POLICY.

102. *See, e.g.,* Mun. Auth. of Union Township, 150 F.3d at 267 ("wrongful profits" approach may be used in assessing economic benefit when "capital investment postponed" approach was inapplicable under factual circumstances).

103. *See, e.g., Powell Duffryn Terminals,* 913 F.2d at 80.

104. 33 U.S.C. § 1319(b).

plement" permit requirements.[105] So long as the equitable relief sought by the government is reasonably calculated to remedy the established wrong and roughly proportional to the violations at issue, courts have granted the government wide berth in establishing appropriate remedial relief.[106]

3. Consent Decrees

Many civil enforcement actions that do not reach trial are settled by consent decree. The Department of Justice will not consent to settlement of an action "to enjoin discharges of pollutants into the environment" without giving the public an opportunity to review and comment upon the proposed decree.[107] Unless extraordinary circumstances dictate otherwise, the department lodges a consent decree with the court at least 30 days before moving for entry of the decree.[108] The government reserves the right to withhold its consent if public comment reveals that the proposed decree is "inappropriate, improper or inadequate,"[109] although this right is rarely exercised.

II. Civil Administrative Enforcement

MARK A. RYAN*

In addition to bringing suit in federal court, the CWA authorizes EPA to enforce the act's provisions by assessing administrative penalties for violations of the act. These include discharges into waters of the United States without a permit (including unauthorized work in wetlands[110] in violation of section 301), violations of

---

* The views expressed here are the author's and do not necessarily reflect those of the United States Environmental Protection Agency or the United States Department of Justice.

105. *See* Natural Res. Def. Council v. Southwest Marine, Inc., 236 F.3d 985, 999–1001 (9th Cir. 2000) (although federal courts do not have authority to impose effluent limitations more stringent than those imposed by EPA, injunctive measures that complement or seek to enforce permits are valid); United States v. Smith, 149 F.3d 1172, No. 96-2450, 1998 WL 325954 (4th Cir. June 18, 1998) (unpublished) (injunction ordering wetlands restoration not abuse of discretion); *Powell Duffryn Terminals*, 913 F.2d at 80 (district court's order enjoining defendant from violating future permits was invalid, while portion of injunction directing defendant not to discharge in violation of current permit was held valid); United States v. Alcoa Inc., 98 F. Supp. 2d 1031, 1038 (N.D. Ind. 2000) (injunction ordering cleanup of contaminated sediments was valid when contamination was direct result of NPDES permit violations).

106. *See Natural Res. Def. Council*, 236 F.3d at 1000; *Alcoa Inc.*, 98 F. Supp. 2d at 1039.

107. 28 C.F.R. § 50.7(a) (2001).

108. *Id.* §§ 50.7(b)–(c) (2001).

109. *Id.* § 50.7(b).

110. Section 309(g) authorizes the Army Corps of Engineers to assess administrative penalties for violations of section 404 permits. EPS, however, has authority to assess administrative penalties for unpermitted discharges violating section 301 that relate to section 404 and for violations of state-issued permits. The Corps and EPA have a memorandum of agreement concerning implementation of administrative penalty authority relating to discharges without permits in violation of section 404.

NPDES permit conditions, and violations of other enumerated statutory provisions, including section 308's information-gathering requirements. The act also allows EPA to issue administrative compliance orders and information requests.

While the large penalties typically are assessed in the federal court cases, the bulk of EPA's enforcement is done administratively under section 309. In 2001, for example, EPA initiated 442 administrative penalty actions and filed 452 administrative compliance orders under the CWA. By contrast, the agency referred to the Department of Justice for litigation in federal court only 76 cases during that same time period.[111]

A. ADMINISTRATIVE COMPLIANCE ORDERS

EPA uses its administrative order authority broadly. Section 309(a) of the CWA authorizes EPA to issue orders requiring compliance with the act.[112] This can include restoration of filled wetlands, completion of BMP plans, and cessation of an ongoing discharge. The courts have held that there is no preenforcement review of section 309(a) orders.[113] If the recipient of an order does not believe it should not be subject to the order, its only options are to comply with the order or to defend in a subsequent federal court action brought by the EPA to enforce the order. One can, of course, always attempt to negotiate compliance with the order with the local EPA office that issued the order.

B. INFORMATION REQUESTS

CWA section 308[114] gives the EPA authority to request information from a person or entity who may be discharging pollutants to waters of the United States. Section

---

111. U.S. EPA FY 2001 ENFORCEMENT AND COMPLIANCE RESULTS. This report is available at: http://es.epa.gov/oeca/main/2001eoy/2001nattot.pdf.

112. "Whenever on the basis of any information available to him the Administrator finds that any person is in violation of section 1311 . . ., or is in violation of any permit condition or limitation implementing any of such sections in a [402 or 404] permit . . ., he shall issue an order requiring such person to comply with such section or requirement, or he shall bring a civil action in accordance with subsection (b) of this section." 33 U.S.C. § 1319(a) (3).

113. Laguna Gatuna, Inc. v. Browner, 58 F.3d 564 (10th Cir. 1995), cert. denied, 516 U.S. 1071 (1995) (administrative cease-and-desist order to prevent brine discharges to salt playa not reviewable in federal court because of lack of subject matter jurisdiction (no preenforcement review)); Southern Ohio Coal v. Office of Surface Mining, 20 F.3d 1418, 1426 (6th Cir. 1994) (district court lacks jurisdiction to review EPA compliance order prior to commencement of enforcement proceedings; court was "persuaded that Congress meant to preclude judicial review of compliance orders under the CWA.").

114. 33 U.S.C. § 1318(a).

308 also is EPA's statutory authority to conduct inspections.[115] Because EPA relies heavily upon self-reporting to police compliance with the CWA, the courts have held that EPA's section 308 authority should be broadly construed.[116] A violation of the act need not be shown as a prerequisite to issuance of a section 308 information request.[117] The EPA can also use section 308 authority to collect information for preparation of NPDES permits, effluent standards, and guidelines.[118]

C. ADMINISTRATIVE PENALTIES

Section 309(g)(2) establishes two classes of penalties, differing in their maximum amount and the process for their assessment.[119] EPA must notify the state in which the violation has occurred before assessing either type of penalty.[120] The

---

115. *See* Sierra Club v. Simkins Industries, Inc., 847 F.2d 1109 (4th Cir. 1988), *cert. denied*, 491 U.S. 904, 109 S. Ct. 3185 (1989) ("Section 308 of the Clean Water Act . . . authorizes the EPA Administrator or his or her authorized representatives a right of entry to an effluent source location or to premises where required records or monitoring equipment are kept."); *In re* Town of Ashland Wastewater Treatment Facility, 9 E.A.D. 661, 671 (EAB 2001), *reconsideration denied*, unpublished order (EAB Apr. 9, 2001) ("The Board has repeatedly found that broad authority is conveyed by CWA section 308(a).").

116. *See* Mobil Oil Corp. v. EPA, 716 F.2d 1187 (7th Cir. 1983) ("Policing compliance with EPA pollution standards is critical to the achievement of [the CWA's goal of eliminating the discharge of pollutants], and section 308(a) eliminates any doubts on that score by expressly authorizing the EPA to check whether someone, such as Mobil, holding a permit to pollute is complying with the pollution limits set forth in its permit. . . . Section 308(a) also expressly authorizes the EPA to collect samples whenever required to develop new permit limits on the discharge of pollutants.").

117. United States v. Hartz Construction Co., 1999 U.S. Dist. LEXIS 9126, 1999 WL 417388 (N.D. Ill. 1999) (defendant's motion to dismiss claims for failure to respond to section 308 information request denied on grounds that EPA had properly alleged cause of action; court rejected argument that EPA could not request information about wetlands fill until it proved it had jurisdiction over wetland).

118. 33 U.S.C. § 1318(a); *see In re* Town of Ashland, 9 E.A.D. 661, 671 ("The Board has repeatedly found that broad authority is conveyed by CWA section 308(a)."; "[T]he monitoring relates to maintaining a State water quality standard, we find nothing in the statute or the implementing regulations that would constrain the Region's authority to include such a monitoring provision." *id.*, 672).

119. 33 U.S.C. § 1319(g)(2).

120. 33 U.S.C. § 1319(g)(1). Failure of EPA to comply with state-notice requirements has been held to be a nonjurisdictional defect. See United States v. City of Colorado Springs, CO, 455 F. Supp. 1364, 1366 (D. Colo. 1978) (notice to the state under section 309(b) is not a condition precedent to federal enforcement of the CWA; failure to notify the state must not result in dismissal of the subsequent federal CWA lawsuit); *In re* City of Kalamazoo Water Reclamation Plant, 3 E.A.D. 109, 113–114 (CJO 1990) (rejecting argument that complaint should be dismissed with prejudice because EPA failed to notify state of action before filing complaint, held that CWA only requires EPA to notify the state prior to *assessment* of the penalty; the filing of the complaint is a *proposed* assessment of a penalty).

procedural rules for administrative litigation differ significantly from the Federal Rules of Civil Procedure. The practitioner should become familiar with EPA's "Consolidated Rules of Practice Governing the Administrative Assessment of Civil Penalties, Issuance of Compliance or Corrective Action Orders, and the Revocation, Termination or Suspension of Permits" found in 40 C.F.R. part 22.[121] In general, administrative litigation before the EPA is much more streamlined than in federal court. For example, discovery is allowed only upon leave of the ALJ[122] and hearsay is generally admissible.[123]

1. Class I Penalty Actions

Class I cases are not conducted under the Administrative Procedures Act (APA).[124] As such, they are designed to proceed more quickly than class II cases, which are presided over by Administrative Law Judges (ALJs) and are subject to the APA. Class I cases are presided over by Regional Judicial Officers (RJOs),[125] who are typically senior EPA lawyers who otherwise have no enforcement duties for the agency. Class I penalties may not exceed $11,000 per violation or $27,500 in total.[126] Before assessing such a penalty, EPA must provide the person to be penalized (the respondent) written notice of the proposed penalty and the opportunity to request a hearing.[127] The respondent has 30 days from receipt of the notice to request a hearing.[128] If requested, EPA must conduct a hearing that provides the respondent a reasonable opportunity to be heard and to present evidence.[129]

2. Class II Penalty Actions

Class II penalties may not exceed $11,000 per day for each day during which the violation continues, or a total of $127,500.[130] EPA assesses class II penalties after

---

121. The preamble to the Consolidated Rules can be found at 64 Fed. Reg. 40138 (July 23, 1999). The preamble offers much useful information regarding the Rules of Procedure.

122. 40 C.F.R. § 22.19(e).

123. *See* 40 C.F.R. § 22.22(a) (all evidence is admissible "which is not irrelevant, unduly repetitious, unreliable, or of little probative value).

124. 33 U.S.C. § 1319(g)(2)(A).

125. 40 C.F.R. § 22.51.

126. 33 U.S.C. § 1319(g)(2)(A); 40 C.F.R. pt. 19 (Adjustment of Civil Penalties for Inflation); *see* note 2 *infra.*

127. 33 U.S.C. § 1319(g)(2)(A).

128. *Id.*; 40 C.F.R. § 22.15(c).

129. *Id.* Class I administrative penalty proceeding are conducted under 40 C.F.R. part 22, subtitle I (Administrative Proceedings Not Governed by Section 554 of the Administrative Procedures Act). Hearing Procedures are set out in 40 C.F.R. part 22, subpart D.

130. 33 U.S.C. § 1319(g)(2)(B); 40 C.F.R. pt. 19; *see* note 2 *infra.*

notice and an opportunity for a hearing on the record in accordance with the APA.[131] EPA initiates the proceeding with an administrative complaint.[132] Settlements, if any, are memorialized in a "Consent Agreement and Final Order."[133] Like all litigants, EPA settles the vast majority of the cases it brings under the CWA. If no settlement can be reached an evidentiary hearing typically is held within six months to a year from the filing of the complaint. Class II cases are heard by ALJs, most of whom are located in Washington, D.C. The ALJs typically travel to the courthouse nearest the respondent for hearings.

3. Factors Affecting Amount of Penalties

Section 309(g)(3) directs EPA to consider the following factors in determining the amount of a penalty: (1) the nature, extent, and gravity of the violations;[134] (2) the respondent's prior compliance history; (3) the respondent's degree of culpability; (4) the economic benefit or savings accrued by the respondent as a result of the violations;[135] (5) the respondent's ability to pay the proposed penalty;[136] and (6) any other factors that justice requires.[137] The trial or hearings judges have

---

131. 33 U.S.C. § 1319(g)(2)(B); *see also* 5 U.S.C. § 554. The procedures for class II penalty hearings are set forth at 40 C.F.R. pt. 22.

132. 40 C.F.R. § 22.14.

133. 40 C.F.R. § 22.18(b)(2).

134. In considering this factor, EPA examines the number, type, duration, and significance of the violations, as well as the actual and potential harm to human health and the environment resulting from the violations. A single operational upset leading to the simultaneous violation of permit limits regarding more than one pollutant is treated as a single violation. 33 U.S.C. § 1319(g)(3).

135. EPA uses the computer program BEN to calculate the avoided and delayed cost savings associated with a respondent's failure to comply with environmental laws. EPA uses BEN primarily for calculating settlement amounts in civil and administrative cases. EPA does not generally use BEN to calculate economic benefit at trial or in an administrative hearing, relying instead on financial experts in those settings.

136. The EAB has held that EPA has the burden of coming forward with evidence to show that it has considered the respondent's ability to pay the proposed penalty. Once EPA has done this, the burden shifts to respondent to prove that it cannot pay the proposed penalty. *In re* New Waterbury, Ltd., 5 E.A.D. 529, 538–39 (EAB 1994).

137. *See In re* B.J. Carney Industries, Inc., 7 E.A.D. 171, 232 n. 82 (EAB 1997), *appeal dismissed*, 192 F.3d 917, 49 ERC 1252 (9th Cir. 1999), *dismissal vacated*, 200 F.3d 1222 (9th Cir. 2000) ("Adjustment under the 'justice' factor may be warranted only if the evidence of those good deeds is 'clear and unequivocal, and the circumstances must be such that a reasonable person would easily agree that not giving some form of credit would be a manifest injustice.'"); *In re* Spang & Co., 6 E.A.D. 226, 250 (EAB 1995) ("[U]se of the justice factor should be far from routine, since application of the other adjustment factors normally produces a penalty that is fair and just.").

broad discretion in assessing a penalty.[138] The Environmental Appeals Board (EAB) gives deference to the ALJs and RJOs on the assessment of the penalty,[139] and will not overturn those penalty decisions unless there has been a clear abuse of discretion.[140] The EAB exercises de novo review of all cases appealed to it.[141]

EPA does not have a written policy governing the calculation of penalty amounts under the CWA as it does under some other environmental statutes. The agency does, however, have a settlement policy[142] that provides guidance for calculating penalties for purposes of settlement.[143]

4. Subpoenas

Section 309(g)(10) authorizes EPA to issue subpoenas for the testimony of witnesses and the production of documents in connection with either class I or II penalty hearings.[144]

Federal district courts have authority to enforce these subpoenas.[145]

5. Rights of Interested Persons

Before assessing a penalty, EPA must give interested persons notice of the penalty and a reasonable opportunity to comment.[146] EPA must also notify all persons who submit comments of any hearing and allow them to be heard and to present evidence at the hearing.[147] EPA must also notify persons who have sub-

---

138. *See* United States v. Smithfield Foods, Inc., 191 F.3d 516, 526–27 (4th Cir. 1999), *cert. denied*, 121 S. Ct. 46, 148 L. Ed. 2d 16 (2000) ("Because of the difficulty of determining an appropriate penalty in a complex case such as this one, we give deference to the 'highly discretionary calculations that take into account multiple factors [that] are necessary in order to set civil penalties under the Clean Water Act.' . . . [T]he Supreme Court has emphasized that under the CWA, the highly discretionary calculations necessary to assess civil penalties are particularly within the purview of trial judges, and we have continually given these determinations wide deference, reviewing them only for abuse of discretion." (citations omitted))

139. *In re* City of Marshall, 10 E.A.D. ___ (EAB 2001) ("[T]he Board has stated on various occasions that it will generally give deference to a presiding officer's findings of fact based upon the testimony of witnesses because the presiding officer has the opportunity to observe witnesses and evaluate their credibility.").

140. *In re* Robert Wallin, 10 E.A.D. ___, CWA Appeal No. 00-3 (EAB 2001), slip op. at 19.

141. 40 C.F.R. § 22.30(f).

142. *See* EPA, Revised Interim Clean Water Act Settlement Penalty Policy (Mar. 1, 1995). This document is available online at: http://www.epa.gov/oeca/ore/water/cwapol.pdf.

143. EPA considers specific penalty calculations to be strictly for internal use and privileged. The Penalty Policy document itself, however, is not privileged.

144. 33 U.S.C. § 1319(g)(10).

145. *Id.*

146. 33 U.S.C. § 1319(g)(4)(A).

147. 33 U.S.C. § 1319(g)(4)(B).

mitted comments of the issuance of a final order assessing the penalty.[148] If EPA does not hold a hearing before issuing the final order, any person who has submitted comments may petition EPA to set aside the order and conduct a hearing.[149] Petitions concerning class I and II penalties are filed with the Regional Administrator or the EAB, depending on whether the region or EPA headquarters initiated the case.[150] If the petitioner presents evidence that is material and was not considered when EPA issued the order, the Regional Administrator or Appeals Board will set aside the order and provide a hearing. If the Regional Administrator or Appeals Board denies a petition for a hearing, it must publish its reasons for the denial in the *Federal Register*.

6. Appeals

The ALJ or RJO, as the case may be, will issue an initial decision to reflect his or her ruling in the case. The parties have 30 days to file an appeal with the EAB.[151] If neither party appeals, the EAB can sua sponte take up the case for review within 45 days of the initial decision.[152] After the 45 days have passed, the initial decision becomes a final order.[153]

Persons who have been assessed a penalty or have commented upon a penalty may seek judicial review of a final penalty order under section 309(g)(8).[154] Federal district courts review class I penalties,[155] while federal courts of appeals review class II penalties.[156] Persons seeking judicial review must file a notice of appeal within 30 days after EPA issues the penalty order.[157] A court will set aside a penalty order only if it finds either that the record lacks substantial evidence to support the finding of a violation or that EPA has abused its discretion in determining the amount of penalty assessed.[158]

---

148. 33 U.S.C. § 1319(g)(4)(C).

149. *Id.*

150. 40 C.F.R. § 22.45(c)(4).

151. 40 C.F.R. § 22.30(a).

152. 40 C.F.R. § 22.30(b).

153. 40 C.F.R. § 22.31(b).

154. 33 U.S.C. § 1319(g)(8).

155. 33 U.S.C. § 1319(g)(8)(A).

156. 33 U.S.C. § 1319(g)(8)(B).

157. 33 U.S.C. § 1319(g)(8).

158. *Id.; see e.g.*, Pepperell Associates v. EPA, 246 F.3d 15 (5th Cir. 2001); General Motors v. EPA, 168 F.3d 1377 (D.C. Cir. 1999).

7. Collection of Unpaid Administrative Penalties

EPA has several means of collecting administrative penalties.[159] First, EPA may refer the matter to the Department of Justice, which can bring an action in federal district court.[160] Second, EPA's Financial Management Division may bring a claim under the Federal Debt Collection Act.[161] And third, EPA may refer debts not exceeding $5,000 directly to a collection agency.[162]

Under EPA regulations, EPA may also "suspend or revoke licenses or other privileges for any inexcusable, prolonged, or repeated failure of a debtor to pay a claim."[163] EPA could, therefore, revoke an NPDES permit for the failure of a discharger to pay an amount assessed in a final penalty order.[164]

D. EFFECT OF ADMINISTRATIVE PROCEEDINGS ON OTHER ENFORCEMENT ACTIONS

Courts may not assess civil penalties under sections 309(d), 311(b), or 505 for CWA violations that EPA is diligently prosecuting in administrative proceedings or for which EPA has already assessed an administrative penalty.[165] Citizen suits for penalties are not barred by administrative action, however, if they are filed before the administrative proceedings begin or if notice of intent to sue is provided before the administrative proceedings begin and suit is filed within 120 days of the notice.[166] Nonpenalty administrative orders largely have been held to not preclude subsequent federal or citizen suits.[167]

---

159. The validity and amount of the underlying penalties are not subject to challenge in collection actions. 33 U.S.C. § 1319(g)(9); *see also* EPA MANUAL ON MONITORING AND ENFORCING ADMINISTRATIVE AND JUDICIAL ORDERS (Feb. 6, 1990).

160. *See* 33 U.S.C. § 1319(g)(9).

161. 33 U.S.C. § 3711; *see also* 4 C.F.R. pt. 102 (general federal collection procedures); 40 C.F.R. pt. 13 (EPA collection procedures).

162. *See* EPA, OFFICE OF ADMINISTRATION AND RESOURCES MANAGEMENT, REFERRAL OF DELINQUENT DEBTS TO COLLECTION AGENCIES (Aug. 1990).

163. 40 C.F.R. § 13.17.

164. To do so, EPA would have to follow applicable permit revocation procedures.

165. 33 U.S.C. § 1319(g)(6)(A). There is a wealth of case law interpreting the phrase "has commenced and is diligently prosecuting." *See e.g.,* Jones v. City of Lakeland, 224 F.3d 518, 51 ERC 1080 (6th Cir. 2000); Knee Deep Cattle Co. v. Bindana Investment Co., 94 F.3d 514 (9th Cir. 1996); United States v. Smithfield Foods, Inc., 972 F. Supp. 338 (E.D. Va. 1997), *affirmed in part, reversed in part,* 191 F.3d 516 (4th Cir. 1999), *cert. denied,* 121 S. Ct. 46, 148 L. Ed. 2d 16 (2000).

166. 33 U.S.C. § 1319(g)(6)(B).

If a state is diligently prosecuting an administrative penalty action or has imposed an administrative penalty for a violation, federal courts may not impose additional penalties under sections 309(d), 311(b), or 505.[168] State administrative penalty actions do not, however, preempt administrative compliance orders under section 309(a), judicial injunctive actions under section 309(b), criminal actions under section 309(c), ongoing judicial civil penalty actions under section 309(d), administrative civil penalty assessments under section 309(g), or any federal enforcement action regarding different CWA violations. Absent compelling circumstances, EPA will not commence a judicial civil penalty action to collect a penalty for any violations for which a state has already collected a penalty or for which a state is diligently prosecuting an administrative penalty action.

III. Criminal Enforcement

JAMES OESTERLE*

A. INTRODUCTION AND OVERVIEW

Water pollution violations are among the most common types of environmental violations that are both investigated and prosecuted as federal crimes. Recent statistics released by the U.S. EPA's Office of Enforcement and Compliance Assistance confirm that both the number of prosecutions and the criminal sanctions imposed for water pollution violations have increased in recent years.[169] In addition, there are several other federal statutes with criminal sanctions for conduct related to water pollution. The Rivers and Harbors Act of 1989; the Marine Protection, Research, and Sanctuaries Act; and the Act to Prevent Pollution from Ships all include criminal sanctions. A brief discussion of these statutes is included at the conclusion of this chapter.

---

* The views expressed here are the author's and do not necessarily reflect those of the United States Environmental Protection Agency or the United States Department of Justice.

167. *See e.g.,* Kara Holding Corp. v. Getty Petroleum Marketing, Inc., 67 F. Supp. 2d 302, 49 ERC 1536 (S.D.N.Y. 1999) (administrative action by state environmental agency does not bar RCRA or CWA citizen suits); United States v. Smithfield Foods, Inc., 972 F. Supp. 338 (E.D. Va. 1997), *affirmed in part, reversed in part,* 191 F.3d 516, 49 ERC 1193 (4th Cir. 1999), *cert. denied,* 121 S. Ct. 46, 148 L. Ed. 2d 16 (2000) (no 309(g)(6)(A) preemption where state issued special orders re compliance, but the orders were not incorporated into the permit in any way and the enforcement scheme used by the state was not sufficiently comparable to section 309); Culbertson v. Coats American Inc., 42 ERC 1162 (N.D. Ga. 1996) (no preemption in citizens suit for violations of copper and zinc limits and state water quality color standard where state action was limited to compliance order).

168. 33 U.S.C. §§ 1319(g)(6)(A)(ii)–(iii).

169. *EPA Achieves Significant Compliance and Enforcement Progress in 2001,* EPA Office of Enforcement and Compliance Assistance.

244 ENFORCEMENT: SECTION 309

The numerous environmental crimes found in the Clean Water Act can generally be separated into the following six categories:

1. direct discharges of pollutants to bodies of water either without a permit or in violation of a permit;
2. indirect discharges from industrial users to publicly owned sewer systems in violation of pretreatment standards;
3. wetlands violations;
4. falsification of information and equipment tampering:
5. knowingly endangering another person; and
6. spills of oil or hazardous substances into bodies of water.

The overwhelming majority of criminal investigations and prosecutions under the CWA have been brought under one of these six categories. Each of these categories will be discussed in greater detail below.

Sections 309(c)(1)(A) and (2)(A) of the Clean Water Act authorize criminal penalties for any person who negligently or knowingly violates sections 301, 302, 306, 307, 308, 311(b)(3), 318, 402, 404, and 405 of the CWA. Sections 309(c)(1)(B) and 309(c)(2)(B) authorize criminal penalties for any person who negligently or knowingly introduces "any pollutant or hazardous substance" into a sewer system or publicly owned treatment works that the person "knew or should have known could cause personal injury or property damage" or causes the treatment works to violate its NPDES permit.

B. THE MENTAL STATE REQUIREMENT

As noted above, the CWA imposes criminal liability for both knowing and negligent violations. The state of mind element that the government must prove to establish criminal liability has been one of the most widely litigated issues in federal criminal prosecutions under the CWA.

1. Knowing Violations

Prior to the 1987 amendments to the CWA, 33 U.S.C. section 1319(c) contained only misdemeanor criminal offenses with a disjunctive willful or negligence state of mind standard. The 1987 amendments divided the central criminal provision into a negligent misdemeanor and a knowing felony.[170]

---

170. The "knowing" standard appears in the Federal Water Pollution Control Act or Clean Water Act (FWPCA or CWA), 33 U.S.C. § 1319(c)(2), the Resource Conservation and Control Act (RCRA), 42 U.S.C. § 6928(d), the Clean Air Act (CAA), 42 U.S.C. § 7413(c), the Ocean Dumping Act (ODA), 33 U.S.C. § 1415(b), the Federal Insecticide, Fungicide, and Rodenticide Act (FIFRA), 7 U.S.C. § 136l(b), and the Act to Prevent Pollution from Ships (APPS), 33 U.S.C. § 1908(a).

Based largely upon various combinations of *United States v. International Minerals and Chemical Corp.*,[171] statutory language, and the purpose of the statutes,[172] courts generally have held that "knowing" environmental offenses require knowledge of the facts, but not knowledge of the law. The government must prove that the defendant knew of the conduct that constituted the violation. The violative acts must be voluntary and intentional and not the result of an accident or mistake of fact. The government is not required to show that the defendant had knowledge of the statute or regulations or knew that his or her conduct was unlawful.[173] Specifically, as applied in CWA criminal cases, the government need not establish that the defendant knew the discharges were prohibited or that the materials being discharged were pollutants as defined under the act.[174]

The case law on the issue of knowledge and permits outside of the RCRA context is more limited. Three circuits have addressed whether the Clean Water Act requires proof that the defendant was aware of its permit status, of the conditions or limitations in such a permit, or of the fact that its actions violated a permit. In *United States v. Weitzenhoff, supra,* a prosecution for discharge of pollutants in violation of a permit condition, the Ninth Circuit concluded that the government did not need to prove that the defendants knew that their acts violated their permit or the CWA. [*Id.* at 1286.] Five judges on the Ninth Circuit dissented from the court's order denying rehearing. In their opinion, the

---

171. 402 U.S. 558, 562–64, 91 S. Ct. 1697, 29 L. Ed. 2d 178 (1971) ("knowing" in environmental prosecutions means only intentionally and voluntarily and not specific knowledge of existing law or of intent to break it).

172. For example, Congress enacted RCRA to provide "nationwide protection against the dangers of improper hazardous waste disposal." H.R. Rep. No. 1491, 94th Cong., 2d Sess. 11, *reprinted in* 5 U.S. CODE CONG. & AD. NEWS 6238, 6249 (1976). It was intended by Congress "to promote the protection of health and the environment . . . by . . . [*inter alia*] regulating the treatment, storage, transportation, and disposal of hazardous wastes which have adverse effects on health and the environment. . . ." 42 U.S.C. § 6902(4).

173. *See, e.g.,* United States v. Laughlin, 10 F.3d 961, 965–67 (2d Cir. 1993) (RCRA, CERCLA), *cert. denied sub nom.* Goldman v. United States, 511 U.S. 1071 (1994); United States v. Weitzenhoff, 35 F.3d 1275, 1283–86 (9th Cir. 1994) (CWA), *cert. denied,* 513 U.S. 1128 (1995); United States v. Buckley, 934 F.2d 84, 88–89 (6th Cir. 1991) (CERCLA); United States v. Reilly, 827 F. Supp. 1076 (D. Del. 1993) (Ocean Dumping Act); United States v. Corbin Farms, 444 F. Supp. 510, 519–20 (E.D. Cal.) (FIFRA), *aff'd,* 578 F.2d 259 (9th Cir. 1978).

174. See *United States v. Weitzenhoff,* 35 F.3d 1275, 1286 (9th Cir. 1993) (government need only prove that defendants were aware that they were discharging the pollutants in question), *cert. denied,*115 S. Ct. 939 (1995). *But see* United States v. Ahmad, 101 F.3d 386 (5th Cir. 1996) (government required to prove knowledge of each element of the offense except for "purely jurisdictional" elements); United States v. Wilson, 133 F.3d 251 (4th Cir. 1997) (government must prove defendants knowledge of facts meeting each of essential elements of the substantive offense).

government should be required to show knowledge that the defendant is violating a permit condition.[175]

In *United States v. Hopkins*,[176] a vice-president in charge of manufacturing was convicted for discharging electroplating wastewater in violation of a permit, falsifying or rendering inaccurate a monitoring method by diluting wastewater samples, and conspiracy to violate the CWA. [*Id.* at 534–535.] The defendant appealed, among other things, the district court's instructions that the government need not prove that the defendant intended to violate the law or had any specific knowledge of the particular statutory, regulatory, or permit requirements imposed by the CWA. [*Id.* at 536.] Based on the holding of *International Minerals*, dicta in *Staples v. United States*, the legislative history of the 1987 amendments to the CWA, and the body of RCRA case law, the Second Circuit upheld the use of the general intent instructions and affirmed the convictions. [*Id.* at 537–540.]

The third case is *United States v. Sinskey*,[177] which also involves an NPDES permit. The Eighth Circuit considered a combination of statutory language, FWPCA legislative history, and its own precedents in cases involving "knowing" mental state standards to conclude that 33 U.S.C. Section 1319(c)(2)(A) requires factual knowledge by a defendant of his or her acts, but not knowledge that such acts violated the statute or the terms and conditions of the permit. [*Id.* at 715–717.]

a. Willful Blindness Doctrine. The "willful blindness" doctrine has been applied in criminal prosecutions brought under the CWA. Under the doctrine, the knowing standard can be met by establishing that the defendant "closed their eyes" to obvious facts or failed to investigate when the defendant knew of facts that demanded further investigation.[178]

b. Responsible Corporate Officer. Under both the CWA and the Clean Air Act, the definition of a "person" criminally liable under the statutes expressly includes "any responsible corporate officer." 33 U.S.C. Section 1319(c)(3); 42 U.S.C. Section 7413(6). The statutes do not, however, define the term. The limited leg-

---

175. 35 F.3d at 1299. Note that in United States v. Cooper, 173 F.3d 1192, 1201 (9th Cir.), *cert. denied*, 528 U.S. 1019 (1999), the district court instructed the jury that the government had to show the defendant's knowledge of the permit; however, that case was unique in that the defendant was a third-party contractor, not the permittee or one of its employees. The Ninth Circuit did not address whether that instruction was necessary, and it did not back away from its *Weitzenhoff* decision. This situation is similar to *Hayes International* and *Speach*, where knowledge of permit status was required for hazardous waste transporters who would be less likely than facility operators to be familiar with permit status.

176. 53 F.3d 533 (2d Cir. 1995), *cert. denied*, 516 U.S. 1072 (1996).

177. 119 F.3d 712 (8th Cir. 1997).

178. *See* United States v. Pacific Hide & Fur Depot, 768 F.2d 1096, 1098–99 (9th Cir. 1985) (a "willful blindness" instruction is properly given when defendant claims a lack of guilty knowledge and proof supports inference of deliberate ignorance).

islative history suggests that Congress intended that environmental prosecutions not be limited to the employees who directly engaged in the illegal conduct:

> [F]or the purpose of liability for criminal penalties the term "person" is defined to include any responsible corporate officer. This is based on a similar definition in the enforcement section of the Federal Water Pollution Control Act. The [Senate] Committee [on Environment and Public Works] intends that criminal penalties be sought against those corporate officers under whose responsibility a violation has taken place, and not just those employees directly involved in the operation of the violating source. [S. Rep. No. 94-717, 94th Cong., 2d Sess. 40 (1976).]

The addition of "responsible corporate officer" to the definition of "person" was meant to expand the classes of individuals responsible under the environmental laws.[179] There are two significant appellate cases in which the "responsible corporate officer" doctrine was applied to impose criminal liability under the CWA. In the first case, United States v. Iverson, 162 F.3d 1015 (9th Cir. 1998), the government sought to convict the president and chairman of the company even though he did not commit the acts himself. Arguing that the defendant's conduct fell within the responsible corporate officer doctrine, the government relied on the fact that the defendant was present when the illegal discharges occurred and did nothing to stop them. The court rejected defendant's arguments that a corporate officer is not "responsible" when he or she does not in fact exercise control over the activity, *id.*:

> Under the CWA, a person is a "responsible corporate officer" if the person has authority to exercise control over the corporation's activity that is causing the discharges. There is no requirement that the officer in fact exercise such authority or that the corporation expressly vest a duty in the officer to oversee the activity. [*Id.* at 1025.]

In a more recent case, the court in *United States v. Hong*[180] affirmed application of the responsible corporate officer doctrine in another pretreatment prosecution, this time in the context of negligent violations.[181]

---

179. *See, e.g.,* United States v. Johnson & Towers, Inc., 741 F.2d 662, 665, n.3 (3rd Cir. 1984).

180. 242 F.3d 528 (4th Cir. 2001).

181. In United States v. Brittain, 931 F.2d 1413 (10th Cir. 1991), a misdemeanor CWA prosecution, the court stated that the rationale of the responsible corporate officer doctrine applies to the CWA. (At the time of the offenses in *Brittain*, the act required that a criminal violation be committed willfully or negligently.) However, the jury in *Brittain* was not presented with this "responsible corporate officer" theory, *id.* at 1420, n.5, and the court of appeals found that there was sufficient evidence in the record to prove that defendant's conduct was "willful and, at the very least, negligent." *Id.* Thus, the court's observations about the applicability of the responsible corporate officer doctrine to misdemeanor CWA violations appear to be dicta.

In summary, the responsible corporate officer doctrine can be a very important tool for the criminal enforcement of environmental laws. Under certain circumstances, corporate agents may be held criminally liable for their failure to prevent violations.[182] Under present case law authority, criminal liability can be based on the failure to act—by an individual with the knowledge, power, and the duty to act.[183] Corporate officers or other corporate agents can be held criminally liable when direct or circumstantial evidence proves that they had knowledge of environmental violations, they were in a position of responsibility and authority to prevent those violations, and they failed to do so.

2. Negligent Violations

The CWA does not define the term "negligently," nor does the legislative history definitively address the issue.[184] To date only one court of appeals decision has defined the government's burden under the negligence standard. In *United States v. Hanousek*,[185] the Ninth Circuit Court of Appeals concluded that the standard in 33 U.S.C. Section 1319(c)(1) is one of simple negligence; and not, as the defendant argued, a heightened gross negligence standard. [176 F.3d at 1120–22.] Affirming the conviction below, the court relied upon the plain wording of the statute and its view that the CWA is a "public welfare" statute, as it previously had determined in *Weitzenhoff*.

C. COMMON CRIMINAL OFFENSES

1. Direct Discharge

A direct pollutant discharge either without or in violation of a permit can be charged as a criminal violation under 33 U.S.C. Section 1319 (c) (1) or (2). The

---

182. *See, e.g., United States v. Park*, 421 U.S. at 658 (duty of "foresight and vigilance" imposed on responsible corporate agents includes, "primarily, a duty to implement measures that will insure that violations will not occur").

183. Of course, under traditional and well-established criminal law, the defendant's knowledge may be proved by direct or circumstantial evidence. This is true for any criminal statute, and it is equally true for the environmental statutes. As the court stated in *Johnson & Towers, Inc.*, the fact that defendants managed, supervised, and directed a substantial portion of the company's operations is circumstantial evidence from which the jury may infer knowledge. 741 F.2d at 670; *see also MacDonald & Watson*, 933 F.2d at 55 (knowledge can be proven from circumstantial evidence, such as a defendant's position and responsibility or willful blindness to the facts constituting the offense).

184. The limited legislative history suggests that Congress intended to create a simple negligence standard. The only recorded commentary on the negligence standard suggests that the act requires proof of simple negligence. Representative Harsha stated during a debate concerning adding criminal penalties for violating EPA orders that such an addition would be unnecessary because "[W]e can already charge a man for simple negligence, we can charge him with a criminal violation under this bill. . . ." *A Legislative History of the Water Pollution Control Act Amendments of 1972*, Vol. 1 at 530 (emphasis added): *reported in* 118 CONG. REC. 10, 644 (1972).

185. 176 F.3d 1116 (9th Cir. 1999), *cert. denied*, 528 U.S. 1102 (2000).

government must prove the following elements beyond a reasonable doubt to establish a violation:

(1) a person
(2) knowingly or negligently
(3) discharged through a point source
(4) a pollutant
(5) into a water of the United States
(6) without or in violation of a permit.

2. Discharges to Sewer Systems/Pretreatment Violations

Conduct associated with discharges to publicly owned sewer systems can be prosecuted under two separate but partially overlapping statutory provisions. First, violations of pretreatment standards, including federally enforceable local pretreatment programs, can be prosecuted under 33 U.S.C. Section 1319(c). This section references 33 U.S.C. Section 1317(d). It prohibits any owner or operator from operating a source in violation of any pretreatment standard. The elements of an offense for violation of a pretreatment standard under 33 U.S.C. Section 1317(d) are:

(1) a person
(2) knowingly/negligently
(3) operated a source (thereby discharged into a sewer system)
(4) in violation of a pretreatment standard
(5) after the effective date of that standard.

The second statutory route through which the government may seek criminal sanctions for pretreatment violations is the distinct negligent or knowing pretreatment crimes under 33 U.S.C. Sections 1319(c)(1) and (2). These statutory provisions reference 33 U.S.C. Sections 1342(a)(3) and (b)(8), making violations of the requirements of a federally approved local pretreatment program subject to federal criminal enforcement. The elements of a pretreatment offense under 33 U.S.C. Sections 1319 (c)(1) and (2) are as follows:

(1) a person
(2) knowingly or negligently;
(3) violated a requirement imposed in a pretreatment program approved under 33 U.S.C. Sections 1342(a)(3) or 1342(b)(8).

3. Wetlands Violations

The central issue in recent CWA criminal prosecutions for wetlands related violations has been the jurisdictional reach of the statute and applicable regulations.[186] As discussed in chapter 6 of this publication (covering CWA section

---

186. *Wilson, supra* note 174.

404), judicial interpretations of the scope of the definition of "waters of the United States" is the key to most enforcement actions, both civil and criminal.

The statutory prohibition upon which a wetlands related violation is based is the same one that underlies the NPDES program, namely, 33 U.S.C. Section 1311(a). Under that provision, "[e]xcept as in compliance with . . . 33 U.S.C. §1344, the discharge of any pollutant by any person shall be unlawful." Also, the same sections that define criminal sanctions for NPDES violations, 33 U.S.C. Section 1319(c)(1)(A) and (2)(A), apply to violations of 33 U.S.C. Section 1344, and those sections make it clear that the federal government can prosecute for violations of either federally issued or state-issued permits. Consequently, the elements of an offense relating to wetlands and dredged or fill material disposal are virtually the same as those for other surface water violations:

(1) a person
(2) discharged a pollutant
(3) from a point source
(4) into a water of the United States (including a wetland)
(5) without a permit or in violation of a federal or state permit under 33 U.S.C. section 1344; and
(6) he or she acted knowingly [or negligently].

4. Falsification and Tampering

As with many other environmental statutes, the effectiveness and integrity of the CWA is heavily dependent upon truthful and accurate self-reporting by the regulated community. There are insufficient government resources available to monitor all water pollutant discharges or activities that have potential adverse environmental impacts.

Federal and state agencies rely upon the regulated community to submit accurate information. Because of its dependence upon the truthful information from the regulated community, the CWA has its own falsification and tampering felony provision, 33 U.S.C. Section 1319(c)(4), which reads as follows:

Any person who knowingly makes any false material statement, representation, or certification in any application, record, report, plan, or other document filed or required to be maintained under this chapter or who knowingly falsifies, tampers with, or renders inaccurate any monitoring device or method required to be maintained under this chapter, shall upon conviction, be punished by a fine of not more than $10,000, or by imprisonment for not more than 2 years, or by both. If a conviction of a person is for a violation committed after a first conviction of such person under this paragraph, punishment shall be by a fine of not more than $20,000 per day of violation, or by imprisonment of not more than 4 years, or by both.

To date this provision has been used primarily in cases involving falsifications of discharge monitoring reports (DMRs) or monthly monitoring reports, which are required to be maintained or submitted to federal or state agencies by holders of NPDES permits, although an increasing number of cases are being prosecuted for unlawful tampering with monitoring devices or methods.[187]

The falsification portion of 33 U.S.C. Section 1319(c)(4) is very similar to the general federal false-statement statute, 18 U.S.C. Section 1001. They are largely interchangeable, and prosecutors may elect to seek charges under either statute.

Offenses under 33 U.S.C. Section 1319(c)(4) include falsifications in documents that must be maintained, as well as in those that must be filed, and they extend to causing inaccuracies in monitoring devices or methods. Similarly, this provision could also be utilized when evaluating information submitted in the context of permit applications. Since states or local government entities may be the ones implementing the statutory programs, the provision is not written in terms of federal requirements only.

The elements of an offense under 33 U.S.C. section 1319(c)(4) are as follows:

(1) a person
(2) makes a false material statement, representation, or certification in any application, report, record, plan, or other document[188] *or*
(3) falsifies, tampers with, or renders inaccurate any monitoring device or method,[189]
(4) and the document was required to be filed or maintained or the device or method was required to be maintained under the Act; and
(5) he or she acted knowingly [or negligently].

5. Knowing Endangerment

The 1987 CWA amendments added a knowing-endangerment provision to the statute.[190] It is modeled on the knowing-endangerment provisions of the RCRA, 42 U.S.C. Sections 6928(e) and (f), as amended in 1984. The1990 Clean Air Act

---

187. *See, e.g.,* United States v. Sinskey, *supra, and* United States v. Hopkins, *supra.*

188. Note that, unlike the corresponding RCRA and Clean Air Act provisions, 42 U.S.C. sections 6928(d)(3) and 7413(c)(2), respectively, this subsection does not specifically criminalize omissions. However, it should be possible to characterize many material omissions in an affirmative manner as falsifications since their ultimate effect is to convey an inaccurate picture of a given situation.

189. *See* United States v. Hopkins, *supra,* for the mental state standard applicable to a 33 U.S.C. section 1319(c)(4) violation.

190. 33 U.S.C. § 1319(c)(3).

amendments included a similar subsection in that statute.[191] While the three are not absolutely identical, they are similar enough that case law interpreting the provisions should be instructive. Under each, if a person commits certain other offenses under the respective statute and knows at the time that they thereby place another person in imminent danger of death or serious bodily injury, they may be found guilty of knowing endangerment. The sanctions for such a crime are up to 15 years' imprisonment and up to a $250,000 fine for an individual or up to a $1,000,000 fine for an organization.

The elements of 33 U.S.C. section 1319(c)(3) offense are as follows:

(1) a person
(2) knowingly committed a specified predicate felony
(3) and he knew at the time that he thereby put another person in imminent danger of death or serious bodily injury.

The predicate offenses for knowing endangerment are nearly the same as those covered in 33 U.S.C. Section 1319(c)(2)(A). Congress added violations of 33 U.S.C. Section 1313 (water quality standards), which cannot be enforced under the act's basic misdemeanor or felony provisions. More importantly, though, in (c)(3) there is no reference to approved state and local pretreatment requirements. Thus, on the face of the statute, it would appear that only violations of federal pretreatment standards (which can include approved state or local pretreatment prohibitions or limitations, according to 40 C.F.R. Sections 403.5(d) and 403.10(e)) can be predicate offenses for knowing endangerment violations. Also missing as predicate offenses are the violations under 33 U.S.C. Section 1319(c)(2)(B).[192]

In *United States v. Borowski*,[193] the defendants were convicted by a jury on two counts of knowing endangerment under the CWA for dumping plating wastes into sinks leading to a municipal sewer system in violation of pretreatment standards and for exposing company employees to health risks. However, the court of appeals vacated the convictions, holding that a prosecution for knowing endangerment under the CWA cannot be premised upon danger that occurs before the pollutant reaches publicly owned sewers or treatment works. Thus, while defendants had knowingly violated pretreatment standards, the court found they had not "thereby" placed the employees in imminent danger since the risk of

---

191. 42 U.S.C. § 7413(c)(5).

192. In most instances violations of 33 U.S.C. section 1319(c)(2)(B) probably can be developed along more-conventional pretreatment felony lines within the scope of 33 U.S.C. section 1317(d), thereby making them predicate offenses for purposes of 33 U.S.C. section 1319(c)(3).

193. 977 F.2d 27, 29–31 (1st Cir. 1992).

harm would have been the same even had the discharge never reached the municipality's sewer system.

The *Borowski* court took a narrow view that pretreatment standards were designed to only protect sewers and sewer workers, and noted that the CWA does not extend to protecting employees working with the wastes at the point of discharge or working *within* the discharging industries, referring to other laws, such as the Occupational Safety and Health Act (OSHA), as protecting industrial health and safety. The court also noted that since the CWA generally does not cover the *handling* of pollutants, the knowing-endangerment provision of the act applies only to persons "downstream" from the point of discharge. Thus, the court adopted the view that the predicate environmental crime must be completed or perfected before "knowing endangerment" can occur.

6. Oil or Hazardous Substances Violations

Congress enacted the Oil Pollution Act (OPA) in 1990. The 1990 amendments chiefly affect section 311 of the CWA.[194] Although the CWA, as it existed before the OPA amendments, already prohibited discharges of oil and hazardous substances, those amendments made that prohibition specifically criminally enforceable, while making the failure to report a spill a felony and restricting the immunity applicable to such a report. The amendments also dramatically increased liability of vessels for cleanup costs and instituted the Oil Spill Liability Trust Fund.

a. Prohibited Discharges of Oil or Hazardous Substances: 33 U.S.C. Section 1321(b)(3)[195].

Section 1321(b)(3) of Title 33 prohibits discharges of oil or hazardous substances in quantities that "may be harmful." Section 1319(c) makes negligent or knowing violation of this prohibition a criminal offense.[196]

The elements of an offense under 33 U.S.C. sections 1319(c) and 1321(b)(3) are as follows:

(1) a person
(2) discharged oil or a hazardous substance
(3) into water of the United States *or*

---

194. 33 U.S.C. § 1321.

195. Depending on the facts of the case, a violation of section 1321(b)(3) also may be a violation of the Act to Prevent Pollution from Ships (APPS), 33 U.S.C. Section 1908, as well as of other statutes. The CWA and APPS have somewhat different elements and penalties. Also, a discharge at sea of a hazardous substance (but not of oil) may constitute a violation of the Ocean Dumping Act, 33 U.S.C. § 1401 *et seq.*

196. The 1990 OPA amendments added section 1321(b)(3) to the list of sections for which violations can be prosecuted under sections 1319(c)(1)(A) and (c)(2)(A). Prior to that amendment, such spills were prosecuted as unpermitted discharges from point sources in violation of 33 U.S.C. section 1311(a), and in some circumstances they still may be. *See, e.g.,* United States v. Hamel, 551 F.2d 107 (6th Cir. 1977).

(4) upon adjoining shorelines *or*

(5) into the contiguous zone *or*

(6) in connection with activities under the Outer Continental Shelf Lands Act or the Deepwater Port Act,[197] *or* that may affect natural resources belonging to the United States

(7) in a quantity that may be harmful;[198] and

(8) he or she acted knowingly [or negligently].

Some discharges of oil under 33 U.S.C. section 1321(b)(3) may be subject to an exception created by the MARPOL Protocol.[199] The MARPOL exception varies depending on the vessel, type of waste, and location. The requirements established by MARPOL, and the exceptions thereto, are set forth in the U.S. Coast Guard's implementing regulation, 33 C.F.R. part 151. For example, 33 U.S.C. Section 1321(b)(3) (A) exempts discharges in the contiguous zone (that is, waters 3 to 12 miles from shore) and in waters outside of the contiguous zone that are from ships operating in compliance with MARPOL. Under MARPOL, ships (other than oil tankers) within 12 miles from shore may discharge oily water if the following limited conditions exist: the oil or oily mixture does not originate from the cargo pump room bilges; the oil or oily mixture does not mix with oil cargo residues; the ship has an operational pollution prevention device known as an oil/water separator (bilge/water separator), and an alarm; and the oil content of the discharge contains less than 15 parts per million.[200] For discharge beyond 12 miles the oil content of the discharge must be less than 100 parts per million.[201] The MARPOL exception in section 1321(b)(3)(A) does not apply to discharges within the navigable waters (waters within three miles of shore and internal waters of the United States).

---

197. The Outer Continental Shelf Lands Act is at 43 U.S.C. § 1331 *et seq.* and the Deepwater Port Act is at 33 U.S.C. §§ 1501 *et seq.*

198. The elements of an offense charged under 33 U.S.C. section 1321(b)(3) differ from an unpermitted discharge under 33 U.S.C. section 1311 in several ways: Under section 1321(b)(3), (1) a discharge need not be from a "point source" (although it is likely to be in any event); (2) geographic jurisdiction is broader, in that the discharge can be to "adjoining shorelines" and the "contiguous zone" (or beyond in some instances), as well as to navigable waters; and (3) the amount discharged must be a quantity that "may be harmful."

199. MARPOL refers to the International Convention for the Prevention of Pollution from Ships, 1973, and the Protocol of 1978 relating to the International Convention for the Prevention of Pollution from Ships, 1973. Together referred to as the MARPOL Protocol or MARPOL 73/78, these treaties, to which the United States is a signatory, contain several general axioms and five annexes that provide specific substantive regulations. Annex I regulates discharges of oil; Annex II covers the discharges of noxious liquid substances in bulk; Annex III regulates harmful substances carried by sea in packaged forms or in freight containers, portable tanks, or road and rail wagons; Annex IV regulates sewage pollution from ships; and Annex V regulates the disposal of sewage (including plastics) from ships.

200. 33 C.F.R. § 151.10(b).

The provision through which violations of the prohibition in 33 U.S.C. Section 1321(b)(3) are prosecuted is 33 U.S.C. Section 1319(c)(1) and (2), discussed earlier in this chapter.

b. Failure to Report Spills: 33 U.S.C. Section 1321(b)(5). The second criminal offense under 33 U.S.C. Section 1321 is the failure to report a spill to the government, a five-year felony with fines tied to the Alternative Fines Act, 18 U.S.C. Section 3571. The elements of the offense are as follows:

(1) a person
(2) in charge of a vessel or of an onshore or offshore facility
(3) from which oil or a hazardous substance is discharged in a reportable quantity (*i.e.,* such quantity as may be harmful)
(4) into a navigable water of the United States [or other area specified in 33 U.S.C. Section 1321(b)(3)]
(5) fails to immediately notify the appropriate federal agency
(6) as soon as he or she has knowledge of the discharge.

Violation of 33 U.S.C. Section 1321(b)(5) is a crime of omission. The only knowledge required is that of the occurrence of the discharge on the part of the person in charge of the vessel or facility. The spill, though, must be of a sufficient amount to constitute a reportable quantity (often referred to as the "RQ" for the material involved). Reportable quantities are the same as "quantities which may be harmful" as discussed above.[202]

Section 1321(b)(5) prohibits the use of spill notifications in criminal prosecutions against "natural persons."[203] Consequently, although individuals who make spill notifications may still be charged criminally, prosecutors and investigators

---

201. 33 C.F.R. § 151.10(a).

202. Note that for hazardous substances in solution, only that portion of the solution that actually is the hazardous substance is counted toward the reportable quantity requirement. For example, the RQ for malathion is 100 pounds. If 100 pounds of a 50-percent (by weight) solution of malathion and water were discharged, the total amount of malathion actually discharged would be only 50 pounds (0.50 x 100); hence the RQ would not have been met. For 100 pounds of the malathion to have been discharged, a total of 200 pounds of the 50-percent solution would have to be discharged. 44 Fed. Reg. 50765, 50767 (Aug. 29, 1979). For exceptions to the reporting requirement, see 40 C.F.R. §§ 117.11–117.14. Also, the reportable quantity of hazardous substance has to have been discharged within a 24-hour period. 40 C.F.R. § 117.21.

203. Note, also, that CERCLA contains a notification requirement, applicable only to releases of hazardous substances, that includes release into the waters. 42 U.S.C. § 9603(b). That provision gives use-immunity to all persons, including corporations, and bars use of information obtained through exploitation of the notification. Thus, where a case involves a properly reported spill of hazardous substances in circumstances where both 33 U.S.C. Section 1321(b)(5) and 42 U.S.C. Section 9603(b) may apply, it must be assumed that the broader use-immunity under CERCLA applies. In those cases, it may be necessary for a "tainted" investigator or lawyer to screen evidence to determine whether it was derived from the immunized report before providing it to the prosecution team.

may not use evidence of a notification against the notifying individual. However, such information may be used against a corporate defendant or against individuals other than the person who made the notification.[204]

D. RELATED WATER POLLUTION STATUTES

The CWA, while it is the most comprehensive, is only one of several federal water pollution statutes that include criminal sanctions. The statutes discussed below present enforcement options thereby allowing prosecutors to select the statute that is most appropriate for a given set of facts.

1. Rivers and Harbors Act of 1899

The Rivers and Harbors Act of 1899 is the oldest federal environmental law. Under the act, it is a misdemeanor to discharge refuse matter of any kind into navigable waters of the United States without a permit.[205] In addition, it is a misdemeanor under the act to excavate, fill, or alter the course, condition, or capacity of any port, harbor, channel, or other areas within reach of the act without a permit.[206] There is no knowledge or negligence requirement articulated in the statute and none has been read into it. In other words, the act has been interpreted as a strict liability statute, at least as it has been applied to corporations.[207] In such cases, therefore, the government need not prove that the defendant acted with knowledge or in a negligent manner.[208]

One district court, in a case against corporate and individual defendants, has concluded, however, that the government must show that a defendant acted with general intent.[209]

2. Marine Protection, Research, and Sanctuaries Act (Ocean Dumping Act)

The Marine Protection, Research, and Sanctuaries Act, which is more commonly known as the Ocean Dumping Act, generally regulates the dumping of material

---

204. Before its amendment by the Oil Pollution Act of 1990, 33 U.S.C. section 1321(b)(5) provided for derivative use immunity by excluding "information obtained by the exploitation of such notification" and extended the use immunity to all persons including corporations. The amendment was intended to narrow substantially the scope of use immunity and to eliminate all derivative use immunity. *See* Conf. Rep. for H.R. 1465, Oil Pollution Act of 1990, July 30, 1990, at 122.

205. 33 U.S.C. §§ 407, 411.

206. 33 U.S.C. §§ 403, 406.

207. Note that in *United States v. Standard Oil*, 384 U.S. 224, 230 (1966), the Supreme Court declined to address the mental state issue for Refuse Act violations. Also, in *United States v. White Fuel Corp.*, 498 F.2d 619, 623–24 (1st Cir. 1974), the First Circuit left open the issue of whether the violation would be treated as a strict liability offense in the case of an individual defendant.

208. *See, e.g., White Fuel Corp.*, 498 F.2d at 622–24; United States v. United States Steel Corp., 328 F. Supp. 354, 356 (N.D. Ind. 1970), *aff'd*, 482 F.2d 439 (7th Cir.), *cert. denied*, 414 U.S. 909 (1973).

209. United States v. Commodore Club, Inc., 418 F. Supp. 311, 319–20 (E.D. Mich. 1976).

into the ocean.[210] The act establishes a permitting system that allows ocean dumping only pursuant to permits issued by EPA and the Army Corps of Engineers.

There are two felony criminal sanctions in the Ocean Dumping Act. First, the Act prohibits transporting material from the United States for the purpose of dumping it into ocean waters without a permit. Second, the Act prohibits the dumping of materials transported from outside the United States into U.S. waters without a permit.[211]

3. Act to Prevent Pollution From Ships

The 1973 International Convention for the Prevention of Pollution From Ships, and its 1978 Protocol, together commonly referred to as the "MARPOL Protocol," establish a comprehensive set of international rules relating to the discharge of oil, plastic, garbage, and other pollutants from ships. The Act to Prevent Pollution From Ships (APPS), 33 U.S.C. Sections 1901 through 1912, implements the MARPOL Protocol and makes it enforceable under federal law. The U.S. Coast Guard is responsible for administering the law and has promulgated a detailed set of regulations addressing vessel pollution. A knowing violation of the MARPOL Protocol, APPS, or regulations implementing APPS can be prosecuted as a felony.[212] The primary provisions underlying the majority of prosecutions relate to oil discharges from vessels and the prohibition on discharging plastic and other garbage.

IV. Citizen Suits

LAIRD LUCAS

Citizen suits have played a prominent role in CWA enforcement. Citizens have been very active as litigants under the CWA for the last 20 years, filing numerous suits each year. Until recently, almost all of the large penalties assessed under the CWA resulted from citizen suits, not suits brought by EPA or the Department of Justice.[213]

---

210. 33 U.S.C. §§ 1401–1445.

211. 33 U.S.C. §§ 1411, 1415(b).

212. 33 U.S.C. § 1908(a).

213. See, e.g., Student Public Interest Research Group v. P.D. Oil and Chemical, 913 F.2d 64 (3d Cir. 1989) (statutory max. ($4,085,000) for 386 effluent violations); Hawaii's Thousand Friends v. City and County of Honolulu, 821 F. Supp. 1368 (D. Hawaii 1993) ($718,000 penalty plus $1 million paid to the Manla Bay Study Commission for additional monitoring of the effects of sewage discharges on public health and the marine environment); Atlantic States Legal Foundation v. Universal Tool & Stamping Co., 786 F. Supp. 743 (N.D. Ind. 1992) ($450,000 for 1,977 violations of NPDES permit prior to installing new equipment); Natural Resources Defense Council v. Texaco Refining and Marketing, Inc., 800 F. Supp. 1, 17 (D. Del. 1992), aff'd in part, rev'd in part on other grounds, 2 F.3d 493 (3d Cir. 1993) ($1,680,000 assessed for 3,360 NPDES violations (included flow, pH, oil and grease, BOD, TOC, phenols, sulfides, bioassay)).

A. STATUTORY AUTHORITY

The CWA, like most federal environmental statutes, grants citizens the right to file suit in federal court to enforce the act. The citizen suit provision provides as follows:

Except as provided in subsection (b) of this section and section 1319(g)(6) of this title, *any citizen* may commence a civil action on his own behalf—

(1) against *any person* (including (i) the United States, and (ii) any other governmental instrumentality or agency to the extent permitted by the eleventh amendment to the Constitution) who is alleged to be *in violation of* (A) *an effluent standard or limitation* under this chapter or (B) *an order* issued by the Administrator or a State with respect to such a standard or limitation, or

(2) against *the Administrator* where there is alleged a *failure* of the Administrator *to perform* any act or *duty* under this chapter which is not *discretionary* with the Administrator.[214]

B. LEGISLATIVE INTENT AND AUTHORITY

Prior to the enactment of the Federal Water Pollution Control Act of 1972, it was widely recognized that the government had failed to adequately enforce the federal water pollution statute.[215] Congress included the citizen suit provision in the 1972 act as part of the response to this enforcement problem.[216]

The structure of the CWA indicates that Congress intended federal and state governments primarily to enforce the CWA, but that citizens would play an important role in filling gaps that remained.[217] Courts thus sometimes refer to citizen-

---

214. 33 U.S.C. § 1365(a) (emphasis added).

215. *See* Dunkleberger, *The Federal Government's Role in Regulating Water Pollution Under the Federal Water Quality Act of 1965*, 3 Nat. Res. L. 3 (1970).

216. *See* S. Rep. No. 414, 92d Cong., 1st Sess. 2–3 (1971), *reprinted in*, 1 Env'tl Policy Div., Cong. Res. Serv., U.S. Library of Cong., A Legislative History of the Water Pollution Control Act of 1972, at 1415, 1420–25 (1973).

217. Gwaltney of Smithfield v. Chesapeake Bay Found., 484 U.S. 49, 108 S. Ct. 376, 98 L. Ed. 2d 306 (1987) (citizen suit provision has "central purpose of permitting citizens to abate pollution when the government cannot or will not command compliance."); North & South Rivers Watershed Ass'n v. Scituate, 949 F.2d 552 (1st Cir. 1991) (citing *Gwaltney*); Coastal Fishermen's Ass'n v. N.Y. City Dept. of Sanitation, 772 F. Supp. 162 (S.D.N.Y. 1991) (citizen suits can proceed where federal and state entities are not fulfilling their enforcement duties).

plaintiffs as "private attorneys general."[218] Reflecting the legislative intent, the courts have rejected efforts to marginalize the role of citizens in CWA enforcement.[219]

Constitutional challenges to the CWA citizen suit provision have been uniformly rejected.[220] But the courts have declined to read implied causes of action not expressly identified in the citizen suit provision.[221]

C. TYPES OF CWA CITIZEN SUITS

Three decades of experience confirms that citizen suits have played an important role in enforcing the CWA's requirements, although concerns that citizen suits have exceeded their anticipated role have been voiced.[222]

As discussed below, citizen suits have been particularly prominent in enforcing pollution discharge permit requirements under section 402,[223] and in enforcing statutory requirements for EPA to approve state water quality standards and

---

218. *See, e.g.*, Sierra Club v. Peterson, 705 F.2d 1475, 1479 (9th Cir. 1983).

219. Sierra Club v. Chevron U.S.A., Inc., 834 F.2d 1517 (9th Cir. 1987) ("Our own review of the legislative history indicates only that citizen suits should be handled liberally, because they perform an important public function: 'It is the Committee's intent that enforcement of these control provisions be immediate, that citizens should be unconstrained to bring these actions, and that the courts should not hesitate to consider them.' ") S. Rep. No. 414, 92nd Cong. 2d Sess. *reprinted in* 1972 U.S. CODE CONG. & ADMIN. NEWS 3746.

220. Atlantic States Legal Foundation, Inc. v. Universal Tool & Stamping Co., 735 F. Supp. 1404 (N.D. Ind. 1990); Natural Resources Defense Council, Inc. v. Bethlehem Steel Corp., 652 F. Supp. 620, 623-26 (D. Md. 1987); Student Public Research Group of New Jersey, Inc. v. Monsanto Co., 600 F. Supp. 1474, 1478–79 (D.N.J. 1985).

221. Middlesex County Sewerage Authority v. National Sea Clammers Ass'n, 453 U.S. 1, 14–15, 101 S. Ct. 2615, 69 L. Ed. 2d 435 (1981); Board of Trustees v. City of Painesville, 200 F.3d 396 (6th Cir. 1999); Walls v. Waste Resource Corp., 761 F.2d 311 (6th Cir.1985).

222. *See* J. Campbell, *Has the Citizen-Suit Provision of the Clean Water Act Exceeded its Supplemental Birth?* 24 WM & MARY ENV'TL L. & POL'Y REV. 305 (Spring 2000); R. Macfarlane and L. Terry, *Citizen Suits: Impacts on Permitting and Agency Enforcement,* 11 NAT. RESOURCES & ENV'T 20 (Spring 1997); D. Hodas, *Enforcement of Environmental Law in a Triangular Federal System: Can Three Not Be a Crowd when Enforcement Authority Is Shared by the United States, the States and Their Citizens?* 54 MD. L. REV. 1552, 1577 (1995).

223. *See, e.g.,* Natural Resources Defense Council v. Southwest Marine, Inc., 236 F.3d 985 (9th Cir. 2000); Sierra Club v. Cedar Point Oil, 73 F.3d 546 (5th Cir. 1996); Committee to Save Makelumne River v. Eat Bay Util. Dist., 13 F.3d 305 (9th Cir. 1993).

TMDLs under section 303.[224] Far less frequently, citizens suits have been used to enforce section 404 "dredge and fill" permit requirements.[225]

1. Section 505(a): Failure to Comply with Act

Subsection 505(a)(1) grants citizens the right to sue any person for violating an effluent standard or limitation, or an order issued with respect to an effluent standard or limitation.[226]

The scope of this section is broad. The CWA defines "person" to include individuals and a wide variety of entities, including corporations, partnerships, associations, municipalities, commissions, and interstate bodies.[227] In addition, under section 505(a)(1), "person" includes the United States and "any other governmental instrumentality or agency to the extent permitted by the eleventh amendment to the Constitution."[228]

---

224. *See* Hayes v. Whitman, 264 F.3d 1017 (10th Cir. 2001); Miccosukee Tribe of Indians v. EPA, 105 F.3d 599 (11th Cir. 1997); Alaska Center for the Environment v. Browner, 20 F.3d 981 (9th Cir. 1994); Scott v. City of Hammond, 741 F.2d 992 (7th Cir. 1984); A. Houck, *TMDLs: The Resurrection of Water Quality Standards-Based Regulation Under The Clean Water Act,* 27 ELR 10329 (1997).

225. *See* Save Our Community v. EPA, 971 F.2d 1155 (5th Cir. 1992); Comment, *Slowing the Net Loss of Wetlands: Citizen Suit Enforcement of Clean Water Act 404 Permit Violations,* 27 ENV'TL L. 245 (1997); M. Blumm & B. Zaleha, *Federal Wetlands Protection Under The Clean Water Act: Regulatory Ambivalence, Intergovernmental Tension, and a Call for Reform,* 60 COLO. L. REV. 695, 753–54 (1989). Most litigation by environmental groups has been against the Corps for alleged violations of 404 requirements, or requirements of NEPA and other laws, in issuing dredge-and-fill permits; these actions are brought under the federal APA, rather than as CWA citizen suits. *See, e.g.,* Sierra Club v. Slater, 120 F.3d 623 (6th Cir. 1997); Friends of the Earth v. U.S. Army Corps of Engineers, 109 F. Supp. 2d 30 (D.D.C. 2000); Save Greers Ferry Lake v. U.S. Army Corps of Engineers, 111 F. Supp. 2d 1135 (E.D. Ark. 2000); Defenders of Wildlife v. Ballard, 73 F. Supp. 2d 1094 (D. Ariz. 1999); Florida Keys Citizens Coalition v. West, 996 F. Supp. 1254 (S.D. Fla. 1998).

226. 33 U.S.C. § 1365(a)(1).

227. 33 U.S.C. § 1362(5).

228. 33 U.S.C. § 1365(a)(1). Federal agencies may thus be sued for violating CWA permit requirements. *See* Legal Env'tl Assistance Found., Inc. v. Hodel, 586 F. Supp. 1163 (E.D. Tenn. 1984). The CWA does not waive state sovereign immunity. Burnette v. Carothers, 192 F.3d 52, 49 (2d Cir. 1999); Froebel v. Meyer, 13 F. Supp. 2d 843 (E.D. Wis. 1998). Nevertheless, state agencies and official may be subject to injunctive relief in enforcement actions, under *ex parte Young. See* Natural Resources Defense Council v. California Dept. of Transp., 96 F.3d 420 (9th Cir. 1996); Bragg v. Robertson, 72 F. Supp. 2d 642 (S.D. W.Va. 1999), *aff'd in part, vacated in part,* 248 F.3d 275 (4th Cir. 2001); Mancuso v. New York State Thruway Authority, 86 F.3d 289 (2nd Cir. 1996).

"Effluent standard or limitation" is defined broadly to include essentially all federal and state standards and limitations established under the CWA.[229] This provision thus embraces enforcement of section 402 requirements that point source discharges must have an NPDES permit, including certain stormwater discharges,[230] as well as enforcement of state-established quality standards or other terms in permits.[231]

A large number of citizen suits have been brought to enforce the NPDES permit requirements of section 402, confirming Congress's intent that citizen enforcement play a vital role in ensuring the cleanup of the nation's waterways.[232]

2. Section 505(b): Government Failure to Comply with Mandatory Duty

The CWA also authorizes citizen suits against EPA for failure to perform nondiscretionary duties.[233] A primary issue in these suits has been whether a particular duty is nondiscretionary.[234] When the CWA requires EPA to take a specific action by a certain date, it creates a nondiscretionary duty.[235] In the last decade, citizen suits

---

229. 33 U.S.C. § 1365(f). In PUD No. 1 of Jefferson County v. Washington Dept. of Ecology, 511 U.S. 700, 114 S. Ct. 1900, 128 L. Ed. 2d 716 (1994), the Supreme Court held that the term "effluent standards and limitations" encompasses conditions upon a federally permitted discharge imposed by states under CWA section 401.

230. *See, e.g.,* Natural Resources Defense Council v. Southwest Marine, Inc., 236 F.3d 985 (9th Cir. 2000) (stormwater permit enforcement action); Driscoll v. Adams, 181 F.3d 1285 (11th Cir. 1999) (property owner liability for stormwater discharges).

231. Northwest Environmental Advocates v. Portland, 56 F.3d 979 (9th Cir. 1995), *cert. denied*, 116 S. Ct. 2550, 135 L. Ed. 2d 1069 (1996) (citizen suits may enforce state-established standards); Upper Chattahoochee Riverkeeper Fund, Inc. v. City of Atlanta, 953 F. Supp. 1541 (N.D. Ga. 1996) (same).

232. The wide array of citizen enforcement cases is illustrated by the following examples: Headwaters, Inc. v. Talent Irrig. Dist., 243 F.3d 526 (9th Cir. 2001) (action against irrigation district for applying aquatic herbicide in ditches); Stone v. Naperville Park Dist. 38 F. Supp. 2d 651 (N.D. Ill. 1999) (injunction against trapshooting facility for unpermitted discharges of lead in waterway); Upper Chattaochee Riverkeeper Fund v. City of Atlanta, 986 F. Supp. 1406 (N.D. Ga. 1997) (action over city wastewater collection and treatment system); Hudson Riverkeeper Fund v. Yorktown Heights Sewer Dist., 949 F. Supp. 210 (S.D.N.Y. 1996) (same); Beartooth Alliance v. Crown Butte Mines, 909 F. Supp. 1168 (D. Mont. 1995) (action over abandoned mine discharges).

233. 33 U.S.C. § 1365(a)(2).

234. *See, e.g.,* Miccosukee Tribe of Indians v. EPA, 105 F.3d 599 (11th Cir. 1997); Alaska Center for the Environment v. Browner, 20 F.3d 981 (9th Cir. 1994); Sun Enterprises v. Train, 532 F.2d 280, 288 (2d Cir. 1976); Sierra Club v. Harkinson, 939 F. Supp. 865 (N.D. Ga. 1996); NRDC v. Fox, 30 F. Supp.2d 369 (S.D.N.Y. 1998).

235. *See* Natural Resources Defense Council v. EPA, 966 F.2d 1292 (9th Cir. 1992) (duty to issue stormwater permit regulations); Natural Resources Defense Council, Inc. v. Train, 510 F.2d 692 (D.C. Cir. 1974); Natural Resources Defense Council, Inc. v. Reilly, 32 Env't Rep. Cas. (BNA) 1969 (D.D.C. 1991).

have been widely used to enforce EPA's mandatory duties under CWA sections 303(c) and (d), in reviewing and approving state water quality standards, list of water quality limited waterbodies, and "total maximum daily loads" (TMDLs).[236]

On the other hand, decisions regarding whether or not to prosecute CWA violations,[237] approve a grant for the construction of an underground sewage retention basin,[238] or whether or not to veto a permit issued by a state are discretionary.[239]

The courts appear to be split on whether 505(b) applies to enforce mandatory duties imposed on the Army Corps of Engineers under section 404, since 505(b) names only the "Administrator."[240]

D. STATUTORY REQUIREMENTS FOR CITIZEN SUITS

1. Notice

The CWA requires plaintiffs to provide 60 days' notice to the alleged violator, the state in which the violation is alleged to be occurring, and EPA before filing suit.[241]

---

236. A merely partial listing of these cases includes: Alaska Center for the Environment v. Browner, 20 F.3d 981 (9th Cir. 1994); Kingman Park Civic Ass'n v. U.S. EPA, 84 F. Supp. 2d 1 (D.D.C. 1999); American Canoe Ass'n v. EPA, 30 F. Supp. 2d 908 (E.D. Va. 1998); Sierra Club v. Hankinson, 939 F. Supp. 865 (N.D. Ga. 1996); Idaho Sportsmen Coalition v. Browner, 951 F. Supp. 962 (W.D. Wa. 1996); NRDC v. Fox, 909 F. Supp. 153 (S.D.N.Y. 1995); Sierra Club v. Browner, 843 F. Supp. 1304 (D. Minn. 1993); Alaska Center for the Env't v. Reilly, 762 F. Supp. 1422 (D. Alaska 1991). *See also* O. Houck, *TMDS, Are We There Yet?: The Long Road Toward Water Quality-Based Regulation Under the Clean Water Act,* 27 ELR 10391 (1997).

237. Sierra Club v. Whitman, 268 F.3d 898 (9th Cir. 2001) (no mandatory duty to prosecute after finding violations); Cross Timbers Concerned Citizens v. Saginaw, 991 F. Supp. 563 (N.D. Tex. 1997) (denying citizen suit to force EPA to issue compliance orders against large feedlot operators). *But see* Save the Valley, Inc. v. U.S. Environmental Protection Agency, 99 F. Supp. 2d 981 (S.D. Ind. 2000) (denying EPA motion to dismiss citizen suit claim that EPA has mandatory duty to issue compliance order upon finding that state NPDES program for industrial hog farms inadequate).

238. Association of Significantly Impacted Neighbors v. City of Livonia, 765 F. Supp. 389, 391 (E.D. Mich. 1991).

239. District of Columbia v. Schramm, 631 F.2d 854 (D.C. Cir. 1980).

240. *See* Preserve Endangered Areas of Cobb's History v. U.S. Army Corps of Engineers, 87 F.3d 1242 (11th Cir. 1996) (CWA did not waive sovereign immunity to sue Corps under 505(b)); Cascade Conservation League v. M.A. Segale, Inc., 921 F. Supp. 692 (W.D. Wash. 1996) (same); National Wildlife Federation v. Hanson, 859 F.2d 313 (4th Cir. 1988) (citizen suits may enforce nondiscretionary duties against Corps); Northwest Environmental Defense Center v. U.S. Army Corps of Engineers, 118 F. Supp. 2d 1115 (D. Or. 2000) (distinguishing *Hanson* because EPA and Corps did not work in tandem).

241. 33 U.S.C. § 1365(b)(1)(A). An exception to the 60-day notice requirement is provided in 33 U.S.C. Section 1365(b), allowing an action to be brought immediately after notification if plaintiff is alleging violation of section 1316 (new source standards) or section 1317(a) (toxic effluent standards).

The purpose of the notice requirement is to allow the parties to negotiate and correct the violations before litigation is launched.[242] EPA has adopted regulations under the CWA setting forth in more detail the requirements of notice letters.[243]

In *Hallstrom v. Tillamook County*,[244] the Supreme Court held that a similar notice requirement in RCRA is mandatory, and that a court must dismiss an action if the plaintiff has failed to provide the required notice.[245] Following *Hallstrom*, courts have held that the CWA's notice requirement is jurisdictional.[246]

The level of detail required in a notice letter is a frequent topic of litigation. The legislative history indicates Congress intended the notice requirement to be liberally construed.[247] Many courts have followed this intent, declining to dismiss citizen suits where adequate notice was deemed to be given identifying the alleged violations.[248] Would-be plaintiffs are well advised to make their notice

---

242. New Mexico Citizens for Clean Air and Water v. Espanola Mercantile Co., Inc., 72 F.3d 830, 833 (10th Cir. 1996) (the purpose of the pre-suit notice is to "allow parties time to 'resolve their conflicts in a nonadversarial time period'"), quoting Hallstrom v. Tillamook County, 493 U.S. 20, 110 S. Ct. 304 (1989).

243. 40 C.F.R. pt. 135.

244. 493 U.S. 20, 110 S. Ct. 304 (1989).

245. *Id.*

246. *See* Washington Trout v. McCain Foods, Inc., 45 F.3d 1351 (9th Cir. 1995) (action dismissed where 60-day notice letter failed to properly identify plaintiffs); Greene v. Reilly, 956 F.2d 593 (6th Cir. 1992) (action dismissed for failure to provide 60-day notice); National Env'tl Found. v. ABC Rail Corp., 926 F.2d 1096, 1097–98 (11th Cir. 1991) (compliance with section 1365(b) is a mandatory prerequisite to citizen suit); Pennsylvania Env'tl Defense Found. v. Mazurkiewicz, 712 F. Supp. 1184, 1190–91 (M.D. Pa. 1989).

247. S. Rep. No. 92-414 at 80 (1971), 92nd Cong. 1st Sess., *reprinted in* 2 LEGISLATIVE HISTORY OF THE WATER POLLUTION CONTROL ACT AMENDMENTS OF 1972 at 1498 (1973), U.S. CODE & ADMIN. NEWS 1972, pp. 3668, 3745 (notice requirement should not place "impossible or unnecessary burdens on citizens but rather should be confined to requiring information necessary to give a clear indication of the citizens' intent," such as "the identity and location of the alleged polluter, a brief description of the activity alleged to be in violation, and the provision of law alleged to be violated").

248. Natural Resources Defense Council v. Southwest Marine, Inc., 236 F.3d 985 (9th Cir. 2000) (plaintiffs gave adequate notice and new notice letter was not required after defendant remedied some of the problems listed in the notice letter); Atlantic States Legal Found. v. Stroh Die Casting, 116 F.3d 814 (7th Cir. 1997), *cert. denied*, 118 S. Ct. 442 (1997) ("[T]he key to notice is to give the accused company the opportunity to correct the problem," and holding that facts showed defendant was adequately on notice); Public Interest Research Group of N.J. v. Hercules, Inc., 50 F.3d 1239 (3d Cir. 1995) (notice not required for violations of same parameter from same outfall identified in earlier notice when discovered after filing of original notice); Friends of Frederick Seig Grove # 94 v. Sonoma County Water Agency, 124 F. Supp. 2d 1161 (N.D. Ca. 2000) (notice was sufficient even though it did not exhaustively list all 326 alleged violations and corresponding dates); Community Assoc. for Restoration of the Env't v. Bosma Dairy, 54 F. Supp. 2d 976 (E.D. Wash. 1999) (notice letter sufficiently apprised defendant of location and nature of violations).

letters as detailed as possible, however, since many claims have been dismissed for lack of adequate notice.[249]

2. Preexisting Prosecutions

The CWA prohibits citizens from bringing suit when either the federal or state government is "diligently prosecuting" a civil or criminal action regarding the same violations.[250] Dismissal of a citizen suit is required when the defendant demonstrates that a state or federal enforcement action has been brought over the same alleged violation(s).[251]

The courts have construed the "diligent prosecution" bar narrowly, to prevent violators from escaping liability.[252] The agency enforcement action thus has to be instituted before a citizen suit is brought for the "diligent prosecution" bar to apply.[253] A state prosecution does not bar a citizen suit if the state law is not "comparable" to the federal Clean Water Act.[254] Administrative sanctions that do

---

249. *See,* e.g., Catskill Mountains Chapter of Trout Unlimited, Inc. v. City of New York, 273 F.3d 481 (2d Cir. 2001) (partial dismissal where notice alleged unlawful sediment but not thermal discharges); Board of Trustees v. City of Painesville, 200 F.3d 396 (6th Cir. 1999); New Mexico Citizens for Clean Air and Water v. Espanola Mercantile Co., 72 F.3d 830 (10th Cir. 1996).

250. 33 U.S.C. §§ 1365(b)(1)(B) & 1319(g)(6).

251. *See, e.g.,* Jones v. City of Lakeland, 175 F.3d 410 (6th Cir. 1999) (district court lacks subject matter jurisdiction over CWA citizen suit when the state environmental agency has issued prior compliance orders); Arkansas Wildlife Federation v. ICI Americas, Inc., 29 F.3d 376, 382 (8th Cir. 1994) (injunctive relief as well as civil penalties foreclosed by comparable state action filed before 60-day notice); Baughman v. Bradford Coal Co., 592 F.2d 215 (3d Cir. 1979), *cert. denied,* 441 U.S. 961, 99 S. Ct. 2406, 60 L. Ed. 2d 1066 (1979).

252. *See,* e.g., Washington Public Interest Research Group v. Pendleton Woolen Mills, Inc., 11 F.3d 883 (9th Cir. 1993) (CWA "unambiguously bars suits only when the EPA has instituted an administrative penalty action"); Student Pub. Interest Research Group, Inc. v. Fritzsche, Dodge & Olcott, Inc., 759 F.2d 1131 (3d Cir. 1985) (previous EPA administrative enforcement action was not a "court" proceeding under section 505(b)(1)(B)); Student Pub. Interest Research Group v. Fritzsche, Dodge & Olcott, Inc., 759 F.2d 1131 (3d Cir. 1985); *When Are Clean Water Act Citizen Suits Precluded by Government Enforcement Actions?,* 30 ELR 10111 (Feb. 2000).

253. Long Island Soundkeeper Fund, Inc. v. New York City Dep't of Env'tl Protection, 27 F. Supp. 2d 380 (E.D.N.Y. 1998); Sierra Club v. Hyundai American Inc., 23 F. Supp. 2d 1177 (D. Or. 1997); Mass. Public Int. Research v. ICI Americas Inc., 777 F. Supp. 1032, 1036 (D. Mass. 1991) (citizens group is not barred if it files its 60-day notice prior to EPA bringing an administrative action).

254. *See* 33 U.S.C. § 1319(g)(6)(A)(ii); Knee Deep Cattle Co. v. Bindana Investment Co., 94 F.3d 514 (9th Cir. 1996); Jones v. City of Lakeland, 224 F.3d 518 (6th Cir. 2000); Idaho Rural Council v. Bosma, 143 F. Supp. 2d 1169 (D. Id. 2001); Atlantic States Legal Foundation, Inc. v. Universal Tool & Stamping Co., 735 F. Supp. 1404 (N.D. Ind. 1990).

not include a comparable penalty as an enforcement action also do not bar a citizen suit.[255]

3. Venue

The CWA requires citizen suits for alleged violations of an effluent standard or limitation to be brought in the district court where the source that caused the alleged violation is located.[256] Suits against EPA for failure to perform a nondiscretionary duty may be brought in any district in which a defendant resides, a substantial part of the events or omissions giving rise to the action occurred, or the plaintiff resides.[257]

E. STANDING

The CWA grants any citizen standing to bring an enforcement action,[258] defining "citizen" as "a person or persons having an interest which is or may be adversely affected."[259] As a constitutional matter, a plaintiff bringing a CWA citizen suit has to establish "standing" to satisfy Article III's "case or controversy" requirement.[260] This requires satisfying a three-part test: (a) actual or threatened injury,

---

255. *See* 33 U.S.C. § 1319(g); Citizens for a Better Environment v. UNOCAL, 83 F.3d 1111 (9th Cir. 1996) (citizen suit not barred "because UNOCAL has not paid a 'penalty'"); NRDC v. Fina Oil & Chem. Co., 806 F. Supp. 145, 146 (E.D. Tex. 1992) (citizen suits not prohibited when EPA issued administrative compliance order but imposed no administrative penalty).

256. 33 U.S.C. § 1365(c)(1).

257. *See* 28 U.S.C. § 1391(e).

258. 33 U.S.C. § 1365(a). States have standing to bring a citizen suit. *See* United States Department of Energy v. Ohio, 503 U.S. 607, 112 S. Ct. 1627, 118 L. Ed. 2d 255 (1992); Commonwealth of Mass. v. U.S. Veterans Admin., 541 F.2d 119, 121 n.1 (1st Cir. 1976).259. 33 U.S.C. § 1365(g). The legislative history indicates that Congress intended to extend standing according to the standard set forth in *Sierra Club v. Morton*, 405 U.S. 727 (1972). *See* A LEGISLATIVE HISTORY OF THE FEDERAL WATER POLLUTION CONTROL ACT OF 1972 at 329.

260. *See* Friends of the Earth, Inc. v. Laidlaw Env'tl Serv's, Inc., 528 U.S.167, 120 S. Ct. 693, 145 L. Ed. 2d 610 (2000); Lujan v. Defenders of Wildlife, 500 U.S. 915, 112 S. Ct. 2130 (1992); Valley Forge Christian College v. Americans United for Separation of Church and State, 454 U.S. 464, 472 (1982). If the plaintiff is an environmental organization, it may establish representational standing by showing that (1) its members would have standing, (2) the interests the organization seeks to protect are germane to its purposes, and (3) neither the claim asserted nor the relief requested requires individual members to participate in the litigation. *See* Hunt v. Washington State Apple Advertising Comm'n, 432 U.S. 333, 343 (1977); Friends of the Earth v. Chevron Chemical, 129 F.3d 826 (5th Cir. 1997); Save Ourselves v. U.S. Army Corps of Eng'rs, 958 F.2d 659, 661 (5th Cir. 1992); Natural Resources Defense Council, Inc. v. Texaco, 800 F. Supp. 1, 7 (D. Del. 1992).

(b) caused by defendant's conduct, (c) redressable by the court.[261] The "standing" requirement has provoked a large amount of litigation under the CWA.[262]

However, the Supreme Court's recent decision in *Friends of the Earth v. Laidlaw* confirmed that citizens may demonstrate the "injury" required for standing under the CWA by showing a reasonable concern about pollution has harmed their aesthetic or recreational interests in a waterbody.[263] Accordingly, the trend in the courts since *Laidlaw* suggests that establishing plaintiff standing under the CWA will be simpler in the future.[264] Even the Fourth Circuit, which recently has been hostile to citizen suits, appears now to have relaxed its scrutiny following *Laidlaw*.[265]

In addition to "injury," the plaintiff must demonstrate a substantial likelihood that the defendant caused his or her injury.[266] The plaintiff need not, however,

---

261. Lujan v. Defenders of Wildlife, 500 U.S. 915, 112 S. Ct. 2130, 2136 (1992).

262. *See, e.g.,* Sierra Club v. Cedar Point Oil Co., 73 F.3d 546 (5th Cir. 1996); Save Our Community v. EPA, 971 F.2d 1155, 1161 (5th Cir. 1992); Public Interest Research Group of New Jersey v. Powell Duffryn Terminals, Inc., 913 F.2d 64, 71 (3d Cir. 1990), *cert. denied*, 498 U.S. 1109 (1991); United States v. Metropolitan St. Louis Sewer Dist., 883 F.2d 54, 56 (8th Cir. 1989); Natural Resources Defense Council, Inc. v. Texaco, 800 F. Supp. 1, 8 (D. Del. 1992). Natural Resources Defense Council, Inc. v. Vygen Corp., 803 F. Supp. 97, 102 (N.D. Ohio 1992); Tobyhanna Conservation Ass'n v. Country Place Waste Treatment Co., 734 F. Supp. 667, 669 (M.D. Pa. 1989).

263. 528 U.S. at 704–05.

264. *See* Natural Resources Defense Council v. Southwest Marine, Inc., 236 F.3d 985 (9th Cir. 2000) (standing found based on curtailed use of bay for recreation due to concern about stormwater discharges); Ecological Rights Foundation v. Pacific Lumber Co., 230 F.3d 1141 (9th Cir. 2000) (standing does not require regular or continuous use of an area); Pennsylvania Public Interest Research Group, Inc. v. P.H. Glatfelter Co., 128 F. Supp. 2d 747 (M.D. Pa. 2001) (standing upheld where plaintiffs alleged their recreational use of stream was adversely affected by the discoloration of the water); Idaho Rural Council v. Bosma, 143 F. Supp. 2d 1169 (D. Id. 2001) (standing to sue neighboring dairy based on alleged contamination of pond).

265. *See* Piney Run Preservation Ass'n v. Comm'r's of Carroll Cty., 268 F.3d 255 (4th Cir. 2001) (plaintiff suing POTW for thermal discharges held to have "injury in fact" where she used river for enjoyment, and expert testimony showed that thermal discharges added to algae build ups in river that detracted from her enjoyment of it); Friends of the Earth v. Gaston Copper Recycling Corp., 204 F.3d 149 (4th Cir. 2000) (en banc) (homeowner who lived downstream of smelter violating NPDES permit had standing based on "reasonable fear and concern about the effects of Gaston Copper's discharge"); Comment, *Pollution, Pollution Everywhere, But Not a Plaintiffs to Be Found; Standing: The Fourth Circuit Judicially Repeals the Citizen Suit Provision of the Clean Water Act*, 39 WASHBURN L. J. 555 (Spring 2000).

266. *See Lujan*, 112 S. Ct. 2130, 2136 (1992); Natural Resources Defense Council, Inc. v. Texaco, 800 F. Supp. 1, 9 (D. Del. 1992).

prove to a scientific certainty that the defendant's unlawful discharge alone caused the plaintiff's precise injury.[267]

Finally, the plaintiff must demonstrate that his or her injuries are likely to be redressed by a favorable decision.[268] When a plaintiff claims injury to waters in which he or she has a cognizable interest, an injunction barring, or civil penalties discouraging, further permit violations will redress the plaintiff's injury.[269]

F. DEFENSES

1. Ongoing Violations and Mootness

The CWA only authorizes citizen suits against a person "alleged to be in violation" of the act.[270] The Supreme Court has construed this language to bar citizen suits over "wholly past" violations.[271] Actionable ongoing violations exist when defendant's violations continued after the date the plaintiff files the complaint, or there is a reasonable likelihood that the defendant will violate the CWA again in the future.[272]

Plaintiffs thus may not sue over one-time violations,[273] although actions such as filling wetlands improperly may be deemed a continuing violation as long as

---

267. *See* Save Our Community v. EPA, 971 F.2d 1155, 1161 (5th Cir. 1992); Public Interest Research Group of N.J., Inc. v. Powell Duffryn Terminals, Inc., 913 F.2d 64, 72 (3d Cir. 1990), *cert. denied*, 489 U.S. 1109, 111 S. Ct. 1018 (1991); Natural Resources Defense Council, Inc. v. Texaco, 800 F. Supp. 1, 9–10 (D. Del. 1992).

268. *See* Valley Forge Christian College v. Americans United for Separation of Church and State, 454 U.S. 464, 472 (D. Del. 1992); Pub. Interest Research Group v. Powell Duffryn Terminals, 913 F.2d 64, 73 (3rd Cir. 1990).

269. *See* Save Our Community v. EPA, 971 F.2d 1155, 1161; Natural Resources Defense Council v. Texaco, 800 F. Supp. 1, 10–11 (D. Del. 1992).

270. 33 U.S.C. § 1365(a)(1).

271. Gwaltney of Smithfield v. Chesapeake Bay Found., 484 U.S. 49, 108 S. Ct. 376, 98 L. Ed. 2d 306 (1987).

272. *See Gwaltney*, 484 U.S. at 108; Sierra Club v. Union Oil Co., 853 F.2d 667, 671 (9th Cir. 1988); Carr v. Altra Verde Indus., Inc., 931 F.2d 1055, 1062 (5th Cir. 1991).

273. *See* Pawtuxet Cove Marina, Inc. v. Ciba-Geigy Corp., 807 F.2d 1089, 1094 (1st Cir. 1986), *cert. denied*, 484 U.S. 975, 108 S. Ct. 484, 98 L. Ed. 2d 483 (1987).

the fill remains.[274] Whether an alleged violation is wholly past or continuing is often an intensely factual issue for the court to resolve.[275]

A defendants' voluntary cessation of discharges that violate the act will not moot a citizen enforcement suit unless it is *"absolutely clear* that the allegedly wrongful behavior could not reasonably be expected to recur."[276]

2. Statute of Limitations

The CWA does not contain a specific statute of limitations. Courts have thus applied the general federal five-year statute of limitations for actions seeking civil penalties to CWA citizen suits,[277] commencing from the date of discovery of the alleged violation.[278] The statute of limitations is tolled either by filing a citizen suit or by providing EPA with a 60-day notice of intent to sue.[279]

---

274. Informed Citizens United, Inc. v. USX Corp., 36 F. Supp. 2d 375 (S.D. Tex. 1999); United States v. Reaves, 923 F. Supp. 1530 (M.D. Fla. 1996); North Carolina Wildlife Federation v. Woodbury, 29 ERC 1941 (E.D.N.C. 1989). *But see* Bettis v. Town of Ontario, 800 F. Supp. 1113 (W.D.N.Y. 1992) (no continuing violation where defendant ceased fill activities but had not removed material); Prisco v. New York, 902 F. Supp. 374 (S.D.N.Y. 1995) (no continuing violation found where defendant discharged to wetland in distant past, but had not continued to do so for years).

275. *See, e.g.,* Russian River Watershed Protection Comm. v. City of Santa Rosa, 142 F.3d 1136 (9th Cir. 1998) (plaintiffs did not establish continuing violations or likely reoccurrence of past sporadic violations); Hamker v. Diamond Shamrock Chemical Co., 756 F.2d 392, 397 (5th Cir. 1985) ("continuing residual effects resulting from a discharge are not equivalent to a continuing discharge"); Friends of Sante Fe Co. v. LAC Minerals, 892 F. Supp. 1333, 1354 (D.N.M. 1995) ("migration of residual contamination resulting from previous releases is not an ongoing discharge"); Sierra Club v. Colorado Refining Co., 838 F. Supp. 1428, 1434 (D. Colo. 1993) (CWA violation occurs if a refinery continues to discharge pollutants into soils and tributary groundwater that then makes its way into water body); Idaho Rural Council v. Bosma, 143 F. Supp. 2d 1169 (D. Id. 2001) (plaintiffs provided sufficient evidence of past violations to argue that violations are likely to recur at CAFO).

276. *Laidlaw Env'tl Serv.*, 528 U.S. at 708, quoting United States v. Concentrated Phosphate Export Assn., 393 U.S. 199, 203, 89 S. Ct. 361, 21 L. Ed. 2d 344 (1968). *See also Carr*, 931 F.2d at 1064; Pawtuxet Cove Marina, Inc. v. Ciba-Geigy Corp., 807 F.2d 1089, 1094 (1st Cir. 1986) (there was no reasonable likelihood of recurring violation where the facility has shut down); San Francisco Baykeeper v. Tidewater Sand & Gravel Co., 46 ERC 1780, 1786 (N.D. Ca. 1997) (possibility of continuing violations found where sand and gravel operator had installed stormwater control devices, but had "not demonstrated that there is no real likelihood that its past noncompliance will recur").

277. 28 U.S.C. § 2462; Public Interest Research Group of N.J., Inc. v. Powell Duffryn Terminals, Inc., 913 F.2d 64, 75 (3d Cir. 1990), *cert. denied*, 489 U.S. 1109, 111 S. Ct. 1018, 112 L. Ed. 2d 1100 (1991); New York v. PVS Chemicals, Inc., 50 F. Supp. 2d 171 (W.D.N.Y. 1998).

278. Public Interest Research Group of New Jersey v. Powell Duffryn Terminals, Inc., 913 F.2d 64 (3d Cir. 1990); Atlantic States Legal Foundation v. Al Tech Specialty Steel Corp., 635 F. Supp. 284, 287 (N.D.N.Y. 1986); Mutual Life Insurance Co. v. Mobil Corp., 1998 U.S. Dist. LEXIS 4513 (N.D.N.Y. Mar. 31, 1998).

279. *See Sierra Club v. Chevron*, 834 F.2d 1517, 1523 (9th Cir. 1987).

G. INTERVENTION

The EPA is entitled to intervene in any citizen suit to which it is not already a party.[280] In appropriate cases, citizen groups or others may also intervene in enforcement actions brought by the United States.[281]

H. REMEDIES

Remedies available to the government under the CWA, such as penalties and injunctive relief, generally are available to citizen plaintiffs. The following discussion points out where the law differs for citizen plaintiffs.

1. Civil Penalties

As with EPA-initiated lawsuits, the CWA gives courts wide latitude to impose in citizen suits "any appropriate civil penalties under section 1319(d)" of the act.[282] Penalties are authorized of up to $27,500 per day per violation.[283] Once a court has determined that a defendant has violated the act, it must impose civil penalties.[284]

Penalties must be paid to the U.S. Treasury, not to the citizen enforcers.[285] This provision, however, does not prohibit settlements requiring defendants to pay funds for other purposes, such as "supplemental environmental projects." If the amount paid to settle a case, however, is not denominated a "penalty," it may carry no preclusive effect for subsequent litigation regarding the same violations.[286]

---

280. 33 U.S.C. § 1365(c)(2).

281. *See* Sierra Club v. EPA, 995 F.2d 1478 (9th Cir. 1993); EPA v. City of Green Forest, Ark., 921 F.2d 1394 (8th Cir. 1990); United States v. Metropolitan St. Louis Sewer Dist., 874 F.2d 588 (8th Cir. 1989).

282. 33 U.S.C. § 1365(a).

283. 33 U.S.C. § 1319(d); 40 C.F.R. pt. 19; *see* note 2 *infra*.

284. *See* Atlantic States Legal Found. v. Tyson Foods, Inc., 897 F.2d 1128, 1142 (11th Cir. 1990); Chesapeake Bay Found. v. Gwaltney of Smithfield, Ltd., 890 F.2d 690, 697 (4th Cir. 1989); Atlantic States Legal Found., Inc. v. Universal Tool & Stamping Co., 786 F. Supp. 743, 754 (N.D. Ind. 1992); Friends of the Earth v. Archer Daniels Midland Co., 780 F. Supp. 95, 100 (N.D.N.Y. 1992).

285. Gwaltney of Smithfield v. Chesapeake Bay Foundation, Inc., 484 U.S. 49, 53, 108 S. Ct. 376, 379, 98 L. Ed. 2d 306 (1987); Sierra Club v. Chevron, USA, Inc., 834 F.2d 1417, 1522 (9th Cir. 1987); Atlantic States Legal Foundation, Inc. v. Universal Tool & Stamping Co., Inc., 786 F. Supp. 743 (N.D. Ind. 1992).

286. Citizens for a Better Environment v. UNOCAL, 83 F.3d 1111 (9th Cir. 1996) (defendant paid $780,000 to settle case, but avoided use of the word "penalty" in the settlement document with the state; hence, because UNOCAL has not paid a "penalty," the section 309(g)(6)(A)(iii) bar to citizen suits did not apply).

2. Department of Justice Comments on Consent Decrees

Under section 505(c)(3), the Department of Justice is also entitled to comment on all consent decrees before they are entered.[287] The department often objects to consent decrees that require the discharger to pay monies to entities other than the U.S. Treasury.[288] The Ninth Circuit has held, however, that "[t]he provisions of the Act provide no limitation on the type of payments to which parties to citizens' suits can agree in a settlement."[289]

The department also sometimes objects to consent decrees that require a defendant to take remedial actions that are not closely related to the alleged CWA violations.[290] In doing so, the federal government usually refers to EPA's Settlement Policy and its "nexus" requirement. Courts are not bound by EPA's Settlement Policy when deciding whether to approve a proposed consent decree.[291] Courts are split, however, regarding whether to apply EPA's nexus requirement in particular cases nonetheless.[292]

3. Attorneys' Fees and Costs

The CWA authorizes courts to award "costs of litigation (including reasonable attorney and expert witness) fees to any party, whenever the court determines [an]

---

287. 33 U.S.C. § 1365(c)(3). *See also* 40 C.F.R. § 135.5 (EPA regulations regarding review of consent decrees).

288. *See* Comment, *Polluter-Financed Environmentally Beneficial Expenditures: Effective Use or Improper Abuse of Citizen Suits Under the Clean Water Act*, 21 ENV'TL L. 175, 197 (1991).

289. Sierra Club v. Electronic Controls Design, Inc., 909 F.2d 1350, 1356 (9th Cir. 1990). The court noted that the legislative history supports settlements that "preserve the punitive nature of enforcement actions while putting the funds collected to use on behalf of environmental protection." *Id.* at 1355.

290. *See* Atlantic States Legal Found., Inc. v. Simco Leather Corp., 755 F. Supp. 59 (N.D.N.Y. 1991); Friends of the Earth v. Archer Daniels Midland Co., 31 Env't Rep. Cas. (BNA) 1779 (N.D.N.Y. 1990), *aff'd on different grounds upon reconsideration*, 780 F. Supp. 95 (N.D.N.Y. 1992); Pennsylvania Env'tl Defense Found. v. Bellefonte Borough, 718 F. Supp. 431, 435 (M.D. Pa. 1989).

291. *Simco Leather*, 755 F. Supp. at 61; Friends of Earth v. Archer Daniels Midland Co., 31 Env't Rep. Cas. (BNA) 1778, 1782 (N.D.N.Y. 1990); *Pennsylvania Env'tl Defense Found.*, 718 F. Supp. 431, 437 (M.D. Pa. 1989).

292. *See Simco Leather*, 755 F. Supp. 59 (approving payment of money for study of nonpoint source pollution in river); Friends of Earth v. Archer Daniels Midland Co., 31 Env't Rep. Cas. (BNA) 1779 (flatly rejecting nexus requirement and concluding that payment of funds to environmental conservation organizations furthered the goals of the Act); Pennsylvania Env'tl Defense Found. v. Bellefonte Borough, 718 F. Supp. 431 (M.D. Pa. 1989) (rejecting consent decree involving payment to Trout Unlimited because there was no requirement that money would be used to address the environmental effects of the defendant's violations).

award is appropriate."[293] Until recently, courts awarded fees when citizen suits were deemed the "catalyst" for a defendants' compliance with the CWA, even if no final judgment resulted.[294] In 2001, the Supreme Court held that the "catalyst theory" is not an appropriate basis for award of fees under two federal civil right statutes that limit fee awards only to the "prevailing party."[295] Because the CWA fee provision does not employ a strict "prevailing party" standard,[296] however, and because the legislative history suggests that Congress expressly intended to provide fees to citizen groups when their enforcement actions result in compliance with the act,[297] fee awards may still be made under the CWA using a "catalyst" approach.

The amount of attorneys' fees awarded in CWA citizen suits typically is determined by the "lodestar" amount.[298] The court determines the number of hours reasonably expended on the case (taking into account the extent of plaintiff's success),[299] times a reasonable hourly rate. A reasonable hourly rate is equal to the prevailing rate in the community for similar work.[300] Evidence on this issue

293. 33 U.S.C. § 1365(d).

294. Armstrong v. Asarco Inc., 138 F.3d 382, 46 ERC 1471 (8th Cir. 1998); Atlantic States Legal Found., Inc. v. Eastman Kodak Co., 933 F.2d 124, 127-28 (2d Cir. 1991); Colorado Env'tl Coalition v. Romer, 796 F. Supp. 457 (D. Colo. 1992). *See also* Idaho Conservation League, Inc. v. Russell, 946 F.2d 717 (9th Cir. 1991) (affirming catalyst theory but denying fees under facts of case).

295. Buckhannon Board and Care Home, Inc. v. West Virginia Dept. of Health and Human Resources, 532 U.S. 598, 121 S. Ct. 1835 (2001).

296. The CWA authorizes fees to a "prevailing party or substantially prevailing party, whenever the court determines such award is appropriate." 33 U.S.C. § 1365(d).

297. The CWA fee provision is similar to that of the Clean Air Act, which also uses a "whenever . . . appropriate" standard. 42 U.S.C. § 7604(d). In Ruckelshaus v. Sierra Club, 463 U.S. 680 (1983), the Supreme Court construed the meaning and intent of this language, and held that it extends "to suit that forced defendants to abandon illegal conduct, although without a formal court order." 463 U.S. at 686. Because *Buckhannon* does not cite *Ruckelshaus,* it does not address the "whenever . . . appropriate" standard of the CWA, CAA, Endangered Species Act, and other similar statutes. *See* Center for Biological Diversity v. Norton, 262 F.3d 1077 (10th Cir. 2001) (holding inapplicable under ESA).

298. *See* Hensley v. Eckerhart, 461 U.S. 424, 433 (1983) (lodestar method is a "useful starting point for determining the amount of a reasonable fee"); Copeland v. Marshall, 641 F.2d 880, 891 (D.C. Cir. 1980) (en banc).

299. Armstrong v. Asarco Inc., 149 F.3d 872 (8th Cir. 1998); Public Interest Research Group of New Jersey v. Air Force Dep't, 51 F.3d 1179 (3d Cir. 1995).

300. Copeland v. Marshall, 641 F.2d at 892; Proffitt v. Municipal Auth. of Morrisville, 716 F. Supp. 845, 852 (E.D. Pa. 1989), *aff'd*, 897 F.2d 523 (3d Cir. 1990).

is usually presented by affidavit.[301] As long as lawyers bringing citizen suits keep accurate, contemporaneous records,[302] they can recover fees at a market-based rate, even though greater than the below-market rates often charged by lawyers practicing public interest law.

---

301. Wilderness Soc'y v. Morton, 495 F.2d 1026, 1037 (D.C. Cir. 1974) (en banc), *rev'd on other grounds sub nom,* Alyeska Pipeline Serv. Co. v. Wilderness Soc., 421 U.S. 240, 95 S. Ct. 1612, 44 L. Ed. 2d 141 (1975).

302. Citizens Coordinating Comm. on Friendship Heights, Inc. v. Washington Metro. Area Transit Auth., 568 F. Supp. 825, 828 (D.D.C. 1983).

CHAPTER 12

Judicial Review: Section 509

KAREN M. MCGAFFEY

I. Jurisdiction

The Clean Water Act (CWA) has several provisions that delineate the jurisdiction of the federal district and appellate courts over suits brought pursuant to the act.[1] Section 509 sets forth the procedure for challenging EPA rule-makings. Section 309 establishes judicial review procedures for EPA and Army Corps of Engineers (Corps) civil and criminal enforcement actions. This chapter focuses on the former, EPA rule-makings. In crafting Section 509, Congress tried to clearly define which lawsuits belonged in which courts. Despite Congress's attempts to clarify the federal court process, uncertainty remains regarding the proper jurisdiction for judicial review of some Environmental Protection Agency (EPA) actions taken under the CWA.

A. FEDERAL COURT OF APPEALS

Clean Water Act Section 509(b)(1)[2] provides for direct review by the federal courts of appeals of seven types of actions taken by the Administrator of the EPA:

1. Standards of performance promulgated under section 306 (33 U.S.C. Section 1316);

---

1. *See* S. Rep. No.1196, 91st Cong., 2d Sess. 40 (1970).
2. 33 U.S.C. § 1369(b)(1).

2. Determinations made pursuant to section 306(b)(1)(C) (33 U.S.C. Section 1316(b)(1)(c));
3. Effluent standards, prohibitions, or pretreatment standards promulgated under section 307 (33 U.S.C. Section 1317);[3]
4. Determinations as to state permit programs submitted under section 402(b) (33 U.S.C. Section 1342(b));[4]
5. The approval or promulgation of effluent limitations or other limitations under section 301, 302, or 306 (33 U.S.C. Section 1311, 1312, or 1316);
6. The issuance or denial of permits under section 402 (33 U.S.C. Section 1342);[5] and
7. The promulgation of individual control strategies under section 304 (33 U.S.C. Section 1314(l)).[6]

Congress included section 509(b)(1) as part of the 1972 amendments to the CWA in the hope of streamlining decision-making and guaranteeing prompt high-level judicial review of the specified administrative actions.[7] In addition to having jurisdiction over these specified actions, the federal courts of appeals also have exclusive jurisdiction over petitions to compel EPA to take these actions.[8]

Courts have often construed section 509(b)(1)'s jurisdictional grant narrowly, insisting that the courts of appeals may review only those EPA actions that are clearly and expressly included among the actions identified in subsections (A) through (G).[9] They reason that the complexity and specificity with which the

---

3. *See* Maier v. EPA, 114 F.3d 1032, 1038 (10th Cir. 1997) (courts of appeals have jurisdiction to review EPA action in denying petition to initiate rule making to establish secondary pretreatment standards), *cert. denied*, 522 U.S. 1014 (1997).

4. *See* American Forest & Paper Ass'n v. EPA, 137 F.3d 291, 295 (5th Cir. 1998).

5. *See* 33 U.S.C. § 1369(b)(1); *see also* City of Ames v. Reilly, 986 F.2d 253 (8th Cir. 1993) (discussing what constitutes issuance or denial).

6. *See* 33 U.S.C. § 1369(b)(1)(G). This section authorizes review of EPA-promulgated individual control strategies only, not EPA decisions to list water segments or dischargers under section 304(l). Lake Cumberland Trust, Inc. v. EPA, 954 F.2d 1218 (6th Cir. 1992); Municipal Auth. of St. Marys v. EPA, 945 F.2d 67 (3d Cir. 1991); Roll Coater, Inc. v. Reilly, 932 F.3d 668 (7th Cir. 1991). It also does not authorize federal appellate review of state listings or individual control strategies under section 304(l), or even EPA approval of those state decisions. Boise Cascade Corp. v. EPA, 942 F.2d 1427 (9th Cir. 1991), P.H. Glatfelter Co. v. EPA, 921 F.2d 516 (4th Cir. 1990).

7. Shell Oil Co. v. Train, 415 F. Supp. 70 (N.D. Cal. 1976), *aff'd*, 585 F.2d 408 (9th Cir. 1978); *see also* Central Hudson Gas & Elec. Corp. v. EPA, 587 F.2d 549 (2d Cir. 1978) (explaining that Congress enacted Section 505(b)(1) in order to save litigants time and procedural steps).

8. *Maier*, 114 F.3d at 1038.

9. *See e.g.,* Pacific Legal Found. v. Costle, 586 F.2d 650 (9th Cir. 1978), *rev'd on other grounds*, 445 U.S. 198,100 S. Ct. 1095, 63 L. Ed. 2d 329 (1980); Bethlehem Steel Corp. v. EPA, 538 F.2d 513 (2d Cir. 1976).

actions in section 509(b)(1) are set forth suggests that Congress intended to strictly limit the jurisdiction of the courts of appeals.[10] Other courts have constructed section 509(b)(1) somewhat more expansively, emphasizing Congress's intent to provide prompt, high-level review of agency actions that can be readily evaluated based on an administrative record developed by the agency.

Subsections 509(b)(1)(E) and (F) authorizing review of the certain against regarding "effluent limitations" and NPDES permits appear to have generated the most confusion and controversy. Subsection (E) authorizes review of EPA's "approval or promulgation of effluent limitations or other limitations under sections 301, 302 or 306." Courts have concluded that this provision authorizes direct appellate review of effluent limitations guidelines promulgated pursuant to section 304[11] and section 316 regulations concerning the location of cooling structures,[12] essentially concluding that they were closely related to effluent limitations promulgated under sections 301 and 306. Meanwhile, courts have concluded that total maximum daily loads (TMDLs),[13] section 309 compliance orders,[14] and antidegradation policies[15] are not effluent limitations subject to direct review by the courts of appeals.

Subsection (F) authorizes appellate review of the EPA "issuance or denial of permits under section 402." This section plainly authorizes review of EPA-issued NPDES permits in the courts of appeals,[16] but it does not authorize federal courts to review state-issued NPDES permits.[17] Under previous Clean Water Act provisions that allowed EPA to veto state-issued permits, EPA's decision to veto a permit was reviewable in the courts of appeals.[18] Under the current statutory structure, however, EPA may object to a state-issued permit and later issue a permit

---

10. Bethlehem Steel Corp. v. EPA, 538 F.2d 513 (2d Cir. 1976).

11. E.I. du Pont de Nemours & Co. v. Train, 430 U.S. 112, 97 S. Ct. 965, 51 L. Ed. 2d 204 (1977).

12. Virginia Elec. & Power Co. v. Costle, 566 F.2d 446 (4th Cir. 1977); *see also* Modine Mfg. Corp. v. Kay, 791 F.2d 267 (3d Cir. 1986) (interpreting subparagraph (C) broadly to permit review of EPA interpretations of the applicability of pretreatment standards).

13. Longview Fibre Co. v. Rasmussen, 980 F.2d 1307 (9th Cir. 1992). TMDLs are addressed in chapter 10.

14. Ackels v. EPA, 7 F.3d 862, 869 (9th Cir. 1993); City of Baton Rouge v. EPA, 620 F.2d 478 (5th Cir. 1980).

15. American Paper Inst. v. EPA, 890 F.2d 869, 877 (7th Cir. 1989).

16. Defenders of Wildlife v. Browner, 191 F.3d 1159, 1162 (9th Cir. 1999).

17. American Paper Inst. v. EPA, 890 F.2d 869, 875 (7th Cir. 1989); District of Columbia v. Schramm, 631 F.2d 854, 863 (D.C. Cir. 1980); Mianus River Preservation Comm. v. Administrator of EPA, 541 F.2d 899, 906 (2d Cir. 1976).

18. Crown Simpson Pulp Co. v. Costle, 445 U.S. 193, 196 (1980); District of Columbia v. Schramm, 631 F.2d 854, 859 (D.C. Cir. 1980).

itself, if the state does not adequately address its objection. EPA's mere objection to a permit is not subject to appellate review,[19] although EPA's ultimate issuance of a permit following objections is subject to review.[20] EPA's decision not to veto or object to a permit is discretionary, and is not reviewable in federal court.[21]

For those EPA actions listed in section 509(b)(1), a petitioner must seek review in the court of appeals for the federal judicial district where the petitioner resides or where the petitioner transacts business that would be affected by the EPA Administrator's action.[22] Petitions for review of these actions must be filed within 120 days of the Administrator's action.[23] A defendant in an administrative, civil, or criminal enforcement proceeding may not challenge the actions listed in section 509(b)(1) "collaterally" as a defense to the enforcement action.[24]

B. DISTRICT COURT JURISDICTION

Petitioners can challenge EPA actions in federal district court on "federal question" grounds,[25] and pursuant to the Administrative Procedure Act[26] and other related statutes,[27] unless section 509(b)(1) vests exclusive jurisdiction in the

---

19. American Paper Inst. v. EPA, 890 F.2d 869, 875 (7th Cir. 1989)

20. City of Ames, Iowa v. Reilly, 986 F.2d 253, 256 (8th Cir. 1993).

21. District of Columbia v. Schramm, 631 F.2d 854, 860 (D.C. Cir. 1980); Mianus River Preservation Comm. v. Administrator of EPA, 541 F.2d 899, 904 (2d Cir. 1976).

22. See Tenneco Oil Co. v. EPA, 592 F.2d 897 (5th Cir. 1979) (holding that the court had jurisdiction and venue to hear the case because the regulation of offshore operations significantly affected the business of the petitioners within the circuit); Peabody Coal Co. v. EPA, 522 F.2d 1152 (8th Cir. 1975) (holding that the court had jurisdiction and venue to hear the case because the petitioner transacted business in the circuit and that business was affected by the challenged permit even though it applied to mining operations located in another circuit).

23. 33 U.S.C. § 1369(b)(1); see also Ackels v. EPA, 7 F.3d 862, 869 (9th Cir. 1993).

24. 33 U.S.C. § 1369(b)(2); see also General Motors Corp. v. EPA, 168 F.3d 1377, 1383 (D.C. Cir. 1999); Public Interest Res. Group. of N.J. v. Powell Duffryn Terminals, Inc., 913 F.2d 64, 78 (3d Cir. 1990), cert denied, 498 U.S. 1109 (1991); Natural Resources Defense Council v. Outboard Marine Corp., 702 F. Supp. 690, 694 (N.D. Ill. 1988).

25. 29 U.S.C. § 1331; see also Natural Resources Defense Council, Inc. v. Callaway, 524 F.2d 79 (2d Cir. 1975).

26. 5 U.S.C. §§ 701–706; Washington v. EPA, 573 F.2d 583 (9th Cir. 1978).

27. 28 U.S.C. § 1361 (mandamus) and 28 U.S.C. § 1337 (commerce and antitrust); see Chesapeake Bay Found., Inc. v. United States, 445 F. Supp. 1349 (E.D. Va. 1978) (mandamus statute grants court jurisdiction to hear claim that an environmental impact statement is required in connection with NPDES but not to hear claim that EPA failed to object to NPDES permit issued by state); P.F.Z. Properties, Inc. v. Train, 393 F. Supp. 1370 (D.D.C. 1975) (court has jurisdiction to hear declaratory judgment action claiming that EPA and Army Corps of Engineers had violated the CWA by attempting to exercise jurisdiction over certain waters).

courts of appeals. The CWA does not impose any time limit for filing challenges to EPA actions in district court.

The CWA grants the federal district courts jurisdiction over suits brought by the EPA Administrator[28] and citizens[29] to enforce the provisions of the CWA. Enforcement actions are addressed more specifically in chapter 8. The CWA does not preempt the right of citizens to bring suit under other statutes or the common law.[30] As several courts have pointed out, Congress intended to create additional enforcement mechanisms, not to eliminate existing ones, when it enacted the CWA citizen suit provision.[31]

II. Justiciability: Ripeness and Exhaustion of Administrative Remedies

A. RIPENESS

The doctrine of ripeness prevents the courts from interfering with administrative decisions until they are final and their effects are felt in a concrete way.[32] The doctrine requires that a reviewing court determine whether the challenged action is fit for review and the denial of judicial review will cause hardship to the parties.[33] An action is fit for review if it is final and concerns purely legal questions.[34]

The doctrine has been applied in a number of CWA cases in order to defeat jurisdiction. In *Municipality of Anchorage v. United States,*[35] for instance, the court held that a challenge to a CWA memorandum of agreement between the Army Corps of Engineers and the EPA was not ripe because the memorandum of agreement had not yet been applied in a particular case. Similarly, in *New*

---

28. 33 U.S.C. § 1319(b).

29. 33 U.S.C. § 1365(a).

30. 33 U.S.C. § 1365(e). *But see* City of Milwaukee v. Illinois and Mich., 451 U.S. 304, 101 S. Ct. 1784, 68 L. Ed. 2d 114 (1981) (holding that state does not have a federal common law remedy for abatement of a nuisance); Middlesex County Sewerage Auth. v. National Sea Clammers Ass'n, 453 U.S. 1, 101 S. Ct. 2615, 69 L. Ed. 2d 435 (1981) (holding that no federal common law nuisance claim is available for alleged damage to fishing grounds caused by discharge of sewage because underlying legal basis for claims was preempted by CWA).

31. Natural Resources Defense Council, Inc. v. Train, 510 F.2d 692 (D.C. Cir. 1974).

32. Abbott Laboratories v. Gardner, 387 U.S. 136, 148, 87 S. Ct. 1507, 1515, 18 L. Ed. 2d 681 (1967), *overruled on other grounds*, Califano v. Sanders, 430 U.S. 99, 97 S. Ct. 980, 51 L. Ed. 2d 192 (1977); *see also* Assiniboine & Sioux Tribes v. Board of Oil & Gas Conservation, 792 F.2d 782 (9th Cir. 1986).

33. *Abbott Laboratories,* 387 U.S. at 148, 87 S. Ct. at 1515.

34. *Id.* at 149; 87 S. Ct. at 1515.

35. 980 F.2d 1320, 1323–25 (9th Cir. 1992).

Hanover Township v. U.S. Army Corps of Engineers,[36] the court held that a challenge to the Corps's decision to allow a landfill to be built pursuant to a general permit was not ripe because the landowner could not begin construction or operation of the landfill until he had obtained several other permits.[37]

B. EXHAUSTION OF REMEDIES

The courts generally require plaintiffs to exhaust their administrative remedies before filing a case in federal court.[38] For example, before challenging an EPA-issued NPDES permit, parties must request an administrative hearing before EPA's Environmental Appeal Board and file an appeal with the Administrator.[39]

---

36. 992 F.2d 470, 472–73 (3d Cir. 1993).

37. *See also* Howell v. U.S. Army Corps of Eng'rs, 794. F. Supp. 1072 (D.N.M. 1992) (holding that a challenge to the Corps's authority to issue cease-and-desist letter under CWA was not ripe for review because no factual determination had been made that property at issue in case contained wetlands and review would not promote effective enforcement by agency).

38. Plaintiffs generally need not exhaust available administrative remedies before filing citizen suits under section 505. *See* Susquehanna Valley Alliance v. Three Mile Island Nuclear Reactor, 619 F.2d 231 (3d Cir. 1980), *cert. denied,* 449 U.S. 1096,101 S. Ct. 893, 66 L. Ed. 2d 824 (1981). For a more detailed discussion of citizen suits, see chapter 8.

39. *See* Ackels v. EPA, 7 F.3d 862, 869 (9th Cir. 1993).

TABLE OF CASES

Abbott Laboratories v. Gardner, 387 U.S. 136, 87 S. Ct. 1507, 1515, 18 L. Ed. 2d 681 (1967), *overruled on other grounds,* Califano v. Sanders, 430 U.S. 99, 97 S. Ct. 980, 51 L. Ed. 2d 192 (1977), 277nn.32, 33

Abenaki Nation of Mississquoi v. Hughes, 805 F. Supp. 234 (D. Vt. 1992), 109n.64

Ackels v. EPA, 7 F.3d 862 (9th Cir. 1993), 275n.14, 276n.23, 278n.39

Advanced Electronics, *In re,* 2000 EPA ALJ LEXIS 64 (Aug. 15, 2000), 87n.27

Alaska Center for the Environment v. Browner, 20 F.3d 981 (9th Cir. 1994), 260n.224, 261n.234, 262n.236

Alaska Center for the Environment v. Reilly, 762 F. Supp. 1422 (W.D. Wash. 1991), *aff'd sub nom.* Alaska Center for the Env't v. Browner, 20 F.3d 981 (9th Cir. 1994), 211n.43, 262n.236

Allegany Env. Action Coalition v. Westinghouse Corp., 46 Env't Rep. Cas. (BNA) 1126 (W.D. Pa. 1998), 15n.46

Allens Creek/Corbetts Glen Pres. Group, Inc. v. West, 2001 WL 87434 (2d Cir. Jan. 31, 2001), 231nn.79, 81

Alyeska Pipeline Serv. Co. v. Wilderness Soc., 421 U.S. 240, 95 S. Ct. 1612, 44 L. Ed. 2d 141 (1975), 272n.301

American Canoe Ass'n, Inc. v. EPA, 30 F. Supp. 2d 908 (E.D. Va. 1998), 210n.35, 211nn.38, 43, 262n.236

American Canoe Ass'n, Inc. v. EPA, 46 F. Supp. 2d 473 (E.D. Va. 1999), 210n.34

American Canoe Ass'n, Inc. v. EPA, 54 F. Supp. 2d 621 (E.D. Va. 1999), 218n.87

American Forest & Paper Ass'n v. EPA, 137 F.3d 291 (5th Cir. 1998), 274n.4

American Frozen Food Inst. v. Train, 539 F.2d 107 (D.C. Cir. 1976), 22n.80

American Iron & Steel Inst. v. EPA, 526 F.2d 1027 (3d Cir. 1975), 22n.80, 23n.88

American Littoral Soc'y v. EPA, 199 F. Supp. 2d 217 (D.N.J. 2002), 213n.51, 218n.87

American Meat Inst. v. EPA, 526 F.2d 442 (7th Cir. 1975), 20n.68

American Mining Congress v. EPA, 965 F.2d 759 (9th Cir. 1992), 165n.12

American Paper Inst. v. EPA, 890 F.2d 869 (7th Cir. 1989), 275nn.15, 17, 276n.19

American Paper Inst. v. Train, 543 F.2d 328 (D.C. Cir. 1976), 22n.81, 23n.89

American Petroleum Inst. v. EPA, 661 F.2d 340 (5th Cir. 1981), 22n.83

Arkansas Poultry Federation v. EPA, 852 F.2d 324 (8th Cir. 1998), 85n.18

Arkansas v. Oklahoma, 503 U.S. 91 (1992), 209n.29

Arkansas Wildlife Federation v. ICI Americas, Inc., 29 F.3d 376 (8th Cir. 1994), 264n.251

Armstrong v. Asarco Inc., 138 F.3d 382 (8th Cir. 1998), 271n.294

Armstrong v. Asarco Inc., 149 F.3d 872 (8th Cir. 1998), 271n.299

Ashcroft v. Department of the Army Corps of Engineers, 526 F. Supp. 660 (W.D. Mich. 1980), 109n.65

Assiniboine & Sioux Tribes v. Board of Oil & Gas Conservation, 792 F.2d 782 (9th Cir. 1986), 277n.32

Association of Pac. Fisheries v. EPA, 615 F.2d 794 (9th Cir. 1980), 22n.83

Association of Significantly Impacted Neighbors v. City of Livonia, 765 F. Supp. 389 (E.D. Mich. 1991), 262n.238

Atlantic States Legal Foundation, Inc. v. Eastman Kodak Co., 933 F.2d 124 (2d Cir. 1991), 271n.294

Atlantic States Legal Foundation, Inc. v. Simco Leather Corp., 755 F. Supp. 59 (N.D.N.Y. 1991), 270nn.290, 291, 292

Atlantic States Legal Foundation, Inc. v. Tyson Foods, Inc., 897 F.2d at 1134, 231nn.77, 78, 233nn.91, 93, 94, 269n.284

Atlantic States Legal Foundation, Inc. v. Universal Tool & Stamping Co., 735 F. Supp. 1404 (N.D. Ind. 1990), 259n.220, 264n.254

Atlantic States Legal Foundation, Inc. v. Universal Tool & Stamping Co., 786 F. Supp. 743 (N.D. Ind. 1992), 257n.213, 269nn.284, 285

Atlantic States Legal Foundation v. A1 Tech Specialty Steel Corp., 635 F. Supp. 284 (N.D.N.Y. 1986), 268n.278

Atlantic States Legal Foundation v. Eastman Kodak Co., 12 F.3d 353 (2d. Cir. 1993), 53n.71, 230n.71

Atlantic States Legal Foundation v. Stroh Die Casting, 116 F.3d 814 (7th Cir. 1997), *cert. denied,* 118 S. Ct. 442 (1997), 263n.248

Avoyelles Sportsmen's League v. Marsh, 715 F.2d 897 (5th Cir. 1983), 108n.50, 121n.145, 122n.146

Baughman v. Bradford Coal Co., 592 F.2d 215 (3d Cir. 1979), *cert. denied,* 441 U.S. 961, 99 S. Ct. 2406, 60 L. Ed. 2d 1066 (1970), 264n.251

B&B Partnership v. United States, 133 F.3d 913 (4th Cir. 1997), 116n.119

Beartooth Alliance v. Crown Butte Mines, 904 F. Supp. 1168, 26 ELR 20639 (D. Mont. 1995), 226n.46, 261n.232

Bersani v. EPA, 850 F.2d 36 (2d Cir. 1988), 115n.113

Bethlehem Steel Corp. v. EPA, 538 F.2d 513 (2d Cir. 1976), 274n.9, 275n.10

Bettis v. Town of Ontario, 800 F. Supp. 1113 (W.D.N.Y. 1992), 268n.274

B.J. Carney Industries, Inc., *In re,* 7 E.A.D. 171 (EAB 1997), *appeal dismissed,* 192 F.3d 917, 49 ERC 1252 (9th Cir. 1999), *dismissal vacated,* 200 F.3d 1222 (9th Cir. 2000), 239n.137

Board of Trustees v. City of Painesville, 200 F.3d 396 (6th Cir. 1999), 259n.221, 264n.249

Boca Ciega Hotel v. Bouchard Transp. Co., 51 F.3d 235 (11th Cir. 1995), 156n.141

Boise Cascade Corp. v. EPA, 942 F.2d 1427 (9th Cir. 1991), 274n.6

Borden Ranch Partnership v. United States Army Corps of Engineers, 261 F.3d 810 (9th Cir. 2001), *aff'd per curium,* 123 S. Ct. 599 (2002), 108n.48, 109n.57, 121n.145, 122nn.150, 152, 227n.54, 233n.94

Borden Ranch Partnership v. United States Army Corps of Engineers, 1999 U.S. Dist LEXIS 21389 (E.D. Cal. 1999), *aff'd,* 261 F.3d 810 (9th Cir. 2001), *aff'd per curium,* 123 S. Ct. 599 (2002), 123n.154

Bragg v. Robertson, 72 F. Supp. 2d 642 (S.D. W.Va. 1999), *aff'd in part, vacated in part,* 248 F.3d 275 (4th Cir. 2001), 260n.228

Broadwater Farms Joint Venture v. United States, 45 Fed. C. 154 (Ct. Cl. 1999), 128

Buckhannon Board and Care Home, Inc. v. West Virginia Dept. of Health and Human Resources, 532 U.S. 598, 121 S. Ct. 1835 (2001), 271n.295

Burnette v. Carothers, 192 F.3d 52 (2d Cir. 1999), 260n.228

Buttrey v. United States, 690 F.2d 1170 (5th Cir. 1982), 117n.126

Califano v. Sanders, 430 U.S. 99, 97 S. Ct. 980, 51 L. Ed. 2d 192 (1977), 277n.32

Carr v. Alta Verde Indus., Inc., 931 F.2d 1055 (5th Cir. 1991), 12n.26, 182n.110, 184n.124, 267n.272, 268n.276

Cascade Conservation League v. M.A. Segale, Inc., 921 F. Supp. 692 (W.D. Wash. 1996), 262n.240

Catskill Mountains Chapter of Trout Unlimited, Inc. v. City of New York, 273 F.3d 481 (2d Cir. 2001), 264n.249

Center for Biological Diversity v. Norton, 262 F.3d 1077 (10th Cir. 2001), 271n.297

Central Hudson Gas & Electric Corp. v. EPA, 587 F.2d 549 (2d Cir. 1978), 274n.7

Cerro Copper Products Co. v. Ruckelshaus, 766 F.2d 1060 (7th Cir. 1985), *transferred to* Natural Resources Defense Council, Inc. v. EPA, 790 F.2d 289 (3rd Cir. 1986), *cert. denied sub nom* Chem. Mfrs. Ass'n v. Natural Resources Defense Council, Inc., 479 U.S. 1084 (1987), 89n.39

Champion Int'l Corp. v. EPA, 850 F.2d 182 (4th Cir. 1988), 52n.65

Chem. Mfrs. Ass'n v. Natural Resources Defense Council, Inc., 470 U.S. 116 (1985), 23n.86

Chem. Mfrs. Ass'n v. Natural Resources Defense Council, Inc., 479 U.S. 1084 (1987), 89n.39

Chesapeake Bay Foundation, Inc. v. United States, 445 F Supp. 1349 (E.D. Va. 1978), 276n.27

Chesapeake Bay Foundation v. Bethlehem Steel Corp., 608 F. Supp. 440 (D. Md. 1985), 228n.59

Chesapeake Bay Foundation v. Gwaltney of Smithfield, Ltd., 890 F.2d 690 (4th Cir. 1989), 269n.284

Citizens Coordinating Comm. on Friendship Heights, Inc. v. Washington Metro. Area Transit Auth., 568 F. Supp. 825 (D.D.C. 1983), 272n.302

Citizens for a Better Environment v. UNOCAL, 83 F.3d 1111 (9th Cir. 1996), 265n.255, 269n.286

Citizens Legal Env'tl Action Network, Inc. v. Premium Standard Farms, Inc., 2000 WL 220464, at *15 (W.D. Mo. Feb. 23, 2000), 223n.19

City National Bank of Miami v. United States, 33 Fed Cl. 759 (Ct. Cl. 1995), 130

City of Alma v. United States, 744 F. Supp. 1546 (S.D. Ga. 1990), 115n.113

City of Ames v. Reilly, 986 F.2d 253 (8th Cir. 1993), 274n.5, 276n.20

City of Baton Rouge v. EPA, 620 F.2d 478 (5th Cir. 1980), 275n.14

City of Kalamazoo Water Reclamation Plant, *In re,* 3 E.A.D. 109 (CJO 1990), 237n.120

City of Marshall, *In re,* 10 E.A.C. (EAB 2001), 240n.139

City of Milwaukee v. Illinois and Michigan, 451 U.S. 304, 101 S. Ct. 1784, 68 L. Ed. 2d 114 (1981), 277n.30

City of New York v. Anglebrook Ltd. P'ship, 891 F. Supp. 900 (S.D.N.Y. 1995), 225n.29

City of Yankton, *In re,* 1993 EPA ALJ LEXIS 288 (Jan. 21, 1993), *aff'd,* 1994 EPA App. LEXIS 44 (July 1994), 86n.20

Coastal Fishermen's Ass'n v. N.Y. City Dept. of Sanitation, 772 F. Supp. 162 (S.D.N.Y. 1991), 258n.217

Colorado Env'tl Coalition v. Romer, 796 F. Supp. 457 (D. Colo. 1992), 271n.294

Commerce Oil Co., *In re,* 847 F.2d 291 (6th Cir. 1988), 232nn.84, 85

Committee to Save Mokelumme River v. East Bay Util. Dist., 13 F.3d 305 (9th Cir. 1993), 12n.21, 259n.223

Commonwealth of Mass. v. U.S. Veterans Admin., 541 F.2d 119, 121n.1 (1st Cir. 1976), 265n.258

Community Ass'n for Restoration of the Env't v. Henry Bosma Dairy, 52 Env't Rep. Cas. (BNA) 1167 (E.D. Wash. 2001), 222n.15

Community Ass'n for Restoration of the Env't v. Henry Bosma Dairy, 65 F. Supp. 2d 1129 (E.D. Wash. 1999), 12n.26, 13n.36, 183n.118

Community Ass'n for Restoration of the Env't v. Sid Koopman Dairy, 54 F. Supp. 2d 976, (E.D. Wash. 1999), 183n.118

Concerned Area Residents for the Environment v. Southview Farm (*Southview Farm*), 34 F.3d 114 (2d Cir. 1994), *cert. denied,* 514 U.S. 1082 (1995), 181n.106, 183n.118, 184, 193n.6

Condor Land Co., *In re,* No. CWA-404-95-106 (ALJ Charneski Dec. 8, 1998), 105

Copeland v. Marshall, 641 F.2d 880 (D.C. Cir. 1980), 271nn.298, 300

Cristina Investment Corp. v. United States, 40 Fed. Cl. 571 (Ct. Cl. 1998), 130n.186

Cross Timbers Concerned Citizens v. Saginaw, 991 F. Supp. 563 (N.D. Tex. 1997), 262n.237

Crown Simpson Pulp Co. v. Costle, 445 U.S. 193 (1980), 275n.18

Culbertson v. Coats American Inc., 42 ERC 1162 (N.D. Ga. 1996), 243n.167

Dague v. City of Burlington, 935 F.2d 1343 (2d Cir. 1991), 12n.28

Defenders of Wildlife v. Ballard, 73 F. Supp. 2d 1094 (D. Ariz. 1999), 260n.225

Defenders of Wildlife v. Browner, 191 F.3d 1159 (9th Cir. 1999), 174, 275n.16

Dioxin/Organochlorine Ctr. v. Clarke, 57 F.3d 1517 (9th Cir. 1995), 212n.46, 213n.53

District of Columbia v. Schramm, 631 F.2d 854 (D.C. Cir. 1980), 52n.65, 262n.239, 275nn.17, 18, 276n.21

Driscoll v. Adams, 181 F.3d 1285 (11th Cir. 1999), 12n.30, 13n.35, 261n.230

Dubois v. Thomas, 820 F.2d 943 (8th Cir. 1987), 223n.22

Ecological Rights Foundation v. Pacific Lumber Co., 230 F.3d 1141 (9th Cir. 2000), 266n.264

E.I. du Pont de Nemours & Co. v. Train, 430 U.S. 112, 97 S. Ct. 965, 51 L. Ed. 2d 204 (1977), 275n.11

EPA v. City of Green Forest, Ark., 921 F.2d 1394 (8th Cir. 1990), 269n.281

Exxon Corp. v. Train, 554 F.2d 1310 (5th Cir. 1977), 15n.46

Fishel v. Westinghouse Electric Corp., 640 F. Supp. 442 (M.D. Pa. 1986), 12n.27

Florida Keys Citizens Coalition v. West, 996 F. Supp. 1254 (S.D. Fla. 1998), 260n.225

Florida Rock Industries v. United States, 18 F.3d 1560 (Fed. Cir. 1994), 124n.157, 127

FMC Corp. v. Train, 539 F.2d 973 (4th Cir. 1976), 22n.80

Forest Properties v. United States, 177 F.3d 1360 (Fed. Cir. 1999), 128

Fox Bay Partners v. U.S. Army Corps of Engineers, 831 F. Supp. 605 (N.D. Ill. 1993), 116n.120

Friends of Frederick Seig Grove # 94 v. Sonoma County Water Agency, 124 F. Supp. 2d 1161 (N.D. Ca. 2000), 263n.248

Friends of Santa Fe County v. LAC Minerals, 892 F. Supp. 1333 (D.N.M. 1995), 15n.48, 268n.275

Friends of the Earth, Inc. v. Laidlaw Env'tl Serv's (TOC), Inc., 528 U.S. 167 (2000), 231n.76, 260, 265, 266, 268n.276

Friends of the Earth v. Archer Daniels Midland Co., 780 S. Supp. 95 (N.D.N.Y. 1992), 269n.284, 270nn.290, 291, 292

Friends of the Earth v. Chevron Chemical, 129 F.3d 826 (5th Cir. 1997), 265n.260

Friends of the Earth v. Gaston Copper Recycling Corp., 204 F.3d 149 (4th Cir. 2000), 266n.265

Friends of the Earth v. Hintz, 800 F.2d 822 (9th Cir. 1986), 117n.125

Friends of the Earth v. U.S. Army Corps of Engineers, 109 F. Supp. 2d 30 (D.D.C. 2000), 260n.225

Friends of the Wild Swan, Inc. v. EPA, 130 F. Supp. 2d 1184 (D. Mont. 1999), 211nn.38, 43, 212n.50, 213nn.51, 52, 216n.73

Froebel v. Meyer, 13 F. Supp. 2d 843 (E.D. Wis. 1998), 109n.59, 260n.228

Gatlin Oil Co. v. United States, 169 F.3d 207 (4th Cir. 1999), 160n.162

Gearhart v. Reilly, Civ. No. 89-6266-HO (D. Or.), 76, 77

Gearhart v. Whitman, Civ. Dist. Ct. No. 89-6266-HO (D. Or.), 78

General Electric Co. v. United States Dept. of Commerce, 128 F.3d 767 (D.C. Cir. 1997), 155n.138

General Motors Corp. v. EPA, 168 F.3d 1377 (D.C. Cir. 1999), 229n.67, 241n.158, 276n.24

Goldman v. United States, 511 U.S. 1071 (1994), 245n.173

Good v. United States, 189 F.3d 1355 (Fed. Cir. 1999), 128

Greene v. Reilly, 956 F.2d 593 (6th Cir. 1992), 263n.246

Gwaltney of Smithfield v. Chesapeake Bay Foundation, Inc., 484 U.S. 49, 108 S. Ct. 376, 98 L. Ed. 2d 306 (1987), 5n.26, 217, 258, 267nn.271, 272, 269n.285

Hallstrom v. Tillamook County, 493 U.S. 20, 110 S. Ct. 304 (1989), 263, 263n.242

Hamker v. Diamond Shamrock Chemical Co., 756 F.2d 392 (5th Cir. 1985), 268n.275

Harmon Industries, Inc. v. Browner, 191 F.3d 894 (8th Cir. 1999), 224n.24

Hawaii's Thousand Friends v. City and County of Honolulu, 821 F. Supp. 1368 (D. Haw. 1993), 257n.213

Hayes v. Browner, 117 F. Supp. 2d 1182 (N.D. Okla. 2000), 211n.43

Hayes v. Whitman, 264 F.3d 1017 (10th Cir. 2001), 210n.33, 211n.43, 212nn.44, 45, 46, 260n.224

Headwaters, Inc. v. Talent Irrigation District, 243 F.3d 526 (9th Cir. 2001), 10, 225n.37, 226n.46, 227n.52, 261n.232

Heck and Associates v. United States, 37 Fed. Cl. 245 (Ct. Cl. 1997), 130n.186

Hensley v. Eckerhart, 461 U.S. 424 (1983), 271n.298

Hobbs v. United States, No. 90-1861, 1991 WL 230202, at *7 (4th Cir. Nov. 8, 1991), 231n.74

Homestake Min. Co. v. EPA, 477 F. Supp. 1279 (D.S.D. 1979), 34nn.151, 154, 158

Howell v. Army Corps of Engineers, 794 F. Supp. 1072 (D. N.M. 1992), 123n.156, 278n.37

Hudson River Fishermen's Ass'n v. City of New York, 751 F. Supp. 1088 (S.D.N.Y. 1990), 11n.13

Hudson Riverkeeper Fund v. Yorktown Heights Sewer Dist., 949 F. Supp. 210 (S.D.N.Y. 1996), 261n.232

Hunt v. Washington State Apple Advertising Comm'n, 432 U.S. 333 (1977), 265n.260

Idaho Conservation League, Inc. v. Russell, 946 F.2d 717 (9th Cir. 1991), 271n.294

Idaho Rural Council v. Bosma, 143 F. Supp. 2d 1169 (D. Idaho 2001), 15nn.46, 48, 264n.254, 266n.264, 268n.276

Idaho Sportsmen's Coalition v. Browner, 951 F. Supp. 962 (W.D. Wash. 1996), 212nn.44, 48, 262n.236

Informed Citizens United, Inc. v. USX Corp., 36 F. Supp. 2d 375 (S.D. Tex. 1999), 121n.141, 268n.274

Inland Steel Co. v. EPA, 574 F.2d 367 (7th Cir. 1978), 53n.68

International Union v. Amerace Corp., 740 F. Supp. 1072 (D.N.J. 1990), 89n.41, 90n.43, 95n.79

Ivani Contracting Corp. v. City of New York, 103 F.3d 257 (2d Cir. 1997), 231n.79

James City County v. EPA, 12 F.3d 1330 (4th Cir. 1993), 115n.113

James River II, Inc. v. State of Washington, Nos. 91–140 *et al.* (Wash. Pollution Control Hrg. Bd. May 15, 1992), 37n.176

Jehovah-Jireh Corp., *In re,* 2001 EPA ALJ LEXIS 42 (July 25, 2001), 87n.26

Johnson v. Colonial Pipeline Co., 830 F. Supp. 309 (E.D. Va. 1993), 156n.141
Jones v. City of Lakeland, 175 F.3d 410 (6th Cir. 1999), 264n.251
Jones v. City of Lakeland, 224 F.3d 518 (6th Cir. 2000), 242n.165, 264n.254

Kara Holding Corp. v. Getty Petroleum Marketing, Inc., 67 F. Supp. 2d 302 (S.D.N.Y. 1999),
    243n.167
Kelly v. United States EPA, 203 F.3d 519 (7th Cir. 2000), 225n.32, 232n.87
Kennecott v. EPA, 780 F.2d 445 (4th Cir. 1985), 22n.80
Ketchikan Pulp Co., In re, 7 E.A.D. 605 (EAB 1998), 53n.68, 230n.70, 231n.74
Kingman Park Civic Ass'n v. EPA, 84 F. Supp. 2d 1 (D.D.C. 1999), 211n.43, 262n.236
Knee Deep Cattle Co. v. Bindana Investment Co., 94 F.3d 514 (9th Cir. 1996), 242n.165,
    264n.254

Laguna Gatuna, Inc. v. Browner, 58 F.3d 564 (10th Cir. 1995), cert. denied, 516 U.S. 1071
    (1995), 236n.113
Lake Cumberland Trust, Inc. v. EPA, 954 F.2d 1218 (6th Cir. 1992), 38n.192, 274n.6
Lakewood Associates v. United States, 45 Fed. Cl. 320 (Ct. Cl. 1999), 130n.186
LCP Chemicals-N.Y., In re, 4 E.A.D. 661 (EAB 1993), 57n.95
League of Wilderness Defenders v. Forsgren, 309 F.3d 1181 (9th Cir. 2002), 187n.138
Legal Environmental Assistance Foundation, Inc. v. Hodel, 586 F. Supp. 1163 (E.D. Tenn.
    1984), 260n.228
Leslie Salt Co. v. United States, 789 F. Supp. 1030 (N.D. Cal. 1991), 123n.156
Leslie Salt Co. v. United States, 896 F.2d 354 (9th Cir. 1990), cert. denied, 498 U.S. 1126,
    111 S. Ct. 1089 (1991), 13n.34, 101
Long Island Soundkeeper Fund, Inc. v. New York City Dep't of Env'tl Protection, 27 F.
    Supp. 2d 380 (E.D.N.Y. 1998), 264n.253
Long Island Soundkeeper Fund v. New York Athletic Club (S.D.N.Y. 1995), 109n.60
Longview Fibre Co. v. Rasmussen, 980 F.2d 1307 (9th Cir. 1992), 210nn.31, 36, 275n.13
Louisiana Wildlife Fed'n v. York, 761 F.2d 1044 (5th Cir. 1985), 117n.130
Loveladies Harbor v. United States, 28 F.3d 1171 (Fed Cir. 1994), 127–128
Lucas v. South Carolina Coastal Council, 505 U.S. 1003, 112 S. Ct. 2886 (1992), 124–126
Lujan v. Defenders of Wildlife, 500 U.S. 915, 112 S. Ct. 2130 (1992), 265n.260, 266nn.261,
    266

MacDonald & Watson, 933 F.2d at 55, 248n.183
Maier v. EPA, 114 F.3d 1032 (10th Cir. 1997), cert. denied, 522 U.S. 1014 (1997),
    274nn.3, 8
Mancuso v. New York State Thruway Authority, 86 F.3d 289 (2nd Cir. 1996), 260n.228
Marine Shale Processors, Inc., In re, 5 E.A.D. 751 (EAB 1995), 231n.75
Massachusetts Public Interest Research v. ICI Americas Inc., 777 F. Supp. 1032 (D. Mass.
    1991), 264n.253
Mianus River Preservation Comm. v. Administrator of EPA, 541 F.2d 899 (2d Cir. 1976),
    275n.17, 276n.21
Miccosukee Tribe of Indians of Florida v. S. Florida Water Mgmt. Dist., 280 F.3d 1364 (11th
    Cir. 2002), 193n.6, 226n.42
Miccosukee Tribe of Indians v. EPA, 105 F.3d 599 (11th Cir. 1997), 260n.224, 261n.234
Midatlantic Nat'l Bank v. New Jersey Dep't of Env'tl Protection, 474 U.S. 494 (1986),
    232n.84
Middlesex County Sewerage Authority v. National Sea Clammers Ass'n, 453 U.S. 1, 101 S.
    Ct. 2615, 69 L. Ed. 2d 435 (1981), 259n.221, 277n.30

Miners Advocacy Council, *In re,* 4 E.A.D. 40 (EAB May 29, 1992), 58n.100

Minnehaha Creek Watershed Dist. v. Hoffman, 597 F.2d 617 (8th Cir. 1979), 108n.53

Missouri Soybean Ass'n v. EPA, 289 F.3d 509 (8th Cir. 2002), 213n.51

Mobil Oil Corp. v. EPA, 716 F.2d 1187 (7th Cir. 1983), *cert. denied,* 466 U.S. 980 (1984), 17n.56, 237n.116

Modine Mfg. Corp. v. Kay, 791 F.2d 267 (3rd Cir. 1986), 87n.31, 275n.12

Molokai Chamber of Commerce v. Kukui (Molokai), Inc., 891 F. Supp. 1389 (D. Haw. 1995), 225n.29

Monongahela Power Co. v. Chief, Office of Water Resources, No. 30105, 2002 WL 1438541 (W. Va. July 1, 2002), 210n.30

Montana v. United States, 440 U.S. 147 (1979), 230n.72

Mulberry Hills Development Corp. v. United States, 772 F. Supp. 1553 (D. Md. 1991), 123n.156

Municipal Auth. of St. Mary's v. EPA, 945 F.2d 67 (3d Cir. 1991), 37n.185, 38nn.195, 196, 274n.6

Municipality of Anchorage v. United States, 980 F.2d 1320 (9th Cir. 1992), 277

Murphy Farms, 1998 U.S. Dist. LEXIS 21402, *4, (E.D.N.C. Dec. 22, 1998), *remanded on other grounds,* 2000 U.S. App. LEXIS 5460 (4th Cir. N.C. Mar. 29, 2000), 184n.124

Mutual Life Insurance Co. v. Mobil Corp., 1998 U.S. Dist. LEXIS 4513 (N.D.N.Y. Mar. 31, 1998), 268n.278

National Ass'n of Metal Finishers v. EPA, 719 F.2d 624 (3d Cir. 1983), *rev'd on other grounds sub nom.* CMA v. NRDC, 470 U.S. 116 (1985), 22n.80, 23n.86

National Environmental Foundation v. ABC Rail Corp., 926 F.2d 1096 (11th Cir. 1991), 263n.246

National Mining Ass'n v. United States Army Corps of Engineers, 145 F.3d 1399 (D.C. Cir. 1998), 108n.46

National Resource Defense Council v. Fox, 93 F. Supp. 2d 531 (S.D.N.Y. 2000), *aff'd in part, vacated in part sub nom.* National Resources Defense Council v. Muszynski, 268 F.3d 91 (2nd Cir. 2001), 211n.39, 212n.44

National Resources Defense Council v. Muszynski, 268 F.3d 91 (2d Cir. 2001), 206n.6, 211n.39

National Wildlife Federation v. Consumers Power Co., 657 F. Supp. 989 (W.D. Mich. 1987), *rev'd on other grounds,* 862 F.2d 580 (6th Cir. 1988), 11n.15, 231n.81

National Wildlife Federation v. Consumers Power Co., 862 F.2d 580 (6th Cir. 1988), 10n.4, 11n.15

National Wildlife Federation v. Gorsuch, 693 F.2d 156 (D.C. Cir. 1982), 10, 11n.12, 226n.44

National Wildlife Federation v. Hanson, 859 F.2d 313 (4th Cir. 1988), 210n.34, 262n.240

Natural Resources Defense Council, Inc. v. Bethlehem Steel Corp., 652 F. Supp. 620 (D. Md. 1987), 259n.220

Natural Resources Defense Council, Inc. v. Callaway, 524 F.2d 79 (2d Cir. 1975), 276n.25

Natural Resources Defense Council, Inc. v. Callaway, 392 F. Supp. 685 (D.D.C. 1975), 101

Natural Resources Defense Council, Inc. v. Costle, 568 F.2d 1369 (D.C. Dir. 1977), 12n.30

Natural Resources Defense Council, Inc. v. EPA, 656 F.2d 768 (D.C. Cir. 1981), 70n.3

Natural Resources Defense Council, Inc. v. EPA, 822 F.2d 104 (D.C. Cir. 1987), 18n.58, 23n.86, 54n.77

Natural Resources Defense Council, Inc. v. EPA, 859 F.2d 156 (D.C. Cir. 1988), 54n.73

Natural Resources Defense Council, Inc. v. Fina Oil & Chemical Co., 806 F. Supp. 145 (E.D. Tex. 1992), 265n.255

Natural Resources Defense Council, Inc. v. Fox, 909 F. Supp. 153 (S.D.N.Y. 1995), 262n.236

Natural Resources Defense Council, Inc. v. Fox, 30 F. Supp. 2d 369 (S.D.N.Y. 1998), 210n.33, 211n.43, 261n.234

Natural Resources Defense Council, Inc. v. Muszynski, 268 F.3d 91 (2nd Cir. 2001), 212n.46, 213n.53

Natural Resources Defense Council, Inc. v. Reilly, 32 Env't Rep. Cas. (BNA) 1969 (D.D.C. 1991), 261n.235

Natural Resources Defense Council, Inc. v. Reilly, Civ. No. 89-2980 (D.D.C. Jan. 30, 1992), 24, 186

Natural Resources Defense Council, Inc. v. Train, 510 F.2d 692 (D.C. Cir. 1974), 261n.235, 277n.31

Natural Resources Defense Council, Inc. v. Train, 396 F. Supp. 1393 (D.D.C. 1975), *aff'd sub nom.* NRDC v. Costle, 568 F.2d 1369 (D.C. Cir. 1977), 12n.30, 42n.4

Natural Resources Defense Council, Inc. v. Vygen Corp., 803 F. Supp. 97 (N.D. Ohio 1992), 266n.262

Natural Resources Defense Council, Inc. v. California Dept. of Transp., 96 F.3d 420 (9th Cir. 1996), 260n.228

Natural Resources Defense Council, Inc. v. EPA, 790 F.2d 289 (3rd Cir. 1986), *cert. denied sub nom.* Chem. Mfrs. Ass'n v. Natural Resources Defense Council, Inc., 479 U.S. 1084 (1987), 89n.39, 91

Natural Resources Defense Council, Inc. v. EPA, 915 F.2d 1314 (9th Cir. 1990), 35n.162, 36n.174, 37

Natural Resources Defense Council, Inc. v. EPA, 966 F.2d 1292 (9th Cir. 1992), 166n.13, 261n.235

Natural Resources Defense Council, Inc. v. Outboard Marine Corp., 702 F. Supp. 690 (N.D. Ill. 1988), 276n.24

Natural Resources Defense Council, Inc. v. Southwest Marine, Inc., 236 F.3d 985 (9th Cir. 2000), 235nn.105, 106, 259n.223, 261n.230, 263n.248, 266n.264

Natural Resources Defense Council, Inc. v. Texaco Refining and Marketing, Inc., 800 F. Supp. 1, 7 (D. Del. 1992), aff'd in part, rev'd in part on other grounds, 2 F.3d 493 (3d Cir. 1993), 257n.213, 265n.260, 266nn.262, 266, 267nn.267, 269

New Hanover Township v. U.S. Army Corps of Engineers, 992 F.2d 470 (3d Cir. 1993), 278

New Mexico Citizens for Clean Air and Water v. Espanola Mercantile Co., Inc., 72 F.3d 830 (10th Cir. 1996), 263n.242, 264n.249

New Waterbury, Ltd., *In re*, 5 E.A.D. 529 (EAB 1994), 239n.136

New York v. PVS Chemicals, Inc., 50 F. Supp. 2d 171 (W.D.N.Y. 1998), 268n.277

Newport Galleria Group v. Deland, 618 F. Supp. 1179 (D.D.C. 1985), 115n.113

No Spray Coalition, Inc. v. City of New York, 200 U.S. Dist. LEXIS 13919 (S.D.N.Y. Sept. 25, 2000), 10

North Carolina Wildlife Ass'n v. Woodbury (E.D.N.C. 1989), 121n.141, 268n.274

North & South Rivers Watershed Ass'n v. Town of Scituate, 949 F.2d 552 (1st Cir. 1991), 258n.217

Northwest Environmental Advocates v. Portland, 56 F.3d 979 (9th Cir. 1995), *cert. denied,* 116 S. Ct. 2550, 135 L. Ed. 2d 1069 (1996), 261n.231

Northwest Environmental Defense Center v. U.S. Army Corps of Engineers, 118 F. Supp. 2d 1115 (D. Or. 2000), 262n.240

Oregon Natural Desert Ass'n v. Dombeck, 151 F.3d 945 (9th Cir. 1998), 193n.6

Oregon Natural Desert Ass'n v. Dombeck, 172 F.3d 1092 (9th Cir. 1998), 217n.80

Oregon Natural Resources Council v. U.S. Forest Service, 834 F.2d 842 (9th Cir. 1987), 200n.27

Orgulf Transp. Co. v. United States, 711 F. Supp. 344 (W.D. Ky, 1989), 136n.13

Pacific Legal Foundation v. Costle, 586 F.2d 650 (9th Cir. 1978), *rev'd on other grounds,* 445 U.S. 198, 100 S. Ct. 1095, 63 L. Ed. 2d 329 (1980), 274n.9

Palazzolo v. Rhode Island, 533 U.S. 606 (2001), 129, 130n.186

Palm Beach Isles Associates v. United States, 231 F.3d at 1357 (Fed. Cir. 2000), 128

Pawtuxet Cove Marina, Inv. v. Ciba-Geigy Corp., 807 F.2d 1089 (1st Cir. 1986), *cert. denied,* 484 U.S. 975, 108 S. Ct. 484, 98 L. Ed. 2d 483 (1987), 267n.273, 268n.276

Peabody Coal Co. v. EPA, 522 F.2d 1152 (8th Cir. 1975), 276n.22

Penn Central Transportation Co. v. New York City, 438 U.S. 104 (1978), 124, 125, 126, 128

Penn Terra Ltd. v. Dep't of Env'tl Res. Pa., 733 F.2d 267 (3d Cir. 1984), 232nn.84, 86

Pennsylvania Environmental Defense Foundation v. Bellefonte Borough, 718 F. Supp. 431, 435 (M.D. Pa. 1989), 270nn.290, 291, 292

Pennsylvania Environmental Defense Foundation v. Mazurkiewicz, 712 F. Supp. 1184 (M.D. Pa. 1989), 263n.246

Pennsylvania Public Interest Research Group, Inc. v. P.H. Glatfelter Co., 128 F. Supp. 2d 747 (M.D. Pa. 2001), 266n.264

Pepperell Associates v. EPA, 246 F.3d 15 (5th Cir. 2001), 241n.158

P.F.Z. Properties, Inc. v. Train, 393 F. Supp. 1370 (D.D.C. 1975), 276n.27

P.H. Glatfelter Co. v. EPA, 921 F.2d 516 (4th Cir. 1990), 38n.193, 274n.6

Piney Run Preservation Ass'n v. County Commissioners of Carroll County, 50 F. Supp. 2d 443 (D. Md. 1999), 11n.9

Piney Run Preservation Ass'n v. County Commissioners of Carroll County, Md., 268 F.3d 255 (4th Cir. 2001, *cert. denied,* 70 U.S.L.W. 3707 (U.S. May 20, 2002)), 53n.69, 230n.71, 266n.265

Potter v. Asarco, 49 Env't Rep. Cas. (BNA) 1982 (D. Nebr. 1999), 15n.46

Preserve Endangered Areas of Cobb's History v. U.S. Army Corps of Engineers, 87 F.3d 1242 (11th Cir. 1996), 262n.240

Prisco v. New York, 902 F. Supp. 374 (S.D.N.Y. 1995), 268n.274

Proffitt v. Municipal Auth. of Morrisville, 716 F. Supp. 845 (E.D. Pa. 1989), *aff'd,* 897 F.2d 523 (3d Cir. 1990), 271n.300

Pronsolino v. Marcus, 91 F. Supp. 2d 1337 (N.D. Cal. 2000), *aff'd sub nom.* Pronsolino v. Nastri, 291 F.3d 1123 (9th Cir. 2002), 200n.28, 216n.76

Pronsolino v. Nastri, 291 F.3d 1123 (9th Cir. 2002), 200n.28, 211n.39, 216n.76

Public Interest Research Group of N.J., Inc. v. Powell Duffryn Terminals, Inc., 913 F.2d 64 (3d Cir. 1990), *cert. denied,* 498 U.S. 1109 (1991), 225n.31, 233nn.91, 94, 96, 234n.103, 235n.105, 266n.262, 267nn.267, 268, 268nn.277, 278, 276n.24

Public Interest Research Group of N.J. v. Air Force Dep't, 51 F.3d 1179 (3d Cir. 1995), 271n.299

Public Interest Research Group of N.J. v. Hercules, Inc., 50 F.3d 1239 (3d Cir. 1995), 263n.248

Public Interest Research Group of N.J. v. United States Metals Ref. Co., 681 F. Supp. 237 (D.N.J. 1987), 229n.66

PUD No. 1 of Jefferson County v. Washington Dep't of Ecology, 511 U.S. 700 (1994), 217n.82, 261n.229

Puerto Rico Sun Oil Co. v. EPA, 8 F.3d 73 (1st Cir. 1993), 48n.41, 62n.123

Puget Soundkeeper Alliance Waste Action Project v. Washington Dep't of Ecology, PCHB No. 00-173, 2001 WL 1502152 (Aug. 29, 2001), 216n.73

Ramsey v. Kantor, 96 F.3d 434 (9th Cir. 1996), 218n.91

Resource Investments Inc. v. United States Army Corps of Engineers, 151 F.3d 1162 (9th Cir. 1998), 109n.61

Rice v. Harken Exploration Co., 250 F.3d 264 (5th Cir. 2001), 155n.133

Robbins v. United States, 46 ERC 1505 (Ct. Cl. 1998), 130n.186

Robert Wallin, *In re,* 10 E.A.C. CWA Appeal No. 00-3 (EAB 2001), slip op. at 19, 240n.140

Roll Coater, Inc. v. Reilly, 932 F.2d 668 (7th Cir. 1991), 38n.195, 274n.6

RSR Corp. v. Browner, 924 F. Supp. 504 (S.D.N.Y. 1996), *aff'd,* 1997 U.S. App. LEXIS 5523 (2d Cir. 1997), 94n.72

Ruckelshaus v. Sierra Club, 463 U.S. 680 (1983), 271n.297

Rueth v. EPA, 13 F.3d 227 (7th Cir. 1993), 123n.156

Russian River Watershed Protection Comm. v. City of Santa Rosa, 142 F.3d 1136 (9th Cir. 1998), 268n.275

Rybacheck v. Environmental Protection Agency, 904 F.2d 1276 (9th Cir. 1990), 10

San Francisco Baykeeper v. Tidewater Sand & Gravel Co. (N.D. Ca. 1997), 268n.276

San Francisco Baykeeper v. Whitman, No. 01-16111, 2002 WL 1560778, at *2, *5–6 (9th Cir. July 17, 2002), 208n.21, 210n.33, 212n.44

Sasser v. EPA, 990 F.2d 127 (4th Cir. 1993), 224n.28

Save Greers Ferry Lake v. U.S. Army Corps of Engineers, 111 F. Supp. 2d 1135 (E.D. Ark. 2000), 260n.225

Save Our Community v. EPA, 971 F.2d 1155 (5th Cir. 1992), 109n.63, 260n.225, 266n.262, 267nn.267, 268, 269

Save Ourselves v. U.S. Army Corps of Eng'rs, 958 F.2d 659 (5th Cir. 1992), 265n.260

Save the Valley, Inc. v. U.S. EPA, 99 F. Supp. 2d 981 (S.D. Ind. 2000), 262n.237

Scott v. City of Hammond, 530 F. Supp. 288 (N.D. Ill. 1981), *aff'd in part, rev'd in part,* 741 F.2d 992 (7th Cir. 1984), 209n.28, 211n.40

Scott v. City of Hammond, 741 F.2d 992 (7th Cir. 1984), 33nn.143, 146, 260n.224

Sekco Energy, Inc. v. M/V Margaret Chouest, 820 F. Supp. 1008 (E.D. La. 1993), 156n.139

Shell Oil Co. v. Train, 415 F. Supp. 70 (N.D. Cal. 1976), *aff'd,* 585 F.2d 408 (9th Cir. 1978), 274n.7

Sierra Club, Lone Star Chapter v. Cedar Point Oil Co., 73 F.3d 546 (5th Cir. 1996), 226nn.44, 47, 259n.223, 266n.262

Sierra Club, Northstar Chapter v. Browner, 843 F. Supp. 1304 (D. Minn. 1993), 212n.44

Sierra Club v. Abston Constr. Co., Inc., 620 F.2d 41 (5th Cir. 1980), 12n.21

Sierra Club v. Babbitt, 65 F.3d 1502 (9th Cir. 1995), 217n.84, 218n.89

Sierra Club v. Browner, 843 F. Supp. 1304 (D. Minn. 1993), 211n.43, 262n.236

Sierra Club v. Chevron U.S.A., Inc., 834 F.2d 1517 (9th Cir. 1987), 259n.219, 268n.279, 269n.285

Sierra Club v. Colorado Refining Co., 838 F. Supp. 1428 (D. Colo. 1993), 15n.48, 268n.275

Sierra Club v. Electronic Controls Design, Inc., 909 F.2d 1350 (9th Cir. 1990), 270n.289

Sierra Club v. EPA, 162 F. Supp. 2d 406 (D. Md. 2001), 211n.43, 213n.51, 218n.88

Sierra Club v. EPA, 995 F.2d 1478 (9th Cir. 1993), 269n.281

Sierra Club v. Hankinson, 939 F. Supp. 865 (N.D. Ga. 1996), 206n.5, 211nn.38, 43, 212nn.44, 49, 261n.234, 262n.236

Sierra Club v. Hyundai American Inc., 23 F. Supp. 2d 1177 (D. Or. 1997), 264n.253

Sierra Club v. Meiburg, No. 01-14587, 2002 WL 1426554 (11th Cir. July 2, 2002), 219n.94

Sierra Club v. Morton, 405 U.S. 727 (1972), 265n.259

Sierra Club v. Peterson, 705 F.2d 1475 (9th Cir. 1983), 259n.218

Sierra Club v. Sierra Point Oil Co., 73 F.3d 546 (5th Cir. 1996), *cert. denied,* 519 U.S. 811 (1996), 226n.46

Sierra Club v. Simkins Industries, Inc., 847 F.2d 1109 (4th Cir. 1988), *cert. denied,* 491 U.S. 904, 109 S. Ct. 3185 (1989), 237n.115

Sierra Club v. Slater, 120 F.3d 623 (6th Cir. 1997), 260n.225

Sierra Club v. Train, 557 F.2d 485 (5th Cir. 1977), 223n.22

Sierra Club v. Union Oil Co., 853 F.2d 667, 671 (9th Cir. 1988), 267n.272

Sierra Club v. Union Oil Co. of Cal., 813 F.2d 1480, *vacated and remanded on other grounds,* 485 U.S. 931 (1988), 228n.58

Sierra Club v. Whitman, 268 F.3d 898 (9th Cir. 2001), 223n.22, 262n.237

Solid Waste Agency of Northern Cook County v. U.S. Army Corps of Engineers (SWANCC), 531 U.S. 159 (2001), 2n.8, 14, 102–103, 227

South Holland Metal Finishing Co. v. Browner, 97 F.3d 932 (7th Cir. 1996), 89n.37

South Port Marine, L.L.C. v. Gulf Oil Ltd. Partnership, 73 F. Supp. 2d 17 (D. Me. 1999), *aff'd in part, rev'd in part on other grounds, remanded,* 2000 U.S. App. LEXIS 31178 (1st Cir. Dec. 7, 2000), 156n.139

Southern Ohio Coal Co. v. Office of Surface Mining, 20 F.3d 1418 (1994), 223n.19, 236n.113

Spang & Co., *In re,* 6 E.A.D. 226 (EAB 1995), 239n.137

Staples v. United States, 511 U.S. 600, 114 S. Ct. 1793, 128 L. Ed. 2d 608 (1994), 246

Star-Kist Caribe, Inc., *In re,* 4 E.A.D. 33 (EAB 1992), 40

State of Missouri *ex rel.* Ashcroft v. Department of the Army Corps of Engineers, 526 F. Supp. 660 (W.D. Mich. 1980), 109n.65

Stewart v. Potts, 996 F. Supp. 668 (S.D. Tex. 1998), 117n.131

Stoddard v. W. Carolina Regional Sewer Authority, 784 F.2d 1200 (4th Cir. 1986), 233n.91

Stone v. Naperville Park District, 38 F. Supp. 651 (N.D. Ill. 1999), 12n.24, 261n.232

Student Public Interest Research Group, Inc. v. Fritzsche, Dodge & Olcott, Inc., 759 F.2d 1131 (3d Cir. 1985), 264n.252

Student Public Research Group of New Jersey, Inc. v. Monsanto Co., 600 F. Supp. 1474 (D.N.J. 1985), 259n.220

Student Public Interest Research Group v. P.D. Oil & Chemical, 913 F.2d 64 (3d Cir. 1989), 257n.213

Sun Enterprises v. Train, 532 F.2d 280 (2d Cir. 1976), 261n.234

Sun Pipe Line Co. v. Conewago Contractors, Inc., No. 4: CV-93-1995, 1994 WL 539326 (M.D. Pa. Aug. 22, 1994), 155n.133

Susquehanna Valley Alliance v. Three Mile Island Nuclear Reactor, 619 F.2d 231 (3d Cir. 1980), *cert. denied,* 449 U.S. 1096, 101 S. Ct. 893, 66 L. Ed. 2d 824 (1981), 278n.38

Sylvester v. U.S. Army Corps of Engineers, 882 F.2d 407 (9th Cir. 1989), 117n.129

Tabb Lakes v. United States, 10 F.3d 796 (Fed. Cir. 1993), 126–127

Tanners' Council of Am. v. Train, 540 F.2d 1188 (4th Cir. 1976), 20n.68

Tenneco Oil Co. v. EPA, 592 F.2d 897 (5th Cir. 1979), 276n.22

Texas Mun. Power Agency v. EPA, 836 F.2d 1482 (5th Cir. 1988), 17n.56

3M Co. (Minn. Mining & Mfg.) v. Browner, 17 F.3d 1453 (D.C. Cir. 1994), 225n.30

Tobyhanna Conservation Ass'n v. Country Place Waste Treatment Co., 734 F. Supp. 667 (M.D. Pa. 1989), 266n.262

Tobyhanna Conservation Ass'n v. Country Place Waste Treatment Facility, 769 F. Supp. 739 (M.D. Pa. 1991), 229n.62

Town of Ashland Wastewater Treatment Facility, *In re,* NPDES Appeal No. 00-15, slip op. at 10 (EAB, Feb. 23, 2001), 57n.96, 237nn.115, 118

Town of Norfolk v. U.S. Army Corps of Engineers, 968 F.2d 1438 (1st Cir. 1992), 118n.135

Train v. Colorado Public Interest Research Group, 426 U.S. 1 (1976), 11n.8

Trustees for Alaska v. EPA, 749 F.2d 549 (9th Cir. 1984), 12n.21

Tull v. United States, 481 U.S. 412 (1987), 228n.55

Umatilla Water Quality Protection Assoc. v. Smith Frozen Foods, Inc., 962 F. Supp. 1312 (D. Or. 1997), 15n.47

United States Department of Energy v. Ohio, 503 U.S. 607, 112 S. Ct. 1627, 118 L. Ed. 2d 255 (1992), 265n.258

United States EPA v. City of Green Forest, Ark., 921 F.2d 1394 (8th Cir. 1990), 233n.94

United States Public Interest Research Group v. Atlantic Salmon of Maine, L.L.C., 2002 WL 242466 (D. Maine 2002), 226n.46

United States v. Ahmad, 101 F.3d 386 (5th Cir. 1996), 245n.175

United States v. Akers, 785 F.2d 814 (9th Cir. 1985), 109n.58, 121n.145, 122n.146, 147

United States v. Alcoa Inc., 98 F. Supp. 2d 1031 (N.D. Ind. 2000), 235nn.105, 106

United States v. Allegheny Ludlum Steel Corp., 187 F. Supp. 2d 426 (W.D. Pa. 2002), 234n.100

United States v. Alley, 755 F. Supp. 771 (N.D. Ill. 1990), 89n.42

United States v. Amtrak, No. 01:CV11121 (D. Mass. June 28, 2001), 223n.17

United States v. Appel, 210 F.3d 385 (9th Cir. 2000), 225n.36

United States v. Banks, 115 F.3d 916 (11th Cir. 1997), 101, 224n.27

United States v. Bay Houston Towing Co., 33 F. Supp. 2d 596 (E.D. Mich. 1999), 108n.54

United States v. Boldt, 929 F.2d 35 (1st Cir. 1991), 232n.83

United States v. Borowski, 977 F.2d 27 (1st Cir. 1992), 252–253

United States v. Brace, 41 F.3d 117 (3d Cir. 1994), 121n.145, 122n.146

United States v. Brittain, 931 F.2d 1413 (10th Cir. 1991), 226n.41, 247n.181

United States v. Buckley, 934 F.2d 84 (6th Cir. 1991), 245n.173

United States v. Buday, 138 F. Supp. 2d 1282 (D. Mont. 2001), 100–101

United States v. Ciampitti, 615 F. Supp. 116 (D.N.J. 1984), 122n.149

United States v. City of Colorado Springs, CO, 455 F. Supp. 1364 (D. Colo. 1978), 237n.120

United States v. City of Erie, Pa., No. 94-281 (W.D. Pa. July 21, 1995), 231n.75

United States v. City of Hoboken, 675 F. Supp. 189 (D.N.J. 1987), 232n.82

United States v. City of Rock Island, 182 F. Supp. 2d 690 (C.D. Ill. 2001), 224n.24

United States v. City of Toledo, 63 F. Supp. 2d 834 (N.D. Ohio 1999), 72

United States v. City of Youngstown, 109 F. Supp. 2d 739 (N.C. Ohio, 2000), 224n.24

United States v. Clark Equip. Co., 1996 WL 363050, 42 ERC 1734 (D.N.D. 1996), 89n.39

United States v. Commodore Club, Inc., 418 F. Supp. 311 (E.D. Mich. 1976), 256n.209

United States v. Concentrated Phosphate Export Ass'n, 393 U.S. 199 (1968), 231n.76, 268n.276

United States v. Conoco, 916 F. Supp. 581 (E.D. La. 1996), 155n.136

United States v. Cooper, 173 F.3d 1192 (9th Cir. 1999), *cert. denied,* 528 U.S. 1019 (1999), 226n.41, 246n.175

United States v. Corbin Farms, 444 F. Supp. 510 (E.D. Cal.), *aff'd,* 578 F.2d 259 (9th Cir. 1978), 245n.173

United States v. CPS Chem. Co., 779 F. Supp. 437 (E.D. Ark. 1991), 229n.63, 231nn.74, 80, 81, 232n.87

United States v. Cumberland Farms of Connecticut, 647 F. Supp. 1166 (D. Mass. 1986), *aff'd,* 826 F.2d 1151 (1st Cir. 1987), 112n.88, 122nn.147, 153, 123n.154

United States v. Cumberland Farms of Connecticut, 826 F.2d 1151 (1st Cir. 1987), 112n.88, 122nn.147, 148, 149, 152

United States v. Deaton, 209 F.3d 331 (4th Cir. 2000), 108n.49, 109n.56

United States v. Earth Sciences, Inc., 599 F.2d 368 (10th Cir. 1979), 12n.20

United States v. Edison, 108 F.3d 1336 (11th Cir. 1997), 13n.35

United States v. Edwards, 667 F. Supp. 1204 (W.D. Tenn. 1987), 122n.149

United States v. Frezzo Bros., 546 F. Supp. 713 (E.D. Pa. 1982), *aff'd,* 703 F.2d 62 (3d Cir.), *cert. denied,* 464 U.S. 829 (1983), 12n.22

United States v. GAF Corp., 389 F. Supp. 1379 (S.D. Tex. 1975), 15n.46

United States v. Gulf States Steel, Inc., 54 F. Supp. 2d 1233 (N.D. Ala. 1999), 229n.68

United States v. Gurley, 43 F.3d 1188 (8th Cir. 1995), 230n.73

United States v. Hallmark Construction Co., 14 F. Supp. 2d 1069 (N.D. Ill. 1998), 121n.140

United States v. Hamel, 551 F.2d 107 (6th Cir. 1977), 226n.46, 253n.196

United States v. Hanousek, 176 F.3d 1116 (9th Cir. 1999), *cert. denied,* 528 U.S. 1102 (2000), 248

United States v. Hartsell, 127 F.3d 343 (4th Cir. 1997), *cert. denied,* 523 U.S. 1030 (1998), 83n.1, 87n.27

United States v. Hartz Construction Co., 1999 U.S. Dist. LEXIS 9126, 1999 WL 417388 (N.D. Ill. 1999), 237n.117

United States v. Holland, 373 F. Supp. 665 (M.D. Fla. 1974), 13n.34

United States v. Hong, 242 F.3d 528 (4th Cir. 2001), *cert. denied,* 122 S. Ct. 60 (2001), 96n.92, 247

United States v. Hopkins, 53 F.3d 533 (2d Cir. 1995), *cert. denied,* 516 U.S. 1072 (1996), 246, 251nn.187, 189

United States v. Huebner, 752 F.2d 1235 (7th Cir. 1985), 121n.145, 122nn.146, 147

United States v. Hyundai Merchant Marine Co., 172 F.3d 1187 (9th Cir. 1999), 155n.136

United States v. International Minerals and Chemical Corp., 402 U.S. 558, 91 S. Ct. 1697, 29 L. Ed. 2d 178 (1971), 245, 246

United States v. Interstate General Co., 152 F. Supp. 2d 843 (D. Md. 2001), 103

United States v. ITT Rayonier, Inc. 627 F.2d 996 (9th Cir. 1980), 231n.75

United States v. Iverson, 162 F.3d 1015 (9th Cir. 1998), 96n.92, 247

United States v. Johnson & Towers, Inc. 741 F.2d 662 (3rd Cir. 1984), 247n.179, 248n.183

United States v. Jones & Laughlin Steel Corp., 804 F.2d 348 (6th Cir. 1986), 232n.86

United States v. Krilich, 209 F.3d 968 (7th Cir. 2000), 227n.50

United States v. Krilich, 126 F.3d 1035 (7th Cir. 1997), 123n.155

United States v. Larkins, 657 F. Supp. 2d 76 (W.D. Ky. 1987), *aff'd* 852 F.2d 189 (6th Cir. 1988), 108n.52, 122n.151

United States v. Larkins, 852 F.2d 189 (6th Cir. 1988), 122n.147

United States v. Laughlin, 10 F.3d 961 (2d Cir. 1993), *cert. denied sub nom.* Goldman v. United States, 511 U.S. 1071 (1994), 245n.173

United States v. Locke, 529 U.S. 89 (2000), 157n.147

United States v. Lopez, 514 U.S. 549 (1995), 99

United States v. Mango, 199 F.3d 85 (2d Cir. 1999), 116n.117

United States v. Material Serv. Corp., 1996 WL 563462, at *2 (N.D. Ill. Sept. 30, 1996), 225n.31

United States v. M.C.C. of Florida, Inc., 772 F.3d 1501 (11th Cir. 1985), 109n.55

United States v. Metropolitan St. Louis Sewer Dist., 874 F.2d 588 (8th Cir. 1989), 269n.281

United States v. Metropolitan St. Louis Sewer Dist., 883 F.2d 54 (8th Cir. 1989), 266n.262

United States v. Municipal Auth. of Union Township, 150 F.3d 259 (3d Cir. 1998), 234nn.97, 102

United States v. Municipality of Penn Hills, 6 F. Supp. 2d 432 (W.D. Pa. 1998), 225n.31

United States v. Murphy Exploration and Production Co., 939 F. Supp. 489 (E.D. La. 1996), 155n.136

United States v. Newdunn Associates, 195 F. Supp. 2d 751 (E.D. Va. 2002), 103

United States v. Oxford Royal Mushroom Prod., Inc., 487 F. Supp. 852 (E.D. Pa. 1980), 13n.34

United States v. Pacific Hide & Fur Depot, 768 F.2d 1096 (9th Cir. 1985), 246n.178

United States v. Park, 421 U.S. 658 (1975), 248n.182

United States v. Parks Banks, 115 F.3d 916 (11th Cir. 1997), 122n.149

United States v. Phelps Dodge, 391 F. Supp. 1181 (D. Ariz. 1975), 13n.34

United States v. Plaza Health Laboratories, Inc., 3 F.3d 643 (2d Cir. 1993), 227n.54

United States v. Reaves, 923 F. Supp. 1530 (M.D. Fla. 1996), 224n.28, 268n.274

United States v. Reilly, 827 F. Supp. 1076 (D. Del. 1993), 245n.173

United States v. Riverside Bayview Homes, 474 U.S. 121 (1985), 100, 102, 103, 126

United States v. Sargent County Water, 876 F. Supp. 1090 (D.N.D. Apr. 6, 1992), 101

United States v. Sheyenne Tooling & Manufacturing Co., 952 F. Supp. 1414 (D.N.D. 1996), *aff'd,* 162 F.3d 1166 (8th Cir. 1998), 94n.72

United States v. Sheyenne Tooling & Manufacturing Co., 1998 WL 544413 (8th Cir. Aug. 27, 1998), 228n.60

United States v. Sinclair, 767 F. Supp. 200 (D. Mont. 1990), 108n.51

United States v. Sinskey, 119 F.3d 712 (8th Cir. 1997), 246, 251n.187

United States v. Smith, 149 F.3d 1172, No. 96-2450, 1998 WL 325954 (4th Cir. June 18, 1998), 235n.105

United States v. Smithfield Foods, Inc., 191 F.3d 516 (4th Cir. 1999), *cert. denied,* 121 S. Ct. 46, 148 L. Ed. 2d 16 (2000), 223n.23, 240n.138

United States v. Smithfield Foods, Inc., 972 F. Supp. 338 (E.D. Va. 1997), *affirmed in part, reversed in part,* 191 F.3d 516 (4th Cir. 1999), *cert. denied,* 121 S. Ct. 46, 148 L. Ed. 2d 16 (2000), 242n.165, 243n.167

United States v. Southern Inv. Co., 876 F.2d 606 (8th Cir. 1989), 101n.20

United States v. Standard Oil, 384 U.S. 224 (1966), 256n.207

United States v. Telluride Co., 146 F.3d 1241 (10th Cir. 1998), 224n.27

United States v. Telluride Co., 884 F. Supp. 404 (D. Colo. 1995), *rev'd on other grounds,* 146 F.3d 1241 (10th Cir. 1998), 225n.30

United States v. Tilton, 705 F.2d 429 (11th Cir. 1983), 101n.16

United States v. Town of Lowell, Ind., 637 F. Supp. 254 (N.D. Ind. 1985), 229n.66

United States v. United States Steel Corp. 328 F. Supp. 354 (N.D. Ind. 1970), *aff'd,* 482 F.2d 439 (7th Cir.), *cert. denied,* 414 U.S. 909 (1973), 256n.208

United States v. Van Leuzen, 816 F. Supp. 1171 (S.D. Tex. 1993), 122n.149

United States v. Wal-Mart Stores, Inc., (WD. Ark. June 7, 2001), 223n.17

United States v. Weisman, 489 F. Supp. 1331 (M.D. Fla. 1980), 12n.25

United States v. Weitzenhoff, 1 F.3d 1523 (9th Cir. 1993), 18n.58

United States v. Weitzenhoff, 35 F.3d 1275 (9th Cir. 1993), *cert. denied,* 513 U.S. 1128 (1995), 229n.65, 245nn.173, 174, 245–246

United States v. West Indies Transport Co., 127 F.3d 299 (3d Cir. 1997), 193n.6

United States v. White Fuel Corp., 498 F.2d 619 (1st Cir. 1974), 256nn.207, 208

United States v. Wilson, 133 F.3d 251 (4th Cir. 1997), 99, 101, 245n.174, 249n.186

Upper Chattahoochee Riverkeeper Fund, Inc. v. City of Atlanta, 953 F. Supp. 1541 (N.D. Ga. 1996), 261n.231

Upper Chattahoochee Riverkeeper Fund, Inc. v. City of Atlanta, 986 F. Supp. 1406 (N.D. Ga. 1997), 261n.232

Valley Forge Christian College v. Americans United for Separation of Church and State, 454 U.S. 464 (1982), 265n.260, 267n.268

Village of Oconomowoc Lake v. Dayton Hudson Corp., 24 F.3d 962 (7th Cir. 1994), 15n.47

Virginia Electric & Power Co. v. Costle, 566 F.2d 446 (4th Cir. 1977), 275n.12

Walls v. Waste Resource Corp., 761 F.2d 311 (6th Cir. 1985), 259n.221

Washington Public Interest Research Group v. Pendleton Woolen Mills, Inc., 11 F.3d 883 (9th Cir. 1993), 264n.252

Washington Trout v. McCain Foods, Inc., 45 F.3d 1351 (9th Cir. 1995), 263n.246

Washington v. EPA, 573 F.2d 583 (9th Cir. 1978), 276n.26

Washington Wilderness Coalition v. Hecla Mining Co., 870 F. Supp. 983 (E.D. Wash. 1994), 12n.21, 15n.48

Waste Action Project v. Dawn Mining Co. 137 F.3d 1426 (9th Cir. 1998), 11n.8

Water Works and Sewer Board City of Birmingham v. U.S. Army Corps of Engineers, 983 F. Supp. 1052 (N.D. Ala. 1997), 113n.95

Waterkeeper Alliance v. Smithfield Foods, 2001 U.S. Dist. LEXIS 21314, *4, *11 (E.D.N.C. Sept. 20, 2001), 183n.118, 184nn.120, 124

Weinberger v. Romero-Barcelo, 456 U.S. 305 (1982), 11n.14, 12n.23

West Virginia Coal Ass'n v. EPA, 932 F.2d 934 (4th Cir. 1991), 109n.62

Wetlands Action Network v. U.S. Army Corps of Engineers, 222 F.3d 1105 (9th Cir. 2000), 116n.116

Wilderness Society v. Morton, 495 F.2d 1026 (D.C. Cir. 1974) (en banc), *rev'd on other grounds sub nom.* Alyeska Pipeline Serv. Co. v. Wilderness Soc., 421 U.S. 240, 95 S. Ct. 1612, 44 L. Ed. 2d 141 (1975), 272n.301

Word v. Commerce Oil Co. (*In re* Commerce Oil Co.), 847 F.2d 291 (6th Cir. 1988), 232n.84

Zabel v. Tabb, 430 F.2d 199 (5th Cir. 1970), *cert. denied,* 401 U.S. 910 (1972), 6n.31

INDEX

A list, 35–36
Aboveground storage tanks, 140n.32
ACP (Area Contingency Plan), 148
Act to Prevent Pollution from Ships (APPS), 137n.18, 243, 244n.170, 253n.195, 257
Acute criteria, 29
Adjacent wetlands, 100–101
Administrative compliance orders, 236
Administrative law judge (ALJ), 56, 65, 238, 239, 240, 241
Administrative penalties, 237–242
  appeals, 241
  class I penalties, 238
  class II penalties, 238–239
  collection of unpaid penalties, 242
  factors affecting the amount of, 239–240
  rights of interested parties, 240–241
  subpoenas, 240
Administrative Procedure Act (APA), 29, 43, 44, 53–54, 161, 238, 276
Affirmative defenses, 120–122, 229–232
  bankruptcy, 232
  degree of harm and good faith, 232
  estoppel, 230–231
  impossibility, 232
  laches, 231
  mootness, 231, 267–268
  nationwide permits, 122
  permit shield, 229–230
  res judicata or claim preclusion, 230
  Section 404(f) exemptions, 121–122
  statute of limitations, 120–121
After-the-fact permits, 112, 120
Agricultural stormwater discharges, 165, 184
ALJ (administrative law judge), 56, 65, 238, 239, 240, 241
Alternative Fines Act, 255
Alternatives, practicable, 116–117
Ambient criteria, 28

Ammonia, 25–26
Animal feeding operations (AFOs), 179. See also Concentrated animal feeding operations (CAFOs)
Animal units, 181
Anti-backsliding provisions, 66–68
Antidegradation, 31–32
APA (Administrative Procedure Act), 29, 43, 44, 53–54, 161, 238, 276
Appeals, 241
APPS (Act to Prevent Pollution from Ships), 137n.18, 243, 244n.170, 253n.195, 257
Aquaculture projects, 189–190
Aquatic animal production facilities, 188–189
Aquatic resources of national importance (ARNIs), 114
Area Committees, 148
Area Contingency Plan (ACP), 148
Army Corps of Engineers, 1, 6, 104. See also Section 404 permit program
  public interest review process, 115–116
ARNIs (aquatic resources of national importance), 114
Assessment reports, 195
Association of State and Interstate Water Pollution Control Administrators, 198
Atomic Energy Act of 1954, 11n.8
Attorney fees and costs, 270–272
Authority to act, 145
Average most probable discharge, 152, 153
"Average of the best" formulation, 20

B list, 36–37
Backsliding, 66–68
Bankruptcy, as defense, 232
Baseline Construction General Permit, 169–170
Baseline General Permit, 169
Baseline monitoring reports, 93

BAT (best available technology), 88
BAT (best available technology economically achievable), 2–3, 6–7, 22
BCT (best conventional pollutant-control technology), 3, 19–20, 21
Beachfront Management Act (South Carolina), 125
BEN computer program, 239n.135
Best available technology (BAT), 88
Best available technology economically achievable (BAT), 2–3, 6–7, 22
Best conventional pollutant-control technology (BCT), 3, 19–20, 21
Best management practices (BMPs), 174, 175, 177–178, 192
Best practicable control technology currently available (BPT), 2, 19–20
Best professional judgment (BPJ), 16, 66–67
Biochemical oxygen demand (BOD), 70
Biological oxygen demand (BOD), 19n.66
BIP standard, 213–214
Blacklisting, 5
BMPs (best management practices), 174, 175, 177–178, 192
BOD (biochemical oxygen demand), 70
BOD (biological oxygen demand), 19n.66
Boilerplate conditions, 17–18
BPJ (best professional judgment), 16, 66–67
BPT (best practicable control technology currently available), 2, 19–20
Building industry, 175–176
Bush, George, 81, 130–131
Bypass, 72, 228–229

C list, 37
CAAPF (concentrated aquatic animal production facility), 188–189
Catalyst theory, 271
Categorical pretreatment standards, 87–91
    applicability of and basis for, 87–89
    combined wastestream formula, 90
    deadlines, 90
    innovative technology deadline extensions, 90–91
Categorical taking, 128
Cease and desist orders, 120
CERCLA (Comprehensive Environmental Response, Compensation, and Liability Act), 14, 134–135, 138n.22, 146, 230, 255n.203
Chicken operations, 182–183
Chlorine, 25–26
Chronic criteria, 29

Citizen suits, 242, 257–272
    defenses, 121, 267–268
        ongoing violations and mootness, 267–268
        statute of limitations, 268
    intervention, 269
    legislative intent and authority, 258–259
    remedies, 269–272
        attorneys' fees and costs, 270–272
        civil penalties, 269
    standing, 265–267
    statutory authority, 258
    statutory requirements, 262–265
        notice, 262–264
        preexisting prosecutions, 264–265
        venue, 265
    TMDLs, 211
    types of, 259–262
        failure to comply with act, 260–261
        government failure to comply with mandatory duty, 261–262
Civil administrative enforcement, 235–243
    administrative compliance orders, 236
    administrative penalties, 237–242
        appeals, 241
        class I penalties, 238
        class II penalties, 238–239
        collection of unpaid penalties, 242
        factors affecting the amount of, 239–240
        rights of interested parties, 240–241
        subpoenas, 240
    effects on other enforcement actions, 242–243
    information requests, 236–237
Civil judicial enforcement, 221–235
    defenses, 228–232
        bankruptcy, 232
        degree of harm and good faith, 232
        estoppel, 230–231
        impossibility, 232
        laches, 231
        mootness, 231
        permit shield, 229–230
        regulatory defenses, 228–229
        res judicata or claim preclusion, 230
    elements of proof, 225–227
        discharge of a pollutant, 226
        navigable waters, 227
        point source, 227
    enforcement trends, 222–223
    EPA's enforcement jurisdiction, 223–224
    remedies, 232–235
        civil penalties, 232–234

consent decrees, 235
injunctions, 234–235
standards of liability, 225
statute of limitations, 224–225
statutory authority, 221–222
trial considerations, 228
DMRs as evidence of liability, 228
prevailing party considerations, 228
right to a jury, 228
venue, 224–225
Civil Monetary Penalties Adjustment Rule, 221n.2
Civil penalties
citizen suits, 269
civil judicial enforcement, 232–234
oil and hazardous substances spills, 161–162
wetlands, 122–123
Claim preclusion, 230
Class I penalties, 161, 238
Class II penalties, 161, 238–239
Clean Air Act, 7, 77–78, 244n.170, 246, 251–252
Clean Water Act (CWA), 245
overview, 1–7
permit program and enforcement, 1–2
Section 208, 194
Section 302, 33–34
Section 303, 205–219
Section 304, 35–38
Section 309, 221–272
Section 311, 133–162
Section 319, 195–200
Section 401, 217
Section 404, 97–132
Section 509, 273–278
spills of hazardous or toxic substances, 4–7
technology-based controls, 2–4
water quality-based controls, 2–4
Clean Water Action Plan, 4, 7, 192, 199, 201, 204
Clinton, Bill, 7, 81, 102, 131, 192, 199
CNMP (comprehensive nutrient management plan), 185–186
Coast Guard, 133–134n.4, 138, 143–144
National Response Unit, 146
Coastal Zone Act Reauthorization Amendments of 1990 (CZARA), 200–201
Coastal Zone Management Act (CZMA), 112, 113, 200
Color, 25–26
Combined sewer overflows (CSOs), 79–80, 190
Combined wastestream formula, 90

Common law nuisance doctrine, 124, 127–128
Compensating for Wetlands Losses under the Clean Water Act, 131
Compensatory mitigation, 119
Compliance deadlines, 175
Compliance orders, 236
Compliance reports, 94
Compliance schedules, 40
Comprehensive Environmental Response, Compensation, and Liability Act (CERCLA), 14, 134–135, 138n.22, 146, 230, 255n.203
Comprehensive nutrient management plan (CNMP), 185–186
Concentrated animal feeding operations (CAFOs), 178–186
definition of CAFO, 179–183
AFOs as CAFOs, by definition, 181–183
AFOs designated as CAFOs, 183
facilities qualifying as AFOs, 179–181
duty to apply for NPDES permit, 184
effluent limitations, 185–186
prohibition on unpermitted discharges, 183–184
proposed revisions to regulations, 186
Concentrated aquatic animal production facility (CAAPF), 188–189
Consent Agreement and Final Order, 239
Consent decrees, 235
Construction activity, 169–170, 175–176
Constructive submission theory, 210–212
Continuing violation theory, 123
Corps of Engineers. *See* Army Corps of Engineers
Cost tests, 21
Credits, for removal, 73, 91–92
Criminal enforcement, 243–257
direct discharge, 248–249
discharges to sewer systems/pretreatment violations, 249
falsification and tampering, 250–251
introduction and overview, 243–244
knowing endangerment, 251–253
mental state requirement, 244–248
oil or hazardous substances violations, 253–256
related water pollution statutes, 256–257
Act to Prevent Pollution from Ships, 257
Marine Protection, Research, and Sanctuaries Act, 256–257
Rivers and Harbors Act of 1899, 256
wetlands violations, 249–250

Criminal sanctions, 162
Criteria
    acute, 29
    ambient, 28
    chronic, 29
    narrative, 31
    numerical chemical-specific, 28–30
    site-specific, 38–39
    for water quality, 28–31
    WET, 30, 72
    whole-effluent numeric toxicity, 30–31
Critical low-flow condition, 39
Cropland, prior converted, 105
CZARA (Coastal Zone Act Reauthorization
        Amendments of 1990), 200–201
CZMA (Coastal Zone Management Act), 112,
        113, 200

Deadlines
    categorical pretreatment standards, 90
    innovative technology, 90–91
    phase I stormwater discharge permits, 175
    phase II stormwater discharge permits, 178
Debt Collection Act of 1997, 161, 162, 242
Deepwater ports, 133n.3, 158
Deepwater Ports Act of 1974, 136, 140n.33,
        254
Defenses. See also Affirmative defenses
    citizen suits, 121, 267–268
    civil judicial enforcement, 228–232
    oil and hazardous substances spills,
        157–158
    regulatory defenses, 228–229
    single operational upset, 233
Degrees of harm, as defense, 232
Delineation manuals, 104–105
Department of Justice, 120, 236, 242
Designated uses, of water bodies, 27
Diligent prosecution, 264–265
Dioxins, 78
Direct discharge, 248–249
Discharge, defined, 10, 135
Discharge Monitoring Reports (DMRs), 17, 251
    as evidence of liability, 228
Discharge of a pollutant, defined, 226
Discharge of dredged material, defined, 107
Discharge of fill material, defined, 107
Discharges associated with industrial activity
    defined, 165–166
    general permits, 42–43, 59
    group permits, 170–172
    individual permits, 168–169
District court jurisdiction, 276–277

DMRs. See Discharge Monitoring Reports
Doctrine of laches, 231
Doctrine of mootness, 231, 267–268
Doctrine of ripeness, 130, 277–278
Doctrine of willful blindness, 246
Domestic Policy Council, 130–131
Draft permits, 46–47
Dredged and fill material discharge, 107–109.
        See also Section 404 permit program
Dredged material, defined, 107–108
Drilling rigs, 59n.110

EAB (Environmental Appeals Board), 48, 56,
        57–58, 240
EAJA (Equal Access to Justice Act), 228n.60
Economic incapability variance, 25
Edible Oil Regulatory Reform Act, 153–154
Edible oils, 153–154
EEZ (Exclusive Economic Zone), 136, 144,
        155, 158
Effluent Guidelines Plan, 24
Effluent limitation guidelines (ELGs), 62, 66
Effluent limitations. See also Water quality-
        based effluent limitations
    CAFOs, 185–186
    numeric effluent limits, 174–175
    POTWs, 70–71
Effluent limitations and standards, EPA,
        3, 16
Effluent standard or limitation, defined, 261
Effluent trading programs, 203–204
EIS (environmental impact statement), 55
Eleventh Amendment, 260
ELGs (effluent limitation guidelines), 62, 66
ELI (Environmental Law Institute), 202–203
Emergency Planning and Community Right-to-
        know Act (EPCRA), 171
Emergency procedures, 111–112
Endangered Species Act (ESA), 112, 114, 128,
        217–218
Energy and Water Development Appropriations
        Act, 104n.31
Enforceable state mechanisms, 202–203
Enforcement, 221–272
    citizen suits, 242, 257–272
    civil administrative enforcement, 235–243
    civil judicial enforcement, 221–235
    criminal enforcement, 243–257
    fines, 255
    hazardous substances spills, penalties for,
        4–5, 160–162
    for indirect dischargers, 96
    of pretreatment program, 249

of pretreatment standards, 96
Section 404 permit program, 119–123
Environmental Appeals Board (EAB), 48, 56,
    57–58, 240
Environmental impact statement (EIS), 55
Environmental Law Institute (ELI), 202–203
EPA (Environmental Protection Agency)
    civil judicial enforcement, 223–224
    effluent limitations guidelines and
        standards, 3, 16
    Environmental Appeals Board, 48, 56,
        57–58, 240
    nonadversary panel procedures and, 56
    nonpoint source management programs,
        196–197
    Office of Enforcement and Compliance
        Assurance, 79, 243
    review of state-issued NPDES permits,
        48–52
    Section 404(b)(1) guidelines, 116–118
    state certification of NPDES permits, 48–52
    state standards review and approval, 49–50
    TMDLs and, 213
EPCRA (Emergency Planning and Community
    Right-to-know Act), 171
Equal Access to Justice Act (EAJA), 228n.60
ESA (Endangered Species Act), 112, 114, 128,
    217–218
Estoppel, 230–231
Exclusive Economic Zone (EEZ), 136, 144,
    155, 158
Exhaustion of remedies, 278
Existing sources, pretreatment standards for
    (PSES), 23, 88
Existing uses, of water bodies, 27
Expiration Dates for Wetlands Jurisdictional
    Delineations, 105–106
Exxon Valdez oil spill, 135, 144–145, 147

FACA (Federal Advisory Committee Act), 79,
    218
Facility, defined, 139n.30
Facility response plans, 148–154
Fact sheet, 46
Failure to comply
    with act, 260–261
    with mandatory duty, 261–262
Failure to report spills, 255–256
Falsification and tampering, 250–251
Farming activity, 165, 184
FDF (fundamentally different factors)
    variances, 24–25, 73, 92–93
Fecal coliform, 19n.66

Federal Advisory Committee Act (FACA), 79,
    218
Federal Court of Appeals, 273–276
Federal Debt Collection Act, 161, 162, 242
Federal Insecticide, Fungicide, and Rodenticide
    Act (FIFRA), 244n.170
Federal lands, 201
Federal On-Scene Coordinator (FOSC), 146
Federal Register, 24, 29, 62, 124, 241
Federal response units, 146
Federal Water Pollution Control Act (FWPCA),
    6, 20n.67, 178, 244n.170, 247, 258
Federalism, 202
Feedlot ELG, 185
FIFRA (Federal Insecticide, Fungicide, and
    Rodenticide Act), 244n.170
Fifth Amendment, 123, 124
Fill material, 107–109. *See also* Section 404
    permit program
Financial responsibility, 158–159
Fines, 255. *See also* Enforcement
Fish and wildlife response plan, 148
Fish and Wildlife Service, U.S. (FWS),
    102–103, 104, 114, 148, 217
Fish hatching, 188–189
Fishable/swimmable uses, 27
Flow conditions, 39
Forestry. *See* Silviculture
Form 2F, 168–169
FOSC (Federal On-Scene Coordinator), 146
Fourteenth Amendment, 125
Fundamentally different factors (FDF)
    variances, 24–25, 73, 92–93
FWPCA (Federal Water Pollution Control Act),
    6, 20n.67, 178, 244n.170, 247, 258
FWS (Fish and Wildlife Service, U.S.),
    102–103, 104, 114, 148, 217

Gas industry, 158
General permits
    appeals, 59
    for discharges associated with industrial
        activity, 42–43, 59
    NPDES, 42–43, 59
General pretreatment requirements, 85–87
Good faith, as defense, 232
Grace period, 56
Grants, 196, 198, 199–200
Groundwater discharges, 15–16
Group permits, 170–172

Harmful quantity, defined, 136
Hazardous substances, defined, 134, 135

Hazardous substances spills. *See* Oil and hazardous substances spills

Hazardous waste, notification of discharge, 95

Heat sources, 213–214
    temperature TMDLs *vs.* thermal TMDLs, 214
    thermal discharges, 213–214

Historic preservation, 112, 113–114

Homeland Security Act of 2002, 134n.4

Homeland Security Department, 134n.4

Hydric soils, 104

Hydrology, 104

Hydrophytic vegetation, 104

ICSs (individual control strategies), 35–38

Immunity from liability, 146

Impossibility, as defense, 232

Incidental fallback, 108

Incineration, 77–78

Independent Agencies Appropriations Act of 1993, 104n.31

Indirect dischargers. *See also* Pretreatment and indirect dischargers
    defined, 84

Individual control strategies (ICSs), 35–38

Individual permits
    for discharges associated with industrial activity, 168–169
    NPDES, 42
    Section 404 permit program, 111
    Section 404 program, 115–116, 118–119
    stormwater discharges, 168–169
    wetlands, 112–118

Industrial activity, discharges associated with
    defined, 165–166
    general permits, 42–43, 59
    group permits, 170–172
    individual permits, 168–169

Industrial stormwater discharges, to storm sewer systems, 167

Industrial users. *See also* Pretreatment and indirect dischargers
    significant industrial users, 74, 85

Industry cost-effectiveness test, 21

Information requests, 236–237

Injunctions, 234–235

Injunctive relief, 122

Innovative technology deadline extensions, 90–91

Integrated Contingency Plans, 140n.34

Intent, 54, 169

Interference, 85

Interim permitting, 174–175

International Convention for the Prevention of Pollution from Ships (MARPOL 73/78), 137–138, 254, 257

Inverse condemnation, 124

Iron, 25–26

Isolated wetlands, 101–104

Judicial review, 273–278
    jurisdiction, 273–277
        district court jurisdiction, 276–277
        federal court of appeals, 273–276
    justiciability, 277–278
        exhaustion of remedies, 278
        ripeness, 277–278
    NPDES permit appeals, 58–59
    oil and hazardous substances spills, 4–5
    right to jury, 228
    of TMDLs, 210

Jurisdictional Determination, 104

Jury trial, right to, 228

Justice Department, 120, 236, 242

Knowing endangerment, 251–253

Knowing violations, 244–248
    responsible corporate officer, 246–248
    willful blindness doctrine, 246

Laches doctrine, 231

Land applied sludges, 77

Lawsuits. *See* Citizen suits

LC (lethal concentration), 31

Letters of permission, 111

Liability. *See also* Oil and hazardous substances spills
    DMRs as evidence of, 228
    immunity from, 146
    standards of, 225
    wetlands, 119–123

Liability Trust Fund, 135, 148, 159–160, 253

Liquid manure system, 182–183

Litigation, TMDLs, 210–213

Load Allocation (LA), 207

Local limits, 86–87

Lodestar amount, 271–272

Long list, 35–36

Magnuson Fishery Conservation and Management Act, 140n.33

Major permit modification, 61–63

Managing Nonpoint Source Pollution: Final Report to Congress on Section 319 of the Clean Water Act, 197

Marine Fisheries Service, 114, 217

Marine Protection, Research, and Sanctuaries Act, 76n.30, 243, 256–257
Marine transportation-related (MTR) facilities, 151–152
MARPOL Protocol, 137–138, 254, 257
Maximum most probable discharge, 152
Medium spill, defined, 150
Memorandum of Agreement (MOA), 49–50, 114
Mental state requirement, 244–248
   knowing violations, 244–248
      responsible corporate officer, 246–248
      willful blindness doctrine, 246
   negligent violations, 248
Migratory Bird Rule, 101–104, 227
Minerals Management Service (MMS), 140n.32
Mining operations, 165
Minor permit modification, 61
Mitigation banking, 118–119
Mitigation policy, 118–119
Mixing zones, 39–40
MOA (Memorandum of Agreement), 49–50, 114
Monitoring requirements
   for indirect dischargers, 93–96
   National Monitoring Program, 197
   NPDES, 16–17
Mootness doctrine, 231, 267–268
MSGP (Multi-Sector General Permit), 169, 171
MS4s (municipal separate storm sewers), 168, 172–173, 176–178
MTR (marine transportation-related) facilities, 151–152
Multi-Sector General Permit (MSGP), 169, 171
Municipal separate storm sewers (MS4s), 168, 172–173, 176–178
Municipal Wastewater Treatment Construction Grant Amendments of 1981, 70n.3
Municipality, defined, 84n.5

NAICS (North American Industrial Classification System), 44n.17
Narrative standards, 31, 206n.5
National categorical pretreatment standards, 85
National Contingency Plan (NCP), 147–148, 159
National CSO Control Strategy, 79
National Emission Standards for Hazardous Air Pollutants (NESHAPs), 77
National Environmental Policy Act (NEPA), 55, 112, 113, 117
National Historic Preservation Act, 113–114
National Marine Fisheries Service, 114, 217

National Monitoring Program, 197
National Oceanographic and Atmospheric Administration (NOAA), 148, 155n.138, 201
National Pollutant Discharge Elimination System. *See* NPDES
National Pretreatment Standards, 84
National Register of Historic Places, 114
National Research Council, 131
National Response Center (NRC), 138
National Response Unit, 146
National Sewage Sludge Survey, 77
National Weather Service, 182n.109
Nationwide permits (NWPs), 109–110, 122
Natural Resource Conservation Service, 131
Natural resource damages, 155n.138
Navigable waters, defined, 12–14, 98, 100, 155n.133, 227
NCP (National Contingency Plan), 147–148, 159
Negligence standard, 248
Negligent violations, 248
NEPA (National Environmental Policy Act), 55, 112, 113, 117
NESHAPs (National Emission Standards for Hazardous Air Pollutants), 77
Net/gross calculation, 93
New discharger, defined, 55n.80
New source performance standards (NSPS), 3, 22–23
New Source Performance Standards under Clean Air Act (CAA), 77–78
New sources
   defined, 54–55
   NPDES requirements, 54–56
   performance standards, 3, 22–23, 77–78
   pretreatment standards, 23, 88–89
NMFS (National Marine Fisheries Service), 114, 217
"No environmental harm" defense, 232
"No net loss" of wetlands policy, 118–119, 130–131
No observed effect concentration (NOEC), 31
NOAA (National Oceanographic and Atmospheric Administration), 148, 155n.138, 201
NOEC (no-observed-effect concentration), 31
NOI (notice of intent), 54, 169
Nonadversary panel proceeding, 56
Nonpoint source agricultural activity, 165, 184
Nonpoint Source Guidance, 196–197
Nonpoint source pollution, defined, 192–193

Nonpoint source pollution control, 191–205
  in coastal areas, 200–201
  definition of nonpoint source pollution,
      192–193
  EPA guidance, 196–197
  future of, 204
  grants for, 196, 199–200
  introduction, 191–192
  original control provisions, 193–194
    CWA Section 208, 194
    CWA Section 303(e), 194
    Water Quality Management Plans, 194
  related programs, 200–204
    Coastal Zone Act Reauthorization
        Amendments of 1990, 200–201
    effluent trading programs, 203–204
    enforceable state mechanisms, 202–203
    watershed management on federal lands,
        201
  Section 319 program, 195–200
    Clean Water Action Plan, 199
    EPA Final Report to Congress, 197
    EPA Nonpoint Source Guidance,
        196–197
    grants for state management programs,
        196
    national monitoring program, 197
    new focus for program guidance, 198
    state assessment reports, 195
    state management programs, 195–196
    supplement guidelines for grants,
        199–200
  water quality inventory, 196–197
Nonpoint Source Program and Grants
    Guidance for Fiscal Year 1997 and
    Future Years, 198
Normal growing season, 180n.103
North American Industrial Classification
    System (NAICS), 44n.17
Notice of intent (NOI), 54, 169
Notice requirement, 46–47, 262–264
Notification of changed discharge, 95–96
NPDES (National Pollutant Discharge
    Elimination System), 1–2, 6, 9–40
  anti-backsliding provisions, 66–68
  APA extension, 53–54
  applicability, 9–16, 41
  conditions for all permits, 16–18
  definitions, 9–14
  discharges to groundwater and wells, 15–16
  draft permits, 46–47
  EPA review of state-issued permits, 49–52
  exclusions, 14–15

  general permits, 42–43
  individual permits, 42
  monitoring, 16–17
  new sources requirements, 54–56
  nonadversary panel procedures, 56
  permit appeals, 56–59
    EAB hearing process, 57–58
    effect of appeal on issued permits, 59
    general permits, 59
    judicial review, 58–59
  permit application requirements, 43–45
  permit issuance process, 45–48
    effective date of application, 46
    final permit decision, 47–48
    public comment/hearing, 47
    review for completeness, 45
    tentative permit decision, draft permit,
        and public notice, 46–47
  permit modification, 60–63
  permit revocation and reissuance, 63
  permit shield, 53, 229–230
  permit term, expiration, and APA extension,
      53–54
  permit termination, 63
  permit transfers, 64
  permit types, 41–43
    general permits, 42–43
    individual permits, 42
  public notice, 46–47
  scope, 9–16, 41
  Section 311 exemptions, 136–137
  special conditions, 18
  standard conditions, 17–18
  state certification, 48–49
    EPA review, 48–52
    MOA agreement, 49–50
    statutory authority to review, 49
    veto of state-issued permits, 50–52
  stormwater discharge permits, 173–174
  technology-based limitations, 16, 18–26
  water quality-based limitations, 16, 26–40
NRC (National Response Center), 138
NSPS (new source performance standards), 3,
    22–23
Nuisance doctrine, 124, 127–128
Numeric effluent limits, 174–175
Numerical chemical-specific criteria, 28–31
NWPs (nationwide permits), 109–110, 122

Occupational Safety and Health Act (OSHA),
    253
Ocean Dumping Act (ODA), 244n.170,
    253n.195, 256–257

Ocean Dumping Ban Act of 1988, 76
Office of Enforcement and Compliance
    Assurance, 79, 243
Office of Wetlands, Oceans and Watersheds,
    196n.21, 201n.32
Offshore oil and gas operations, 158
Oil, defined, 135
Oil and grease, 19n.66
Oil and hazardous substances spills, 4–7,
    133–162
    Comprehensive Environmental Response,
        Compensation, and Liability Act
        (CERCLA), 134–135
    definitions, 135
    enforcement of penalties, 4–5,
        160–162
        civil penalties, 161–162
        criminal sanctions, 162
        enforcement provisions, 160–161
    exemption, 136–138
    facility response plans, 148–154
        edible oils, 153–154
        marine transportation-related facilities,
            151–152
        nontransportation-related facilities,
            149–151
        Section 311 requirements, 148–149
    federal response contingency plans,
        147–148
    general discharge prohibition, 135–136
    historical background, 5–7
    introduction and scope, 133–138
    judicial review, 4–5
    liability for response costs and damages,
        154–160
        defenses and exclusions, 157–158
        financial responsibility, 158–159
        liability for oil discharges, 155–156
        limits of liability, 156–157
        Oil Spill Liability Trust Fund (OSLTF),
            159–160
    Oil Pollution Act (OPA), 135
    removal and response authority,
        144–146
        authority to act, 145
        federal response units, 146
        responder immunity, 146
        threats to public health or welfare,
            145–146
    spill notification requirement, 138
    spill prevention, 138–144
        marine facilities and vessels, 143–144
        SPCC plans, 139–142

vessel response plans, 152–153
violations, 253–256
    failure to report spills, 255–256
    prohibited discharges, 253–255
Oil Pollution Act (OPA), 133, 135, 256n.204
    authority to act, 145
    defenses and exclusions to liability,
        157–158
    financial responsibility requirements,
        158–159
    liability for oil discharges, 155–156
    limits of liability for response costs and
        damages, 156–157
    responder immunity, 146
    violations, 253
Oil Spill Liability Trust Fund (OSLTF), 135,
    148, 159–160, 253
OPA. *See* Oil Pollution Act
OSHA (Occupational Safety and Health Act),
    253
OSLTF (Oil Spill Liability Trust Fund), 135,
    148, 159–160, 253
Outer Continental Shelf Lands Act, 136,
    140n.33, 254
Outstanding national resource waters,
    27n.112

Pass-through, 85
PCBs (polychlorinated biphenyls), 78
PDN (predischarge notification), 110
Penalties. *See* Enforcement
"Per day for each violation," 233
Periodic reports, 94
Permit modification
    major, 61–63
    minor, 61
Permit shield, 53, 229–230
Permit transfers, 64
Person, defined, 246–247
pH, 19n.66, 70
Phase I stormwater discharges. *See* Stormwater
    discharges
Phase II stormwater discharges. *See* Stormwater
    discharges
Phenols, 25–26
Point source, defined, 11–12, 227
Point source discharges, 33–34. *See also* "Wet
    weather" discharges
Pollutant, defined, 10–11, 214, 226
Pollutants, priority, 6
Pollution, defined, 214–215
Pollution sources, and TMDLs, 214–215
Polychlorinated biphenyls (PCBs), 78

POTWs (publicly-owned treatment works), 69–81
  applicability, 69
  cost-comparison test, 21
  defined, 84
  effluent limitations, 70–71
  exemptions, 137
  indirect dischargers to, 3
  NPDES permit requirements, 71–72
  pretreatment programs, 72–76
    applicability, 73
    categorical standards, 73
    modifications, 75–76
    pretreatment standards, 73–74
    prohibited discharge standards, 74
    submission and approval procedures, 75
    substantive requirements, 74
  scope, 69
  sewage sludge use and disposal, 76–78
  sewer overflows, 78–81
  technology-based limitations, 70–71
  water quality-based limitations, 71
Poultry operations, 182–183
Practicable alternatives, 116–117
Predicting Soil Erosion by Water, 175–176
Predischarge notification (PDN), 110
Preenforcement review, 123
Preexisting prosecutions, 264–265
Presidential authority, 138–139, 145, 147, 148, 157
Pretreatment, defined, 84
Pretreatment and indirect dischargers, 83–96
  applicability, 84–85
  categorical standards, 87–91
    applicability of and basis for, 87–89
    combined wastestream formula, 90
    deadlines, 90
    fundamentally different factors variances, 92–93
    innovative technology deadline extensions, 90–91
    modifications of and variances from, 91–93
    net/gross calculation, 93
    removal credits, 91–92
  definitions, 84
  enforcement of standards, 96
  general pretreatment requirements, 85–87
  industrial users not subject to categorical standards, 94–95
  industrial users subject to categorical standards
    baseline monitoring reports, 93
    compliance reports, 94
    periodic reports, 94
  national categorical standards, 85
  notification of changed discharge, 95–96
  notification of hazardous waste discharges, 95
  objectives, 83
  overview, 83–85
  records maintenance, 96
  removal credits, 91–92
  reporting, 93, 94
  slug load notification, 95
Pretreatment standards for existing sources (PSES), 23, 88
Pretreatment standards for new sources (PSNS), 23, 88–89
"Prevailing party" standard, 228, 271
Prior converted cropland, 105
Priority pollutants, 6
Programmatic permits, 111
Project decision schedule, 46
Proof, elements of, 225–227
PSES (pretreatment standards for existing sources), 23, 88
PSNS (pretreatment standards for new sources), 23, 88–89
Public comment, 47
Public health threats, 145–146
Public interest review, 115–116
Public notice, 46–47, 262–264
Publicly-owned treatment works. *See* POTWs

Rainfall erosivity factor, 175–176
RCRA (Resource Conservation and Recovery Act), 95, 165, 224n.24, 244n.170, 245, 246, 251
Reasonably ascertainable issues, 58
Recapture provision, 121
Records maintenance, 96
Refuse Act, 256n.207
Regional Judicial Officers (RJOs), 238, 240, 241
Regional permits, 110–111
Regulatory defenses, 228–229
Regulatory Flexibility Act, 43n.7
Regulatory guidance letter (RGL), 105–106
Remedies
  citizen suits, 269–272
  civil judicial enforcement, 232–235
  exhaustion of, 278
  wetlands, 122–123
Removal and response authority, 144–146
Removal credits, 73, 91–92

Reportable quantity, 136, 255
Reporting requirements
    assessment reports, 195
    baseline monitoring reports, 93
    compliance reports, 94
    Discharge Monitoring Reports, 17, 228, 251
    for indirect dischargers, 93, 94
    for industrial users, 93, 94
    periodic reports, 94
    state assessment reports, 195
Res judicata, 230
Resource Conservation and Recovery Act
        (RCRA), 95, 165, 224n.24,
        244n.170, 245, 246, 251
Responder immunity, 146
Response planning, 148–154. *See also* Oil and
        hazardous substances spills
Responsible corporate officer, defined, 96
"Responsible corporate officer" doctrine,
        246–248
Revised universal soil loss equation rule
        (RUSLE), 175–176
RGL (regulatory guidance letter), 105–106
Right to jury, 228
Ripeness doctrine, 130, 277–278
Rivers and Harbors Act of 1899, 5–7, 243, 256
RJOs (Regional Judicial Officers), 238, 240,
        241
Rules of Civil Procedure, 238
RUSLE (revised universal soil loss equation
        rule), 175–176

Safe Drinking Water Act, 16
Sampling, 17
SAMPs (Special Area Management Plans), 111
Sanitary sewer overflows (SSOs), 80–81, 190
SCS (Soil Conservation Service), 104
Secondary treatment, 70
Section 311, 133–162
    exemption from coverage, 136–138
    facility response plans, 148–149
Section 319 program, 195–200. *See also*
        Nonpoint source pollution control
Section 404 permit program, 107–119
    enforcement, 119–123
    individual permits
        EPA's section 404(b)(1) guidelines,
            116–118
        mitigation policy and banking, 118–119
        public interest review, 115–116
        "no net loss" of wetlands policy, 118–119,
            130–131
    state authority to implement, 130

takings issue, 123–130
violations
    administrative enforcement, 119–120
    civil enforcement, 120–123
    preenforcement review, 123
Section 404(b)(1) guidelines, 116–118
Seventh Amendment, 228
Sewage sludge
    defined, 76
    incineration, 77–78
    land application, 77
    surface disposal, 77
    use and disposal, 76–78
        round one regulations, 76–78
        round two regulations, 78
Sewer overflows, 78–82
    combined sewer overflows, 79–80
    sanitary sewer overflows, 80–81
Sheen test, 136n.13
SIC (Standard Industrial Classification) codes,
        44
Signature requirements, 45
Significant degradation, 117
Significant industrial users (SIUs)
    defined, 85
    slug control plan for, 74
Silvicultural point source, defined, 186–187
Silviculture, 186–188
"Single operational upset" (SOU) defense, 233
Site-specific criteria, 38–39
SIUs (significant industrial users)
    defined, 85
    slug control program for, 74
Sludge. *See* Sewage sludge
Slug discharges, 74, 95
Slug load notification, 95
Small spill, defined, 150
Soil Conservation Service (SCS), 104
SOU ("single operational upset") defense, 233
South Carolina Beachfront Management Act,
        125
Sovereign immunity, 260n.228
SPCC (Spill Prevention, Control, and
        Countermeasures) Plan, 139–142
Special aquatic sites, 117
Special Area Management Plans (SAMPs), 111
Spill notification, 138
Spill Prevention, Control, and Countermeasures
        (SPCC) Plan, 139–142
SSOs (sanitary sewer overflows), 80–81, 190
Standard Industrial Classification (SIC) codes,
        44
Standards of liability, 225

Standing, 265–267

State assessment reports, 195

State management programs, 195–196

State mechanisms, enforceable, 202–203

State responsibilities

    authority to implement Section 404 program, 130

    EPA review and approval of standards, 49–50

    Section 304(l) program, 35–37

    TMDLs and, 209–210

State sovereign immunity, 260n.228

State-issued NPDES permits

    EPA review, 49–52

    veto of, 50–52

Statement of basis, 46n.26

Statute of limitations

    civil judicial enforcement, 224–225

    as defense, 120–121, 268

Stipulated penalties, 123

Storm sewer systems, industrial stormwater discharges to, 167

Stormwater, defined, 165

Stormwater discharges, 163–178

    associated with industrial activity, 165–172

        conditional exclusion for "no exposure," 167–168

        discharges to storm sewer systems, 167

        exclusions, 167

        types of permits for, 168–172

    general permits, 169–170

    group permits, 170–172

    individual permits, 168–169

    from large and medium municipal separate storm sewer systems, 172–175

        application requirements, 172–173

        compliance deadlines, 175

        NPDES permit conditions, 173–174

    permit application deadlines, 178

    phase I discharges, 165–175

    phase II discharges, 175–178

    from small construction activity, 175–176

    from small municipal separate storm sewer systems, 176–178

Stormwater pollution prevention plans (SWPPPs), 169, 171

Subpoenas, 240

Substantial harm facilities, 150, 151

Supplemental Environmental Projects, 222

Surface disposal of sludge, 77

SWPPPs (stormwater pollution prevention plans), 169, 171

"Take" of listed species, 218n.91

Takings issue, 123–130

Tampering, 250–251

Technology-based controls, 2–4

Technology-based limitations, 16, 18–26

    developing, 23–24

    levels of control, 19–23

        BAT, 22

        BCT, 21

        BPT, 19–20

        NSPS, 22–23

        PSES and PSNS, 23

    POTWs, 70–71

    variances, 24–26

        BAT variances, 25–26

        fundamentally different factors variance, 24–25

Temperature TMDLs, 214

Temporary taking, 126

Thermal discharges, 214

Thermal TMDLs, 214

TMDLs (Total Maximum Daily Load), 4, 7, 199–200, 205–219

    citizen suits, 211

    components of, 206–207

    Endangered Species Act and, 217–218

    EPA responsibilities, 213

    heat sources, 213–214

        temperature TMDLs *vs.* thermal TMDLs, 214

        thermal discharges, 213–214

    implementation, 215–217

        nonpoint sources, 216

        point sources, 215–216

        sources requiring Section 401 certification, 217

    introduction, 205–206

    July 2000 TMDL rule, 218–219

    litigation, 210–213

        challenges to substance of TMDLs, 212–213

        constructive submission theory, 210–212

        EPA's expanded authority, 213

        judicial review, 210

    multistate issues, 209–210

    pollution sources, 214–215

    substance and timing of submittals, 207–208

    trading, 208–209

Total Maximum Daily Load. *See* TMDLs

Total suspended solids (TSS), 19n.66, 70

Toxic substance spills, 4–7. *See also* Oil and hazardous substances spills
Toxic Substances Control Act, 134n.6
Toxicity criteria, 30–31
Trading programs, 203–204, 208–209
Trans-Alaska Pipeline Authorization Act, 158
Transportation Department, 133n.4, 138–139
Transportation facilities, 151–152
Treasury Department, 233, 269
Tree farming. *See* Silviculture
Trials, 228
TSS (total suspended solids), 19n.66, 70

Underground Injection Program, 16
Underground storage tanks, 140n.32
Upset, 228–229
    defined, 18n.59
Urbanized area, defined, 176
U.S. Department of Agriculture (USDA), 179
U.S. Minerals Management Service (MMS), 140n.32

Variances, 24–26
    BAT variances, 25–26
    economic incapability variance, 25
    FDF, 24–25, 73, 92–93
    for indirect dischargers, 91–93
    site-specific, 38–39
    for technology-based limitations, 24–26
Vegetation, hydrophytic, 104
Vegetation exemption, 180–181
Venue, 224–225, 265
Vessel response plans, 152–153
Vessel spill prevention, 143–144
Veto of state-issued NPDES permits, 50–52
    basis for, 50–51
    procedures for, 52

Wasteload Allocation (WLA), 207
Water bodies, uses of, 27
Water Pollution Control Act, 6, 20n.67, 178, 244n.170, 247, 258
Water pollution violations, 243
Water Quality Act Amendments, 67
Water Quality Act of 1965, 6
Water Quality Act of 1987, 29, 67, 71n.4, 91
Water quality certification (WQC), 114
Water quality criteria, 28–31
Water Quality Inventory Reports, 196–197
Water quality limited segments (WQLSs), 207, 208
Water Quality Management (WQM) plans, 194

Water quality standards, 26–32
    criteria, 28–31
    CSOs and, 79–80
Water Quality Standards Handbook, 32
Water quality-based controls, 2–4
Water quality-based effluent limitations, 16, 26–40
    implementation, 38–40
        compliance schedules, 40
        flows, 39
        mixing zones, 39–40
        site-specific criteria and variances, 38–39
    individual control strategies, 35–38
        A list, 35–36
        B list, 36–37
        C list, 37
        EPA responsibilities, 37–38
        individual control strategies, 37
        state responsibilities, 35–37
    POTWs, 71
    standards review and approval process, 32–33
    supplemental limitations, 33–34
    total maximum daily loads, 34–35
    water quality criteria, 28–31
        narrative criteria, 31
        numeric chemical-specific criteria, 28–30
        whole-effluent numeric toxicity criteria, 30–31
    water quality standards, 26–32
        antidegradation, 31–32
        designated uses, 27
Waters of the United States
    defined, 97, 250
    isolated waters and wetlands, 101–104
    Migratory Bird Rule, 101–104, 227
    wetlands definition, 98–99, 101
    wetlands delineation, 104–106
Watershed management, on federal lands, 201
Watershed planning, 201
Wells, discharges to, 15–16
"Wet weather" discharges, 163–190
    aquatic animal production or aquaculture, 188–190
    concentrated animal feeding operations, 178–186
    sewer overflows, 190
    silviculture, 186–188
    stormwater, 163–178

Wet Weather Water Quality Act of 2000, 80n.53
WET (whole-effluent toxicity) criteria, 30, 72
Wetlands, 97–132
  adjacent wetlands, 100–101
  affirmative defenses, 120–122
    nationwide permits, 122
    Section 404(f) exemptions, 121–122
    statute of limitations, 120–121
  defined, 98–100
  enforcement, 119–123
    agency roles and administrative enforcement, 119–120
    civil enforcement, 120–123
  individual permits
    EPA guidelines, 116–118
    permitting decision considerations, 115–118
    permitting process, 112–115
    public interest review, 115–116
  introduction and scope, 97–98
  isolated wetlands, 101–104
  jurisdiction, 98–106
  longevity of wetlands delineations, 105–106
  Migratory Bird Rule, 101–104
  mitigation policy and banking, 118–119
  as navigable waters, 13n.32
  "no net loss" policy, 118–119, 130–131
  permit types, 109–112
    after-the-fact permits, 112
    emergency procedures, 111–112
    individual permits, 111
    letters of permission, 111
    nationwide permits, 109–110
    programmatic permits, 111
    regional permits, 110–111
  preenforcement review, 123
  remedies, 122–123
    civil penalties, 122–123
    injunctive relief, 122
  Section 404 permit program, 107–119
  state authority
    to implement Section 404 permit program, 130
    in light of *SWANCC,* 106
  suggestions for addressing Section 404, 131–132
  takings issue, 123–130
  violations, 249–250
  wetlands delineation manuals, 104–105
Wetlands delineation manuals, 104–105
Whole-effluent numeric toxicity criteria, 30–31
Whole-effluent toxicity (WET) criteria, 30, 72
Wholly past violations, as defense, 267–268
Willful blindness doctrine, 246
WLA (Wasteload Allocation), 207
Worst-case discharge, 150, 151
WQC (water quality certification), 114
WQLSs (water quality limited segments), 207, 208
WQM (Water Quality Management) plans, 194